Bibliotherapy Sourcebook

Bibliotherapy Sourcebook

Edited by
Rhea Joyce Rubin

A Neal-Schuman
Professional Book

 ORYX PRESS
1978

Operation Oryx, started more than 10 years ago at the Phoenix Zoo to save the rare white antelope—believed to have inspired the unicorn of mythology—has apparently succeeded.

An original herd of nine, put together through Operation Oryx by five world organizations, now numbers 34 in Phoenix with another 22 farmed out to the San Diego Wild Game Farm.

The operation was launched in 1962 when it became evident that the animals were facing extinction in their native habitat of the Arabian peninsula.

Copyright © 1978 by Rhea Joyce Rubin
Published by The Oryx Press
3930 E. Camelback Road
Phoenix, AZ 85018

Published simultaneously in Canada

Printed and Bound in the United States of America

Distributed outside North America by
Mansell Information/Publishing Limited
3 Bloomsbury Place
London WC1A 2QA, England
ISBN 0-7201-0805-5

Library of Congress Cataloging in Publication Data

Main entry under title:

Bibliotherapy sourcebook.

   (A Neal-Schuman professional book)
   Bibliography: p.
   Includes index.
   1. Bibliotherapy—Addresses, essays, lectures.
I. Rubin, Rhea Joyce.
RC489.B48B5   615'.8516   78-939
ISBN 0-912700-04-1

To my dad, Harold Rubin

Contents

Preface

This anthology represents the first collection in book form of articles on bibliotherapy. An abundance of material was available: librarians, educators, psychologists, doctors, and others have been writing about bibliotherapy since the nineteenth centry. The concept has been used since the Greeks called their libraries pharmacies of "medicine for the souls," and the Romans felt that orations could be read by patients to improve their mental health. Bibliotherapy has developed from the basic idea that literature has therapeutic properties. The term "bibliotherapy" comes from *biblion* (book) plus *oepatteid* (healing). Bibliotherapy *per se* is the harnessing of the power of literature into a specific activity.

Samuel McChord Crothers coined the word in an *Atlantic Monthly* article of 1916, but the first definition didn't appear until 1941 when *Dorland's Illustrated Medical Dictionary* printed the definition that is still used in the current edition: "The employment of books and the reading of them in the treatment of nervous disease." Twenty years later, *Webster's Third New International Dictionary* offered a definition which was accepted in 1966 as the official definition of the American Library Association: "The use of selected reading materials as therapeutic adjuvants in medicine and psychiatry; also, guidance in the solution of personal problems through directed reading." The 1966 edition of the *Random House Dictionary* followed with this definition: "The use of reading as an ameliorative adjunct to therapy." The author prefers her own definition which is:

> A program of activity based on the interactive processes of the use of print and nonprint material whether imaginative or informational, facilitated by a librarian or other professional, to achieve insight into normal development or to effect changes in emotionally disturbed behavior.

The earliest use of books for therapeutic purposes was in the Middle Ages. In 1272 the Al-Mansur Hospital in Cairo provided readings of the Koran as a part of treatment. The provision of religious materials to hospital patients and prison inmates continued throughout the years. In the eighteenth century, humanitarians in Europe began providing recreation, including reading materials, to the insane. By the beginning of the nineteenth century these reforms had spread to America where Benjamin Rush became the first American to recommend reading, including nonreligious materials, for the sick (1802) and for the mentally ill (1810). Another American physician, John

Minson Galt II, wrote the seminal article on bibliotherapy in 1846, but is better known for his 1853 essay entitled "On Reading, Recreation and Amusements for the Insane." E. Kathleen Jones, administrator of libraries at the McLean Hospital in Waverly, Mass., was the first trained librarian to use books in the treatment of the mentally ill in 1904.

Library services to the general population were also changing in the late eighteenth and early nineteenth centry. Justin Winsor established a precedent when he opened the stacks to students in 1877 and allowed books to circulate; this was the beginning of reference services. In 1876 the first proposal for an actual program of assistance to readers was made and by 1883, Boston Public Library, the largest public library of the time, had a full-time assistance position. In the 1920's and 1930's, reference service was well-established, and readers' advisory service became the new idea in public libraries. In 1924, Jennie M. Flexner was hired to be the first readers' advisor for the New York Public Library. She worked both with individuals and with groups, advising on book selection and developing personalized reading courses.

Concomitant with changes in the American treatment of mental patients and library services to patrons, the field of psychology also experienced change. The concept of group therapy was developed in the early 1900's (the term itself was coined by Joseph Moreno in 1931). Throughout the first half of the century, experimentation with group therapy was popular, but World War II forced its use on the public. More wounded soldiers required attention than could be dealt with in private therapy; group therapy became standard. Library service to hospitalized soldiers also became the standard—and the fields of psychotherapy, library science, and medical treatment were joined.

Bibliotherapy is an interdisciplinary field in which many professions are active. This volume represents the interests of librarians, educators, social workers, occupational therapists, psychologists, psychiatrists, doctors, counselors, and many other groups of people who currently employ bibliotherapy as a powerful technique to promote self-growth.

Acknowledgements

Although the selection of articles for inclusion in this anthology was done by the author, she thanks her teachers and colleagues who have influenced her and, therefore, her choices. Staff members at both the Washington State Library and the Oregon State Library were extremely helpful in obtaining many of the materials which appear here. Lyn Stuckey and Joan Crawford of Oryx Press edited the book and prepared the biographical notes; Susan Ruth Stein did the index. Special thanks go to my husband, Lawrence Berman, for guidance and support.

Rhea Joyce Rubin
February 1, 1978

Suggestions for Further Reading

William K. Beatty, "A Historical Review of Bibliotherapy," *Library Trends* 11:106-117 (October 1962).

Samuel McChord Crothers, "A Literary Clinic," *Atlantic Monthly* 118:291 (1916).

E. K. Jones, "Library Work Among the Insane," *American Library Assn. Bulletin* 6:310-324 (July 1912).

Margaret Monroe, *Library Adult Education* (Metuchen, New Jersey: Scarecrow, 1963).

Margaret Monroe and Rhea Rubin, "Bibliotherapy: Trends in the U.S." *Libri* 25:156-162 (1975).

Pauline Opler, "The Origins and Trends of Bibliotherapy as a Device in Mental Hospital Libraries," MLS thesis, San Jose State College (1969).

Samuel Rothstein, *The Development of Reference Services* (Chicago: A.C.R.L., 1955).

Rhea Joyce Rubin, *Using Bibliotherapy: A Guide to Theory and Practice* (Phoenix: Oryx Press, 1978).

Ruth Tews, "Bibliotherapy," in Allen Kent and Harold Lancour, eds. *Encyclopedia of Library and Information Science* (New York: Marcel Dekker, 1969).

Philip J. Weimerskirch, "Benjamin Rush and John Minson Galt II: Pioneers of Bibliotherapy in America," *Medical Library Assn. Bulletin* 53:510-525 (1965).

Contributors

Rosa Horn Alexander, "Bibliotherapy with Chronic Schizophrenics: The Therapeutic Function of the Psychiatric Librarian in a State Mental Hospital," reprinted with permission from *The Journal of Rehabilitation* 55:26-27,42 (November-December 1967). Copyright © 1967 by The National Rehabilitation Association. This article, co-authored with Stephen E. Buggie, is a summary of her Master's thesis, written when she was a graduate student in library science at San Jose State College, California.

Edwin F. Alston is Clinical Professor of Psychiatry at the University of California, San Francisco. "Bibliotherapy and Psychotherapy" is reprinted with permission from *Library Trends* 11:159-176 (October 1962).

H. A. Altmann, Ed.D., is Professor, Department of Educational Psychology, The University of Calgary, Alberta, Canada. "Books and Empathy Help Troubled Children," co-authored with B. Nielsen, is reprinted with permission from *The Canadian Library Journal* 31: 284-287 (1974).

Franklin M. Berry, Ph.D., is Professor of Psychology, Columbus College, Georgia. "Contemporary Bibliotherapy: Systematizing the Field" is an original paper based on notes from the Third Bibliotherapy Round Table, held in conjunction with the Annual Meeting of Mental Health Librarians and the American Psychiatric Association's Institute on Hospital and Community Psychiatry, Altanta (September 1976) and the Fourth Bibliotherapy Round Table co-sponsored by the National Council on Aging, Inc., Washington, DC (January 1977).

Alice I. Bryan, Ph.D., is Professor Emeritus, School of Library Science, Columbia University, New York. "The Psychology of the Reader" is reprinted from *The Library Journal* 64:7-12 (January 1939). Published by R. R. Bowker Co. (A Xerox Company). Copyright © 1939 by Xerox Corporation. Dr. Bryan was Consulting Psychologist, School of Library Science, Columbia University, when this article was published.

Stephen E. Buggie, Ph.D., is currently Lecturer in Experimental Psychology, University of Zambia, Lusaka. This article, which was Rosa Horn Alexander's thesis project, was summarized with the assistance of Dr. Buggie when he was a candidate for a B.A. in psy-

chology at San Jose State College. "Bibliotherapy with Chronic
Schizophrenics: The Therapeutic Function of the Psychiatric Librar-
ian in a State Mental Hospital," co-authored with Rosa Horn Alex-
ander, is reprinted with permission from *The Journal of Rehabilitation,*
Vol. 55, (November-December 1967). Copyright © 1967 by The
National Rehabilitation Association.

S. D. Coomaraswamy, M.A., M.Sc., A.B.P.S., is Senior Clinical
Psychologist and Head of the Department of Clinical Psychology at
Queen Elizabeth II Hospital, Welwyn Garden City, England. "Therapeutic Aspects of a Library Service to Hospital Patients" is reprinted
with permission from *Health and Welfare Libraries Quarterly* 2(2-4):
29-32 (June-December 1975).

Ella Yensen Fierman, "Bibliotherapy in Psychiatry," co-
authored with Louis B. Fierman, pp. 163-174, in *Occupational Therapy:
Principles and Practice* by Dunton and Licht, 1952, is reprinted with
permission from Charles C Thomas, Springfield, Illinois. She is now
Executive Director, Psychotherapy Associates, New Haven, Connecticut.

Louis B. Fierman, M.D., is Medical Director of the Elmcrest Psychiatric Institute in Portland, Connecticut. "Bibliotherapy in Psychiatry," co-authored with Ella Y. Fierman, pp. 163-174, in *Occupational
Therapy: Principles and Practice* by Dunton and Licht, 1952, is reprinted
with permission from Charles C Thomas, Springfield, Illinois. Dr.
Fierman was Instructor and Chief Resident in Psychiatry, Yale
University School of Medicine at the time this article was first published.

Kenneth Gorelick, " 'Great' Literature as a Teaching Tool in the
Education of Mental Health Professionals" is reprinted with permis-
sion from *Libri* 25(2):138-143 (1975). Copyright © 1975 by Danmarks
Biblioteksskole, Copenhagen, Denmark. Gorelick is a Faculty Mem-
ber of the Psychiatry Training Branch at Overholser Division of
Training, Saint Elizabeths Hospital, Washington, DC.

Louis A. Gottschalk, M.D., is Professor and Chairman, Department of Psychiatry and Human Behavior, College of Medicine,
University of California, Irvine; Director, Psychiatric Service, University of California, Irvine, Medical Center, Orange, California; Training and Supervising Analyst, Southern California Psychoanalytic
Institute. "Bibliotherapy as an Adjuvant in Psychotherapy" is reprinted from the *American Journal of Psychiatry* 104:632-637 (1948).
Copyright © 1948, The American Psychiatric Association. Reprinted
by permission. Dr. Gottschalk was Assistant Surgeon, U.S. Public
Health Service, when this article was first published.

Margaret C. Hannigan was formerly Coordinator of Library
Services to State Institutions and to the Physically Handicapped, Divi-

sion of Library Programs, United States Office of Education, Washington, DC. "Narcotic Addicts Take Up Reading," co-authored with William T. Henderson, is reprinted with permission from *Bookmark* 22:281-286 (July 1963). At the time this article was written Hannigan was Librarian, Library Extension Division, New York State Library. She retired in August 1974.

Molly Harrower, Ph.D., is Professor Emeritus at the University of Florida, Gainesville, and Editor, *American Lectures in Psychology.* "The Therapy of Poetry," from *Current Psychiatric Therapies,* pp. 97-105, is reprinted by permission of Grune & Stratton, Inc. and the author, 1974.

William T. Henderson is Library Specialist to State Agencies, State Library Government Program, Michigan Department of Education, State Library Services, Lansing. "Narcotic Addicts Take Up Reading," co-authored with Margaret C. Hannigan, is reprinted with permission from *Bookmark* 22:281-286 (July 1963). At the time this article was written Henderson was Librarian, Library Extension Division, New York State Library.

Inez Huntting, now retired, was Director of Occupational Therapy at the Cleveland Psychiatric Institute and Hospital, Ohio, at the time her article was originally published. "The Role of the Occupational Therapist as Related to Bibliotherapy" is reprinted with permission from *Library Trends* 11:207-216 (October 1962).

Arleen Hynes, C.P.T., is Librarian, Circulating Library at Saint Elizabeths Hospital, Washington, DC. "Bibliotherapy in the Circulating Library at Saint Elizabeths Hospital" is reprinted with permission from *Libri* 25(2):144-148 (1975). Copyright © 1975 by Danmarks Biblioteksskole, Copenhagen, Denmark.

Evalene P. Jackson was Director of the Division of Librarianship at Emory University, Atlanta, Georgia, from 1954 to 1964. She died April 2, 1974. "Bibliotherapy and Reading Guidance: A Tentative Approach to Theory" is reprinted with permission from *Library Trends* 11:118-126 (October 1962).

Clara E. Lack is Bibliotherapist and Outreach Supervising Librarian at Santa Clara County Library, 1095 North Seventh Street, San Jose, California. "Systems Analysis of a Bibliotherapy Session at Agnews State Hospital" is printed here for the first time with the author's permission.

Archie L. Lejeune is Coordinator, High School Relations at Louisiana State University, Baton Rouge., "Bibliocounseling as a Guidance Technique" is reprinted with permission from *Catholic Library World* 41:156-164 (November 1969). Copyright © 1969 by the Catholic Library Association. This article was a speech presented at the Special Libraries Association-California Library Association Dinner Meeting, April 6, 1969, New Orleans.

Duncan Leys, a retired Fellow of the Royal College of Physicians, was Consultant Physician at Farnborough Hospital, Kent, England. "The Place of Literature in Healing," Chapter V, pp. 44-50, in *Hospital Libraries and Work with the Disabled,* M. E. Going, editor, is reprinted with permission from The Library Association, London (1963).

R. W. Medlicott, M.B., ChB., is Medical Director of Ashburn Hall, Dunedin, New Zealand, and Personal Professor in Graduate Studies in Psychiatry, Otago University Medical School. "Bibliotherapy" is reprinted with permission from *New Zealand Libraries* 38(4):205-208 (August 1975) and the author.

William C. Menninger, M.D., who died in 1966, was President of The Menninger Foundation, Topeka, Kansas. "Bibliotherapy" is reprinted with permission from *The Menninger Clinic Bulletin,* Volume 1, Number 8, pages 263-274. Copyright © 1937 by The Menninger Foundation.

A. M. Miller was Hospital Librarian in Kharkhov, United Soviet Socialist Republic at the time the article was originally published. "U.S.S.R. 1970: The Reading Matter of Patients," *International Library Review* 4:373-377 (1972) is reprinted with permission from Academic Press, London and V.A.A.P., Moscow. Copyright © 1972 by Academic Press, London.

Eugéne Moerdijk was Librarian, Department of Prisons, South Africa, at the time this article was originally published. "Suggestions for Rehabilitation and Bibliotherapy in South African Prisons" is reprinted with permission from *Libri Natales* 11-15 (July 1974).

Margaret E. Monroe, DLS, is Professor of Library Science at the University of Wisconsin, Madison. Dr. Monroe, who received her DLS from Columbia University in 1962, is a Member and Consultant to the American Library Association's Bibliotherapy Committee. "A Bibliotherapeutic Model for Library Service" is published here for the first time.

Mildred T. Moody was Librarian at the Glen Lake Sanitorium, Minnetonka, Minnesota, at the time the article was originally published. "Bibliotherapy for Chronic Illnesses" is reprinted with permission from *Hospital Progress,* January 1964. Copyright © 1964 by the Catholic Hospital Association.

Harold A. Moses is Associate Professor of Educational Psychology at the University of Illinois, Urbana. "Bibliotherapy in an Educational Context: Rationale and Principles," co-authored with J. S.

Zaccaria, is reprinted with permission from *High School Journal* 52:401-411 (1969). Copyright © 1969 by the University of North Carolina Press.

Beatrice F. Nielsen is currently on leave from the Calgary Board of Education, Calgary, Alberta, where she was employed as a librarian. She is a full-time doctoral student at Brigham Young University and teaches two undergraduate courses in children's literature. "Books and Empathy Help Troubled Children," co-authored with H. Altmann, is reprinted with permission from *The Canadian Library Journal* 31:284-287 (1974).

Sadie Peterson-Delaney died in 1958 while serving as Chief Librarian, United States Veterans Administration Hospital, Tuskegee, Alabama. "The Place of Bibliotherapy in a Hospital" was originally published in *Opportunity-Journal of Negro Life* 18:53-56 (February 1938) and is reprinted here from *Library Journal* 63:305-308 (April 1938). Published by R. R. Bowker Co. (A Xerox Company). Copyright © 1938 by Xerox Corporation.

Elizabeth Pomeroy was Director, Veterans Administration Library Service, Washington, DC, from 1923 to her retirement in 1946. She died in 1966. "Book Therapy in Veterans' Hospitals" is a United States Government Publication originally published in 1927.

Louis A. Rongione, O.S.A., is Professor of Library Science and Director of Falvey Memorial Library at Villanova University, Villanova, Pennsylvania. "Bibliotherapy: Its Nature and Uses" is reprinted with permission from *Catholic Library World* 43:495-500 (May/June 1972). Copyright © 1972 by the Catholic Library Association.

David H. Russell, Ph.D., now deceased, was Professor of English at the University of California, Berkeley. "Contributions of Research in Bibliotherapy to the Language-Arts Programs, Parts I and II," co-authored with C. Shrodes, is reprinted with permission from *School Review* 58:335-342 (September 1950); 58:411-420 (October 1950). Copyright © 1950 by the University of Chicago Press.

Barbro Schmidt, deceased, was a Hospital Librarian in Lund, Sweden. This article originally appeared in a Swedish newspaper in 1948. "Reading Therapy in the Service of the Sick" is reprinted with permission from "The Hospital Library in Sweden," Pamphlet #23 (London: The Library Association, 1962).

Jerome M. Schneck, M.D., formerly Clinical Associate Professor of Psychiatry, State University of New York, Downstate Medical Center, Brooklyn, is currently Attending Psychiatrist, Division of Psychiatric Training and Education, Saint Vincent's Hospital and Medical Center of New York. He was involved in research in bibliotherapy at The Menninger Clinic when this article was first published. "Bibliotherapy for Neuropsychiatric Patients: Report of Two Cases" is reprinted with permission of *The Bulletin of the Menninger Clinic,* Volume 10, Number 1, pages 18-25. Copyright © 1946 by The Menninger Foundation.

Michael Shiryon, Ph.D., is Chief Psychologist at the Department of Psychiatry, Kaiser Permanente Medical Center-Kaiser Foundation Hospital in Oakland, California. "Literatherapy: Theory and Application" is an unpublished speech presented at the Annual Meeting of the Western Psychological Association, April 13, 1973, at Anaheim, California, and is printed with the author's permission.

Caroline Shrodes, Ph.D., was Professor and Chairman of the English Department at San Francisco State University, California. Dr. Shrodes is now Emeritus Professor of English and Core Faculty Member of Union Graduate School. "Application of Dynamic Personality Theory to the Dynamics of the Aesthetic Experience," (Chapter VI) and "Implications for Psychotherapy," (Chapter VIII) from "Bibliotherapy: A Theoretical and Clinical-Experimental Study," Ph.D. dissertation, University of California (1949). "Contributions of Research in Bibliotherapy to the Language-Arts Program, Parts I and II," co-authored with D. H. Russell, is reprinted with permission from *School Review* 58:335-342 (September 1950); 58:411-420 (October 1950). Copyright © 1950 by the University of Chicago Press.

Sylva Simsova, MPhil, FLA, is Lecturer of Librarianship at the Polytechnic of North London, England. "Nicholas Rubakin and Bibliopsychology" is reprinted with permission from *Libri* 16(2):118-129 (1966). Copyright © 1966 by Danmarks Biblioteksskole, Copenhagen, Denmark.

George D. Spache, Ph.D., is Professor Emeritus of Psychology, University of Florida and President, Readings Research Service Institute. "Using Books to Help Solve Children's Problems," Chapter III in *Good Reading for Poor Readers* is reprinted with permission from Garrard Publishing Co., Champaign, Illinois. Copyright © 1974 by George D. Spache.

Daniel Sweeney, Ph.D., is Staff Psychologist, Division of Forensics, Saint Elizabeths Hospital, Washington, DC. "Bibliotherapy and the Elderly," a speech given at the East Coast Bibliotherapy Round Table on January 11, 1976, is included here with the author's permission.

Ruth M. Tews, before her retirement, was Supervisor, Patients' Library at the Mayo Clinic, Rochester, Minnesota. "The Role of the Librarian on the Interdisciplinary Team," pp. 57-62, In: Monroe, Margaret E., *Reading Guidance and Bibliotherapy in Public, Hospital and Institution Libraries,* is reprinted with permission from the University of Wisconsin Library School and the author. The book is a selection of papers presented at a series of Adult Services Institutes at the University of Wisconsin (1971).

Louis Hollenback Twyeffort, A.M., M.D., was associated with the Institute of the Pennsylvania Hospital at the time this chapter was first published. He died in 1953. "Therapy in Psychoneurosis (Bibliotherapy)" is reprinted with permission from *Cyclopedia of Medicine, Surgery, and Specialities,* Volume 12. Copyright © 1940 by F. A. Davis Co.

Joseph S. Zaccaria, Ed.D., is Professor of Educational Psychology at the University of Illinois, Urbana. "Bibliotherapy in an Educational Context: Rationale and Principles," co-authored with H. A. Moses, is reprinted with permission from *High School Journal* 52: 401-411 (1969). Copyright © 1969 by the University of North Carolina Press.

PART

I

CLASSIC WORKS ON BIBLIOTHERAPY (1927-1949)

Introductory Comments

The first published article "On Reading, Recreation and Amusements for the Insane" appeared in 1853, although most researchers only date bibliotherapy literature back to the first World War when the term "bibliotherapy" was coined. Perhaps the first bibliotherapy article of the twentieth century was "The Therapeutic Use of a Hospital Library" published in 1919. It was co-authored by a librarian and a neurologist. Since that time, library and medical professionals have contributed many articles on bibliotherapy.

During the 1920s, eighteen articles and reports on bibliotherapy for the adult hospitalized patient were published. Most notable were "The Therapeutic Value of Books" by Josephine Jackson in 1925 and "Book Therapy in Veterans' Hospitals" by Elizabeth Pomeroy. The latter is reprinted here. Pomeroy, who was the Superintendent of Hospital Libraries for the Veterans' Administration, continued publishing on bibliotherapy throughout the 1930s. In 1927, she was already a staunch supporter of bibliotherapy, although she had no scientific evidence of its efficacy:

> The effect of the printed page is far-reaching—how far, it is impossible to measure in any satisfactory way. The hospital librarian can only watch carefully her books and her opportunities for applying them, knowing that her part as a curative agent in the hospital must be done quietly and unobtrusively with results intangible but none the less sure.

A decade later, Pomeroy published an article offering 1,538 case studies as a basis for her belief in the field.

Bibliotherapy may have received a large impetus during World War I, but it was not until the 1930s that the concept really came into its own. The amount of articles published tripled, and some 63 percent were published in fields outside of library science. As in the 1920's, all dealt with hospitalized patients. Both of the eminent Menninger brothers of the Menninger Clinic were proponents of bibliotherapy. Dr. Karl Menninger published his book *The Human Mind* in 1930 and was overwhelmed with readers who claimed that it had had a therapeutic effect. Inspired by this response, he compiled *A Guide to Psychiatric Books* for librarians to use when helping patrons. His brother, Dr. William Menninger, also presented papers advocating the use of literature for therapeutic purposes. One of these, presented to the American Psychiatric Association in 1937, is reprinted here. His paper is mainly of historic interest today; many of his ideas have (justly) gone out of vogue, such as the concept that reading prescription should be "directed by the physician. The librarian is the tool who carries out the mechanics and reports the observations."

Alice I. Bryan, Consulting Psychologist to the School of Library Service at Columbia University, was the foremost bibliotherapy theoretician of the 1930s. In "The Psychology of The Reader" (reprinted here), published in 1939 and followed by articles in August and October—the last one entitled "Can There Be A Science of Bibliotherapy?"—she answered her own question in the affirmative, stating that the field already had a philosophical justification, a working hypothesis, and a definition, but greatly needed experimental data and scientifically trained workers.

A third major contributor in the 1930s was Sadie Peterson-Delaney, a librarian at the Veterans' Administration Hospital, Tuskegee, Alabama, whose 1938 article "The Place of Bibliotherapy in a Hospital" appears here. (The fact that both Pomeroy and Delaney were librarians with the Veterans' Administration is not coincidental—the Veterans' Administration's involvement in bibliotherapy has been notable throughout the past sixty years.) Delaney realized that "many people never have the leisure to read until a period of hospitalization is necessary" and she used that opportunity to make readers out of many mental patients.

The growth of interest in bibliotherapy was demonstrated in the 1940s, and by 1950, more than 400 journal articles on bibliotherapy had been published. Many authors concentrated on methodology and research. Ruth Tews and Margaret Kinney (both librarians), and Salomon Gagnon and Jerome Schneck (both doctors) began publishing and continued appearing in print for many years. Dr. Jerome Schneck, who was doing research in bibliotherapy at the Menninger Clinic at the time, published a series of four articles on his work. His "Bibliotherapy for Neuropsychiatric Patients" appears here as it is an excellent example of the case study approach to research. "Additional case material is desirable in order to encourage further trials, substantiate findings, furnish data for broader and more complete evaluations, and aid generally in the development of another therapeutic method." Another good case history report was originally published in 1948 by Dr. Louis A. Gottschalk and is reprinted here primarily because of the introduction which discusses how prescribed reading works, requisites of suitable patients, indications and techniques. The article also includes a long bibliography typical of the time.

In 1940, a prestigious medical work, *Cyclopedia of Medicine, Surgery, and Specialities*, included a chapter on "Therapy in Psychoneurosis (Bibliotherapy)" by Dr. Louis H. Twyeffort. It summarizes the prevalent theories and techniques of the period and was written specifically to help the general practitioner deal with patients who are troubled but are not in psychotherapy. He defined bibliotherapy as "an aid to treatment which aims at the acquisition, through reading, of a fuller and better knowledge of oneself and one's reactions, resulting in a better adjustment to life. It also connotes the relief of suffering by the psychological processes induced by reading."

These processes were thoroughly analyzed by Caroline Shrodes in her doctoral dissertation written in 1949. Hers was the first doctoral dissertation on bibliotherapy per se, and it remains the theoretical framework for the field. Since it has never been published, and is extremely difficult to obtain, two chapters — "Application of Dynamic Personality Theory to the Dynamics of the Aesthetic Experience" and "Implications for Psychotherapy" — are reprinted here so that the reader can study this important work first-hand.

Book Therapy in Veterans' Hospitals

by Elizabeth Pomeroy

At the Hospital Libraries Round Table recently held in connection with the fiftieth anniversary meeting of the American Library Association, one of the speakers gave as the three essentials to good hospital library service an organized central library, an appropriation specifically for books, and a trained librarian. To make her points more emphatic she made comparison with the Roosevelt Dam, saying that the organized central library and the book appropriation might be likened to the water and the masonry construction—the trained librarian with her knowledge of books and human nature to the mechanism for getting the water out.

The importance of selecting the hospital librarian, not only with adequate training but with personality adapted to dealing with the sick, cannot be overemphasized. She may know her books perfectly, but if she lacks the ability to gain the confidence of the patient—to put herself figuratively in his place and get his mental outlook—she will fall short of success in her work.

Given, then, the well-trained librarian with a broad knowledge of books, a pleasing personality, and a sympathetic and understanding nature, how is she to use her equipment to aid the physician in the recovery of his patient, because it is for this purpose and no other that she has been given a place on the hospital staff. As a librarian she is as much interested in circulating her books as the merchant is in selling his goods. As a hospital librarian she must remember that sometimes an overdose of reading, as well as reading the wrong book, may be detrimental to the recovery of the patient. She is thrilled when she hears, as we of the veterans' hospitals often do, that this or that man is reading a book through for the first time in his life, and she thinks with enthusiasm of the vistas of learning she may be instrumental in opening to him. In her zeal to spread the gospel of books she must always remember that every patient is temporarily more or less abnormal and the responsibility for the wise choice of his mental food rests with her as surely as the proper preparation of his regular meal rests with the dietitian. It must be right in quantity as well as in quality, giving to his mind healthy thoughts and causing temporary forgetfulness of his ailment.

Statistics of book circulation from a hospital library are, in a measure, valuable and interesting and give some idea of the use made of the library, but it should never be considered that quantity reading can be taken as a basis for estimating the therapeutic value of books. Neither can emphasis be placed on quality as this term is understood in public library usage. One patient suffering great pain may find a rousing detective story a sedative, while to another of a different type of mind Mark Sullivan's *Our Times* or Wells's *Outline of History* may serve the same purpose. In such instances the hospital library has fulfilled its purpose as much in the former as the latter case.

The librarian should be able to get the viewpoint of the patient and should be tactful in her approach, not giving to him the idea that she is trying to force him to read. If he is listless and disinterested yet strong enough to read if so minded, she may find, possibly from the nurse or doctor if not from the patient himself, what his occupation and interest in life had been previous to hospitalization. He may have been a cartoonist. Very well, the next day when the bookcart makes its rounds a copy of Briggs' *How to Draw Cartoons* will "accidentally" repose on the side of the cart nearest his bed. It may be as well not to pause when passing but as the cart is wheeled between the beds to make selection for the man next at hand it so happens that the cartoon literature is within easy reach and nine times out of ten the first patient will reach for it and inquire what else the library has on the subject, expressing surprise that there are real books and not just western and detective stories in the library. With interest once aroused, this man is going to be a more contented patient and therefore more amenable to treatment than he was before.

Many instances might be cited to show how the resources of the library and the librarian have been instrumental through this indirect therapy in keeping patients from leaving the hospital against medical advice. Just one case will be mentioned, that of a patient in a tuberculosis hospital who had been threatening to "sign out," as the boys say. After thinking the matter over he confessed to the librarian: "I've decided not to go. I got to thinking about it and there's nothing to do while you take the cure here or at home except read, and I said to myself, shucks, boy, you know you can't get library service at home like you can here and you can't afford to buy all the books you'd have to have so you'd better stick around awhile longer."

What encouragement and hope comes to a tuberculous patient after reading the life of Trudeau or Stevenson? And what discouragement and depression may result from reading books—fiction it may be but real to the reader—describing in detail, as several recent novels do, the unsuccessful struggles of a victim of tuberculosis in combating the disease. The latter type of book may be as disastrous in its effects upon a tuberculous patient as a rarebit or a fudge shortcake upon a dyspeptic.

Dr. D. MacDougall King in his book called, *The Battle with Tuber-*

culosis and How to Win It, tells us that a book which causes deep concentration of the mind requires as much energy as spending the day performing physical exercise and that the sick man is much more liable to have his body affected by his mind than the well man is. He says also that a person suffering from tuberculosis is on the verge of nervous excitement at all times and the little things of life, which in health are passed over, have often a profound effect upon the invalid's mind, which, in turn, seriously interferes with the normal working of bodily functions.

The librarian then in "prescribing" books in a tuberculosis hospital must always remember that there are times when the highly exciting book as well as the depressing one must not be given to the tuberculous patient and that he must not be overtired by reading. When because of his diligent pursuit of the cure he feels better, or when perhaps a change of climate has produced the same effect, then must he be guarded from "overreading" while reading enough to keep contented and in a peaceful state of mind.

The librarian of the Veterans' Tuberculosis Hospital, Legion, Texas, keeps a card record of the men who are reading, when they stop and why, and also has space on each man's card for notes as to his likes, dislikes, condition, and needs. A check of the infirmary roll of patients in one month showed that out of 102 patients all except 16 had active cards for books, and most of the men took magazines also. As this was the ward having the most serious cases the conclusion is that practically all the patients who were able to do so made use of the library. A later check during the same month showed that out of 84 patients in a ward all except 7 were taking either books or magazines from the bookcart as the librarian made her rounds. Her plan in checking up on the reading in the wards is to find if there are particular reasons why certain patients are not reading, what these reasons are, and whether the library is failing in any way to meet their needs.

While the library technique in all types of bureau hospitals is practically the same, the technique of the librarian in her contact with patients varies according to the type of patients hospitalized; with less variation perhaps from the public library type of reader in a general hospital than in those for the tuberculous or neuropsychiatric patient.

The report of the librarian from one bureau general hospital gives a few of the books and subjects called for in one month as follows: Drummond's *Natural Law in the Spiritual World,* Ibsen's *Doll's House,* Milton's *Paradise Lost,* studies in Spanish, early bronze and stone ages, prehistoric animals, geologic formations, social psychology, automobile repair work, woodworking, poultry raising, astronomy, astrology, civics, contracting, building, etc.

With what would the men who made the above requests have occupied their minds during that month in the hospital had not the library and the librarian been there? It is a safe guess that they would have read whatever came to hand and not what they were most interested in, and perhaps have become discontented and left the hospital before it was safe to do so. The librarian, trained in her line, gets for the man the book he wants. Sometimes it is not in her library, for there must be some limitation in the subjects covered by the hospital library, but by means of interlibrary loan she can borrow from neighboring and state libraries and satisfy her readers. In the rare instances when she is not able to do so it is a gratification to the patient to know she is doing her best at any rate to meet his needs.

One patient in a general hospital recently remarked to the librarian as he was leaving the hospital: "I cannot say enough in thanking you for the use of the splendid books I have had while here and for your help in selecting them for me. I have to return later for an operation and I will really look forward to coming back to this splendid hospital." What is it worth to have a patient go out feeling that he has been in a hospital so "splendid" that he can look forward to returning for an operation? Another patient tells the librarian that he has learned more by reading the library books of the Veterans' Bureau than he had learned in many years at school. He is going to be a better citizen as a result of his stay in the hospital and is not going to be afraid to patronize the public library when he gets home.

How the eyes of the Italian or the Greek patient light up when in looking hopelessly at the collection of books on the cart he spies one in his own language. It cannot be—a book just for him? "Yes," says the librarian, "and we have others you will like." He had been painfully laboring a few hours each day with words in an English primer—homesick, with no one who spoke his language. What are the therapeutic values of the right book to such a man?

One radical socialist in a hospital is said to have asked "the price of having the books to read," and when told they were free, said: "It is a shock to find people so kind to give books for nothing."

The librarian in a neuropsychiatric hospital has as entirely different a problem from the librarian in a general hospital as the latter has from the one in the tuberculosis type. She is dealing with patients mentally abnormal who must be attracted and interested in reading to begin with. Some of these are incapable of any continuous concentration and their reading must be carefully directed. To do this successfully a study of the individual patient must be made, and when necessary the case record consulted for this purpose. The confidential nature of such record must at all times be kept in mind and its contents discussed only with the ward surgeon whose advice should always be sought in difficult situations.

Mrs. Minnie D. Miller, hospital librarian at the Veterans' Hospital, North Little Rock, Arkansas, says:

> If the patient can be brought to the library it is very helpful, as being temporarily off the ward changes his thoughts and the library environment is interesting and stimulating in itself. The doctors advocate a psychological approach

to the patient, but not a psychiatric; that is, workers are advised to go with a sympathetic understanding of moods and underlying motives without assuming that they are in any wise abnormal; to deal with them as individuals, in an unhurried fashion for, being childish in their reactions, their needs must be treated accordingly. . . . Each man requires individual understanding and there is also a wide difference of word and manner in getting the same idea across. We have to remember that the image which our words and expressions evoke is rarely what we think it is or what we desire it to be. This transference of ideas demands much and we come to hold our stereotyped ideas lightly and modify them gladly. . . . The aim of the neuropsychiatric hospital library, through books and allied tools, is to aid in the restoration of the nonpsychotic to society and the gradual reeducation of the psychotic; that is, the library claims to be a potent help to some of the patients all of the time and to others some of the time. The process is subtle, indirect, deferred; its reactions are positive enough though not possible of exhibit in showroom or bazaar but are a certain and persistent corrective of adverse moods which in time has a happy and substantial effect in mitigating or curing of psychic unbalance or personality disturbances.

The mind naturally occupies itself with that which is put before it and it is the responsibility of the hospital librarian if the patient gets from the library the type of literature which upsets his tranquility to a harmful extent. She is not to be blamed for salacious or depressing literature which visitors may bring him but it is often her privilege at an opportune time to replace such material with that more wholesome and which will have a quieting rather than a disturbing effect on the patient.

Marcus Aurelius says "Tranquility is nothing else than the good ordering of the mind," and who in the hospital has a better opportunity than the librarian to bring tranquility to the disturbed mind?

One librarian reported in August that a patient had just told her of carrying in his pocket since January parts of a magazine she had taken to his ward. He said the short article and a poem had proven a real medicine to him every time he felt himself getting "down" (depressed).

In reading the printed page a mental picture is made. For the patient in a neuropsychiatric hospital this picture must not be one of gruesome murders with the sordid and depressing background of criminal plots, drug and rum smuggling rings or surroundings primarily sexual in appeal. Books of a psychological nature and those recalling the horrors of war too vividly are not the right mental food for this type of patient.

In these days of realism in literature an undue number of books seem disqualified when it comes to making additions to the library of the neuropsychiatric hospital, and for that matter to any hospital, for the depressing and sordid book is not wholesome reading for the mentally or physically ill.

The new school of novelists may be right that we should face the bare facts of life and its dubious problems as they choose to present them, but certainly they are not considerate of the problems of the hospital librarian in thus placing emphasis on all that encourages intro-spection and discontent among her readers.

The effect of the printed page is far-reaching—how far, it is impossible to measure in any satisfactory way.

The hospital librarian can only watch carefully her books and her opportunities for applying them; knowing that her part as a curative agent in the hospital must be done quietly and unobtrusively with results intangible but none the less sure.

Bibliotherapy

by William C. Menninger

It is the purpose of this paper to present and discuss two closely allied subjects of interest to the psychiatrist: first, the method of utilization by the average layman of popular literature on psychiatric and psychologic subjects, and second, the prescription of reading material as a therapeutic measure in hospitalized psychiatric patients.

MENTAL HYGIENE LITERATURE FOR THE LAYMAN

There has apparently been a widespread demand by the laity for books dealing with personality formation, structure, and adjustment. Most of these books have been written chiefly for the laity, and since they are concerned primarily with mental health and ill health, they are usually referred to as "mental hygiene literature." Some of the best known are: Bernard Hart's *Psychology of Insanity,* Myerson's *The Nervous Housewife,* Jackson and Salisbury's *Outwitting Our Nerves,* Pratt's *Your Mind and You,* Menninger's *The Human Mind,* Burnham's *The Normal Mind,* Strecker and Appel's *Discovering Ourselves,* Adamson's *So You're Going to a Psychiatrist.* It is not my purpose to attempt to describe the merits or demerits of particular books, but to investigate the effect of some of these books on the readers.

A few of these books have been among the "best sellers." There is a sufficient demand for all of them to lead most book stores to carry a steady supply of them. Some of them are consistently prescribed as therapeutic reading matter by physicians, with the purpose of giving the individual some information about himself or his family, or to afford him insight into his own difficulty, or, in the case of books regarding children, to aid a parent in the management of his child.

The persons who buy this type of book spontaneously may be divided into five groups, according to their reasons for doing so. First, there are undoubtedly many individuals who buy such books because of a catchy title made to appeal to the narcissism of the average man and to lead him to believe that he will learn something about himself. Second, there must be many individuals who seek such books because of concern about themselves or about some member of their family. Some people buy a particular book on the urgent recommendation of a friend, with the belief that it may be of personal benefit. Fourth, probably many individuals become interested in these books through some group study, through contact with a mental hygiene society, or through general popularity—e.g., hearing them discussed at the luncheon or bridge table. A fifth group of individuals, because of their interest in the field of psychiatry as it relates to their business or their profession, obtain and read this type of literature for the information it contains.

Results of Such Reading

It is probably impossible to evaluate adequately such reading by the general public, since there is no way to examine the motives or the benefits from a cross-section of the readers of such books. However, I have had the opportunity to analyze 400 letters written spontaneously by the readers of one of these books, *The Human Mind,* a popular presentation of the field of psychiatry, to the author, my brother Karl A. Menninger. The great majority of these were written by individuals entirely unknown to the author. One would probably be correct in assuming that this group did not represent a cross-section of the readers of the book, rather only those who were so affected by it that they felt the urge to convey their feelings in a letter.

An attempt was made to classify the content of these letters in order to gain some leads as to the nature of the effect of the book on the individual. Many letters were written for more than one purpose, e.g., to express approval as well as to indicate some self-help gained. The percentage figures used below indicate the frequency with which an opinion was expressed in the total group of letters studied.

Per cent of letters

Praise was expressed (in many instances the chief purpose of the letter)	79
Personal help was reported	18
Problems were submitted to the author for solution or requests made for information	31
Data that the writer believed would be of interest to the author was given	12
Unfavorable criticisms were made or attention was called to mistakes	8

It was the express purpose of 18 per cent of them in writing to report that they believed themselves benefited. Unfortunately, it is not possible to analyze the specific ways in which they were helped except from such remarks as, "I gained a better understanding of myself," "How were you able to obtain all my characteristics without knowing anything about me?" "I have quit worrying and am in better mental health since reading it," "Reading it affected me with a sounder outlook, knowing that I'm not the sole sufferer," "It has given me an enlarged sense of being and knowing that is at once tonic and catharsis to my soul." In a few instances the writers specified changes that had resulted from reading the book: thus, one man who, as the result of a great disappointment and loss, had become very depressed, suicidal, and hostile towards the world, was deeply impressed by a section in the book dealing with the personality-environmental struggle. As a direct result he was led to some remarkable constructive efforts in bringing happiness to a large group. A second individual reported that he had suffered from migraine attacks all his life which had not responded to any medical help, but which as a result of reading the book, entirely disappeared.

It is quite possible that some individuals are made worse by reading this type of literature, though these are probably few in number. We can assume that in the reading, they can find corroboration of their introspective doubts and fears for themselves. They support their self-destructive or aggressive tendencies by distortion or misapplication of the material they read.

As judged from the superficial remarks in these letters, no reader seems to have been harmed by reading the book. However, probably the great majority of readers are not materially affected by what they read. Insofar as the material may be new or entertaining, or may agree with their own conceptions, the particular book meets approval, but has little effect even on the conscious attitude or behavior. The influence from reading is an important question with patients undergoing psychoanalytic treatment. Psychoanalysts usually advise their patients against any psychiatric or psychoanalytic reading during the analysis. However, even under such circumstances, the patient may express an enthusiastic verbal acceptance of a particular book without producing any real change in his attitude or his behavior. On the basis of this experience, the question may be raised as to whether the difficulties arising from reading during psychoanalysis have not been over-emphasized. It is perhaps conservative to avoid prescribing or recommending mental hygiene reading to any individual whose situation or understanding is such that he may distort the ideas so gained to meet his own unconscious aggressive or self-destructive desires.

PRESENT STATUS OF BIBLIOTHERAPY IN PSYCHIATRIC INSTITUTIONS

In order to determine the present status of reading as used as a therapeutic measure in psychiatric institutions, I sought information from the superintendents of eighteen outstanding hospitals. It is my impression that the majority of these answers were as optimistic as the facts would permit. There was a general approbation of the use of bibliotherapy, but there was an apparent indifference to the execution of it as a treatment method, and no effort to evaluate results. Every institution had some sort of a library and several availed themselves of the use of libraries in the city in which they were located. (Such a plan is well described by Berry.[1]) The methods in prescribing the books or selecting the reading as a treatment method were for the most part unorganized. Five of the hospitals reported that they had no scientific program in operation. In seven, the program was left entirely to the librarian. In one institution it was mentioned that the books were surveyed by the physician before they were purchased. At another, the comment was made that the physician gave occasional suggestions about the library. In only three instances did a physician give specific recommendations relative to the reading matter, though the impression was gained from these reports that in other cases the physician did occasionally manifest interest in the program. In two institutions assigned readings were made from the educational classes. (The use of this plan has been outlined by Millar as applied to hobbies.[8]) The librarian in all instances was directly responsible for whatever activities were carried on, the choice and the prescription of books, the direction of the program, and the evaluation of the results being left largely to her.

The Purpose of Bibliotherapy

Over a period of five years we have carried out a program of bibliotherapy directly under the physician's supervision. On the basis of this experience we believe the purpose of bibliotherapy to be threefold. One of these purposes is education. As an educational effort, reading has been prescribed with several aims in view: as a source of information; to encourage the individual to invest some interest outside of himself; to establish or to assist the patient in maintaining contacts with external reality, and to gain insight into the nature of his problem.

The second purpose of bibliotherapy would seem to be to provide a form of recreation or amusement in which it has been the aim to supply reading material merely as a source of gratification for the patient. The third purpose is to help the individual identify himself with the social group, as has been possible through the formation of a book review club, the patients' forum, and the library column of the patients' publication.

THE PRESCRIPTION OF BIBLIOTHERAPY

The Basis for the Prescription

In considering the basis for the prescription of reading we have taken into account three factors: the present therapeutic needs; the background of the individual; and the symptomatic picture. In "therapeutic needs" we consider the purposes of bibliotherapy to be essentially those indicated above, namely, whether it is intended for education or to help the individual gain psychological insight, or to aid in his resocialization, or to provide merely a form of recreation. In considering the background it has been essential that we give attention to the patient's intelligence, his previous interests both as they concern reading and the much broader field of life interest, the sex of the individual, and the occupation. We have not found it practical to base the prescription entirely on the diagnostic category,[3] etiological factors, or merely types of personality, but rather on the individual's present psychological status—namely, his emotional state, the amount of his withdrawal from reality, and his capacity at the moment to read and to gain something from what he reads.

The Technique of the Prescription

In the development of our program we have evolved a plan by which certain responsibilities are delegated to the physician and certain other responsibilities to the librarian. It is the established attitude that reading is a treatment method and as such, must be directed by the physician. The librarian is the tool who carries out the mechanics and reports the observations.

The physician is responsible for at least six functions with regard to the program. First, he is responsible for the contents of the library and must approve the books before they are purchased. It is expected that the librarian will make herself familiar with new literature available, and prepare the recommended list of books to purchase. Much help can be gained from the Quarterly Hospital Book List prepared by the Hospital Libraries Committee of the American Hospital Association. Second, he must approve the weekly list of current reading assignments to the patients as submitted by the librarian. Third, he prescribes the first reading assignment given to a patient after having interviewed the patient; this is not only to insure a wise choice but also to enlist the patient's interest in it. Fourth, he holds weekly conferences with the librarian regarding problems that have arisen and the results that have been obtained. Fifth, it is his responsibility to communicate the historical data and the psychological status of each new patient, along with the patient's particular reading habits and interests, to the librarian for her aid and guidance. Last, he must express a personal interest in and carry on frequent discussions with the patient regarding his therapeutic reading.

The librarian's responsibilities include first, the mechanics of purchasing and maintaining and distributing the books. Second, she must have a personal acquaintance with the books that she lends to the patients. Third, she interviews each patient as to the impressions and satisfaction gained from each assigned or chosen reading. Last, she is responsible for making a written report of the patients' comments and reactions to their reading for the physician's information.

In the mechanics of the prescription of the reading, we have found it desirable for the physician to interview the patient regarding his reading interests and to enlist his cooperation prior to the first assignment. The physician's influence has proven far more effective than that of the librarian in initiating the reading program of his patient. Subsequent assignments are determined by the patient's choice, by the librarian's guidance, and (perhaps most important) by the physician's suggestion. Certain types of reading, particularly that given for the purpose of aiding the patient in gaining psychological insight is always given to the patient only on the physician's order. This applies particularly to mental hygiene literature and to religious reading.

THE RESULTS OF BIBLIOTHERAPY

The evaluation of the results of reading as a treatment measure is extremely difficult because of the large number of variables. There is a wide variety of therapeutic needs, types of personalities, and a limitless variety of reading material. The psychological mechanisms by which the individual gains benefit or harm are frequently very different. In every instance, the reading is only a small part in a total program of therapy.

In attempting to evaluate the results one cannot overlook the significance that books, papers, or magazines may have for the individual. Thus, we see many persons who have never owned a book. To them books are strange and useless or worthless things. At the other extreme, we find the individual who may be nearly as unfamiliar with them as the first cited type, but whose "love of books" leads him to collect them. Books for such persons have a symbolic significance of great value. Thus, in one instance, a patient was so attached to his books that he had a good portion of his library shipped to the hospital so that he might surround himself with them. He purchased many during his stay in the hospital. Through psychoanalytic study it was possible to determine that these books had for him a symbolic connection with his mother, and their mere presence was far more significant than their content. In another instance, a patient subscribed for four daily papers. The majority of these he did not even unwrap, but would hoard them in a rack that he constructed especially to hold them until the rack was full; then he would throw them all out and begin his accumulation anew. In some instances the collector is an omnivorous reader; he not only wants to be surrounded, but also wishes to incorporate the love object.

The results from bibliotherapy as we have observed them have come about through a variety of psychological mechanisms. We have repeatedly been able to see a close parallelism between the recovery or the improvement of the patient and his renewed or awakened interest in books. Whether the therapeutic aim was to afford the patient recreation or to give him knowledge or insight, the benefit in each instance was gained through some degree of incorporation by the patient of the particular reading material. We have observed at least four methods by which benefit seems to be gained.

Perhaps the most common therapeutic benefit from bibliotherapy is derived by identification of the patient with some particular character or experience in the book with a subsequent abreaction of emotion regarding the material absorbed. In such identification the person obtained vicarious gratification from the hero's struggle and victory. He may obtain relief from the recognition that other people have problems similar to his own. This method of benefit has been especially noted from reading fiction, particularly in instances where the hero or heroine has a struggle and does achieve. Thus, one elderly patient who felt that her family had deserted her found great satisfaction in reading Pearl Buck's *Exile*. The struggle that the author's mother experienced stimulated the patient to write of her own mother, but it was apparent that she was writing a good deal about herself. Another patient whose home had been temporarily closed by her married children found a great deal of solace and satisfaction in reading Hale's *A Man Without a Country*. Still another patient was very definitely benefited by reading Ludwig's *Marie Antoinette*. In this instance our patient had been told by her husband that he would not live with her again, and she identified herself with Marie Antoinette, feeling that the heroine was unappreciated and that the king should have been in Marie's shoes. This same mechanism of identification and abreaction has at times a deleterious or at least dubiously beneficial effect. Thus, a paranoid woman whose delusions centered about clothes that other women wore, but which she claimed as her designs, was always greatly disturbed by fashion magazines. A hypomanic woman, who proclaimed and exhibited her hypererotic desires, was always demanding sex stories and risque books. A young married man, whose impotence and masturbation were the chief factors in his coming for treatment, had secretly collected illustrated pornographic literature in great quantities which he would read as he masturbated. A schizophrenic lad whose parents had lead him to believe he was to become a poetic genius, would ask for Swinburne and Pope but never read them.

A special form of identification in which benefits are apparently derived is through the mechanism of projection in which the patient uses the opportunity to attribute his or her own traits to some villain in the story, or to the "bad parents" or to the "unfaithful partner." By so doing, he vicariously expresses these traits with varying degrees of relief. Thus, one patient who consciously had a great deal of hostility for her husband felt that Rhett Butler, the character in Mitchell's *Gone With the Wind*, was by all odds the best character in the book. This ruthless individualist who in the story runs the blockade, speculates in food supplies, and finances a prostitute, she could identify with her husband and could project on to him her own character and wishes. Another patient could read into the character of Scarlett in the same book her own single-tracked and one-minded purpose to defy the doctors, her husband, and her friends. It may be recalled that it was Scarlett's one object in life to regain the family plantation; it was this patient's one aim in life to disregard all obstacles and opinions that she might return to a particular project she wished to carry out. A young schizophrenic girl who had a great deal of unconscious hostility towards her mother, but consciously thought that she chose her mother in preference to her father, found much satisfaction in Pearl Buck's *Exile* in which the author indicated a greater fondness for her mother than for her father. It is observed that many of our neurotic patients addicted to alcohol have preferred murder and mystery stories, and apparently have derived some therapeutic benefit by reading these and finding a character who was murderous or deceitful. One alcoholic expressed this very bluntly by stating that he "liked to find a murder on every page."

Therapeutic benefit results when the patient is stimulated by his reading to make a comparison between the author's standards or ideas and his own. This is particularly true when the author's statements or principles have been such that the patient could accept and adopt them. Thus, one individual with an agitated depression had found some ideas in Jackson's *Outwitting Our Nerves* which were apparently of more help for her insomnia than any direct psychotherapy that the physician had been able to give her. Another patient, a schizophrenic girl, who had been perplexed about her sexual life, found something in Strecker and Appel's *Discovering Ourselves* which prompted her to urge the book on everyone else, as the "most valuable thing she had ever read."

Beneficial results have been obtained in various ways through affording the patient some narcissistic gratification. This we feel has been accomplished by several different methods. First, by the patient finding a means of fantasy expression in some reading material whereby he momentarily escapes his own conflict. Particularly is this true with books of fiction, as illustrated by the case of a paranoid schizophrenic young man who found satisfaction and benefit in Jim Tully's novels. Frequently we see such escapes in adventure fiction such as Zane Grey's books in which the identification mechanism of the patient with the hero is not so apparent as is the momentary escape from conflict. The choice of mystery stories by patients addicted to alcohol seems in part to be beneficial because of this form of gratification.

A second type of narcissistic gratification is seen in those individuals who make an effort to maintain their contact with reality through reading newspapers and magazines. This is well illustrated by an instance of an epileptic patient whose mental age was not more than 12 years, who insisted on receiving *Time, The Review of Reviews, The Nation's Business,* and the *Wall Street Journal* with unfailing regularity. It was apparent that he never gained very much information from his reading of any of these, and yet the narcissistic value to himself was of great importance in maintaining his self-respect. Another patient, a schizophrenic woman of middle age, called a great deal of attention to herself and derived much satisfaction from clipping from every magazine and newspaper any data about her hero, the Prince of Wales. She made a scrapbook of this, enlisting the help of a good many other patients to collect the material. Curiously enough, she did little other reading of newspapers unless it pertained to England. It was conspicuous that her interest as well as the size of the scrapbook paralleled her improvement. This type of gratification may also be regarded as beneficial therapy when it prevents further deterioration.[7]

A third method of gaining narcissistic gratification is seen in the patients who want to increase their general fund of knowledge and perhaps thus strengthen and enhance the ego. This has been particularly noticeable in physician-patients who in many instances have asked for various medical journals from the hospital library. One patient voluntarily chose such books as Stockard's *The Physical Basis of Personality*, Carrel's *Man, The Unknown*, Zinsser's *Rats, Lice, and History*, and Merejkowski's *The Romance of Leonardo Da Vinci*.

A fourth method of obtaining narcissistic gratification has apparently been through the patient's desire to gain social approval, often through the therapist's or the physician's interest and affection. This has been shown by various patients who have accepted books and attempted to read them but, we felt, gained little by the reading, making the attempt chiefly because they felt it was the proper thing to do. In some instances this was because the group was doing it and in other instances because they thought the physician wanted them to do it.

EXPERIENCES WITH CERTAIN TYPES
OF BIBLIOTHERAPY

It may be of help to note certain specific failures or mistakes in bibliotherapy. In general, we have found from experience that religious reading has been detrimental. It has been permitted when it was not used to the exclusion of other reading and when it was not used to support delusional trends. Many times religious reading of any kind has appeared to increase, rather than to decrease, the mental illness. In a very few instances we have prescribed religious reading, specifically the Bible, in illnesses in elderly patients who previously had maintained a compensation only with the aid of religion.

The question of when to prescribe mental hygiene literature has received much attention.[6, 7] In general, we have found it inadvisable to permit psychotic patients or individuals with obsessional neuroses and anxiety states to have such books. It is not advised for psychoanalytic cases under treatment. In the milder neuroses, it is tolerated. We have found it practical to prescribe it for individuals with alcohol addiction prior to psychoanalytic treatment, for near-recovered psychotic individuals; and occasionally for intelligent neurotic individuals in conjunction with psychotherapy. It has often been helpful for the relatives of the patient; and, we have occasionally found that the mental hygiene books regarding children, written for parents, have been more helpful than the mental hygiene books written for the adult.

SUMMARY

The purpose of this paper has been to present an analysis of the reader's response to popular presentations of psychiatry, and the effects of reading as a therapeutic measure in a psychiatric hospital.

REFERENCES

1. L. Berry, "Hospital Library Service," Paper read before International Catholic Federation of Nurses, (July 7, 1930).
2. E. P. Bledsoe, "The Library as a Therapeutic Agent," Paper read before American Library Assn., (1923).
3. F. G. Ebaugh, "Library Facilities for Mental Patients," Read before American Library Assn., in Denver, Colorado, (June 28, 1935).
4. M. B. Graham, "Motivation of Reading among Neuropsychiatric Patients," *U. S. Vet. Bur. Med. Bull.* 6:1088-1090 (December 1930).
5. G. O. Ireland, "Bibliotherapy as an Aid in Treating Mental Cases," *Modern Hospital* 34:87-91 (June 1930).
6. E. K. Jones, "The Library in the Mental Hospital," *Modern Hospital* 18:535 (June 1922).
7. G. R. Kamman, "The Doctor and the Patients Library," *Trans. of Am. Hospital Assn.* 36:374-384 (1934).
8. F. G. A. Millar, "Patients Fly Their Hobbies to the Hospital Library," *Occup. Therapy and Rehab.* 14:121-129 (April 1935).
9. G. B. Webb, "The Prescription of Literature," *Am. J. Surg.* 12:153-163 (April 1931).

The Psychology
of the Reader

by Alice I. Bryan

Many and varied are the approaches which have been made towards
an understanding of that curious phenomenon of human society — the
gentle reader. From the viewpoint of the one who writes, the approach
to his audience may range all the way from the avowed indifference of
the narcissistic artist, creating solely to express his own ego, to the
calculated objectivity of the advertiser or propagandist whose only
purpose in writing is to sell a reader a product or an idea. Between
these extremes are the countless, more or less purposeful attempts to
evoke in the reader some emotional or intellectual reaction. What
effect all this stimulation has upon the people who are exposed to it is a
question of absorbing interest and importance to everyone whose business it is to deal with human nature.

Thousands of dollars are spent by the advertiser to measure the
effect of his printed message upon the readers he aims to influence.
Scientific techniques have been devised which enable him to compare
the "pulling power" of various types of sales appeal upon any specified
group of readers. His solvency, as well as that of the manufacturer who
employs him, depends directly upon his success in understanding the
psychology of the reader. Much more difficult to evaluate are the
efforts of the propagandist, who seeks to influence fundamental
attitudes and behavior in ways which are not so objectively measurable. Yet, that propaganda pays could hardly be doubted by anyone
who has observed its effects upon the public opinion of our times. The
anti-democratic propaganda now assailing a large number of the
readers of the world is regarded by many as the greatest menace
civilization has ever had to fight.

In view of the power attributed to the printed word by those who
see its effects upon millions of readers, it is difficult to understand the
attitude towards books and reading adopted by certain groups of con-

temporary educators. According to their philosophy, reading is but a substitute activity, much inferior to "real" life experience. Printed materials, they believe, should be used in education for reference purposes or to provide vicarious experience when opportunity for first-hand knowledge is not available or feasible. They hold that young children should be protected from books until the age of nine or ten, so that they will have an opportunity to learn about life first-hand, uncontaminated by the impressions of more sophisticated observers. Textbooks especially are anathema to these educators, for they present systematically organized facts and conclusions which deprive their readers of the opportunity to gather these facts from primary sources and reason out their own conclusions instead of accepting the pre-digested opinions of experienced specialists. Learning, they hold, takes place only through one's own doing and thinking, not by reading about what other people are doing and thinking.

The implications of this theory are very far-reaching. The amount of purposeful activity, especially manual manipulation, overtly exhibited by the learner tends to become the criterion of satisfactory development. The child who keeps busy building a doghouse, baking a cake, or sailing a boat is assumed to be more wholesomely occupied than the child who seizes every possible opportunity to "bury his nose in a book." The adult who spends his leisure time playing bridge, going to church, and engaging in other extravertive social activities is assumed to be a better adjusted individual than he who prefers to stay at home and read.

Americans have been adversely criticized for being a nation of spectators, sitting by the thousands in grandstands and moving-picture theaters, lecture halls and concert stadia, watching, listening, participating only through applause, while a handful of professionals put on a show. Worse still, it is complained, we often do not even exert ourselves to attend the performance, but sit at home and listen to the symphony over the radio, hear the prize fight described by the special sports reporters, and read the speeches of our public men in the morning newspapers. We read about life in books and magazines and the daily press instead of participating actively in first-hand adventure. It has even been proposed, to remedy this deplorable condition, that we take a lesson from Russia or Germany and organize mass group performances where the people engage vigorously in athletics, folk dancing, and pageants while the reviewing stands are reserved for the dignitaries.

This conception of life experience as muscular and glandular activity, together with its corollary that learning can occur only through overt trial-and-error experimentation, presents an extremely limited view of human behavior. In the absence of any experimental proof of its validity, it would seem rather absurd to make it the foundation stone of a philosophy of education and guidance. Furthermore, this mechanistic theory of behavior has been effectively challenged by theories of more recent vintage which reject this over-simplification of human nature and which are based upon important new experimental data on the nature of the development, perceptual, and learning processes.

The customary lag between the findings of science and their application to educational practice may help to explain why these new points of view have, as yet, had comparatively little influence in shaping educational policies. One of their chief applications, oddly enough, has been in the field of reading, where they have revolutionized the process of teaching this skill. But although it is now generally recognized that the child learns to read more effectively by first perceiving patterns and meaningful relationships and then proceeding to analysis, this principle does not seem to have been applied very widely to understanding the effects of reading and its tremendously important role in the educative process. The emphasis seems to have been almost entirely upon the improvement of reading as a useful mechanical skill or tool, rather than upon attempting to re-evaluate the contribution which reading can make in presenting organized and meaningful patterns of experience, the elements of which can later be analyzed in more concrete terms. If synthesis should precede analysis in the development of a perceptual skill, such as reading, why not in the acquisition of knowledge and in the development of the ability to think?

Furthermore, it shall be my contention that the reading of books or other printed material may be just as real and vital an experience as playing a game of tennis, building a radio, painting a picture, or marching in a parade. The relative stimulus value of any of these activities depends upon the capacity of the individual to perceive them as meaningful situations, to assimilate their meaning with reference to his own previous and future experiences, and to make any adjustments necessary to bring the new experience into acceptable relationship with his own basic motivation. The effects of reading a book, like the effects of any other experience, must be measured in terms of the changes in attitude and behavior induced in a particular individual, at a particular time.

Thus, the same physical pattern of black marks on white paper may so threaten the emotional insecurity of one reader that he will fight to have it censored, so reinforce the attitudes of another that he will contribute a sum of money to the cause it sponsors, while a third reader may find it so meaningless that he will return it to the shelf half read with a request for something more interesting. I venture to suggest that newspaper and radio accounts during the past few months of events occurring three thousand miles away, to people we have never met, have induced in most of us more intense emotional reaction than any personal "real life" experience during the same period.

This problem of the function of reading in the educational process seems of vital importance to the librarian as well as to the professional educator. Although philosophies of librarianship may vary in some respects, it seems safe to say that one of the chief concerns of the library profession is to encourage as many people as possible to utilize the resources of the library in ways which will enrich their experience and contribute to their personal and social effectiveness.

Three major problems seem to be involved in the fulfillment of this aim: first, the problem of providing those resources in terms of buildings, reading materials, and trained personnel; second, that of motivating and equipping the reader to avail himself of these resources; and third, providing guidance to those who need it in the selection of reading materials best adapted to their purposes and needs. All three problems require for their solution an understanding of the psychology of the reader, but it is the third problem — that of reader guidance — to which particular attention will be directed in this paper.

Before guidance of any form can be undertaken, it is necessary first to know what the goal or objective of the guidance is to be, and secondly, how this goal is to be achieved. The former may be termed the philosophy of guidance, while the latter is concerned with guidance techniques. Differences of opinion exist among specialists with respect to both these aspects. One of the most fundamental questions that has been raised is whether the attempt to assist the individual to adjust to life under present economic and social conditions is worth the effort.

Several years ago an eminent psychiatrist, Dr. Frankwood E. Williams, went on record in a public address just a few months before his death to the effect that individual guidance had in his opinion become practically futile. He testified that thirty years of work in the field of mental hygiene had convinced him that the only fruitful approach to the solution of basic human problems must be through the avenue of social change. A new world order must be established which would permit the individual to function freely and harmoniously before personal happiness could become a reality for the majority of human beings. He announced his intention to devote all of his professional efforts in the future to the recreating of society, rather than to the adjustment of the individual to the present order, and he urged all professional workers in the field of guidance to redirect their energies similarly.

This point of view has also found expression from time to time in other quarters. It raises very fundamental issues regarding the function and province of the specialist in human adjustments. Must work with the individual be abandoned entirely or, at best, be considered alleviative rather than educative or therapeutic in its function and effects? Is it true that economic and social maladjustments of contemporary civilization must necessarily thwart or dwarf all individual development and negate all therapeutic effort which does not directly attack or reform existing institutions or environmental conditions? To me this seems like defeatism in the face of one of the greatest challenges that has ever been presented to the teachers of humanity.

Moreover, it would seem to involve a fundamental fallacy in the assumptions it implies regarding the nature of human adjustment.

A more tenable philosophy, in the opinion of many, is the point of view that the function of guidance is to assist the individual, and through the individual the group, to acquire the resources and techniques necessary for attacking his problems more effectively, rather than attempting (even if that were possible) to solve his problems for him. Mankind is now in the process of working out tremendously complicated problems of social adjustment. Many of these problems involve variables which, so far as we know, have never confronted the human race before. We have no precedents or formulae for their control.

A variety of solutions has been suggested and some of these, in the form of different political and economic systems, are being experimented with in various parts of the world. The absence of unanimity in evaluating their success indicates the complexity of the problem. It is possible that the ultimate solution may involve the development of an entirely new system of international organization. The survival of our civilization through the present period of conflict, chaos, and crisis would seem to depend upon the capacity of our generation to comprehend the meaning and the implications of these problems and to apply a technique of adjustment which will at least give us time to attempt a constructive solution before disaster overwhelms us. The educational system under which we have been trained to meet life is now on trial. We are tensely watching an exhibition of problem-solving, on a vast scale, with life or death for millions as the eventual stake.

Whatever the immediate outcome of the present international crisis, no one can doubt that dangerous and difficult times lie ahead. At such a moment, it would seem, the agencies of education and guidance cannot, while they search for ultimate solutions of their own, turn aside from their task of assisting individuals, who depend upon them for guidance, to comprehend and adjust to the changing conditions of life. Guidance is now more needed than ever to give insight into the nature of the problems the world is facing, to combat mendacious and pernicious propaganda, and to help the individual to retain his emotional and intellectual balance while values and standards shift, change, and disappear.

Differences of opinion arise, also, with respect to the techniques, as well as the philosophy, of guidance. One school of thought holds that guidance should be passive in nature, affording merely an opportunity for the individual to carry on a process of emotional catharsis in order to rid his system of the accumulated poisons of repression and frustration. Other schools advocate that guidance be a more active, educational process. They attempt to give the individual increasing insight into the genesis and nature of his problems, to help him analyze the adequacy of his own behavior, and to assist him to work out more effective modes of adjustment.

Whichever technique is employed, it would seem that the librarian who specializes in reader guidance should approach the individual from a psychological point of view. This would mean that an attempt should be made to obtain as much insight as possible into the fundamental motivation which lies behind the individual's special interest in reading. Thus, it might be possible that a woman who asks advice in planning a course of reading on contemporary affairs is motivated by a feeling of insecurity in her marital relationship. She may be seeking to hold, against outside competition, an intellectually superior husband who has ceased to respond to her physical appeal. She may rationalize her interest in contemporary affairs by saying that she wants to be able to help her daughter with her high school homework in social science. If the librarian knows and understands the implications of this situation, he may be able to suggest books which will help her deal with her problem much more directly and with greater likelihood of working out a constructive adjustment.

Another woman in the same neighborhood, of about the same age, intelligence, and socio-economic level, may also come seeking a course of reading in contemporary affairs. She, too, says she wants to help her daughter with her homework. But her motivation may be entirely different from that of her neighbor. She has a husband whom she dominates completely and towards whom she is very protective. She noticed at a dinner party the other night that he was conspicuously ignorant of current events. She intends to read up on these matters and force him to listen while she summarizes for his benefit.

Now let us imagine one more woman of the same general type who asks for the same course of reading and who also wants to help her daughter. She is a person of thwarted ambition, married to a man who is content with very little. She has identified herself almost completely with her daughter, whom she plans to make a teacher, a career she herself always wanted to follow. Her daughter has been failing in her social science work. The mother wants to help her, for she fears that she may drop out of high school and take up tap-dancing. The daughter has been hinting that this is what she really wants to do and the father thinks it might be a good idea. From a psychological point of view, each of these three women is attempting to adjust to a basic personal problem, each very different in nature and with only a very superficial relationship to their mutual reading interest. There may be books in that library which would help each one to gain some insight into her real problem and make it possible for her to obtain satisfaction for her basic drive, but they would probably not be books on current events.

The librarian's task of "finding the right book, for the right reader, at the right time" is really a threefold problem. He must know his books, he must know the reader, and he must know what effect will be produced from bringing the two together. A psychologist interested in the problem of research in reader guidance put the question this

way: We must find out "what books, do what things, to what people."
He might have added "at what times, and under what circumstances."
It would seem that the ideal person for the job of readers' adviser
should be a combination of professional librarian and professional psychologist. Or, better still, that the reader should have the benefit of the
combined judgment of the psychologist and the librarian, working
together to understand his needs and to provide for them.

Much emphasis has been given to the study and analysis of
readers' interests. Elaborate lists have been compiled of the reading interests of children at various levels of development and of the reading
interests of adults in different vocational or socio-economic groups.
This material is valuable, as far as it goes, but in some respects, at least,
it seems a rather superficial approach to the psychology of the reader.
When readers are classified according to some developmental or
sociological typology, the individual as a dynamic personality may
remain completely undiscovered. The case study approach, which has
been applied with interesting results by several investigators, seems to
offer a much more fruitful method for understanding the reader.

Another line of research which has interesting possibilities is the
study of change in attitudes resulting from exposure to various types
of printed material. When a larger number and variety of these studies
are available, they should be very useful in helping us to evaluate the
effects of propaganda of different types upon the attitudes of different
groups. An interesting research study, now in progress by a librarian,
is concerned with measuring the effects of fictional material, presenting the Negro in a favorable light, upon the attitudes of white children
in southern schools. The chief limitation of this type of study is the tendency of group averages to mask individual differences. Interpretation
and application must necessarily be limited by the fact that we are
dealing with groups rather than individuals.

When it is a question of advising the individual reader, the results
of available research on reading interests and attitudes will, I fear, be
of comparatively little help. If guidance is to be more than a very
superficial service, the reader must be understood as a whole personality, and his reading planned in terms of his personal needs, goals,
frustrations, and conflicts. The librarian will be helped to gain this
insight by a study of the adjustment process in general and the various
mechanisms of adjustment which are commonly adopted by individuals in working out their problems. Thus, when an individual meets
an obstacle which interferes with the realization of a basic drive, he
may attempt to adjust in a variety of ways. These might include the development of defense mechanisms, attempts at compensation, day-
dreaming or fantasy, the development of phobias, psychoneurotic ail-
ments, or chronic states of anxiety or worry.

The techniques of guidance and re-education employed by the
psychologist in helping the individual to work out a constructive and
realistic solution to his problems could be applied to good advantage

by the reader's adviser. While the librarian, naturally, could not expect to explore as deeply into the reader's problems as the consulting psychologist, he could learn to gain rapport and confidence, to help build desirable attitudes, and to give the reader a feeling of security in availing himself of the resources of the library. It is a well recognized fact that professional psychiatric and psychological assistance is available to only a small proportion of those who need it. The contribution which can be made by the trained layman, such as the teacher, parent, and social worker, in preventative mental hygiene has been shown to be of the utmost importance in supplementing professional work in this field. The teacher training curriculum is heavily weighted with this point of view and with specific courses in psychology; the social worker likewise is well trained in this approach. But for some reason the potential role of the librarian in the mental hygiene program seems to have been overlooked, although in some respects he is even more strategically situated to render constructive guidance than any other lay worker.

L. F. Shaffer[1] stresses the part played by parents, teachers, social workers, and employers in preserving the mental health of the nation, but he does not mention the librarian. He defines the work of the layman as follows:

> The practice of mental hygiene is not limited to the work of clinics, or the treatment of maladjusted persons. In a very real sense, everyone is engaged in mental hygiene, whether he intends it or not. . . . preventative action in mental hygiene is of more fundamental importance than is remedial work to repair damages already done. If all persons who deal with others, especially parents, teachers and employers, governed their influence by principles of mental hygiene, there would be fewer lame and deficient personalities for clinicians to treat. The constructive measures that are applied to create effective personality have been termed *positive mental hygiene*. . . . As far as pronounced disorders of behavior are concerned, laymen need only to know how to identify them, to learn to consider them from an objective rather than a moralistic viewpoint, and to seek such expert assistance as may be available. In the everyday problems of the development and training of emotional and other habits, the intelligent and informed parent or teacher can contribute directly to the building of an effective personality. Also, just as parents bind up the child's little wounds of physical injury, so some remedial service may be rendered on the occurrence of simpler and more common maladjustments.

In addition to exercising this general function of preventative mental hygiene, it would seem that the reader's adviser could render a highly specialized type of psychological guidance through the effective use of the resources of the library. Psychological counsellors have long since made use of books for purposes of instruction, interpretation, motivation, relaxation, and other forms of psychotherapy. The term "bibliotherapy" has been used by Karl Menninger to designate the use of carefully selected books on mental hygiene for therapeutic purposes. It seems clear that the reading of certain types of material may have beneficial effects upon certain people in re-educating attitudes, helping to overcome feelings of guilt, fear, and insecurity, and giving insight and aid in the solution of personal problems.

I see no reason why bibliotherapy, as a technique of guidance, should not be extended scientifically to include types of literature other than that specifically relating to mental hygiene. Why should not novels, poetry, plays, works on philosophy and ethics, religion, art, history, and science be placed in readers' hands for the specific purpose of helping them to face their life problems more effectively and to gain greater freedom and happiness in their personal adjustments. Everyone who has ever been deeply moved and influenced by reading the right book at just the right moment knows how crucial such an experience can be in shaping his destiny. Autobiographies of many prominent people bear witness to the effect of particular books upon their subsequent attitudes and behavior. Why leave the selection of these books to accident? For every reader who has been fortunate enough to find what he needed at the psychological moment, there must be countless thousands who have not. And yet the books were there for the asking, if there had been someone to know and to understand their needs, and someone to know what books to give them.

So far as I know, the psychologist's training does not in any sense prepare him for expert guidance in book selection, as does the training of the librarian. Psychologists are probably as well read, on the whole, as any professional group. But the very nature of their highly specialized, technical work makes it impossible for them to give the time to acquiring the broad and detailed knowledge of the resources of the world of literature which is the working equipment of the trained librarian. On the other hand, it is equally unlikely that the librarian who specializes in the work of reader guidance has had time or opportunity to acquire the scientific knowledge and understanding of the problems of the reader which are the province of the professional psychologist. Thus, the psychologist is limited to the choice of a comparatively small collection of books, while the librarian is limited to dealing with a comparatively small area of problems.

The most effective solution for this difficulty would seem to be the recognition by both the psychological and the library professions of the necessity, or at least the desirability, of cooperative effort. I would recommend that a professional librarian, specializing in readers' advisory work, be appointed as a staff member in every psychological clinic that could support such a service, either on a full-time or a consulting basis. He should read the case histories, interview the clients to obtain the information he needs on reading habits and interests, attend the staff conferences, contribute when possible to the diagnosing of the problem, and when bibliotherapy is indicated take responsibility for carrying out this part of the treatment and reporting upon its progress.

Next, I would recommend that every public library that could find funds to support such a service should employ a consulting psychologist, either full- or part-time, to cooperate with the readers' adviser in diagnosing the needs and problems of readers who appear to require this service. It would seem almost certain in these troubled times that a number of the readers who are now seeking this advisory service are maladjusted in some respect in their personal lives and are really seeking advice on these deeper problems. They may be quite unaware of their real motivation and entirely sincere in believing that all they want is help in outlining a course of study which is only remotely connected with their actual problem. For example, one of the more frequently noted ways of attempting to adjust to feelings of inferiority is through the acquisition of specialized knowledge. This may or may not be a constructive adjustment, depending upon the nature of the problem and the ability of the individual to solve it this way.

It would also seem important that the library schools should include in their curriculum a course in psychological adjustments, designed to give the librarian the background he needs for understanding the psychology of the reader. This course would be especially valuable to the readers' adviser, but almost equally so to any librarian who plans to work in an educational institution, such as a school or college library. The specialist in library personnel would also find the point of view and the materials of such a course very helpful in dealing with problems of adjustment among library workers. All would profit from the increased understanding they would acquire of their own motivation and adjustment mechanisms. Such a course was given for the first time this past summer session in the Columbia Library School, so there is already a precedent for this recommendation.

Finally, I should like to see closer cooperation between librarians and psychologists in studying and discussing their mutual problems. It was a revelation to find, in the curriculum of the library school, courses and materials so definitely psychological in nature and content. Courses such as Children's Reading Interests, Reading Interests of Adults, Personnel Problems, The School Library, The College Library, are dealing with subjects of vital interest and importance to the educational psychologist. In Kansas City, at the A.L.A. convention, I attended a session at which a paper was given on "Developments in Scientific Instruction and Evaluation of Reading" which was one of many on subjects of psychological interest. Likewise, at the recent Columbus meeting of the American Psychological Association and the American Association of Applied Psychology, papers were read that I am sure would have been instructive and enjoyable to many librarians. In the field of research there are many common problems which could be worked upon cooperatively, with benefit to both professions.

These cooperative activities might take the form of joint programs at meetings and conventions, panel discussions with different points of view represented, joint committees to study problems and make reports on subjects of mutual interest. We might then go a step further and hold an inter-professional conference of librarians, educators, psychologists, psychiatrists, social workers, and parents, where a theme of common concern would be discussed from all angles and united action might be taken in a cause vital to all. An appropriate theme for such a conference might be the new National Health Program, with especial emphasis on the provisions for mental health.

Who shall take the lead in coordinating such a conference? Why not the librarians, whose specific function it is to promote the dissemination of knowledge, and to prevent the inbreeding of ideas, in the interests of greater intellectual fertility.

REFERENCE

1. L. F. Shaffer, *Psychology of Adjustment* (Boston: Houghton Mifflin, 1936).

The Place of Bibliotherapy in a Hospital

by Sadie Peterson-Delaney

Books, like medicine, have a definite effect on the physical, mental and moral welfare of those who are unfortunately handicapped by illness.

Bibliotherapy means the treatment of a patient through selective reading. A brief record of the patient's diagnosis, treatment and prognosis is furnished the librarian, who, having more than the layman's knowledge of the more common cases, selects the books for the individual which will give him not only knowledge and entertainment, but stimulation toward the development of a wholesome interest in subjects which will relieve his mind from his malady and worries. What is good for one person might be detrimental to another, therefore, this careful and intelligent selection of reading matter for each individual is of great importance.

The library then has become a laboratory and a work shop for those interested in the improvement and development of the whole individual. Here, minds long imprisoned in lethargy are awakened. This has been evident at the hospital library of the Veterans Administration Facility, Tuskegee, Alabama, for fourteen years.

The atmosphere of the library is conducive to reading. Its green walls are hung with maps, paintings, and pictures of Negro leaders and authors of books as well as other outstanding persons who have attained great heights through books.

There are nearly 6,000 volumes in the general collection, and a separate collection of books by and about the Negro. Throngs of readers use the library daily and their requests for reference and research material equal that of a public library. Many choose a vocation or a hobby through books and some complete their educational preparation through the library.

The bibliotherapy unit is composed of the mental patients who come from the closed wards daily, with an attendant, to the library. Here they are aided in the development of their dormant qualities through books, and are given individual attention and sympathetic direction.

Reprinted from *Library Journal* 63:305-308 (April 1938). Published by R. R. Bowker Co. (a Xerox Company). Copyright © 1938 by Xerox Corporation.

The librarian is guided by the ward surgeon, through the information he has gathered from the patient's diagnosis, and the patient's progress or reaction to reading is noted.

Sometimes a musician or an artist, an inventor, or a craftsman in trades discovers absorbing material on the theme of his art, his invention or his trade. Through the clipping and binding services of this department, a reading interest is created by the making of scrap books on various subjects and these are used in their discussions of current events. At first, the reading and collection of such material may be a hobby with the patient. Usually, it becomes a serious and steady business with him as the urge awakens within him to return his energies to the perfecting of his former interest, and once again he is alive with the enthusiasm and joy derived from activity. The satisfaction he realizes from being supplied with ample material, both old and new, is evidenced by his testimonials, his obvious improvement mentally and spiritually, and the doctors' reports of steps towards recovery.

The library service to the bed patients is most important. This consists of the librarian's daily visits to the bedsides on the various wards with a library book cart filled with carefully selected reading material and pictures. This gives the patient who must spend long hours in bed, an opportunity through books, to build up hope, relieve his mental tension, absorb his worries and alleviate his pain. Reading interest awakened in a bed patient, often stays with the patient during his entire period of hospitalization.

Reading interest is aroused in the new patient entering the hospital through personal contact by the librarian and the circulation of book lists and compiled pamphlets. Weekly radio talks by the librarian, suggested books and synopses, as well as talks on the wards, keep the patients informed. The library activities have done much in establishing self-confidence, in affording an outlet to the patient who has previously felt himself inadequate.

As the restless patient becomes absorbed in newspapers, magazines, and library activities, he becomes more calm, the introvert becomes communicative, the grandiose finds an outlet, the depressed finds an incentive to live, and many become leaders and public speakers, returning to their communities as useful citizens. In many cases they organize press clubs at home.

In the Library Press Club a weekly Monday morning meeting is held where patients review books they have read, to their comrades. In the Thursday evening meetings of this same club, they select a speaker from among their number who often gains the respect of his audience and develops a certain pride of achievement.

The Philatelic (stamp) Club stimulates interest in books of travel, history, and literature. It also creates stamp collectors who become absorbed in this worth while hobby.

The Library Debate Club (the patients' forum) encourages discussion. A great deal of reading is done by patients in their efforts to prepare for their subjects and before the current topic is closed they are seeking information for another.

The Library Department for the Blind has brought light to men who have been shut out by darkness and has given them a desire to take an active part in life. They are taught "Standard Braille" by the librarian and they are able to keep abreast through current magazines and books in braille. Talking Books are supplied. These, they enjoy in the library and on their wards. Through braille book lists they are given a chance to make a selection of books such as, *Hitting the Dark Trail*—Hawkes; *North to the Orient* — Lindbergh; *Anne Sullivan Macy, The Life Behind Helen Keller*—Braddy; *Cappy Ricks*—Kyne; *Short History of the World*—Wells; Shakespeare's plays and many other eminent authors' books.

The titles in braille on the Talking Book Records bring great satisfaction to the blind reader in making his selection. These books, they review weekly in the library causing the sighted reader to become so interested that they request the same books. Each afternoon the blind patients come in groups to the library and enjoy competitive reading in braille. They give sentences in "Oral Braille" in history and philosophy, braille having been made a language in these departments as well as a text. New men are continually being added to this group and are taught braille. Most of these blind patients are mental cases who, through this therapy, are conquering their mental handicap. The deteriorated blind are cheered and soothed by the Talking Books which are taken to them on their wards and quite often a regressed patient requests the title of some book he has heard previously.

There is a Medical Library, which is accessible to the medical staff only, containing nearly 500 volumes and a large number of medical journals for research and reference.

The World War left a vast number of men broken in body and spirit and suffering from various disabilites. Some must put in long periods of hospitalization and in an effort to aid in their recovery, the Veterans Administration Hospital Libraries bridge the gap between the hospital and the outside world; aiding them in their adjustment to present conditions and fostering hope for a future. Some interesting examples are cited:

(A) Surgical case. This patient was obliged to lie in one position for long periods and had the use of only one arm. He was very discouraged about his condition and became a chronic complainer. He was finally persuaded, by the librarian, to read books. He soon became interested in such books as *Ask Me Another*—Spafford and Esty, *Five Thousand New Answers to Questions*—Haskin. Soon he took delight in encouraging other patients who visited him. He read all current magazines and *The Negro in Our History*—Woodson. He was gratified at being so popular and became optimistic and cheerful. He was given a book review and is now among the best informed patients on his ward. He is greatly improved and cooperative.

(B) Mental case. This man was uncommunicative; was almost mute. It was difficult to have him respond, even to questioning. He sat and stared blankly, dully. He was brought to the library with the bibliotherapy group each day. He was given books of poetry to read. Later he began copying poems. Daily, poems were selected from his copies for circulation to bed patients. He was given selected editorials and essays to read at each Library Press Club meeting. This gave him a chance to talk. Also he would read aloud to other patients. Gradually, by reading aloud, he has become communicative for periods and it is felt that with continued treatment, he may become normal.

(C) Mental case. This patient was deteriorated. He was at last brought to the library with the bibliotherapy group. It was found that he had previously had some training in art. He was given drawing ink and books with photographs of artists. He became calm and subdued and not only made reproductions but steadily improved them greatly. He improved daily in drawing and reading. He requested information on all he was copying. Later he was given oils and painted pictures of Sir Galahad and Pushkin and Lord Byron. He prepares for an art exhibit held in the library annually.

(D) Mental case. This patient was paroled to the library. He had a fair educational background. An effort was made to aid him in view of his weakness. He became interested in the clipping service and collected valuable articles on many subjects. He read extensively and attended the library daily. After ground parole he continued his interest. He read *Habits That Handicap*—Towns; *He Can Who Thinks He Can* and *Everybody Ahead*—Marden, along with biographies of men who have succeeded. He began to gain the confidence of his associates. He assisted his daughter in the preparation of her valedictory for graduation, with material he read in the library. He improved rapidly and was discharged. It was reported that he has become a community leader and has adjusted himself satisfactorily.

(E) Mental case. This patient was paroled to the library; he was found to have had a splendid educational background, but was apathetic and discouraged at first. He soon began to take interest in the library. He improved gradually and became a zealous reader. Finally he asked to be given some library training. He assisted in library desk work. This gave him great pride in his accomplishments. His ward surgeon noticed his rapid improvement. He participated in the Library Debate Club, also the Press Club. His interest in books seemed to lead him to a new world. Home difficulties arose but his interest in books seemed to fortify him. He has been giving his entire day at the library and is an asset. He is composed, interested in his personal appearance and hopes to secure enough training to become an assistant in some library.

(F) This patient (mental case) because of family difficulties, had become bitter toward life and anti-socially inclined. He had been a practicing physician. He was given parole to the library. The librarian interested him in reading. He first read *A Fortune to Share* and *Let's Start Over Again*—Young. He used these books at the Library Press Club meetings. He soon found great interest in reading and requested each time to review his books to the patient group. He is so influential with the patients, that he serves in an official capacity with them. He is now accountable and makes excellent talks in the library to patient groups in their library meetings, and in Saturday Debates, assisting in the selection of reference material. His entire personality has changed. He sent book lists and reviews to his family and through this interest a family adjustment has been brought about. This serves to extend new ways to him for his future. He is allowed time daily to study and soon hopes to be given trial furlough to make plans to resume his practice.

(G) General Ward case. Wheel-chair case. This patient was a bed patient for a long period and then progressed to a wheel chair. His chronic condition made him despondent at first. He became interested in reading and read on the average of a book a day and kept abreast through many newspapers and magazines. He soon began to give reviews of his books to his ward mates and recommended to them the books he had read. This gave him such prestige with his associates that he lost sight of his condition. Although it seems that he will always be incapacitated, he looks forward to being a bookshop owner when discharged.

Thus the library has proven a factor in the medical service of hospitals and is classed as an effective therapeutic measure in the rehabilitation of all types of patients.

It is true that, as David Grayson says in his interesting book *Adventures in Solitude,* many people never have leisure to read until a period of hospitalization is necessary.

Well chosen books ameliorate disturbing thoughts, as well as tend to soothe and build up hope, and the hospitalized veteran benefits from this valuable therapy.

Few people, even veterans, realize the haunting tragedy of scores of men, once young, ambitious, and physically and mentally fit, who came back from the World War pitiable shadows of their former selves.

The Veterans Hospitals are playing a tremendous part in rehabilitating these men and in that process the bibliotherapy unit has been found to be invaluable.

Bibliotherapy for Neuropsychiatric Patients:* Report of Two Cases

by Jerome M. Schneck

The purpose of this report is to present clinical data on bibliotherapy in an effort to encourage further research with this form of treatment. Relatively little information on the subject is available in medical literature.

During the course of research on bibliotherapy at the Menninger Clinic a plan of study has been outlined,[1] two bibliographies prepared[2,3] and a review of the literature presented.[4] Reference to these publications will furnish the background for the development of interest in this field, demonstrating at the same time how very much remains to be accomplished.

This paper deals with two cases in which bibliotherapy has been used as an aid in treatment. In the first case it was incorporated into psychotherapeutic interviews, and in the second it was used as an adjunct to hypnotherapy. In neither instance was an attempt made to utilize bibliotherapy as the only therapeutic technique. This is hardly practicable because a separation in fact from "psychotherapy" is probably inconceivable; the first term virtually implies the second. No claim is made for the indispensability of bibliotherapy in the treatment of these patients; it has simply been a valuable aid in both cases.

The technique of bibliotherapy varies with the physician and patient. With an increase in our knowledge and experience, techniques may probably be standardized, although flexibility will undoubtedly be necessary in accordance with the requirements of the patient and the predilections of the therapist.

The various possible approaches in utilizing reading as treatment will not be discussed. Rather the methods employed with these two patients will be presented with comments or explanations as indicated.

*Part of a research in bibliotherapy, The Menninger Foundation, Topeka, Kansas. For other reports, see papers listed at end of this article.

CASE REPORTS†

Case I

The patient, a 40-year-old housewife, sought treatment for periodic depressions.

Historical Data: The family history was not remarkable. The patient was the third of six siblings, born and reared on a farm in a small midwestern community. Her social relationships in childhood and adolescence were good. She obtained a college education, paying for some of her expenses by part-time work, and then married a professional man. They had three children, one of whom died in early childhood. The patient taught school for several years. Her husband was friendly and sociable and both he and she were active in organizational activities.

Present Illness: Six years prior to the onset of the depression the patient had received thyroid medication for "nervousness" with questionable results. When the feeling of depression started she received estrogenic medication with no beneficial effect. Menopausal changes as indicated by oligomenorrhea began two years after the onset of the depression. The depressive episodes recurred in cycles for five years starting in the fall and ending by mid-January or February. During the last three cycles there was mild euphoria in the spring with resumption of normal behavior in the summer. When depressed the patient experienced feelings of inferiority with an inclination to limit her social contacts and loss of interest in household activities. She had feelings of unworthiness as a mother and wife and had thoughts of suicide. When mildly euphoric she was also hyperactive, reengaging enthusiastically in household and social activities. There was decreasing interest in sexual relationships in recent years.

Examinational Data: Physical and neurological examinations were essentially negative and findings on routine blood, urine and x-ray examinations were within normal limits. The BMR was minus 2.1%.

The clinical psychiatric examination revealed no perceptual defects. Recent and remote memory were good and accessibility was moderate. Historical information was furnished in organized fashion and no disharmony of affect was observed. The patient appeared mildly depressed. She had a characteristic bland facial expression which persisted unchanged throughout the period of study and treatment.

The Bellevue Scale revealed an I.Q. in the superior range. The Performance I.Q. was in the bright-normal range with the discrepancy indicating the depressive trend. There was no evidence of attention disturbance during the psychological testing procedures although some concentration disturbance was apparent. Anxieties seemed to be

†Out-Patient Department, The Menninger Clinic.

kept out of consciousness. Learning efficiency was excellent with everyday concept-formation superior in quality although it showed depressive narrowing. The diagnostic personality tests indicated a pre-morbid compulsive adjustment with clear-cut depressive stereotypy and meticulous thinking. There were also indications of obsessive inclinations. The Rorschach and Association Tests reflected a great tension of aggressions, and the Thematic Apperception Test revealed a sensitive woman with refined feelings and considerable versatility of associations. Despair and suicidal ideas were expressed but there was also an expression of hope for a better future.

On the basis of the history, clinical findings and psychology tests, a diagnosis of neurotic depression was made.

Treatment

The first book used in treatment was *Love Against Hate* by Karl Menninger. This was recommended when conflicts arose about mixed feelings which the patient recognized she might possibly have had toward her son during his fatal illness. This therapeutic approach was attempted because of the patient's intelligence and apparent receptiveness to psychological ideas. When this reading recommendation was made the patient was told that books were to be used in her treatment in order to enable therapeutic procedures to extend beyond the time limited to interviews.

Reading the book prompted discussion of her relative frigidity in sexual relations with her husband. This material arose in direct association with portions of the subject matter in the book. While reading *Love Against Hate* she was stimulated to consider her relationship with both her husband and her deceased son. Also while discussing the book various types of psychiatric treatment were referred to and the patient inquired about the distinguishing features between psychotherapy and psychoanalysis. Misapprehensions were clarified and the discussion as a whole served an educational function for the patient. Rapport between patient and examiner thus seemed enhanced.

Further discussion of material in *Love Against Hate* led directly to an evaluation of the patient's relationship with her parents and siblings, and her school and social activities. The patient was only moderately accessible when treatment was started and the discussion of her reading seemed definitely to increase accessibility. Through association with subject matter in this book the patient was led into a discussion of her relationship with her children, feelings of guilt involved, ideas about childhood masturbation and her own conflicts about this.

After finishing *Love Against Hate* the patient spontaneously requested further reading recommendations. In order to increase accessibility even further *The Human Mind* by the same author was recommended and conflict material likewise elicited. In addition to *The Human Mind* the patient was given the November 1944 issue of *The Bulletin of the Menninger Clinic* (Pediatrics Number). This was highly effective, functioning in the same manner as the aforementioned books. While reading *The Human Mind* the concept of resistance in treatment arose. The patient recognized both intellectually and emotionally its application to herself.

Man Against Himself by Karl Menninger was then used and the patient found the sections on suicide depressing and unenjoyable. It made her uneasy, thus confirming the impression of other workers in this field that it is inadvisable to recommend reading material dealing with suicide to depressed patients. In view of the patient's tendency to re-read various sections of books prescribed, she was advised specifically to refrain from re-reading the subject matter dealing with suicide and she readily accepted the suggestion. No difficulties were encountered.

In the same way that the concept of resistance was encountered and discussed, the concept of ambivalence was likewise evaluated in relation to the patient's family and social relationships. Additional psychiatric terms and ideas were dealt with in this way.

After reading the aforementioned psychological material the patient continued to seek additional recommendations. Her various interests were discussed and it was learned that the patient's social outlook was broad and that she was anxious to learn about people in geographical and social settings different from her own. The writings of J. P. Marquand were mentioned to her and three of his books recommended— *The Late George Apley, So Little Time,* and *H. M. Pulham, Esq.* The patient had improved greatly by this time and reading was prescribed as much for recreational and educational purposes now as for nuclear material for further discussion.

Further discussions of books and interests revealed a long standing desire to learn the elements of astronomy, and reading recommendations were made in accordance with this.

Shortly before treatment was terminated the patient was considering the possiblity of working on a voluntary basis at an Army hospital. Among the possibilities she considered was library work, in view of her previous experience in this field while at college and her renewed interest in books. When treatment was concluded the patient requested further suggestions for reading, especially of psychological material. It was felt that this preference could be satisfied while supplying at the same time books with both recreational and educational value. The following were suggested: Gregory Zilboorg's *Mind, Medicine and Man;* Helen E. Marshall's *Dorothea Dix— The Forgotten Samaritan;* Dorothy Blitzsten's *Psychoanalysis Explained;* Clifford Beers' *The Mind that Found Itself;* and William A. White's *Autobiography of a Purpose.* A brief description of each was given and apparently the patient's wishes were satisfied.

Case II

This patient was a 50-year-old married woman who sought treatment for symptoms which had been disturbing her for the preceding four months. These consisted of various somatic complaints, insomnia, irritability and a constant feeling of fatigue without the ability to relax.

Historical Data: The patient was one of six siblings, born and reared on a midwestern farm. A maternal aunt was a patient in a mental hospital but there was no history of nervous or mental disease in any other members of the family.

The patient's scholastic record through high school was good and she attended a business college following her graduation. She worked steadily as a stenographer for six years and then married a man whose occupation was that of grocery dealer but who, in more recent years, operated a small farm. For many years the patient carried the burden of business transactions in association with her husband's work and, in addition, she did part-time stenographic work. She disliked housekeeping. She was interested in women's clubs and church work, actively engaging in social activities associated with the latter. The patient had two children, one of whom was dead at birth and the other living and well at 18 years of age. She was described by her husband as being meticulously clean about her person and home.

Present Illness: Although some of the patient's difficulties started during the four or five year period prior to treatment, they had increased in intensity four to five months before she appeared at the Clinic. At that time her menstrual flow had stopped completely. She complained of "nerves," frontal headaches, generalized headaches, a sensation of fullness over the bridge of her nose, insomnia, a feeling of fatigue without the ability to relax, irritability when conversing with friends and intermittent substernal pain of ten to fifteen seconds duration with aching of her arms, precipitated by emotional disturbances but not by physical exertion.

Osteopathic treatments had been of no aid and she then received six electroshock treatments at another sanitarium, obtaining temporary relief. She then complained, however, of a peculiar, painful sensation over the areas to which the electrodes had been placed.

Examinational Data: The physical and neurological examinations were essentially negative. Blood studies and urine analysis yielded results within normal limits. Chest and skull x-rays were negative. Four leads on an electrocardiogram revealed a sinus rhythm with normal P waves and T waves and slight slurring of QRS complexes in all leads. It was interpreted as an essentially normal EKG with the appearance of no abnormalities after exercise.

In the clinical interview situation the patient's physical appearance seemed to be somewhat younger than her stated 50 years. She seemed tense, but when it was suggested to her she leaned back in her chair and attempted to relax. There was sighing and slow shrugging of her shoulders giving the impression of fatigue. She was only moderately accessible and quite circumstantial, avoiding conflict material when probing was attempted. Cooperativeness in other respects was good. She was alert, well oriented in all spheres, with good recent and remote memory. No perceptual defects were elicited. Thought content centered largely on her somatic complaints. Her intelligence and fund of knowledge seemed average. Judgment was slightly impaired. The patient was usually tearful and manifested moderate anxiety. No disharmony of affect was evident.

The psychological tests corroborated the clinical impression of neurasthenia. The Bellevue Scale revealed an average I.Q. with the performance level below the verbal level. The original I.Q. seemed probably to have been in the bright normal range. Learning efficiency was fair but every day concept formation very weak. The diagnostic personality tests confirmed the given diagnosis. The association test was relatively well ordered. The Thematic Apperception Test revealed extremely weakly integrated stories with minor perceptual misrecognitions and lapses of logic. Personal relationships appeared weakly represented.

Treatment: During the first few interviews hypnotherapy was used. The production of muscular phenomena was fair. The patient was able, under hypnosis, to furnish additional details of a dream which she was unable to do in the waking state. Manifestations of posthypnotic amnesia were poor. The patient occasionally followed a posthypnotic suggestion. The most marked effect of hypnosis was to produce a state of relaxation which the patient could not initiate spontaneously in the waking state. The disadvantages involved were the temporary effect of benefits derived and the lack of contact with the patient during intervals between visits. Pharmacologic aids such as seconal, acetyl salicylic acid and benzedrine for the production of relaxation, control of headaches and induction of a sensation of well-being were also of temporary value, but the danger existed of producing sustained reliance on barbiturates.

When bibliotherapy was started its initial purpose was to aid in eliciting conflict material difficult to obtain even under hypnosis. The idea again was to produce material by means of associations with reading matter. The bibliotherapeutic approach could thus be incorporated into hypnotherapeutic interviews or it could be used only as an adjunct to hypnosis if this were desired.

On questioning it was learned that the patient was reading books very little but she perused newspapers and magazines. The patient was told that books were going to be used as part of her treatment and that this approach had been found to be particularly effective in illnesses such as hers. A random choice of novel was made when Graham's *Earth and High Heaven* was prescribed. The patient was specifically directed to read at bed time starting as much as one hour before her usual hour of sleep and she was advised not to discontinue reading in the event that headaches appeared. It was suggested that no other books be read at this time although no control was attempted of newspaper and magazine reading. No time limits were set. Shortly after this novel was prescribed the patient obtained and read the book. Discussion of the story led to material dealing with the social and economic conditions in the patient's home town. This in turn led to a discussion of personalities of friends and neighbors with an evaluation of the patient's social relationships at home. The conversation turned to the patient's father about whom much conflict existed. It was interesting to conjecture about the possibility that discussion of her father was initiated through an association with a section in the story wherein attention was called to the hands of one of the characters. It had been observed during the interviews that the patient was at times somewhat preoccupied with observing her own hands and the hands of the examiner. On more than one occasion also she had remarked that her father's hands were one of the most outstanding features about him.

The patient manifested an inadequate appreciation of the feelings of one of the characters in the story toward her father. At this time she attempted to avoid a detailed examination and evaluation of her relationship with her own father.

With the avoidance of conflict material the patient expressed concurrently a sense of relaxation when reading, maintaining that her attention was diverted from her own symptoms. This feeling of relaxation persisted even after she discontinued reading.

Because of the patient's preoccupation with physical disabilities in people and the anxiety which appeared when confronted with them, Butler's *The Little Locksmith* was recommended in an effort to initiate associational material which might in turn lead to an understanding of this difficulty. The story dealing with the problem of physical disability put the patient in a "dither." She reacted to this by expressing boredom with the story and did not finish the last few pages. She rationalized her feelings by maintaining that her own educational background was limited in the field apparently of uppermost interest to the main character of the book. Following discussion of this book the patient forgot to take it with her, leaving it in the therapist's office. She expressed later a reluctance to finish it and no insistence was used.

In view of the patient's symptomatic improvement without recourse to dealing with deeper conflicts, attempts to use books for the latter purpose were discontinued. Reading was recommended for diversion, relaxation and education and the advantages of this approach were discussed with the patient whose interest had been aroused and maintained. Suggestions were made for correlating reading with her hobby of collecting antiques. The frequency of visits was decreased and during the interval periods she followed the reading recommendations. Partial symptomatic improvement continued.

On a return visit it was felt that hypnotherapy could be used again for its immediate bolstering effect in inducing relaxation and alleviating symptoms, and it proved effective. The ability to induce relaxation by this means was invaluable but limitations existed in that contact with the patient could not, of course, be maintained in this way during interval periods. Bibliotherapy was thus an extremely valuable adjunct.

The patient began to request further reading recommendations spontaneously. She remarked of her own accord that reading had helped to induce in her a feeling of relaxation, satisfaction and comfort.

The books recommended, therefore, for an interval period were as follows: R. McKenny's *My Sister Eileen;* Dorothy Parker's *Here Lies;* Hendrick VanLoon's *Lives;* Evelyn Eaton's *Quietly My Captain Waits;* and J. P. Marquand's *So Little Time.*

The patient continued to improve symptomatically and she began to average three hours a day at reading, expressing an opinion about the soothing effect, mentioning her great interest in it and appreciating her ability to utilize spare time effectively and fruitfully in this way. She continued to seek further suggestions. Additional recommendations were Kenneth Robert's *Northwest Passage;* P. G. Wodehouse's *Code of the Woosters* and other writings by this author; J. P. Marquand's *H. M. Pulham, Esq.* and *Wickford Point;* and Bowen's *Yankee from Olympus.* These books were discussed with the patient with suggestions as to extending the range of reading of her own accord along lines of interest, concentrating on the authors preferred most.

DISCUSSION

Bibliotherapy was definitely advantageous in treating these patients. The educational and recreational merits have been mentioned. Its aid in eliciting conflict material was important; it was felt that treatment time was abbreviated, especially with the first patient. In addition, the prescription of reading matter enabled treatment to continue during the patient's absence from the therapist, contact thus being maintained between therapist and patient. This contact may be maintained not only during interval periods in treatment but for some time after termination of psychotherapeutic interviews if it is desired to continue a therapeutic relationship with the patient after he returns home. Sudden termination of treatment is thereby avoided.

A follow-up study of these patients is not presented at this time. It is not essential for the purpose of this paper since no attempt has been made to evaluate the bibliotherapeutic technique from the viewpoint of its relationship to prognosis. The aim has been rather to elucidate the technique with case material citing merits and mentioning some shortcomings.

Care must be taken in prescribing certain types of literature. This is illustrated by the first case wherein reading material dealing with suicide disturbed the patient. In some instances the author has used books in treatment with the purpose of producing anxiety but details of various types of reading material to be used or avoided are not given here since this paper is not intended to present an over-all picture of applied bibliotherapy. Again in the first case the patient's obsessional inclinations caused her to dwell on certain features of the psychological material. No marked difficulties were encountered but some misinterpretations had to be clarified. This need cause no concern if one is prepared for it.

To achieve the several aims of bibliotherapy many forms of literature may be used. Psychological literature is by no means necessary although it is employed often. A shift from psychological non-fiction to novels is demonstrated in one patient and avoidance of psychological material following an initial trial is described in the other. One may have a good idea about the type of reading desired in some instances, whereas in others trial and error may be unavoidable, at least until standardization in technique is effected. Regardless of standardization, however, the maintenance of some flexibility is desirable, depending upon the tastes and aptitude of the therapist.

SUMMARY AND CONCLUSIONS

Two applications of bibliotherapy have been discussed. In one case it was incorporated into psychotherapeutic interviews, and in the other it was used as an adjunct to hypnotherapy. In presenting these cases historical and examinational data have been given but the treatment described has been limited largely to bibliotherapy itself with little information about details of treatment as a whole. The progress of each patient has been indicated, however.

Further experimentation with bibliotherapy would seem to be desirable because it may possibly facilitate and perhaps hasten treatment in certain cases. Its recreational and educational merits may be valuable for some patients. Further potentialities ought to be explored and more scientific evaluations attempted. Presentation of additional case material is desirable in order to encourage further trials, substantiate findings, furnish data for broader and more complete evaluation and aid generally in the development of another therapeutic method.

REFERENCES

1. Jerome M. Schneck, "Studies in Bibliotherapy in a Neuropsychiatric Hospital," *Occupational Therapy and Rehabilitation* 23:316-323 (December 1944).
2. Jerome M. Schneck, "A Bibliography on Bibliotherapy and Libraries in Mental Hospitals," *Bulletin of the Menninger Clinic* 9:170-174 (September 1945).

3. Jerome M. Schneck, "A Bibliography on Bibliotherapy and Hospital Library Activities," *Bulletin of the Medical Library Association* 33:341-356 (July 1945).

4. Jerome M. Schneck, "Bibliotherapy and Hospital Library Activities for Neuropsychiatric Patients: A Review of the Literature with Comments on Trends," *Psychiatry* 8:207-228 (May 1945).

Bibliotherapy as an Adjuvant in Psychotherapy

by Louis A. Gottschalk

INTRODUCTION

Bibliotherapy may be described simply as a means of psychotherapy through reading. It is not something new or recently discovered. Reading has been used for centuries to disseminate new ideas, alter old attitudes and activities, and initiate new ones. The power of the printed word has gained steadily through the years as more and more people have learned to communicate with one another by writing and reading symbols as well as by speaking and hearing symbols. The impressive growth of literature as a means of swaying the actions of men has been exemplified by the martyrdoms because of what was written in the Bible, the murderings because of what was written in a military order, and the mass paranoias because of what was written in a newspaper. And any reader knows, from his personal experience, the myriads of hopes and solaces that can be engendered by what he has read.

The use of reading as a therapeutic adjuvant in patients with personality disorders has been overlooked by many psychotherapists. Few serious efforts have been made to develop its possibilities. At a time when the need for psychiatric treatment is out of proportion to the means, when group therapy and short psychotherapy have gained considerable attention as effective and economical methods of therapy per unit time per patient, bibliotherapy might well present a promising area for further study.

It is the purpose of this discussion to consider the application of bibliotherapy to psychotherapy and to encourage further research in this field. The discussion will be limited to bibliotherapeutic possibilities offered by that technique in which reading is prescribed by the trained therapist, rather than by reading in which the patient's own choice or a haphazard choosing determines what is read. Studies of other applications of bibliotherapy have been limited; a comprehensive bibliography of the literature is given by J. M. Schneck.[8]

(*American Journal of Psychiatry*, vol. 104, pp. 632-637, 1948) Copyright © 1948, The American Psychiatric Association. Reprinted by permission.

HOW PRESCRIBED READING WORKS

Various analyses have been made of how the prescription of reading may effect improvement in the psychiatric patient.[1, 4, 10] The substance of these analyses and some original observations are listed:

1. Prescribed reading may help the patient understand better his own psychological and physiological reactions to frustration and conflict. It may instruct the patient in the mechanics of mental function more clearly, completely and rapidly than the usual interview or question and answer technique. It may help remedy those maladjustments resulting from insufficient or erroneous knowledge.

2. It may help the patient understand some of the terminology used in psychology and psychiatry so that communication between the therapist and patient may be facilitated.

3. It may help or stimulate the patient to verbalize problems which he ordinarily finds difficult to discuss freely because of fear, shame or guilt. If, through the reading chosen for him, the patient discovers his own problems in the vicissitudes of others, his frequent feeling of being different from others may be dispelled. If he learns that others have had to face situations similar to those that contributed to or precipitated his personality malfunctioning or if he finds that others have attacked with success problems similar to his, his self-esteem may be buoyed and his eagerness stimulated to seek an adjustment that will lessen his conflicts.

4. It may help stimulate the patient to think constructively between interviews and to analyze and synthesize further his attitudes and behavior patterns. It may provide therapeutically planned vicarious life experiences which the patient has previously adjusted to only with considerable conflict, without exposing him to the real dangers of the actual experiences.

5. It may reinforce, by precept and example, our social and cultural patterns and inhibit infantile patterns of behavior.

6. It may stimulate imagination, afford vicarious satisfactions or enlarge the patient's sphere of interests.

PREREQUISITES OF SUITABLE PATIENTS

What patients are most amenable to this therapeutic aid?

1. The patient who seeks psychotherapeutic help is a better candidate than one who does not.[7] Furthermore, if the patient asks the therapist whether there is some reading matter that will help, one may expect that the reading will be done more enthusiastically and conscientiously and that the results will be more beneficial.[1]

2. The patient's age should make no significant difference. Twyeffort[10] has nicely outlined recommended reading based on the specific needs of various life epochs, and he has supplied an extensive bibliography, including instructive comments pertinent to each recommended book or article.

C. Bradley and E. S. Bosquet[2] in an article on the "Use of Books for Psychotherapy with Children," have included detailed reading lists which may serve as a guide to the therapist.

C. Kircher and T. V. Moore[4] have discussed the applications of bibliotherapy to the behavior problems of children and have listed and commented on 263 "character-building" titles.

There are few specific studies of the application of supervised reading in the psychotherapy of personality disorders in the adult age groups.[1, 6, 9, 10]

3. Patients in the habit of reading and with good intellectual ability are preferable candidates. Conversely patients not in the habit of reading, or who will not or cannot read, are poor candidates.

4. In general, patients with mild psychoneurotic disturbances are the most favorable candidates for supervised reading. Psychotic or severe psychoneurotic patients are less likely to benefit from this method. However, the author feels that its use in severe illnesses has not been fully exploited by trained therapists and that considerably more experimentation is needed to determine when and how such a method may be used and what results may be expected. Certainly, with hospitalized patients prescribed bibliotherapy of the type described here would seem to be feasible only when the patient has entered a remission stage of a psychosis or has partially recovered from an acute depressive or anxiety state. One study has been reported in which reading prescribed by the librarian working in close co-operation with the doctor was used as a psychological aid for patients still grossly psychotic and receiving insulin shock therapy, but the results of this experiment were indefinite.[5]

INDICATIONS AND TECHNIQUES

Some instructive facts are known about specific situations in which prescribed reading may be valuable, and some hints are available about when and how reading prescriptions may be made.

CHILDREN AND ADOLESCENTS

1. The importance of enlightened, factual, progressive sexual education for children is now realized to be a means of preventing emotional maladjustments in later life. Many parents are too modest or are unable to formulate and present the facts, and they may request the psychotherapist's advice. Prescribed reading may be valuable at the level of understanding of both the child and the parent. Through reading the child may gain help directly, and the parent may get an objective understanding of the facts and a means of presenting the difficult subject to the child.

2. Planned reading may be useful to help develop new interests and hobbies in the child with too narrow interests or too much occupied with its own problems and feelings.

3. T. V. Moore[4] makes helpful recommendations in using bibliotherapy with children. He advises that bibliotherapy should not be the
first procedure attempted when its use appears feasible with a problem
child. With a small child rapport is more easily established by play
therapy. With adolescents, matters may be best talked over in first interviews. Bibliotherapy is best introduced after the child has developed a friendly attitude towards the therapist and is quite willing to
talk over problems. Little children often refuse any book the therapist
offers and insist on one of their own selection. In such instances, one
may get the child to pick out the book desired by pulling it well out on
the shelf so that the cover design is in full view. Older children may be
quite willing to read any book given them when they are friendly with
the therapist.

ADULTS

1. With adults who appear to satisfy most of the prerequisites necessary for the success of this technique, before specific reading is
assigned, a sufficient number of interviews should have taken place so
that the therapist understands fairly thoroughly the nature of the patient's personality disturbance and the outstanding areas of conflict.
Furthermore, the therapist should know enough about the patient's
ordinary habit patterns to be able to foresee that the reading will not
seriously disturb the patient and will not upset a previously close and
congenial patient-therapist relationship. Occasionally, of course, reading may be prescribed which is calculated by the therapist, for diagnostic or therapeutic reasons, to provoke the patient's resentment or
open aggression.

2. The therapist should be thoroughly familiar with his reading
prescriptions so that he can appreciate his patient's reactions to what is
read and can discuss the subject matter with him. The therapist must
always individualize with his patients and should allow for considerable flexibility in using this therapeutic aid, developing its use to fit his
own psychiatric convictions and techniques.

ILLUSTRATIVE CASES

Following are three cases which illustrate some of the ways in
which bibliotherapy may be used in psychotherapy.

Case I

Margaret Wilson Gerard,[3] in the recent contribution of Alexander
and French on short psychoanalytic therapy, reviews a case of a 35-
year-old married woman who came for treatment because of
vaginismus, dyspareunia, and fatigue from overwork. This patient had
been inadequately prepared for the sexual experiences of marriage by
her parents, who were "very religious, Puritanical, but devoted

parents." At the end of the second interview, after she had discussed the attitudes of various people toward sexual activity and her own attitudes of guilt, she expressed interest in the anatomy and physiology of sex. The therapist lent her a book on sex. In the subsequent interview her reading led to an open discussion of her hostility towards her parents for their repression and deprivation of her normal sexual desires. Before therapy was terminated her presenting symptoms were gone, her social life was more contented and she felt less impelled to compete with her husband. "She was able to accept sexuality as a woman; her need to deny her femininity through masculine strivings became no longer necessary." Though prescribed reading was only a minor factor in accomplishing this therapeutic result, it undoubtedly facilitated recovery.

Case II

One of the author's patients was an intelligent, 42-year-old, married woman who became markedly depressed, agitated and indecisive, scratched her skin continually until she produced a definite dermatitis, and expressed strong suicidal ideas. She has always been a person of high activity level, outwardly overbearing and demanding and inwardly insecure. She was very dependent, particularly on her aggressive and dictatorial father. She had tried to avoid emotional dependence on her husband in their twenty years of married life, and had successfully maneuvered and controlled him so that she might live near her father and go and come as she pleased. She was enraged that her father remarried at the age of 73 after her mother's death, and was openly jealous and disapproving of her elderly stepmother. Her illness had its onset shortly after her father indicated to her that he might desert her, for he moved away from the patient at his elderly wife's insistence.

Hospitalization of the patient was necessary. She was too disturbed and depressed on admission for effective interview-psychotherapy. Fifteen subshock insulin treatments and three electro-convulsive treatments were given. Her anxiety and depression improved considerably, but she remained indecisive and restless and indirectly indicated that she was not ready to return home to her husband who lived about 500 miles away.

She was eventually discharged from the hospital and seen as an out-patient in weekly interviews. During her hospitalization her avoidance of sexual topics was notable; when such topics were approached she tended to refer to various somatic complaints or otherwise digress. As an out-patient, while discussing her vague fears of returning home to her husband, she complained of a troublesome vaginal discharge and modestly mentioned her dyspareunia. She then asked whether there was anything she could read about sexual matters and was given "The Marriage Manual" by Stone and Stone (see Bibliotherapeutic

Bibliography). During the ensuing interviews she revealed her fears of sexual intercourse with her husband, her feelings that sexual relations were disgusting and bestial, but admitted that she had orgasms without dyspareunia if her husband began his sexual approaches with foreplay when she was asleep. Then she recalled how her parents punished her as a child for interest in her genitals. Finally, she expressed feelings that her mother and father had rejected her in favor of an older brother. It seemed to her that she had to deny her sexual drives and act like her brother to win her parents' approval.

Her reading had thus stimulated her to discuss subjects of great significance in her maladjusted personality, helped dispel her guilt about her sexual needs, and surely hastened recovery. Like Dr. M. W. Gerard's patient, she became much more passive, less overbearing, preferred to spend more time at home with her husband and to relax her guilty attachment to her father. Her neurotic excoriations, vaginal discharge and dyspareunia all disappeared.

Case III

Another illustrative case is that of a 32-year-old married dentist, overprotected by his mother as a child because of delicate health. To gain group acceptance among his contemporaries in late adolescence, he felt called upon to indulge in forbidden activities, including smoking, mild drinking and eventually illicit heterosexual activities, all of which occasioned considerable guilt and anxiety. In adolescence, the first time his mother discovered he was carrying cigarettes, he suffered marked hysterical and anxiety symptoms including palpitation, dizziness, headaches, generalized numbness, a feeling of a lump in his throat, shortness of breath, and dreams that he was deserted by his parents. Although he occasionally suffered transient symptoms of this sort during his college years and professional training and wondered sometimes whether he "might not be going crazy," he built up a successful dental practice, was respected as a part-time instructor at a grade A dental school, and was married and had two children when he first appeared for treatment. His symptoms of childhood had reappeared suddenly without apparent cause, in more distressing and disabling form than ever.

A series of ten weekly interviews revealed that he had always felt insecure and strongly dependent but had denied his insecurities and had always behaved as if he were unafraid, self-reliant and a man of the world. The recurrence of childhood symptoms was evoked largely by interpersonal difficulties with his wife, who took him literally, made no attempts to over-indulge him, took lightly his vague somatic complaints and tried to insinuate her mildly dominating tendencies into his business affairs. He countered by seeking an extra-marital sexual relationship, boasting of his conquest to his colleagues, and managing to make several obvious slips so that his wife might suspect his philandering.

During his therapy an opportune occasion presented itself to use bibliotherapy. He was given "The Happy Family" by Levy and Munroe (see Bibliotherapeutic Bibliography), which deals in lay terms with some of the common problems in marriage and with some of the specific psychological mechanisms related to his problems. He not only read the book but had his wife read it, and they were able to discuss frankly some of their differences.

He achieved a new understanding of his vulnerabilities before psychotherapy was terminated, has been free of symptoms for a year, and his family life has been considerably more congenial.

This discussion attempts to demonstrate a few of the applications of bibliotherapy when used in conjunction with other types of psychotherapy. Obviously, to rely solely on bibliotherapy to develop more satisfactory habit patterns would be futile. But its value is undeniable as a tool in hastening therapy, whether or not the therapist's goal is to teach the patient to live with his symptoms and habits or alter them. The wisest rule for the therapist to remember in using any collection of books for therapeutic reasons is to know each book and understand its action as thoroughly as the physician seeks to know the ingredients and actions of a medical prescription.

A bibliography follows which may be found useful in prescribing reading. Its contents are to be regarded as suggestions to guide the psychotherapist and are offered with the full realization that many other books are available which might prove equally as valuable. The therapist may be familiar with books not listed that he feels are more suitable to the specific therapeutic problems with which he is dealing. Or he may feel that psychotherapeutic use of some of the books listed is inadvisable. The discretion and originality of the therapist is anticipated in using this bibliography.

BIBLIOTHERAPEUTIC BIBLIOGRAPHY

Personality Disorders in Children and Adolescents

(Reading for the child and parent)

C. A. Aldrich, *Cultivating the Child's Appetite.* (New York: The Macmillan Co., 1932.)

S. Blatz, and H. Bott, *Parents and the Preschool Child.* (New York: William Morrow and Co., 1929.)

B. C. Cady, and V. M. Cady, *The Way Life Begins.* (New York: American Social Hygiene Assn., 1917.)

H. C. Cameron, *The Nervous Child.* (New York: Oxford University Press, 1926.)

George W. Corner, *Attaining Manhood.* (New York: Harper Bros., 1938.)

George W. Corner, *Attaining Womanhood.* (New York: Harper Bros., 1939.)

W. DeKok, *Guiding Your Child Through the Formative Years.* (New York: Emerson Books, 1935.)

K. de Schweinitz, *Growing Up.* (New York: The Macmillan Co., 1935.)

E. Harris, *Twenty-one.* (New York: R. Long and R. Smith, Inc., 1931.)

S. Isaacs, *The Nursery Years.* (New York: Vanguard Press, 1936.)

H. D. Kitson, *How to Find the Right Vocation.* (New York: Harper Bros., 1929.)

E. Mannin, *Common Sense and the Child.* (Philadelphia: Lippincott, 1932.)

L. H. Meek, *Your Child's Development and Guidance—Told in Pictures.* (Philadelphia: Lippincott, 1940.)

A. S. Neill, *The Problem Child.* (New York: McBride, 1927.)

F. H. Richardson, *The Nervous Child and His Parents.* (New York: Putnam's, 1928.)

W. V. Richmond, *The Adolescent Boy.* (New York: Farrar and Rinehart, 1933.)

F. B. Strain, *Being Born.* (New York: Appleton-Century, 1936.)

F. B. Strain, *New Patterns in Sex Training.* (New York: Appleton-Century, 1934.)

M. B. Sayles, *The Problem Child at Home.* (New York: Commonwealth Fund, Division of Publications, 1928.)

D. A. Thom, *Everyday Problems of the Everyday Child.* (New York: Appleton-Century, 1929.)

Williams-Ellis, *How You Began—A Child's Introduction to Biology.* (New York: Coward-McCann, 1929.)

A. W. M. Wolf, *The Parents' Manual.* (New York: Simon and Schuster, Inc., 1941.)

Premarital and Marital Problems

O. M. Butterfield, *Marriage and Sexual Harmony.* (New York: Emerson Books, Inc., 1937.)

L. Clark, *Emotional Adjustment in Marriage.* (Saint Louis: C. V. Mosby Co., 1937.)

E. R. Groves, *Preparation for Marriage.* (New York: Greenberg, Publisher, Inc., 1936.)

M. E. Harding, *The Way of All Women.* (New York: Longmans, Green and Co., 1935.)

N. Himes, *Practical Birth Control Methods.* (New York: Modern Age Books, 1938.)

I. E. Hutton, *The Sex Technique in Marriage.* (New York: Emerson Books, 1932.)

P. Poponoe, *Preparation for Marriage.* (New York: Macmillan, 1940.)

H. Stone and A. Stone, *A Marriage Manual.* (New York: Simon and Schuster, Inc., 1935.)

I. S. Wile, *The Man Takes a Wife: A Study of a Man's Problems in and Through Marriage.* (New York: Greenberg, Publisher, Inc., 1937.)

H. Wright, *The Sex Factor in Marriage.* (New York: Vanguard Press, 1931.)

The Unmarried Adult

L. Hutton, *The Single Woman and Her Emotional Problems.* (Baltimore: Wm. Wood and Co., 1937.)

O. Knopf, *The Art of Being a Woman.* (Boston: Blue Ribbon Books: Little, Brown and Co., 1932.)

A. F. Riggs, *Intelligent Living.* (New York: Doubleday, Doran and Co., 1929.)

I. S. Wile, *The Sex Life of the Unmarried Adult.* (New York: Vanguard Press, 1934.)

Adult Maladjustments in General

A. Adler, *Understanding Human Nature.* (New York: Greenberg, Publisher, Inc., 1927.)

A. Adler, *What Life Should Mean to You.* (Boston: Little, Brown and Co., 1932.)

R. Benedict, *Patterns of Culture.* (New York: Penguin Books, Inc., 1946.)

Earl R. Carlson, *Born That Way.* (New York: John Day Co., 1941.)

G. Coster, *Psychoanalysis for Normal People.* (New York: Oxford University Press, 1932.)

I. Edman, *The Candle in the Dark.* (New York: Viking Press, 1939.)

E. Jacobson, *You Must Relax.* (London: McGraw-Hill Book Co., 1934.)

E. Jacobson, *Progressive Relaxation.* (Chicago: University of Chicago Press, 1938.)

J. Levy and R. Munroe, *The Happy Family.* (New York: Knopf, 1941.)

W. Osler, *A Way of Life.* (Baltimore: Norman Remington, 1932.)

W. B. Pitkin, *Life Begins at Forty.* (London: McGraw-Hill Book Co., 1932.)

W. B. Pitkin, *Careers After Forty.* (London: McGraw-Hill Book Co., 1937.)

W. Rhoades, *The Self You Have to Live With.* (Philadelphia: Lippincott, 1938.)

A. F. Riggs, *Intelligent Living.* (New York: Doubleday, Doran and Co., 1936.)

A. F. Riggs, *Just Nerves.* (Boston: Houghton Mifflin Co., 1922.)

A. F. Riggs, *Play-recreation in a Balanced Life.* (New York: Doubleday, Doran and Co., 1935.)

F. L. Ruch, C. N. MacKensie, and M. McClean, *People Are Important.* (New York: Scott, Foresman, 1941.)

E. A. Strecker and K. E. Appel, *Discovering Ourselves.* (New York: The Macmillan Co., 1931.)

W. B. Wolfe, *How to Be Happy though Human.* (New York: Farrar and Rinehart, Inc., 1931.)

W. B. Wolfe, *Calm Your Nerves.* (New York: Farrar and Rinehart, Inc., 1933.)

M. Wright, *Getting Along with People.* (New York: Whittlesey House, 1935.)

The Climacteric and Old Age

I. E. Hutton, *Woman's Prime of Life.* (New York: Emerson Books, Inc., 1937.)

A. F. Riggs, *Intelligent Living.* (New York: Doubleday, Doran and Co., 1929.)

W. B. Wolfe, *A Woman's Best Years.* (New York: Emerson Books, Inc., 1937.)

REFERENCES

1. K. E. Appel, "Psychiatric Therapy," *Behavior and the Personality Disorders,* vol. 2, ed. by J. McV. Hunt (New York: The Ronald Press Company, 1944), p. 1107.

2. C. Bradley and E. S. Bosquet, "Use of Books for Psychotherapy with Children," *Am. J. Orthopsychiat.* 6:23 (January 1936).

3. M. W. Gerard (By F. Alexander and T. M. French, et al.), "Alleviation of Rigid Standards," *Psychoanalytic Therapy* (New York: The Ronald Press Company, 1946), p. 233.

4. C. J. Kircher (Introduction by T. V. Moore), *Character Formation Through Books: A Bibliography* (Washington, D.C.: Catholic University of America Press, 1945).

5. E. Mascarino and D. Goode, "Reading as a Psychological Aid in the Hypoglycemic Treatment of Schizophrenia," *Medical Bulletin of the Veterans' Administration* 17:61 (July 1940).

6. W. C. Menninger, "Bibliotherapy," *Bulletin of the Menninger Clinic* 1:262 (1937).

7. C. P. Oberndorf, "The Nature of Psychogenic Cure," *Am. J. Psychiat.* 101:91 (1944).

8. J. M. Schneck, "A Bibliography of Bibliotherapy and Hospital Libraries," *Bulletin of the Medical Library Association* 33:341 (July 1945).

9. J. M. Schneck, "Studies in Bibliotherapy in a Neuropsychiatric Hospital," *Occupational Therapy and Rehabilitation* 23:316 (December 1944).

10. L. H. Twyeffort, "Therapy in Psychoneurosis (Bibliotherapy)," *The Cyclopedia of Medicine, Surgery, and Specialities,* vol. 12 (Philadelphia: F. A. Davis Company, 1940), p. 971.

Therapy in Psychoneurosis (Bibliotherapy)

by Louis Hollenback Twyeffort

It has been said that 70 per cent of cases seen in average general medical practice possess an overwhelming functional element. It follows that an immense field of opportunities lies before the psychiatrically minded general practitioner who has trained himself to recognize the emotional factors as they present themselves in many forms of illness, both those complicating "organic" as well as "nervous" forms of sickness. The terms "functional" illness and "neurotic" illness are essentially equivalent, and include the clear-cut psychoneurotic reactions as well as the variegated neurotic overlay present in many "organic diseases." In view, therefore, of the widespread prevalence of the psychoneuroses in their protean manifestations, only the most acute cases will find their way (often too late) to the office of the psychiatrist, and the bulk of these disturbances will remain untreated unless the general practitioner becomes himself equipped and trained to handle the milder forms of these disorders. Furthermore, he occupies an enviable position in which an early recognition of functional nervous disorders is possible, and therefore has a definite advantage over the psychiatrist. He is thus faced with a twofold challenge in prophylaxis, i.e., that of being in a position to abort forms of illness which might otherwise cripple an individual for life, as far as such a person's social usefulness or happiness in life is concerned; or, having detected more serious signs of emotional imbalance, he will then be in a position to refer the patient immediately for more intensive psychiatric care to the specialist.

The aim of this article is not to teach the general practitioner how to become a practicing psychiatrist. Its purpose is two-fold: (1) To orient the practicing physician along the channels through which he may acquire a superficial yet common-sense bit of knowledge which will equip him to recognize early the emotional elements in the more common functional nervous disorders, and at the same time to be able to handle such cases in helpful fashion so as to forestall eventual incapacitating illness; (2) to assist the physician in dealing with certain of these cases through an important adjunct to treatment—a manner of approach which has not received sufficient emphasis in the past, i.e., the judicious prescribing of reading material of therapeutic value to the patients themselves.

The bulk of the neuroses arise on a basis of maladjustment to life. By "bibliotherapy" is meant an aid to treatment which aims at the acquisition, through reading, of a fuller and better knowledge of oneself and one's reactions, resulting in a better adjustment to life. It also connotes "the relief of suffering by the psychological processes induced by reading." It is a method of approach subsidiary to the accepted forms of psychotherapy.

AIMS OF BIBLIOTHERAPY

The eventual results of successful psychotherapy depend upon the development of true insight—an emotional as well as an intellectual appreciation of the causes of the illness. In helping the patient to achieve this advancement, which often includes a need for emotional growth away from infantile reaction-patterns, the mapping out of an individualized, specially prescribed amount of reading may prove a valuable adjunct to treatment. Indiscriminate reading along these lines may be decidedly harmful. Such material should be prescribed, keeping in mind: (a) the particular needs of that particular patient; (b) the various aims of this method of treatment.

Given a suitable patient, prescribed reading may be of decided assistance in a variety of ways:

1. It may assist the patient toward a better understanding of the manifold functions of the personality, especially the role of the emotions; the nature of "complexes" which so often determine functional illness.

2. Frequently a patient experiences great difficulty in stating the actual nature of his emotional difficulties, even when these are on a conscious level. Reading along prescribed lines frequently helps him to verbalize his problems.

3. In connection with the preceding statement, the patient is often assisted in formulating his underlying difficulties if he has the opportunity of viewing these same problems objectively as they occur in other individuals. At times the patient who cannot talk about himself may "loosen up" if through the reading chosen for him he discovers his own problems in the vicissitudes of others.

4. Reading of this sort may help dispel in part his sense of isolation. Almost every psychoneurotic feels that his problems are "somewhat different" from those of other people, that "his case" is probably more serious than the average. A measure of reassurance will come to him as he becomes desensitized to his conviction of the uniqueness of his particular experience.

5. Where the source of the emotional conflict lies not in character traits but rather in situational factors, i.e., where the primary fault

does not lie with the patient (e.g., interference from a second party, unhappy home or business situation, domineering relatives, etc.), if the patient is confronted with similar situations in the prescribed reading, a sense of reticence may be overcome and an objective discussion of the difficulty facilitated.

6. When the difficulties spring rather from personality liabilities, considerable helpfulness may result from the individual being able to see how other persons have faced and tackled apparent failure with success.

7. In this connection, such planned reading may greatly assist in the redetermination and reweighing of values coupled with reorientation as to life goals.

8. Genuine insight into emotional difficulties invariably necessitates a frank stock-taking which can be facilitated by prescribed reading.

Well chosen reading material may also be helpful in other ways. It may help stimulate the patient to think between interviews, and to digest and synthesize what he has learned about himself. It may result in creating "movement" in the refractory patient who is inclined to keep close to superficialities and finds it hard or may be unwilling at the start, to "dig in." At times it can be suggested to the patient to write down specific thoughts, reflections, or questionings which come to him during the course of his reading, for later discussion during interviews. Other general aims of bibliotherapy will be considered later.

More specific uses for prescribed reading arise in occasional cases where it is felt advisable to stimulate fantasy, to make possible vicarious satisfaction, to stimulate new and creative interests, to enlarge the sphere of already existing or latent interests, to assist in achieving greater skill in abilities already present, and finally for general cultural advancement and amusement.

DECIDING ON THE NATURE OF PRESCRIBED READING

The following considerations should be kept in mind by the physician when deciding upon the type of reading to be pursued:

(1) What has been the nature of the patient's chief thwartings?

(2) What elements have made for the emotional conflict which the patient has tried ineffectively to solve by a compromise formation resulting in symptom formation? Inasmuch as the nature of emotional conflicts varies considerably from decade to decade in an individual's life, the chief problems and dangers of man's most significant life epochs will be taken up separately and considered from both the standpoint of prophylaxis and of therapy. It will be seen that the causes of many life maladjustments have been insufficient or erroneous knowledge. Bibliotherapy aims at supplying or correcting this selfsame deficiency, if possible before the damage has resulted, by taking into consideration the specific needs of each of these life epochs.

The physician must himself be familiar with the reading matter with which he supplies his patient. The assigned material will usually be more effective if it is "prescribed" to the patient chapter by chapter for later discussion between patient and physician. It should never be viewed in the nature of imposed "homework," else it immediately loses its value. The helpfulness of the patient's jotting down some of his coincident reflections has already been mentioned.

REQUIREMENTS ON THE PART OF THE PATIENT

In determining whether a specific patient may be a suitable candidate for bibliotherapy, certain prerequisites exist. The *sine qua non* in any form of psychotherapy need scarcely to be insisted upon, i.e., that the patient must want help. There must be present a fair degree of intelligence, the ability to grasp meanings, the readiness to synthesize knowledge acquired, and at least the willingness to ponder ideas not necessarily in accord with the reader's own preconceptions. The rigid type of personality is always a poor subject for any form of psychotherapy. It cannot be too strongly emphasized that supervised reading is merely a useful adjunct to the treatment of certain minor emotional disorders, that it should not be looked upon as a form of self-treatment which relieves the physician of any responsibility. Also, it must be insisted upon that bibliotherapy is not to be considered in any cases which show any suggestion of psychotic or severe psychoneurotic behavior. Cases beyond the stage of mild incipiency belong in the hands of the expert psychiatrist.

VARIETIES OF FUNCTIONAL DISORDERS
WHICH MAY BENEFIT

Generally speaking, collateral reading may prove helpful in two main groups of psychoneurotic disturbances: (a) mild anxiety reactions; (b) incipient neurasthenic reactions. Fortunately, these form the bulk of functional disturbances. The true hysterias and the obsessive-compulsive states should not be handled by the general practitioner, who will have more than accomplished his duty to the latter two groups if he is able to recognize these in their incipiency, and refers them immediately to a competent psychiatrist. A psychoneurosis is a definite clinical entity and should be recognized as such by the psychiatrically-minded clinician without there being a necessity to arrive at such a diagnosis merely by exclusion, i.e., "because the case cannot be fitted into any other diagnosis," or "as a last resort."

Under the heading of mild anxiety states and early neurasthenic reactions, such conditions as the following may be found who may profit from selected reading: the timid, lonely, oversensitive individual handicapped by feelings of inadequacy and of inferiority; frustrated persons with mild conversion symptoms, labelled usually by the practicing physician as essentially "neurotic"; the "nervously upset" individual; persons fatigued and abnormally exhausted; broken-down personalities who look upon themselves as "failures"; the man who "must make another start," whose temporary failure has resulted from force of circumstances rather than from character inadequacies. Bibliotherapy may be used with advantage at times where there is excessive day-dreaming in a poorly adjusted individual; for the shy, retiring person; and for those individuals who seek escape from reality in the abuse of alcohol.

SPECIFIC READING RECOMMENDATIONS BASED ON SPECIFIC NEEDS OF VARIOUS LIFE EPOCHS*

Childhood It goes without saying that the type of literature in which any child becomes interested may exert a great influence on the later personality development. The prophylactic value of properly selected reading is readily apparent, as well as its use in working with the child who already presents a behavior problem. The many opportunities along this line of bibliotherapy are clearly set forth by C. Bradley and E. S. Bosquet[1] in an article on "Use of Books for Psychotherapy with Children" to which detailed reading lists are appended. They stress the need of literature which will primarily absorb the child's interest and yet stimulate him along desirable lines, depending upon his immediate emotional problem. Such selected reading may assist in overcoming the child's resistance to interviews with the physician, or his resistance to schooling when the school-assigned readings have made no appeal to that individual child's specific interests and emotional needs. In the case of the introverted child, too occupied with his own problems and feelings, planned reading may help develop new interests and new hobbies and so interfere with introverted tendencies which in later years might lead to schizophrenic reactions. Well-chosen books at the child's disposal act also as a means of enlarging an inadequate social and cultural background. They also tend to produce maturing effects by the vicarious experience and inspiration which they offer. They serve also in a degree as a means of controlling the child's environment.

The experience of psychiatrists, mental hygiene clinics, and educators has put increasing emphasis upon the importance of enlightened, factual, progressive sexual education for children as a means of preventing a great proportion of the emotional maladjustments, breakdowns and neurotic illness in later life. Guided education in matters pertaining to sex should be a gradual and supervised process of learning. Inasmuch as many parents are still extremely hesitant to impart such information to their children, or else do not know how to formu-

---

*The number of books herein referred to is necessarily limited, and the choice of those mentioned has had to be dictated by the author's experience and by that of immediate associates. Some excellent books remain unacknowledged.

late and present the facts, this responsibility becomes the challenging privilege of the family physician. He may with the parents' consent talk directly with the child or provide the family with the needed literature. A most helpful book for the young child is *Growing Up* by K. de Schweinitz,[2] which, for children a little older, can be followed by *Being Born* by F. B. Strain,[3] or by *The Way Life Begins*, B. C. Cady and V. M. Cady.[4] A child may read these books alone, or more preferably aloud to some adult whom he trusts.

Books which may be of special help to parents in supervising the sexual education of the child are "The Sex Side of Life" (a pamphlet) by M. W. Dennett,[5] and F. B. Strain's[6] *New Patterns in Sex Teaching*, which latter is especially aimed at the instruction of parents in this task. Various emotional problems with which the growing child may be confronted are well presented in the following texts, which may prove useful to the intelligent parent: *Parents and the Pre-School Child*, S. Blatz and H. Bott;[7] *The Problem Child at Home*, M. B. Sayles;[8] and *Everyday Problems of the Everyday Child*, D. A. Thom.[9]

The physician desirous of increasing his own understanding of the problems pertinent to this age epoch will find the following texts helpful: *Parents' Questions*,[10] *The Nervous Child*, H. C. Cameron,[11] *Mental Health of the Child*, D. A. Thom,[12] and *Child Guidance*, S. Blanton and M. Blanton.[13] A discussion of Freudian concepts of the developmental problems in childhood is briefly set forth in Anna Freud's[14] *Psychoanalysis for Teachers and Parents*.

Adolescence The problems of adolescence center chiefly around the need for ever-increasing social adjustments, the extroversion of interests, and the establishment of life-values and ambitions culminating in the choice of a life work. Stress should also be laid upon the importance of the acquisition of avocations, hobbies, and interests whose greatest usefulness may not be appreciated until later years. Supervised sexual enlightenment is also greatly needed during this period. Specific emphasis must be placed upon the importance of preparing the growing girl for the onset of her menstruation, and the growing boy for the first signs of nocturnal pollutions. The onset of these phenomena in the child ignorant of sexual physiology may result in fearful concern, of which the emotional reverberations may even effect aversely later adult sexual adjustments.

In understanding the emotional difficulties which may spring up during these years, the following texts will be helpful to the general practitioner as well as to the parent: *Adolescence: Studies in Mental Hygiene*, F. E. Williams;[15] *Normal Youth and Its Everyday Problems*, D. A. Thom;[16] *The Adolescent Girl*, P. Blanchard;[17] *The Unadjusted Girl*, W. I. Thomas.[18]

In the matter of life orientation and the consideration of a career, the reading of biographies and autobiographies may prove especially stimulating. Here the proper choice of the material by the physician so as to suit the emotional needs of the individual case is especially important because unselected biographical reading is apt to have little appeal to the adolescent mind. Written from the point of view of adolescent orientation (for boys) is a book entitled, *Twenty-One*, E. Harris,[19] which covers in comprehensive fashion all the major decisions with which the boy approaching manhood finds himself confronted. There are a number of books on vocational guidance, which in an occasional case may be of help. A well-known work of this type is *How to Find the Right Vocation*, H. D. Kitson.[20]

Texts which will prove useful in the sexual enlightenment of adolescents may be chosen from the books referred to either in the preceding or in the next section, depending upon the individual requirements of the case.

Of especial help to the general practitioner in the early detection of those child and adolescent emotional difficulties which need expert psychiatric help will be the reading of *Common Neuroses of Children and Adults*, O. S. English and G. H. J. Pearson.[21] In this book there appear some especially interesting sections on the emotional background of disorders of the gastrointestinal and urinary tracts.

Adult Life: Adjustments and Maladjustments *Premarital and Marital Problems*—The practicing psychiatrist is invariably struck with the appalling incidence of adult maladjustments and chronic invalidism, especially in women patients, due to conflicts arising on the sexual level. Some of these unfortunate situations are due to faulty personality traits, but a great many cases result merely from ignorance of general sexual facts, and could be entirely prevented by early, suitable instruction. More frequently than is generally appreciated, the lack of authoritative information is traceable to both marital partners. In the field of preventative medicine, bibliotherapy can be of especial use in helping to spread enlightened sexual knowledge. Recently there have appeared several texts which cover the problem of marital adjustment in a straightforward, scientific fashion. A pamphlet which very aptly covers all the essential material of the larger texts is that entitled "Marriage and Sexual Harmony," O. M. Butterfield,[22] which has been tried out extensively by a well recognized clinic for marital problems and has been found most satisfactory. The questions arising in the minds of those who consult a physician about difficulties in marital adjustments are clearly presented in a recent publication entitled *Emotional Adjustment in Marriage*, L. Clark.[23] This book covers very adequately the problems which come to the average normal individual. Other recommendable books are: *The Sex Technique in Marriage*, I. Hutton;[24] *Preparation for Marriage*, E. R. Groves;[25] *A Marriage Manual*, H. Stone and A. Stone.[26] In most of these books, the primary emphasis centers around woman's adjustment to the marital situation. A recent publication which has viewed the relationship from a somewhat different angle is I. S. Wile's[27] *The Man Takes a Wife: A Study of Man's Problems in and Through Marriage*. The psychology of women and the normal emotional problems of the feminine sex are clearly presented in

M. E. Harding's[28] *The Way of All Women.* The method of approach is that of the Jungian school of psychology.

It is in prescribed reading along lines of sexual enlightenment that the general practitioner can obtain some of his most satisfying therapeutic results in bibliotherapy. In a great many cases it is possible to effect a relief of apprehension and to bring about an attitude of confidence based upon an adequate understanding of the anatomical and physiological facts of normal sex life. Through frank consideration of normal sexual phenomena, many quite normal but harassed individuals will learn that their experiences, seemingly unique and dreaded as unnatural, are no more than the common manifestations of sexuality. Much of what passes for frigidity in women patients is actually the result of apathy or repugnance of the feminine partner to sexual realities which are unsatisfactory because of lack of knowledge on the part of the husband, of some of the most elemental facts of sexual physiology. Gratifying results are also often obtained through the correction, by reading, of wrong ideals centering around the "degradation" of sex, the "baseness" of its physical aspects, etc. Naturally where such attitudes are the results of early miseducation, the prognosis is more serious and the handling of such cases should immediately be entrusted to the psychiatrist. Likewise, the treatment of impotence in the male and of other abnormal manifestations of sexuality, should not be attempted by the general practitioner. In these cases the patients should be referred for skilled psychiatric treatment. The duty of the general practitioner resolves itself into forestalling trouble and if it has developed, in seeing that adequate specialized help is given. This he can do by helping to make more universal the securing of competent sexual information by both partners prior to marriage, including medically accepted contraceptive knowledge when it is required, and also by stressing the importance of premarital examinations.

The Unmarried Adult—The case of the unmarried adult is one which presents its own specific emotional problems, and their nature, as regards the single woman, is well depicted in L. Hutton's[29] *The Single Woman and Her Emotional Problems.* This same problem, in addition to other aspects of woman's emotional life, is covered by O. Knopf's[30] *The Art of Being a Woman,* the approach to the subject being along Adlerian lines. A short enlightening presentation of this entire subject, and of the contention that marriage is not necessary to happiness, forms the substance of a chapter entitled "The Problem of the Unmarried" in A. F. Riggs,[31] *Intelligent Living.* All of the above books are written from the patient's point of view and can be suggested as prescribed reading. Recommendable to the physician and to the occasional patient is the work of I. S. Wile on *The Sex Life of the Unmarried Adult.*[32]

Adult Maladjustments in General—Books Recommendable to Patients—The basis of all adult maladjustments and the essential foundation of most of the neuroses lies in an individual's being unable to adjust himself on a satisfactory basis to his environment, especially in its social implications (family, friends, associates, etc.). The chief purpose of mental hygiene, in which the general practitioner is privileged to play a significant role, lies in the prevention of such maladaptations or in their readjustment when detected in time. This can be achieved in many cases by the practical application of psychology to the art of living. This is the theme of one of the most helpful books that has been written for the maladjusted individual, i.e., A. F. Riggs' *Intelligent Living*,[34] as well as being the purpose of his shorter monograph, *Just Nerves*.[33] The aim of these books is the development of the personality in terms of individual usefulness, serviceability to mankind, and a constructive fitting into the environment. It is this author's contention that breakdowns never truly result from overwork, but rather from a lack of expression of those qualities which make for the "happy, balanced life." Very often a faulty emotional development is at fault, based primarily on the individual's having been unable to adapt or handle his instinctive emotions, chiefly because of having been unwilling to accept the fact of their existence. In helping the individual to understand the source and potentialities of instinctive urges, these books are often of distinct help in persons whose maladjustments are relatively superficial. They are also helpful in clarifying the confusion which often exists in the poorly adjusted individual's mind between means and ends, which state of affairs has usually in the past led to an overvaluation of means and to an undervaluation of ends. The patient handicapped by his "sensitivity" will likewise profit from these two books which also aim to show how sensitiveness may be harnessed to intelligence and so be made to achieve useful ends. Another theme emphasized in Riggs' writings is that too much attention is usually paid to reconstructive or preventative technique, and not enough stress is placed on the concept that "restoration of ability to serve, not relief of symptoms . . . is clearly the main objective of mental as well as of physical hygiene"—success in human relationships being the true key to happiness. Readjustment implies the proper working out of a balance between those activities which make for successful living: work (physical and mental); rest (relaxation and recuperation); play (especially constructive leisure pursuits); love (companionship, social adaptation, family relationships); exercise; and contemplation (worship, philosophy of life). The achieving of a proper balance between these activities results in acquisition of the much coveted "art of living," and in learning to discipline one's life anew.

Written along somewhat less superficial lines, and aimed at presenting a useful and helpful understanding of some of the modern psychological concepts, is E. A. Strecker and K. E. Appel's book *Discovering Ourselves*.[35] In nontechnical language it explains clearly the nature of mental processes, the important role of unconscious mental activities and the various mental mechanisms, an appreciation of which enables the individual to acquire a much truer understanding of his own reactions by realizing that "nervousness" is not a disease of the nerves, and to obtain an insight into the constructive potentialities of the human mind. For the person keenly anxious to tackle the underlying causes of his maladjustment, and where these are less superficial, this book may prove of real value. The nature of complexes and their role in emotional conflicts are clearly illustrated, as well as the nature of those mental mechanisms which make for compromise solutions of conflicts, self-deception, and maladaptation. The patient suffering from mild neurotic physical symptoms, provided he is not too firmly entrenched in his preconceptions of organic causation, may be lead to comprehend the role of the forces of repression in mental conflicts and their conversion into physical symptoms. The patient with mild, latent aggressions can through such reading occasionally be helped to comprehend the real source of his attempts at projection and rationalization, of his fault-finding. In other cases, an intellectual comprehension of the mechanism of displacement may gradually help toward an emotional understanding of the anxiety reaction, by reason of which the fear engendered by factors which threaten the personality from within is often mistakenly attributed to unrelated causes in the environment, or experienced merely as unconnected anxiety while the real threat remains repressed. Through the increasing self-knowledge gained through his reading, the patient is often able to effect a sublimation of his conflicts along constructive and satisfying lines of activities, substituted for the compromise solutions which were attempted as long as he remained unaware of the true nature of his underlying emotional difficulties.

Other writings suitable for assigned reading to patients are A. Adler's[36, 37] *Understanding Human Nature,* and his *What Life Should Mean To You.* The views of this former disciple of Freud's, who later founded his own psychological principles in education. Two recent publications, written in a rather popular style, which aim at promoting mental hygiene, are W. Beran Wolfe's[38, 39] *How to Be Happy Though Human* and *Calm Your Nerves.*

Because of their extreme technicality and the fact that they deal with concepts centering around mental processes which are chiefly unconscious, works on psychoanalysis are of little use to the average patient, and would incline to prove harmful. Nevertheless, there is a very short work entitled *Psychoanalysis for Normal People,* by G. Coster,[40] which can be included in prescribed reading with impunity. This little book in clear, entirely nontechnical language presents the essentials of the outstanding, more generally accepted Freudian concepts, devoid of the customary sexual nomenclature in which they are usually presented in the literature. It will also interest the general practitioner who has never read any analytical works.

Although overwork, tension from external factors, etc., are rarely if ever the actual causes for "nervous breakdowns," excessive tension which characterizes daily living, especially in this country, may be reduced by the individual to help produce physical relaxation, as discussed in, *You Must Relax,* by E. Jacobson.[41] For the physician, this author's larger treatise *Progressive Relaxation*[42] contains much of interest concerning the physiology of muscular states and their significance in psychology and medical practice. Some practical hints can be obtained from this work with reference to the securing of rest in states of fatigue and in organic conditions characterized by spastic visceral conditions, where relaxation and freedom from muscular tensions are essential.

A very frequent variety of adult readjustment problems centers around the person who around middle-age finds himself deprived of his job. Helpful timely suggestions given in such circumstances may materially help offset the sense of failure and accompanying feelings of depression which may ensue. The lay press contains a variety of books which may prove of some assistance at such times, examples of which may be cited having certain stimulating observations about new work opportunities for the middle-aged, as set forth in two books by W. B. Pitkin[43,44] — *Life Begins at Forty* and *Careers After Forty.* Such reading may be of help in capitalizing potential personality assets.

Bibliotherapy also finds its application in any variety of lengthy convalescence, be it from the more severe nervous disorders or from disabling physical illness. Especiallv in the latter type of convalescence, a well selected course of prescribed reading may offset the dangers of a neurotic reaction of invalidism which is frequently the lot of those discouraged by chronic afflictions. A course of reading might assist a patient in becoming an expert in some small field of knowledge toward which he may have had a life-long inclination, although never the necessary leisure.

Books of Use to the General Practitioner — In his endeavor to familiarize himself with the emotional factors underlying functional illness, the general practitioner is usually faced with the difficulty of now knowing what works to read in the extensive psychiatric literature. As it is, very few texts have been written with the special needs of the practicing physician in mind. The average psychiatric work, with its rather specialized terminology, may be understandable by the young physician just out of medical school, but the older practitioner feels singularly at sea when confronted with psychiatric nomenclature. With these considerations in mind, the following texts are suggested as a cursory introduction to a superficial understanding of the etiology of functional illness, and as an aid in treating intelligently some of the less advanced cases. It is also suggested that the books be read in the order in which they are listed.

As a brief review of neurological concepts and as a bridge from organic to psychological processes, S. Cobb's[45] *A Preface to Nervous Disease* is recommended. Of inestimable value to the general practitioner, and written especially with his needs in mind, is T. A. Ross'[46] *The Common Neuroses: Their Treatment by Psychotherapy.* Quoting from the author's preface: "It is my belief that the great bulk of functional nervous disorders can be treated successfully by the general practitioner. It is to him and not to the specialist that the book is addressed. If he is not to do the work it cannot be done at all, for these conditions are among the commonest that he meets on his daily rounds." Each page of this relatively short work is full of significance to the practicing physician. The greater part of the book deals with the etiology, symptomatology, and treatment of "the anxiety reaction," which is the essential mechanism underlying the physical and mental findings in the anxiety and neurasthenic states. Only brief space is given to the hysterical and to the obsessive reactions whose treatment should be relegated to the expert psychiatrist.

Because of the ever-growing and far-reaching effects of the Freudian psychoanalytical doctrines which at present give promise of revolutionizing certain medical concepts of organic disease, the enterprising practitioner will profit from even a superficial acquaintance with some of the more generally accepted Freudian doctrines. A recent very short book entitled *Psychoanalysis Explained* by D. R. Blitzsten[47] will serve as a suitable introduction. A second book by T. A. Ross,[48] *An Introduction to Analytical Psychotherapy*, illustrates the practical application of certain of the psychoanalytical concepts, to the treatment of some of the more severe forms of psychoneurosis. This book, like the author's previously cited work, expresses psychiatric concepts, and reinterprets the Freudian concepts, in a terminology readily comprehended by any medical man. Strictly in keeping with psychoanalytical terminology, but written for the benefit of the lay reader and of the physician is I. Hendrick's[49] *Facts and Theories of Psychoanalysis.*

A very valuable book which gives an excellent portrayal of the neurotic personality as a total concept is *The Neurotic Personality of Our Time* by K. Horney.[50] Special emphasis is placed upon present-day culture and civilization as an important contributing factor to neuroses. Although the method of approach uses many psychoanalytical concepts, the author does not consistently agree with Freud. This work, also written in style suited to the general reader, is of especial help in understanding the mechanisms which underlie feelings of hostility and of aggression, of guilt, and of insecurity.

To assist the physician in understanding the contributions which psychoanalysis is making today toward a better understanding of the origin of illness—even organic illness—the general practitioner should familiarize himself with F. Alexander's[51] *The Medical Value of Psychoanalysis* which will serve as a good introduction to the subject of psychosomatic (mind-body) interrelationships—a new field of investigation which is receiving increasing attention. According to psychoanalytical concepts, the forced internalization of strong instinctive drives (because of the forces of "repression") will lead to morbid organ tensions ("organ neuroses"). Such tensions lead to disturbed physiology, spasms or dilatations of hollow organs, trophic disorders, etc. If long-sustained, such disturbed function may result in organic cellular pathology. If the disturbed physiology is of short duration, the tissue changes may still be reversible. On the other hand, prolonged maintenance of altered physiology may lead to a stage of irreversibility of these alterations, i.e., "organic disease." Within the past 25 years, an extensive literature has been accumulating on this problem of psychosomatic interrelationships which has most ably been surveyed and extensively abstracted by H. F. Dunbar[52] in a volume entitled *Emotions and Bodily Changes.* The pertinent literature, covering the period between 1915 and 1938, and forming a bibliography of 2358 separate titles, is reclassified and listed under individual organ systems. It is a work with which every physician should become acquainted as an extremely stimulating source book. This same field will consistently be covered by the quarterly review, *Psychosomatic Medicine* which appeared in January, 1939.

Because of the historical as well as the present-day value of the contributions of Adler and of Jung, reference will be made in passing to *The Neurotic Constitution* by A. Adler[53] and to C. G. Jung's[54] *Contributions to Analytical Psychology* and to his *Modern Man in Search of a Soul.*[55]

Within recent years much progress has been made in the successful therapy of a number of cases of chronic alcoholic addiction through a new method of approach which looks upon a great number of these cases as examples of neurotic behavior—faulty and inadequate adjustments to reality on the part of emotionally immature individuals who use the beverage as a temporary escape mechanism. Successful results are to be obtained only by the expert psychotherapeutist who has devoted much time to these types of reactions. The following two books are mentioned merely to acquaint the general practitioner with this new method of approach, and to enable him to suggest these works to the occasional alcoholic who appears really anxious for help, so that the afflicted individual may become aware of this new hope for rehabilitation. The works referred to are R. R. Peabody's[56] *The Common Sense of Drinking* and E. A. Strecker and F. T. Chambers, Jr.'s[57] *Alcohol: One Man's Meat.*

Of considerable interest to the general practitioner interested in emotional maladjustments and occasionally of use in a selected patient are autobiographical works which describe personally experienced emotional conflicts. Only a few such books will be listed: C. Beers'[58] *A Mind That Found Itself,* the author of which later became the founder of the international Mental Hygiene movement; and J. R. Oliver's[59] *Foursquare, Victim and Victor* and *Fear,* which should preferably be read in this order. For their inspirational value to the physician himself in his dealings with his patients, as well as for the treasury of common sense which they contain for the emotionally maladjusted patient, the following works by some of American medicine's best-known names are here appended: Sir William Osler's[60] *A Way of Life* and his[61] *Aequanimitas,* Harvey Cushing's[62] *Consecratio Medici,* and Richard C. Cabot's[63] *What Men Live By, Honesty,*[64] and, in collaboration with R. L. Dicks,[65] *The Art of Ministering to the Sick.*

The general practitioner who would familiarize himself with the origin and treatment of functional illnesses must also gain some knowledge of the manifestations of the more serious forms of mental illness (the psychoses), especially of their early signs. If he can develop a certain degree of skill in their early recognition, he will be rendering to the community an inestimable service by immediate referral of such cases to the proper sources for psychiatric care. Such insight will also aid him in refraining from attempting to treat such cases himself. The following books or articles are suggested to the general practitioner and it is advisable that they be read in the order given: B. Hart's[66] *Psychology of Insanity,* a brief but excellent, nontechnical book, and the same author's[67] *Psychopathology: Its Development and Its Place in Medicine;* A. P. Noyes'[68] *Modern Clinical Psychiatry; The Recognition and the Management of the Beginning of Mental Disease* by E. A. Strecker and H. D. Palmer[69] and *Treatment in Psychiatry* by O. Diethelm.[70]

The Climacteric   Another life epoch frought with the dangers of emotional instability is the climacteric, especially in women. Much of the anxiety and tension which accompanies the menopause is unrelated to the physiological changes in the organism but conditioned by the fear with which many women approach this period. Much of this perturbation has its origin in the misconceptions inherent in the minds of the laity, based upon unscientific popular traditions, especially that of impending insanity. It is of the utmost prophylactic importance that every woman be provided with a certain amount of accurate knowledge concerning this phase of life, covering the nature of the physiological changes and especially of the "normal symptoms" which are liable to be experienced. Many women are also unaware of the fact that the menopause need in no way hinder their subsequent sexual adjustment in marriage or impair its satisfaction. The dearth of accurate knowledge concerning the above facts has made for unnecessary suffering on the part of countless women. Unfortunately, little has been written for the lay public upon this pertinent problem. Recently an excellent small book has been contributed by I. E. Hutton[71] entitled *Woman's Prime of Life,* which covers the subject in a very satisfactory and authoritative fashion. The subject is also taken up in W. B. Wolfe's[72] *A Woman's Best Years,* which treats of the problems confronting the mature woman of today. The chapter on "The Balanced Life" in Riggs'[33] *Intelligent Living* gives an expert short account of those attitudes of mind, based on an accurate factual knowledge, which best prepare both women and men for entrance into this somewhat critical, but transient, period of life.

Old Age   Preparation for this final life epoch should have started many years prior to its appearance. Especial emphasis should be laid upon the importance of avocations and hobbies for all persons, as useful equipment with which to approach life's declining years. The ideal emotional approach to old age is well delineated in the last chapter of Riggs' *Intelligent Living*. Whether a greater measure of persons will increasingly achieve "a healthy life, a happy life, and all things being equal, a long life," will depend largely upon the efficiency of the general practitioner not only as the guardian of their physical well-being, but of their emotional health as well.

REFERENCES

1. C. Bradley, and E. S. Bosquet, "Use of Books for Psychotherapy with Children " *Am. J. Orthopsychiat.* 6:23 (January 1936).
2. K. de Schweinitz, *Growing Up* (New York: The Macmillan Co., 1935).
3. F. B. Strain, *Being Born* (New York: D. Appleton-Century Co., 1936).
4. B. C. Cady and V. M. Cady, *The Way Life Begins* (New York: Am. Social Hyg. Assoc., 1917).
5. M. W. Dennett, *The Sex Side of Life*, 7th ed. (Astoria, L.I., NY: By the Author, 1927).
6. F. B. Strain, *New Patterns in Sex Teaching* (New York: D. Appleton-Century Co., 1934).
7. S. Blatz and H. Bott, *Parents and the Pre-school Child* (New York: William Morrow and Co., Inc., 1929).
8. M. B. Sayles, *The Problem Child at Home* (New York: Commonwealth Fund, Division of Publications, 1928).
9. D. A. Thom, *Everyday Problems of the Everyday Child* (New York: D. Appleton-Century Co., 1927).
10. "Parents' Questions," Child Study Association of America (New York: Harper Bros., 1936).
11. H. C. Cameron, *The Nervous Child* (New York: Oxford University Press, 1929).
12. D. A. Thom, *Mental Health of the Child* (Boston: Harvard University Press, 1928).
13. S. Blanton and M. Blanton, *Child Guidance* (New York: Century Co., 1927).
14. Anna Freud, *Psychoanalysis for Teachers and Parents* (New York: Emerson Books, Inc., 1925).
15. F. E. Williams, *Adolescence: Studies in Mental Hygiene* (New York: Farrar and Rinehart, Inc., 1930).

16. D. A. Thom, *Normal Youth and Its Everyday Problems* (New York: Appleton-Century Co., 1932).

17. P. Blanchard, *The Adolescent Girl* (New York: Dodd, Mead and Co., Inc., 1926).

18. W. I. Thomas, *The Unadjusted Girl* (Boston: Little, Brown and Co., 1931).

19. E. Harris, *Twenty One* (New York: R. Long and R. Smith, Inc., 1931).

20. H. D. Kitson, *How to Find the Right Vocation* (New York: Harper Bros., 1929).

21. O. Spurgeon English and G. H. J. Pearson, *Common Neuroses of Children and Adults* (New York: W. W. Norton and Co., 1937).

22. O. M. Butterfield, *Marriage and Sexual Harmony* (New York: Emerson Books, Inc., 1937).

23. L. Clark, *Emotional Adjustment in Marriage* (St. Louis: C. V. Mosby Co., 1937).

24. I. G. E. Hutton, *The Sex Technique in Marriage* (New York: Emerson Books, Inc., 1936).

25. E. R. Groves, *Preparation for Marriage* (New York: Greenberg, Publisher, Inc., 1936).

26. A. Stone and H. Stone, *A Marriage Manual* (New York: Simon and Schuster, Inc., 1935).

27. I. S. Wile, *The Man Takes a Wife: A Study of a Man's Problems in and Through Marriage* (New York: Greenberg, Publisher, Inc., 1937).

28. M. E. Harding, *The Way of All Women* (New York: Longmans, Green and Co., 1935).

29. L. Hutton, *The Single Woman and Her Emotional Problems* (Baltimore: Wm. Wood and Co., 1937).

30. O. Knopf, *The Art of Being a Woman* (Blue Ribbon Books) (Boston: Little, Brown and Co., 1932).

31. A. F. Riggs, *Intelligent Living* (New York: Doubleday, Doran and Co., 1929).

32. I. S. Wile, *The Sex Life of the Unmarried Adult* (New York: Vanguard Press, 1934).

33. A. F. Riggs, *Just Nerves* (Boston: Houghton Mifflin Co., 1922).

34. A. F. Riggs, *Intelligent Living* (3rd ed.; New York: Doubleday, Doran and Co., 1936).

35. E. A. Strecker and K. E. Appel, *Discovering Ourselves* (New York: The Macmillan Co., 1931).

36. A. Adler, *Understanding Human Nature* (New York: Greenberg, Publisher, Inc., 1927).

37. A. Adler, *What Life Should Mean to You* (Boston: Little, Brown and Co., 1932).

38. W. B. Wolfe, *How to Be Happy Though Human* (New York: Farrar and Rinehart, Inc., 1931).

39. W. B. Wolfe, *Calm Your Nerves* (New York: Farrar and Rinehart, Inc., 1933).

40. G. Coster, *Psychoanalysis for Normal People* (New York: Oxford University Press, 1932).

41. E. Jacobson, *You Must Relax* (London: McGraw-Hill Book Co., 1934).

42. E. Jacobson, *Progressive Relaxation* (Chicago: University of Chicago, 1938).

43. W. B. Pitkin, *Life Begins at Forty* (London: McGraw-Hill Book Co., 1932).

44. W. B. Pitkin, *Careers After Forty* (London: McGraw-Hill Book Co., 1937).

45. S. Cobb, *A Preface to Nervous Diseases* (Baltimore: Williams and Wilkins, 1936).

46. T. A. Ross, *The Common Neuroses: Their Treatment by Psychotherapy* (2nd ed.; Baltimore: Wm. Wood and Co., 1937).

47. D. R. Blitzsten, *Psychoanalysis Explained* (New York: Coward-McCann, Inc., 1936).

48. T. A. Ross, *An Introduction to Analytical Psychotherapy* (New York: Longmans, Green and Co., 1932).

49. I. Hendrick, *Facts and Theories of Psychoanalysis* (New York: A. A. Knopf, 1934).

50. K. Horney, *The Neurotic Personality of Our Time* (New York: W. W. Norton and Co., Inc., 1937).

51. F. Alexander, *The Medical Value of Psychoanalysis* (New York: W. W. Norton and Co., Inc., 1936).

52. H. F. Dunbar, *Emotions and Bodily Changes* (New York: Columbia University Press, 1938).

53. A. Adler, *The Neurotic Constitution* (New York: Dodd, Mead and Co., 1926).

54. C. G. Jung, *Contributions to Analytical Psychology* (New York: Harcourt, Brace and Co., Inc., 1928).

55. C. G. Jung, *Modern Man in Search of a Soul* (New York: Harcourt, Brace and Co., Inc., 1933).

56. R. R. Peabody, *The Common Sense of Drinking* (Boston: Little, Brown and Co., 1937).

57. E. A. Strecker and F. T. Chambers, Jr., *Alcohol: One Man's Meat* (New York: The Macmillan Co., 1938).

58. C. Beers, *A Mind That Found Itself* (New York: Doubleday, Doran and Co., 1936).

59. J. R. Oliver, *Foursquare; Victim and Victor;* and *Fear* (New York: The Macmillan Co., 1927).

60. Sir William Osler, *A Way of Life* (Baltimore: Norman, Remington Co., 1932).

61. Sir William Osler, *Aequanimitas* (Philadelphia: P. Blakiston's Sons and Co., 1904).

62. Harvey Cushing, *Consecratio Medici* (Boston: Little, Brown and Co., 1928).

63. R. C. Cabot, *What Men Live By* (Boston: Houghton Mifflin Co., 1914).

64. R. C. Cabot, *Honesty* (New York: The Macmillan Co., 1938).

65. R. C. Cabot and R. L. Dicks, *The Art of Ministering to the Sick* (New York: The Macmillan Co., 1936).

66. B. Hart, *Psychology of Insanity* (New York: The Macmillan Co., 1931).

67. B. Hart, *Psychopathology: Its Development and Its Place in Medicine* (New York: The Macmillan Co., 1927).

68. A. P. Noyes, *Modern Clinical Psychiatry* (Philadelphia: W. B. Saunders Co., 1935).

69. E. A. Strecker and H. D. Palmer, "The Recognition and the Management of the Beginning of Mental Disease," *Oxford Medicine,* VII (1936), p. 132.

70. O. Diethelm, *Treatment in Psychiatry* (New York: The Macmillan Co., 1936).

71. I. E. Hutton, *Woman's Prime of Life* (New York: Emerson Books, Inc., 1937).

72. W. B. Wolfe, *A Woman's Best Years* (New York: Emerson Books, Inc., 1937).

ADDITIONAL REFERENCES

W. C. Menninger, "Bibliotherapy," *Bulletin of the Menninger Clinic* 1:263 (November 1937).

W. C. Menninger, "Address on Bibliotherapy and Mental Disorders," at A. P. A. meeting in Pittsburgh, Pa., (May 13, 1937).

E. H. Mudd and J. L. Whitehall, "Use and Misuse of Books in Counselling," (Marriage Counsel Bureau), *Parent Education* 4:3 (February 1928).

P. D. White, "Doctors and Books," *New England J. Med.* 218:338 (February 24, 1938).

Application of Dynamic Personality Theory to the Dynamics of the Aesthetic Experience

by Caroline Shrodes

The heart has its reasons which the mind cannot know.
Pascal

LITERATURE AS PSYCHOLOGICAL FIELD

That the reading process, like all other human behavior, is a function of the total personality and the result of its interaction with the environment is a conclusion which seems inevitable in the light of the theories presented in the last chapter concerning man's psychobiological nature and its effects upon his perception and cognition. The novels and plays a man reads may constitute a significant aspect of his total life experience inasmuch as they may serve to differentiate and integrate his present life space. Since the psychological field consists of everything in the individual's environment, currently *experienced* by him, to the extent that the reader emotionally participates in the experiences represented in the book he reads, those experiences become a part of his psychological field. The nature and extent of the dynamic interaction between the reader and the reading matter and the ultimate significance of these experiences in terms of cognitive reorganization are the product of a confluence of such factors as his needs and goals, the neural processes in the brain, and his modes of adaptation to experience. In addition to these functional factors, the purely structural properties of the field must be considered; namely, the structural and affective properties inherent in literature as a

This article is Chapter VI from the author's Ph.D. dissertation. The bibliography follows the next article.

Gestalt and the further structurization of his reading through the posing of salient questions for him to answer.

In a world of dynamic equilibrium, in which living beings are constantly interchanging substance with the environment through the process of symbolization (identification, projection, transference, etc.), imaginative literature must inevitably constitute a potentially significant variant in the individual's psychological field. When the organism is conceived as a system of energy rather than as a machine, it may be considered as reactive to all phases of the enrivonment with which it is in interaction; hence energy may be displaced on a character by means of which his traits may be incorporated by the reader. Or a situation in a book may be interchanged with his previous life experience, whereby the former becomes endowed with the affective character of the latter. The change in cognitive force which may be effected by this vicarious experience may be adaptive, leading to intensification of effort toward a goal; the perception may be reorganized so far as the means of reaching the goal is concerned; or it may result in the substitution of an accessible goal for an inaccessible one. That is, literature as a field may merely reflect, and not change or modify, such existing modes of adaptation as repression, rationalization, identification, or projection. But regardless of the nature of the reaction, "for every change in the phenomenology of experience, there is a change in the structure of the underlying dynamic field."[14] How literature becomes a part of the experienced world of the individual is, as has been said, an instance of the process of symbolization, whereby the symbol becomes interchanged with actual experience by means of a transfer of affect from the total situation to the symbol of it. A portrayal of a personal relationship, a conversation, a reflection of a mood, a traumatic experience, an act of aggression, represented in literature may become for the reader a symbolic equivalent of a personal relationship, a conversation, a mood, a traumatic experience, an act of aggression in his own life. As such it must evoke, at least in part, the same affective response as did the original experience. These situations or characters assume importance for the reader because they reflect his own need, fulfill his own wish, or remind him of his own frustrations which are embedded in similar psychical units. The reader's state of tension, having its origin in his biological needs, may then readily communicate with a state of tension represented in the literature.

A novel or a play, as a condensation and ordering of life experience, represents life in microcosm. A character in a play moves about in topological space, which includes the quasi-physical regions of inanimate things and forces, the quasi-social regions of interpersonal relationships, and the quasi-conceptual realm of fantasies, ideas, and values. The ease of his locomotion through these boundaries depends upon the fluidity of the regions, on the distribution of barriers, and on his own psychobiological nature. The latter determines which regions will possess valences of attraction and repulsion for him, and subsequently the magnitude and direction of the vector. The interplay of his valence and tension system will determine, for example, whether the conflict situation in which he is enmeshed will be resolved and how it will be resolved. Under the impact of forces of equal magnitude, he may regress, his psychical energy bound to a region on a low level of reality; on the other hand, the attractiveness of a valence in one region may upset the equilibrium of the opposing forces and result in freeing his psychical energy so that he may move through more differentiated regions of life space.

This formulation of Lewin may be applied to the character, Dion, in *The Great God Brown*. Dion, a sensitive, introverted architect, moves most happily in the region of quasi-physical facts in which he may manipulate objects and create out of them designs and structures of beauty; however, because of the impermeability for him of the quasi-social region, he lives most of the time in the quasi-conceptual region of fantasies, ideas, and values. Because here he is safe from the confusing and threatening interpersonal relationships, this region has a powerful valence of attraction. Although he occasionally manages to move back and forth between the quasi-physical and quasi-conceptual regions, so that for a moment they comprise a single region with a high degree of reality, most of the time he moves on the lesser plane of reality—the quasi-conceptual region—in which his dreams and wishes exert a stronger positive valence than does the world of action. When he does move into the quasi-social region, certain individuals have for him a negative valence. From them he quickly retreats and moves to the one woman for whom he feels a valence of attraction. The movement to regions of positive valence is symbolized by his removal of the mask. A spatial construct could easily be made to show all the possible logical constructs about the positional relationships of the characters. In the end, he moves from a plane of relative reality to a plane of lesser reality as the boundaries of his life space become further separated and as his psychical energy becomes further divorced from his ego. In this state of irreality he is vulnerable to the destructive forces of his environment as well as those in himself.

But the reader too is subject to barriers to locomotion when he moves into the quasi-conceptual region of the play. He may be blocked by a physical barrier such as the difficulty of translating the symbol within the symbol. Or his locomotion might be obstructed by social barriers, a lack of ability in this instance to accept the mores reflected by Dion's unconventionality; or he might be deterred by conceptual barriers, a limited capacity to differentiate the characters and integrate the ideas. Any of these barriers may be the result of a need for protection against further anxiety. Or the play may lack psychological reality for him. If he does not recognize the similarity of his need with that embedded in Dion's total pattern of behavior, there cannot be a communication in their needs-tension systems.

Literature, being at once a fantasy and a realistic portrayal of human behavior, permits the reader, paradoxically, both an illusion of psychic distance and immediacy of experience. He dares to venture in the symbolic field where he dare not in life. The reality-irreality level of the book chosen is crucial in determining its potential impact upon the reader. The more illusion of reality the book conveys, the firmer it is embedded in the reader's mind and the more compelling it becomes in influencing future behavior. Obviously books appealing to the reader's interests, needs, and preoccupations will have a high level of reality and hence be more susceptible to intraception. Although living vicariously may have a lesser degree of reality than actual life experience, it must not be forgotten that the life endowed upon the character is the life the reader, as well as the writer, has endowed upon them, a life which, insofar as his intellect has been sharpened, his perception quickened, his sympathies elicited, and his emotions aroused, may reflect both his powers of differentiation and integration. Hence, to the extent that he has endowed situations and characters with life, the reader's life space may become both more highly differentiated and integrated on a plane of greater reality.

Because of the greater fluidity of movement made possible through the medium of literature, the reader may not only see the field as a whole, comparable to the regions in his own life space, but he may move into remote and complex regions and relationships inaccessible to him in his own insulated life. Through the psychological distance that literature provides he may further observe the field with a certain amount of detachment and objectivity. Engulfed in his own problems, the individual is rarely able to perceive the meaning and complexity of his interpersonal relationships, the varying degrees of reality with which he adapts to the world, the full significance of his past experiences for his present life, or the significance of his present experiences for his future life. Moreover, so enmeshed is he in his own limited but demanding membership groups that he is unaware of other membership groups or other kinds of relationships possible within the same genus of membership groups. Since his attitudes tend to reflect the attitudes of these limited membership groups, his conceptual world is likely also to be limited. Also, objectivity is impossible during states of intense conflict. The conflict implies an impasse, forbidding freedom of movement. Hence one is likely to see only one's own needs, goals, desired position; to be acutely conscious only of one's own physiological state; and hence to act with a diffuse discharge of tension in conformity with the thalamic needs. But with the freedom of movement which literature permits, the whole field may be perceived from a more objective point of view, since there is no immediate compulsion to act; hence man's evaluative and critical faculties may be exercised under the impact of strong emotion detached from personal involvement. Or it may permit the symbolic discharge of tension which the reality situation does not allow.

However, it is also possible that the reader's own inner personal tensions are too acute for him to achieve objectivity even in the more fluid medium of vicarious experience. In this event he may distort the text to conform to his wishes and his needs either by the rejection of meanings uncongenial to his ego or by inattention to the forces directing certain characters or to the regions in which their movements are contained. His failure to see more than a partial field would reflect a lack of ability to differentiate between himself and his environment and suggest that he is living on a low level of reality. Such parataxic distortions, however, on becoming conscious, may permit him later to overcome the barrier in the original plane of reality.

A problematic situation is conceived to be unstructured life space. The problems dramatized in literature are not only structured but highly differentiated. The subregions are connected by defined paths not only from region to region, but from reality level to irreality level, from past to present, and from part to whole. Whether it represents a symbolization or extension of one's own experience, a novel or play is concerned with the same physical, social, and conceptual world in which the reader lives and with human beings whose emotions, needs, hopes, and goals are different only in degree from his own. The reader may thus perceive the inner personal regions of the character as they serve as an impetus or deterrent to transversing the barriers in his environment. He may discover that the barriers which impede the character do not impede him; that barriers which do not obstruct the character's progress do obstruct him. In the very perception of the barriers, in the awareness of the inner personal regions of the character, integration may take place. To the extent that the reader participates emotionally in this journey through topological space, he has recognized or extended his own life space. Certain barriers have been passed through symbolically and can be penetrated again; certain inner personal regions have been recognized or revealed to him and can be recognized again; certain valences may have become attractive or repellent and hence have aroused certain vectors which will steer his subsequent behavior. What had formerly seemed unreal may have become real; what had formerly seemed real may have become unreal. Since a character's life is often presented over a period of years, his behavior may be observed in terms of its effects, remote in time, and far-reaching in its relation to large groups of people with a resultant extension on the part of the reader of his own goals into the future.

What one introjects from one's reading depends on one's needs and goals, his neural traces, and his characteristic modes of adaptation. Just as the psychological field of a given individual may differ from his real environment (as judged by an objective observer), so the psychological space traversed in a book differs from reader to reader. For no two persons can there be an absolute equivalence of symbols, for no two people have identical psychological fields. The laws of perception and cognition, operating in the reading of a work of imaginative literature, may account for variations in response.

LITERATURE AS SYMBOL

It was stated above that the symbol for a total affective experience may become interchanged with the experience itself. According to Whitehead, symbolically conditioned action, lying midway between instinctive and rational modes of behavior, is the primary method by which man attunes himself to his surroundings. It is not reason nor instinct which holds man together but the modification of the automatic instinctive impulse, namely symbolic reference.[49] Symbolization may take the form of inability to discriminate between a character whose life is depicted in a novel and a person of whom he reminds one, including oneself; or to distinguish between a situation dramatized in literature and an event in one's past life of which it is reminiscent. This lack of discrimination, however, operates on more than one level of reality. It may simply imply that literature has been so successful a catalyst that during the reading of the novel neural traces in the brain have come in active contact with the symbolic interplay of human experience, so that temporarily the reader has an illusion of being an active participant in the situations portrayed in the novel. The reading experience has provided a momentary relief from reality, and on thinking over or recording one's impressions of the experience, the reader is sharply brought back to reality and says something like this: "I felt while reading that I was Tim; he had many of the same problems that I have had, and I felt exactly the way he did in confronting them. But while there are many similarities in our lives, my problem was different in many respects . . . ." And he will proceed to discriminate some of the differences in motivation or feeling or resolution of the problem. In making this comparative analysis, he may come to a sharper understanding of his own motivations and problems. At the other extreme, the reader may unconsciously identify with a character, and in his subsequent interpretation of the character's motives or behavior, he may impute to the character his own motives or ascribe to him his own feelings although a concensus of trained readers may have judged the motives to be quite different in the light of the "facts" presented by the author. This kind of projection may even be extended to the ascription to the author of a certain philosophy of life neither explicitly nor implicitly contained in the book. While man's proneness to confuse the symbol with the reality may thus be a cause and manifestation of parataxic distortion, it may also be a means to reality testing and insight.

FUNCTIONALLY SELECTIVE PERCEPTION

So strongly do man's basic needs operate in the perceptual process that even the professional critic displays in his responses to literature the same characteristic modes of adaptation that he reflects in his total life pattern. Thus Samuel Johnson's authoritarian character structure determined his distrust of Fielding and his predilection for Richard-son. The goodfellow morality of the former, who regarded sensuality as an amiable weakness in the otherwise virtuous, aroused his ire; the latter's teaching of the passions to move at the command of virtue won his approbation.[60] Shakespeare he lauded for his provision of the "inner check." His works, Johnson stated, may be collected into a system of civil and economic prudence. His greatest limitation was to sacrifice virtue to convenience and to fail sometimes to show disap-probation of the wicked. It is not surprising, therefore, that Johnson should dismiss Bolingbroke from his consideration because of his "impiety" and that he should be so vehement in his censure of Rousseau, who glorified man's instinctual behavior and would liberate the passions, that he would condemn him as a felon and sentence him to hard labor. Since Johnson conceived of men as preying upon the quiet of each other or of themselves, he would demand of literature the protection of "the beadle within." In light of the relationship that exists between the dynamics of the personality and the dynamics of the esthetic experience, his judgments are what we should expect from a man who married a woman old enough to be his mother, and after her death surrounded himself with crotchety old women to whose bullying he willingly submitted. Although altruistic motives may have led him to substitute this seraglio of superannuated females for the one that he had often envisioned of ladies bedecked in gowns of vegetable substance (to insure cleanliness!), with Boswell in the role of eunuch, it is plain that Johnson was often obsessed by thoughts of sex. His jour-nal frequently includes sharp self-accusatory remarks concerning his sensuality. His authoritarian conscience invariably came to the rescue, however, as in the instance of his confession to Garrick:

> I'll come no more behind your scenes, David; for the silk stockings and white bosoms of your actresses excite my amorous propensities.

Johnson's selective perceptions of literature are simply reflections of his own most characteristic mechanism of adjustment, the reaction for-mation.

THE RELATION OF THE SELF CONCEPT TO PERCEPTION

At which extreme of the continuum the reader will fall depends on such psychological factors as the degree of differentiation and integra-tion in his life space and his characteristic mode of adjustment. These, in turn, determine the magnitude and direction of the valence of attraction or repulsion symbolized in the book. To the degree that symbolization occurs at all, which symbols will become endowed with life for the reader? Those related to a favorable self concept are more readily incorporated and integrated into the self. Those inducing anx-iety because they are threatening to the self concept are likely to be unattended or disassociated:

> Availability of the trace . . . depends upon proper connection between the trace systems and the Ego. Now this connection depends upon a host of factors, among which the so-called conative ones are probably of paramount importance. If a trace is derived from a process which was directly connected with a person's interests, then it will have its place in a field formed by processes of high intensity and will be in particularly close connection with the Ego system. Such traces then are favored for many reasons. Belonging to a sphere of interest, these traces will find ready a trace system with which they will communicate, and ever new traces will be formed which communicate with the same system, enlarging and stabilizing it continually.[64]

According to Schachtel, the possibilities for such stabilization and enlargement are due in part to the very process of evoking the memory trace, which often loses in the isolation of the unconscious all connection with the present. Human behavior, as it is symbolized in literature, is not only surcharged with emotion, but the particular microcosm of life represented has been selected to conform to the reader's interests and hence is especially prone to evoke contact with traces already formed and to leave new traces. Since the adult memory functions largely in terms of recalling stereotyped and conventional schemata of experiences, rather than the experiences themselves, the mere conceptualization of experience has less chance than the actual objects of experience to penetrate the clichés.[99] Literature, in its direct and concrete representations of experiences and in its implicit judgment of such experiences, enables the reader to recapture experience and view it freshly, not embedded in the stereotypes of the past. This new consciousness of the past, linked freshly to the present, brings about a reorganization of the perceptual field, permitting the release of psychic energy and preparing the way for a change in the self concept.

Not only does the symbolic portrait of direct experience related to the reader's interests and favorable to his self concept evoke memory traces whereby the past may become linked to present consciousness, but it may also become endowed with meaning for him. That which is meaningfully perceived is that which evokes attitudes:

> Only when they elicit . . . attitudes in us, do we understand words. These attitudes may be of an affective nature towards poetry, of a practical nature towards questions and comments . . . in all cases they are responsible for understanding.[90]

Since the very essence of the novel or drama is a conflict situation in which the author presents the multiple forces playing upon the character, an attitude of sympathy, scepticism, contempt, friendliness, hostility, or love is engendered. One cannot remain neutral in the presence of human beings in action. However, the meaning or attitude evoked cannot be divorced from the reader's own needs (1):

> Meaning is the evaluation of the perceived situation with relation to the current balance of motivation of the percipient as correlated with past experience, whether consciously remembered or not. The same applies to all forms of symbolization.[75]

According to Pear, the registration of a perception is not "merely a change in the subject's experience, not something which drops into a previous nothingness."[90] Rather it is a modification of consciousness. How the consciousness is modified depends on the strength of the emotional attitudes engendered. If a character has a strong valence of attraction for the reader, a positive identification will be made; if the character has a valence of repulsion for the reader, a negative identification will be made. These identifications constitute transferences of affect from a previous experience to the present experience. A positive identification, being favorable to the self concept, is usually one of projection of the ego ideal upon the character and hence one that provides a readiness for introjection of the ego ideal, one favorable to emulation, change, and growth. A negative identification, being engendered because of threat to the self concept, is one of projection of those qualities upon the character which are incompatible to the ego ideal and hence unfavorable to the development of insight. However, in inducing these projections, the reading process paves the way for enabling them to become conscious:

> Better to make allies than enemies of one's emotions. To rid oneself of troublesome projections one must become aware of them, make allowances for them in judging and by constant practice check their sovereignty.[85]

NATURE IMITATES ART

It is apparent from the foregoing that the character identified with need have none of the traits attributed to him; they may be purely a function of the needs and wishes of the reader. There is abundant evidence of the partial truth of Oscar Wilde's familiar paradox that nature imitates art rather than art, nature. It is reflected in the mass phenomena of seventy million avid comic strip readers, many of whom are demonstrably influenced in speech, dress, custom, and attitude by what they have read and seen. The death of such characters has been the occasion for widespread mourning. The adult will idealize and imitate those who have achieved satisfaction in a field of endeavor that concerns him.[75] It is also apparent in the response of millions to the romances and success stories purveyed by Hollywood. The mass identifications with hero and heroine of the screen provide the witness or reader an escape from the dullness or limitation of his own personality and enable him to emerge resplendent with a flattering image of himself as a Bogart or Bacall. Less obvious is the mass search for meaning in life reflected in the tremendous popularity of such "self-help" books as Dale Carnegie's stereotyped and cynical observations on the personality or Edgar A. Guest's comforting clichés, which exalt the homely and the sentimental. But since it is latent, if not overt, in man's nature to strive for the actualization of his potentialities,[46] and since the ego has needs beyond, and different from, those of the unconscious components of the personality, the reader may also respond to books of an adult and realistic nature whereby he may identify with personalities of greater dimension and complexity than his own. The goal-seeking nature of the organism permits as ready a response to real goals and constructive purposes as to autistic or neurotic needs if they are brought to the attention. Through the mechanism of identification, the reader at once fulfills his need for autonomy and homonomy. Identification with comic strip characters or movie stars provides only an illusion of self-mastery and belongingness inasmuch as they are not grounded on a realistic appraisal of motives and consequences. The figures currently most susceptible to identification tend to represent such stereotyped summations of experiences as are conveyed in such familiar aphorisms as the following: success at any cost or against all odds; you can't change human nature: mother knows best; the sanctity of the home; everything works out for the best; it was meant to be; virtue wins out in the end; good is rewarded and evil is punished. But the same needs may be fulfilled through providing the reader with identifications and summations of experience that will at once satisfy the need for self-mastery and belongingness on a realistic level. The problem is to extend both the complexity and range of the reader's identifications, so that he may recognize his motivations, his latent potentialities, and the means for their realization.

EXAMPLES OF IDENTIFICATION IN READING

The reader's latent capacities, feelings, and needs, submerged by the overlays of the cultural definition of them, may be newly aroused by the emotional impact of imaginative literature. If the reader has been filled with a sense of guilt because of his own "unworthiness," with the semi-detachment which reading permits, his whole perceptual field may be altered by means of an identification with a character who is likewise considered unworthy by his parents. In providing an escape from the reality of his own harsh circumstances at home, the reading will satisfy the same need as would autistic thinking. In satisfying this need, the reader has less need for the support lent to him by his customary schematization of experience and hence it is rendered less potent. In being thus disarmed, he becomes receptive to the full emotional impact of the author's implied meaning and susceptible to the incorporation of new concepts. Or the reader may identify with a character who must inevitably fail in achieving his goal were he to continue to act in the light of inconsistent or unrealistic attitudes, and who must assuredly succeed by accepting new attitudes. Through the identification aroused by a presentation of such a person, the reader, feeling personally involved in the character's destiny, and disarmed by his feeling of sympathy, will detect the dangerous nature of the character's attitudes when he might not be conscious of the same inconsistency in himself. Or the reader may have suffered from failure and frustration due to unfortunate situational aspects in his own life. In perceiving the same forces at work on a character with whom he sympathetically identifies, his concept of self may change from one of inadequacy and inferiority to one of acceptance of the inevitability of his own failure in the light of the harsh circumstances of his life. If the reader is currently experiencing an overt conflict between two goals, one more realistic than the other, he will be peculiarly susceptible to making an identification with an ego ideal. The latter may be selected to give preponderant strength to the more realistic motive. If an adolescent, torn between slavish obedience to his parents and independence, identifies with a figure who is also experiencing such a conflict, he may perceive the emotional dependence of the parents as the contributing cause and in reevaluating his responsibility to himself achieve emancipation.

The reader's identifications may extend to prototypes of characters with whom he is in present conflict or with whom he has been in conflict. Inasmuch as one brings to one's reading experience the available sum total of one's life experience, one brings to the interpersonal relationships depicted in literature the same needs, hostilities, and fears which one brings to any of one's actual interpersonal relationships. Hence one "transfers" to the father figure in a novel the same resentment one has felt or currently feels for one's own father; one demands of the feminine counterpart of one's loved one the same perfection one demands of one's prospective mate. The son who is in conflict with his mother and feels ambivalent toward her may recognize her problem through the mother prototype represented in literature. The very fact that he is ambivalent makes possible a projection of sympathy and love toward her as well as toward the self figure. At the same time he may project on the mother antagonist the hate and resentment he had felt but which he has not been able to express. By means of this dual identification a reconciliation of these opposing forces may take place, culminating in catharsis, which at the least may provide a safety valve for the accumulated hostility and at best may, in making conscious his ambivalent feelings for the character, produce insight into his own situation.

Moreover, embedded in every dramatic presentation of human living is an implicit judgment of the particular human experience portrayed. The writer too has made both positive and negative identifications which are reflected in his presentation of the "facts." Human needs and values have been placed by him in a kind of hierarchical arrangement so that his total value system emerges. A book like Carey McWilliams' *Factories in the Fields,* appearing almost concomitantly with Steinbeck's *Grapes of Wrath,* was probably read by a few thousand intellectuals, whereas the novel was not only read by millions of people but undoubtedly read meaningfully, to the point that attitudes were engendered and sympathies enlisted for the plight of the "Oakies." We know that the person's value system guides and organizes competing motives. A reader with unformulated or vaguely formulated goals and ideals may recognize his own semi-conscious, unarticulated or conceptualized wishes through the medium of fiction or drama to the point where they may be actively incorporated into his behavior patterns.

Since one's attitudes are determined largely by one's membership groups, literature can introduce new membership groups with which the reader may wish to align himself. If his membership group has been an elite group, and he has incorporated attitudes of the group which are untenable in the light of man's biological nature or incompatible with democratic living, a substitute membership group may be introduced to him through the medium of fiction or drama, so that he may find the same satisfactions of group belongingness and approval that the earlier membership group provided, but one with attitudes in greater correspondence to the demands of reality.

INSIGHT AND COGNITIVE REORGANIZATION

The important question is whether the identification will be accompanied by insight, that is whether cognitive reorganization will take place. Not only may literature invoke a state of heightened emotion, it may also give the reader something to organize, interpret, or analyze. This in itself is an integrating activity. The degree to which this organization will take place is a product of a number of factors, such as the nature and strength of the identification, the need of the reader to maintain his defenses, the nature of his defenses, the evocative power of the piece of literature, and the way in which the problem is structured for him. Relevant here are not only the affective and structural properties of literature itself, but also the manner in which the reader is invited to attack his reading. The latter consideration will be discussed in a later chapter.

An accidental event may be consciously related to the life of an individual and incorporated into his subsequent thinking and behavior. A simple suggestion may fall into a prepared and polarized field and thus release the dynamic attitudes involved. Furthermore, periods of incomplete action, relaxation, or slight mental dissociation are the most favorable to insight.[52] Such are the conditions which obtain in the reading of imaginative literature. The manner in which the reader's present tension system may communicate with a previously held tension system, with a resultant revival of forgotten incidents, which on becoming conscious, may be related and assimilated to the present situation of the reader has already been described. In the coalescing of past and present experience, integration occurs. The actual recall is significant, for the traumatic nature of an event is lessened when it achieves consciousness. Its traumatic elements can be understood in a new context as irrelevant to the present, meaningful only to the past. Through clarification and dissolution of the previously unconscious traumatic content, energy is set free for the pursuit of volitional goals.

Even if not presently integrated into a pattern of behavior, the suggestions implicit in literature may leave a memory trace which in turn may communicate at some future date with a state of tension, leading utlimately to tension reduction.[52] Intellectual awareness is not enough to effect cognitive reorganization; there must be more:

> And that more has to do with the spontaneous reorganization of these acquired elements under the aegis of an event which is in reality not a mere addendum to, but rather an interpenetration of the levels of mental experience. And as a result one not only *creates something*; he *becomes something* as well.[52]

Just as the child develops and grows and becomes socialized as the result of the extended interpersonal relationships to which he is exposed, so too the adult may develop and grow through an extension of his experience beyond the narrow confines of the individual life pattern. In supplying both a more complex and extended field for his selective perception, literature opens up the possibilities for the recognition of present needs and the creation of new needs, the reduction of present tension and the arousal of new tensions, leading to new goal-seeking activities. If the characteristic modes of adaptation are too firmly embedded to permit a reorganization of the perceptual field through the incorporation of new attitudes, then at least the reading of imaginative literature reflects these modes of adaptation and provides a useful tool for psychodiagnosis and a new approach to therapy.

AFFECTIVE AND STRUCTURAL PROPERTIES OF LITERATURE AS A FIELD

In addition to the intrinsic needs of the reader, the crucial role of the structural and affective properties of literature in eliciting the dynamic processes must be discussed. It is of concern here only to elucidate those qualities of literature which pertain to realistic fiction, biography, poetry or drama. By "realistic" is meant that the author deals with recognizably real people in real situations rather than stereotypes of people or situations contrived to demonstrate popular schematizations of experience. The characters will thus be governed by motives which are clearly recognizable as universally valid human motives, and the events will follow one another in an inevitable and logical sequence as the result of the interaction of the characters' psychobiological natures with the world in which they have their being. Realistic literature presents not only the phenomena of experience but its genesis. Differing causes for the same behavior manifestations are revealed in such a way that the reader is never left in doubt as to the internal consistency and the lawfulness of the personalities depicted. Lewin has said that the most complete and concrete descriptions of situations are those which such writers as Dostoevski have given us, for they show how different facts in the individual's environment are related to each other and to the individual himself. The whole situation is presented with specific structure. Single factors of the situation are not combined arbitrarily in a summative way.[70] Masserman also acknowledges that the writer pictures the personality as dynamic in a context of interpersonal relationships and total environment. Therefore the reader can view human behavior in a dynamic situation. Great writers do not picture human beings as automatons reacting with mechanical precision but rather with dynamic subtleties and resonant depths.[75]

The affective and the structural properties of literature are thus not to be conceived as separate entities. The structure of the whole is governed by its affective properties, and the affective properties are evoked by the structure. They are indissolubly intertwined, each illumining the other. The concept has been reiterated that the symbol for an experience may elicit the same reaction as the total affective experience itself. Words are affectively charged, and in certain contexts their affective powers may be reduced, changed, or enhanced. Words are surcharged with emotion for man. They were the first medium of communication between the child and his mother; they were the means by which he established his own identity and the means of his growing self-awareness; they were the means by which he staved off fright, called for help, felt approval and love, and felt disapproval or indifference. It is through words that he first learns to think well or poorly of himself; through them he is subject to praise or blame. He uses words from his first cries of rage and frustration to his relatively articulate verbalizations of desires, loves, and hates. Emotion and expression have been linked in intricate, unconscious patterns as he was scolded or caressed by his mother, spanked or pampered by his father, as he quarreled or rejoiced with his brothers and sisters, played football on the corner lot, listened to the crooning of Frankie Sinatra, whispered his behind-the-garage discoveries in the realm of sex, survived the depression, lived his adolescent years in a world at war, and dreamed of tomorrow.

Words in the novel or drama are mainly used to depict interpersonal relationships and hence are peculiarly efficacious in arousing affective responses and in transforming the reader's own experience. As has been stated, one's prevailing attitudes to an extent determine and limit one's identifications. However, the equation is reversible. Under favorable conditions, in periods of intense emotion, one's identifications can be modified or extended, and on being so changed, they can alter one's attitudes. The recreation of intimate human relationships through the medium of literature is a condition favorable to new identifications because of its heightened feeling-tone, which Mueller-Freienfels defines as follows:

> We do not mean only its pleasure or displeasure character in general, but that feeling excitability which allows for its getting into connection with our interests. Interests, however, are feeling-attitudes, and the availability of memory-contents depends on their relations to these. Thus, in order to make a content available we have to keep its feeling-tone fresh and lively. A content strong in

feeling always strives toward the foreground, especially when it is feeling charged in the direction of the dominant interests.[90]

There is no need here to elaborate on the heightened feeling-tone of literature. Its subject matter since the earliest Greeks has been the primary human emotions, of love and anger and fear and hate. From Aeschylus to Henry Miller we find the recurrent themes of human conflict, from the child's world of undifferentiated sense experience to the adult's highly differentiated and complex world of maladjustment or achievement. These themes may be traced by the artist from the fierce loyalties and hostilities of the child's earliest years to their recapitulation in the loves and aggressions of his adult life. They range from the tabooed incestuous feelings to mature heterosexual love; from the autistic fancies of the dabbler in the arts to the profound convictions and manifest integrity of the highly creative artist; from the flights from reality of the pseudo-Bohemian to the triumph over personal misfortune of the man of courage; from the capitulation to expediency of the frightened to the full expression of human dignity and grandeur of the tragic hero. In short, literature is concerned with the portrayal of the molar aspects of human behavior.

At the same time that literature represents universal human experience and man's basic needs and strivings, it depicts the particular, the concrete, and the individual aspects of experience. The artist "of imagination all compact" provides the local habitation and the name. When Freud first developed the technique and practice of psychoanalysis, he confessed bewilderment at the fact that he, a respectable neuropathologist, should find himself writing case histories which read like novels, a form of presentation required by the subject matter.[66] Werthem points out that the research of the scientist and the research of the artist find a common meeting ground; each aims to relate the detail, the symbol, to the living organism as a whole.[113] The very naming of the object, rendering it concrete, is a differentiating process which permits the reader to differentiate and objectify his own experience. T. S. Eliot uses the phrase, objective correlative, to suggest the nature of the symbol-making and image-evoking faculty of the artist. He achieves his emotional impact by

> . . . finding "an objective correlative"; in other words, a set of objects, a situation, a chain of events which shall be the formula of that *particular* emotion; such that when the external facts are given, the emotion is immediately evoked.[27]

Or in Arnold's words, the artist attaches emotion to the idea; the idea becomes the fact. The universal aspects of experience are thus revealed through concrete action; the general is made particular; the irrelevant, the subsidiary, the flat, and the trivial are excluded in the artist's effort to communicate something beyond truth to fact. In so presenting the particular and concrete in an ordered whole the artist reduces the confusion, strangeness, and unintelligibility of human experience. By means of the selection and ordering of the multiplicity of facts available to him, he can create order out of chaos, unity out of multiplicity, and structure out of the amorphous. In so doing he fuses emotion and intellect in the intricate web of human experience. Flugel states that a great artistic production is sometimes truer to reality than is ordinary perception of the external world:

> It assembles or re-creates in a single entity . . . aspects of reality that may be widely separated in space and time, and thus presents them in a more comprehensible, enlightening, and satisfying manner.[34]

Thus Joyce in *Ulysses* permits the reader to share the introspections of Stephen Daedelus over a period of only twenty-four hours. But the world reflected in these introspections was sufficiently complex to take over a thousand pages to record. And so Proust makes a mockery of conventional notions of time and space. In the seven volumes of *Remembrance of Things Past,* time is not measured by the passage of the years but rather in terms of the intensity of the feeling, the sadness of a human soul imprisoned by his memories.

What are the means by which the artist achieves this transcendence of reality? The Gestalt principle that the whole is greater than the sum of its parts has special relevance to the structure of imaginative literature. A novel or a play is not a sum of words added together. Rather it constitutes a Gestalt in which words, images, and situations are cumulative in effect rather than merely additive, integrated logically rather than strung together at random, and climactic rather than equalized. The total structure determines the selection and arrangement of the part. There is no such thing as local determination in the mind of the artist. He weaves together the multiple factors in such an order that he achieves an "architectonic" whole. Compare, for example, the summary of a Shakespearian plot with the actual text. When the mere plot of *Lear* or *Othello* or *Hamlet* is recorded, it reads like a horror story as it might be printed in a newspaper. In the stark detail of horror piled upon horror, the reader is usually left incredulous and uncomprehending, and hence often impervious to the reading experience. In the Shakespearian text, however, the characters assume life, take on flesh and blood, act in accordance with motives not unlike the reader's own, oscillate between retreat and advancement, feel love and despair, hatred and vengeance. Hence they engage the reader's "willing suspension of disbelief" which makes identification possible. Truth *is* stranger than fiction, and the artist selects these facts and embodies them in situations which will create in the reader an illusion of reality. As Aristotle said, a convincing improbability is more suitable for the subject matter of drama than an unconvincing possibility. Until the writer places the character in a specific situation, until he gives lawfulness to the character's motives, he does not achieve verisimilitude. In other words, the structure of the novel or drama is one composed of figure and ground. The character is thrown into relief as he is juxtaposed with another character in the same environment; he is differentiated from the specific situation in which he is participating, from the environmental pressure to which he is subjected; he is seen in interaction with other human beings with whom he is intimately involved—his family, his loved one, his peers, his membership groups; he is viewed striving for perfection, striving for acceptance, striving to force his antagonist into submission, searching for meaning and value in life. Through the repeated exposure of the character in interaction with the various and complex forces of his environment, the writer endows him with consistency and unity.

The structural unity of a piece of literature throws into relief the needs and aspirations of the character. At the same time, the author's hierarchy of values is implicit in the whole. As the reader views experience through his eyes, he may also add it up and evaluate it through what he has observed and felt, thus integrating his own competing motives. But while the artist structures the piece of literature, it is also structured by the reader. If the repeated representations of the character's personality are ignored, or if the multiplication of salient aspects of his environment in which he is in interaction are not perceived, then the intent of the artist is missed; then it is evident that the needs and anxieties and the wishes of the reader are too strong to be overcome without therapy. From the point of view of the application and use of the dynamic processes invoked by reading imaginative literature, it is important to know what identifications are made and rejected, what additions to and subtractions from that which is given are made by the reader.

THE RELATIONSHIP OF PSYCHOANALYTIC AND DYNAMIC PERSONALITY THEORY

Dynamic personality theory as it relates to the dynamics of the aesthetic experience has been presented in Chapters IV, V, and VI as it has been formulated by both psychoanalytic writers and field theorists. The psychoanalytic approach emphasizes the genesis of the subject's response whereas field theory concentrates upon the present experienced world of the subject. While both schools recognize that the personality is conditioned by past experiences, the former is concerned primarily with tracing them to their emotional roots whereas the latter is concerned with their immediate effects upon perception and cognition. In spite of the difference in terminology and emphasis, the two approaches are congruent if looked at from the point of view of the dynamics of the personality.

Freud, no less than the contemporary field theorist, viewed the world in dynamic equilibrium, whereby living beings change substance with their environment. Man's proneness toward symbolization, which the field theorists emphasize, is simply his exercise of such familiar Freudian mechanisms as identification, projection, and introjection. What Burrow calls the confusion of the social symbol, and

Sullivan, parataxic distortion, Freud called the transference, whereby emotion is directed at a given stimulus in terms of a previous affective experience. Freud's principle of stability, providing for the release of tension and leading to a reconciliation of pleasure and reality, and his principle of surplus energy, providing for a substitutive release of energy acceptable to the ego and the super ego, are consistent with a dynamic psychology which holds that all behavior is an attempt to preserve the organismic integrity of the personality by homeostatic restorations of equilibrium.[36] While Freud speaks of the executive function of the ego, whereby separated and independent impulses are drawn into integration, creating order out of chaos, the field theorist stresses the possibility of extending the perceptual field of the subject, whereby his cognition of the world will be in conformity to reality, culminating in a restructuring of the personality. Freud developed many of his theories as the result of his observation of the errors and mistakes of everyday life which reflect the unconscious wishes of the subject. The field theorist develops a parallel concept in his analysis of perception as functionally selective in accordance with the subject's needs and goals. Both schools emphasize the significance of the projective mechanism, which is a reflection of the subject's private world and represents his distortion of reality. Both schools recognize the need for bringing the projections into consciousness, in Freudian terminology so that id may become ego, and in field terms, so that the personality may become a Gestalt. While Freudian theory is highly deterministic, field theory accepts the functional autonomy of motives; while the former emphasizes the polarities in man's nature, the field theorist views these polarities not as dichotomous but at opposite ends of a continuum; while the Freudian concept of the id is, in Fromm's words, a secular version of original sin which stresses the hostile aspects of man's instincts, the latter emphasizes the instincts as sources of energy for self actualization.

The above are the major theories from which application to aesthetic experience has been drawn. Psychoanalytic theory has derived largely from clinical experience; field theory has derived largely from the laboratory. In spite of a different vocabulary and a different emphasis, they need not be regarded as autonomous systems but rather as differing approaches to the understanding of the personality. In their common recognition of the existence of unconscious forces which, in the drawing away of energy from conscious use or in displacement upon the symbol, influence man's cognition of reality, they are on common ground. It is on this common ground that the implications for psychodiagnosis and psychotherapy are rooted.

FOOTNOTE

(1) The description in the press of the last hours of James V. Forrestal offers material for speculation concerning the dynamic processes

involved in his perusal of Greek drama. We are told that in his bedroom was an anthology opened to selections from Sophocles and Euripides. In the back of the volume was a piece of paper on which he had begun copying the *Chorus* from Ajax, which relates the agonies of Ajax, who lost his mind after becoming famous for valor in time of war. The lines copied portray the legendary Greek hero as being "comfortless, nameless, hopeless, save in the dark aspects of the yawning grave." The lines immediately following were not copied:

> When reason's day sets rayless, joyless, quenched in cold decay, better to die and sleep the never waking sleep than linger on and dare to live when the soul's life is gone.

Nor was there a recording of the lines on the opposite page from Euripides' *Chorus from Alcestis:* "The dead thou wilt not awaken from all thy weeping again." The conviction is inescapable that Forrestal made an identification with the war hero; the passage copied down indicates the selective nature of his perception in terms of his own immediate stressful situation. The fact that the lines uncopied reflect in the first instance the choice of death over life, and in the second the promise of relief from stress, suggests that they may have provided, in Burke's phrase, a strategy for encompassing a situation. We do not have sufficient facts to say that this reading experience might have been a precipitating factor in his suicide, but it provides a dramatic and empirical illustration of the dynamics of identification and its possible relation to subsequent behavior. Obviously, literature will not induce in a reader an affective response that is not already latent in him. The fact that Forrestal had made at least one previous attempt at suicide suggests that his reading served as a rationalization for his intention to commit suicide rather than that it brought to the center of consciousness an unconscious death wish. With another reader and another equilibrium of forces, the mere reading of the lines might have produced a substitutive release and the symbolic experience might have sufficed as a relief from tension. The incident further provides a salutary warning, in terms of the application of the dynamic processes of reading to the practice of bibliotherapy, that as with all other therapeutic techniques "interpretations" of experience should not be given beyond the capacity of the person to receive them; that although the wisdom of the psyche may protect the reader from introjecting ideas which are threatening to it, one must exert extreme caution in making recommendations of reading materials without full knowledge of the dynamics of the personality.

Implications For Psychotherapy

by Caroline Shrodes

'And this,' he said, 'is the reason why the cure of many diseases is unknown to the physicians of Hellas, because they are ignorant of the whole, which ought to be studied also; for the part can never be well unless the whole is well. . . . if the head and body are to be well, you must begin by curing the soul; that is the first thing. And the cure, my dear youth, has to be effected by the use of certain charms, and these charms are fair words. . . .'

Plato

Granted that the most crucial aspect of psychotherapy lies in the inter-personal relationship established with the therapist, nonetheless there are certain complementary and supplementary functions which biblio-therapy serves which might in many instances render extended psy-chotherapy unnecessary and which in most cases would facilitate its progress. The dynamic processes of the aesthetic experience corre-spond in both substance and function to the major phases of psycho-therapy. This similarity of response to books and to psychotherapy permits the two techniques to interact with and facilitate each other to the mutual advantage of patient and therapist.

PARALLELS IN AESTHETIC EXPERIENCE AND PSYCHOTHERAPY

First of all there are the common materials: the dream and the fan-tasy are alike used in art and analysis. Freud observed that the dreams invented by writers stand in the same relation to analysis as do genu-ine dreams. Whereas he felt originally that dreams were in the service of the pleasure principle rather than with the reality principle, he later concluded that in psychic life there is a repetition compulsion going beyond the pleasure principle, that dreams are attempts at restoring control of the stimuli by developing apprehension, the pretermission of which caused the traumatic neurosis. The dream is therefore the

---

This article is Chapter VIII from the author's Ph.D. dissertation. The bibliography applies to the preceding article as well.

effort to restore the traumatic situation in order to master it. Might not a compulsion similar to that which provokes a repetition of the same latent content in dreams create a receptivity to materials of art which bear a close relationship to the reader's traumatic experience? Art also provides the path from fantasy back to reality for both artist and appreciator. The artist knows how to find his way back to reality; he understands how to elaborate daydreams so that they lose their personal note.[38, 41] Compare this with Charles Lamb's distinction: "The poet dreams being awake. He is not possessed by his subject but has dominion over it." Dalbiez comments on the parallels between the dream and art and suggests that in each case the fundamental process is that of liberation of the instinct by means of the symbol:

> . . . whereas the dream is a symptom rather than a symbol, an expressive affect of the deep psychic life rather than a cognition, art is cognitive symbolism and not an acognitive symptom, a playful preparation for the exact knowledge which is on its way, and not a result of the transposition of past knowledge.[24]

A dream is, among other things, a projection, an externalization of an internal process.[38] So too is a work of art. Other similarities are to be found in the latent versus the manifest dream work which corresponds to the real and symbolic content of the work of art. Our immediate perception of both is in a disguised and distorted form. Of the many complexes in the latent dream, only a fragment passes over into the manifest content. The latent elements sharing common characteristics are put together in the manifest dream and blended into a single whole.[40] Much the same process occurs when the artist weaves into an organic whole those details of experience which will give emphasis to his conscious or unconscious wishes. The artist achieves unity by the same processes the dreamer utilizes; condensation, secondary elaboration, symbolism, and distortion. Or, as Ellis puts it,

> As a part of the harmony of art, which is necessarily made out of conflict, we have to view that perpetual seeming alteration between the two planes—the plane of vision and the plane of creation, the form within the garment that clothes it—which may sometimes distract the artist himself.[28]

What are the experiences that constitute the latent content of both dream and work of art? According to Jung the artist as well as the neurotic reproduces in detail the myths derived from the ritual experiences of primitive man. Basic to art are the age-old patterns of central human experience. Art is the reflection of man's collective unconscious, the precipitate of humanity's typical forms of reaction since its earliest beginnings in situations of general human character: fear, danger, struggle against superior force, the relation of the sexes, of children to parents, hate and love, birth and death.[54]

According to Freud, the artist expresses unconscious fantasies and daydreams, investing them with a great deal of affect. The driving power behind the fantasies is unsatisfied wishes. In this disguise of the infantile self in adult clothing the reader is afforded an increment of pleasure. True pleasure in literature proceeds from the release of tension in the reader's mind; he is put in a position in which he can enjoy his own daydreams without reproach or shame.[10]

In Rank's study the creative artist can be placed between the dreamer and the neurotic, both of whose psychological processes are alike. The artist, turning to the world with the intention of winning its acclaim, finds his way back to reality through productivity. Artistic creation, having its roots in suffering and conditioned by conflicts from within which the artist cannot control by normal means, involves a discharge of affect, a displacement of psychical intensity.[10]

According to Brill, art is an oral outlet, through words and phrases, for expressing genuine emotion—a sensuous or mystic outlet through words, or, as it were, a chewing and sucking of nice words and phrases. The artist compulsively repeats the whole process of oral gratification, and like the infant, his affective state can be pacified only through the rhythmical expression of pleasant sounds as in early breast sucking.[10]

In Reik's view the artist gives expression to unfulfilled experience. The fantasies which precede conception do not take material from memory—"it was that way"—but are bound up with the imagined "it might have been that way." Accordingly, what the fate of the artist might have been becomes the fate of the fictitious character, whether happy or unhappy.[10]

According to Bergler, every writer is a voyeur who utilizes his exhibitionistic tendencies as a defense against scoptophilic impulses. He feels that the writer's type of neurotic orality consists of a spiteful desire for oral independence, whereby the artist identifies himself with the giving mother out of aggression toward her, and thus eliminates her. The oedipus complex reflected in writing is merely used as a defense against more deeply imbedded oral material. In the light of his analytical experience with writers Bergler views their creations as unconscious defense mechanisms against unconscious wishes.[10]

A more logical position would seem to be that of Freud who regards the writer as the neurotic *plus* his art, which enables him to understand and alter reality.[37] It would seem further that there is the same range of motivation in the writer that is to be found in all human beings; that writers, not unlike all others of the human species, may have attained widely differing positions on the continuum from infantilism to maturity, autism to creativity, and narcism to relatedness to their fellowmen. However, Freud and his adherents saw man's instincts as evil components of his nature which must be sublimated rather than as sources of productivity and creativity in their own right.

From the point of view of the effect of artistic creations upon the reader, these comments on the motivation of the writer are almost irrelevant except as they emphasize the unconscious source material of the writer, compounded of universal human impulses, which inevitably appeals to the unconscious as well as to the consciousness of the reader and invites his participation in the action of the drama or the novel. This process of identification Hans Sachs describes as follows:

> The readers of a work of art are taken out of their ordinary surroundings and put into the realm of illusion. This illusion enriches the individual life with experience beyond the personal horizon, but never imposes on it to such an extent that the critical function which distinguishes between reality and fantasy is suspended. The writer shapes the characters and their emotional life so they seem to have their own individual existence and yet represents the universal. He appeals to the unconscious of the reader without bringing it into conflict with his censor. The emotional reaction which he produces in him means an involuntary admission that his own repressed wishes are the same as those of the writer. In this way he is brought out of his isolation.[96]

Pepper speaks of the emotional stimulation which art affords as doubly derived, by which he means that it differs from genuine or primary emotion only in degree. It lacks all or many of the sensory stimuli and instinctive reflex dynamics of the source act. Moreover, the emotion is under complete or nearly complete voluntary control, and it is greatly reduced in intensity. Art generates no special kind of emotion not experienced in life but only elaborates the kind of emotional activity common in real life. Its biological importance lies in giving a foretaste of source emotion so that it may be avoided, if painful, and sought, if pleasurable.[87]

On the other hand, Edman suggests that our emotions and sensations are intensified through our aesthetic response. In the routine of our lives successively similar situations have produced successively similar emotional reactions. In the clear and artful discipline of the novel or drama, our emotions become reinstated into a kind of pure intensity. Hence a tragedy like *Hamlet* or a novel like *Anna Karenina* clarify and deepen for us the emotional incidents of familiar human situations. He concludes by saying that for many people it is literature rather than life that teaches them what their native emotions are. He reminds us that the refinement of feeling, affection, and thought which is the aim of most moral systems begins with the senses, and it is to the refinements of sensuous experience that the arts are in the first instance addressed. The art of prose becomes the incidental instrument of an imaginative synthesis, a fictional or created world.[26] Fiction enables us to share imaginatively in the fortunes of created beings without paying the price in time or defect for their triumphs and frustrations: "one moves with them in lands where one has never been, experiences loves one has never known. And this entrance into lives wider and more various than our own in turn enables us more nicely to appreciate and more intensively to live the lives we do know."[26] Edman's interpretation is more in harmony than is Pepper's with what is known from dynamic psychology of the unconscious factors that operate and, in large part, control the emotional response to the symbol.

The means by which this effect is achieved is further described by Allen. He states that aesthetic enjoyment depends on the fact that, when the emotional situation is depicted, we share sympathetically in appropriate emotions and thus obtain vicariously valuable experience which would otherwise be denied. Art conveys a feeling of freedom from instinctive and bodily limitations; it provides an enhancement of selfhood by the feeling of power, comparable to that evoked by the fulfillment of what is often called the constructive instinct. This impulse to the enhancement of selfhood is attained through the sense of being able to impress some permanent or semi-permanent alteration on external reality in accordance with the will of self. The reader is at once participating in the emotional situation and yet is a more or less detached spectator. The artist, using an indirect method to communicate, transfigures experience, enlarges it by the wealth of associative meaning he can provide, and hence it remains something from which the self has at once detached itself, and in which, as total experience, he is still able to feel a certain freedom of self-enjoyment.[4] Hence in an attitude of concomitant detachment and involvement the reader is enabled to express his deepest feelings.

IDENTIFICATION

Identification made with characters in literature may facilitate the therapeutic process. Having made an identification with a character, the reader may discuss his own feelings under the guise of talking about the character. Hence the identification paradoxically provides both psychological distance (which many patients will not willingly surrender) and greater accessibility (which the therapist is striving to achieve). Although all therapists do not agree with Freud that symptoms vanish when their unconscious antecedents are made conscious,[38] it may certainly be said that identifications are central to self recognition, and that self recognition is a crucial step in growth. The hearer of the Oedipus reacts, Freud states, as though by self analysis he had detected the oedipus complex in himself and had recognized the will of the gods and the oracle as glorified disguises of his own unconscious.[38]

Jung emphasizes the importance of experiencing as a human being the images, symbols, and visions rising out of the unconscious. One must take them in actively and confront them with full consciousness. Since it is Jung's conviction that over-differentiation of man's superior function leads to tensions, it would obviously in his view be only through extension of one's own limited conscious experience that one would be able to recognize and utilize other functions latent in his nature. Moreover, the self-recognition that literature often permits should help the reader to identify his persona, which, if it becomes automatic and stiffens, causes the individual to stiffen, shrivel, and become the mask. Since the neglected function and the unlived attitude revolt and demand exercise, if need be through neurosis,[54] it is of vital importance to extend the individual's experience and identifications.

Jones points out that the appreciation of resemblances facilitates the assimilation of new experience. The process of fusion or identification, as it aids our grasp of reality and makes it possible to deal with it more adequately, profoundly influences the course of further mental development along both affective lines and intellectual ones.[56] In addition to the individual "shock of recognition," making both catharsis and insight possible, literature may provide an objective recognition of others that the exigencies of intimate living with them do not permit; moreover, it extends the range of one's identifications to personalities alien to one's own and remote from one's immediate environment. The importance for therapy of recognition of familiar figures in one's environment through the emotional impact of imaginative literature may be seen by reviewing the primary function of identification. It is the child's strong unconscious ambivalence toward the parent figures which initially creates a determinative need to identify with one or both of them. Identification provides a complete and permanent solution. That aspect of identification transcending imitation or fantasy is an actual unconscious creation of a permanent personality trait. No longer merely a reaction to one individual in one situation, it has become a component of his total reaction to all situations. As such it constitutes the emotional counterpart of learning. After the child leaves the family circle, he is influenced by other human associations and builds, again by identification with those he loves, hates, and emulates, the rudiments of his own philosophy of life:

> The resulting blends of identification of this period determine standards of caste, religion, race, culture, so decisive in the social configuration of the adult. Later, identifications with personified ideals, those of art and philosophy, add their components to his final character.[48]

It would seem that identification is a permanent and healthful solution to ambivalence only if the ambivalence is made conscious. If the reader meets the prototypes of parent figures in literature, this end may be achieved. He may recognize their "hatefulness" and their limitations, but he may also recognize the forces that produced them. In place of the need for over-protestation of his parents' goodness, the reader may admit their faults without threat to his super ego, for concomitantly he can condone them in the light of the forces that created them. For example, one student found that on the first reading of *To the Lighthouse,* she was very angry with the mother and identified only with the daughter, but on a voluntary rereading of the novel, she extended her identifications to the mother and found herself explaining her faults and sympathizing with her because of the pressures to which she too had been subjected. Another student, a Chinese American girl, who had felt guilty because she had defied her parents by attending college, recognized in the parents in *The Way of All Flesh* the same forces which operated in making her parents so severe, and she was able to substitute for her previously unrecognized ambivalence toward them a realistic appraisal of them in the light of their conditioning, a fact which made it possible for her to continue college without feelings of guilt. A third student, in her first spontaneous comments on reading *The Great God Brown,* expressed sympathy for certain of the characters. In her later recorded, more considered judgment of the characters, she found herself being very angry with the very same characters who had aroused her sympathy. In conference she expressed extreme bewilderment at the inconsistency of her appraisal. After mulling over her reactions she decided that since the book had broken down her defenses, her reactions to people must be very unstable. *Ann Veronica* was given to her subsequently as a different exploration of a similar theme. Again she observed that she had shifted her reactions to the characters. "And what is very strange, I am doing the same thing to people who used to bore me and whom I couldn't stand. I keep asking myself, 'What makes them tick?' and I find I am trying to discover what makes them stupid and conventional. And as I realize that they are afraid to be anything else, I can't hate them any more. And then I begin asking myself why I have to be such a rebel and unconventional. And maybe it's the same reason—maybe it's because I think people don't like me and I'm afraid they won't like me. So I give them a good reason for not liking me. And since I've thought of all this, I find it easier to conform outwardly even when it seems silly. Sometimes it's kinder to do the conforming thing, and it doesn't make me angry any longer to have to conform."

These illustrations show how the subject may progress from ambivalence toward, or blame of, his parents (or other membership groups) to understanding of the social forces responsible for the deficiencies of his childhood.

> For freedom from neurosis begins where the adult individual is put in a position to identify with his own ego-identity and apply that which is given to that which must be done.[30]

This process of rendering conscious the childhood identifications, especially with parent figures, is in line with what most neo-Freudians consider the primary function of psychotherapy. Horney believes that the aim of therapy is not to help the patient gain mastery over his instincts but rather to lessen his anxiety to such an extent that he can dispense with his neurotic trends. Beyond this aim the therapeutic goal is to restore the individual to himself, help him regain his spontaneity and find his center of gravity in himself.[51] Similarly Appel, in his discussion of dynamic growth therapy, emphasizes the importance in therapy of the release of repressed, clogging, and disrupting emotions through expression, recognition, and acceptance of the subject's feelings. The subject must learn to grow out of hindering identifications and work through to new individuality in order to achieve a satisfying and constructive personality.[8] Finally, Alexander and French stress the importance of undergoing a new emotional experience to undo the morbid effects of past emotional experiences. To re-experience the old, unsettled conflict but with a new ending is the secret of every penetrating therapeutic result. Only the actual experiencing of a new solution in the transference situation or in everyday life gives the subject the conviction that a new solution is possible and induces him to give up his old neurotic patterns.[3] Identification with characters and situations in literature permits a re-experience of the old, unsettled conflict but with a new solution. This is illustrated in the case of Ethel, who re-experienced the old conflict with her mother when reading *Sons and Lovers*. In experiencing Paul's victimization by his mother, she not only relived her own childhood and adolescence, but she was able to view these years from a fresh frame of reference. With the perspective and objectivity thus permitted, she gained courage and justification for breaking the bonds that had made her life miserable.

It is important for therapy that the individual should extend his experiences beyond the familiar and immediate that he may develop both a sense of belongingness to all other human beings and a feeling of tolerance and sympathy for lives alien to his own. Literature may stimulate the perception of his fundamental identity with others and promote his socialization. As the insecure adolescent recognizes that he is not alone, that his fears and guilt feelings are shared by others of his age, his sense of difference and isolation is reduced. Since literature provides an awareness of the essential dignity and worth of the individual human life, however humble or unsuccessful in the world's view, the reader may gain a sense of self respect. Identification with such characters as Ma Joad or Tom Joad in *The Grapes of Wrath* or with Jordan in *For Whom the Bell Tolls,* or with some of Pearl Buck's Chinese women, may lead to re-examination of what constitutes human worth and dignity. Literature may encourage identification with healthy sub-cultures or with the "cultural creators." It may enrich the reader's understanding of other people and lessen his fear of the "stranger," for it reaches his emotions as well as his intellect. He may share the plight of the sharecroppers in the South; he may become homeless with the displaced persons in Europe; he may be excluded from public places with the Negro; he may be forced underground with the anti-fascists. If he extends his experience of love and hate, of pity and fear, he can no longer remain insular and chauvinistic. He becomes aware of man's universal struggle against the forces which impede the full development of his potentiality. The recognition of human likeness helps to dissolve the barriers between sex, nationality, race, and class. The variety of human beings whose lives are projected through the pages of a book forbid the viewing of people as all evil or all good. A healthy relativism is engendered as a corrective for the protopathic response which fails to perceive the nuances and complexities of human behavior.

Moreover, it is vital for therapy that the subject should understand not only his own motivations and those of his fellow human beings but also the complexity of interpersonal relationships. The theories of Fromm and Sullivan, attesting to the primacy of interpersonal relations in the determination of the personality, suggest the value of vicarious experience in a context of interpersonal relationships. Through the identifications that literature provides, the reader may become acquainted with emotional capacities which his particular situation does not permit him to exercise as well as with interpersonal situations which may assume a valence of attraction for him. It is of the essence of situation therapy that the patient should be placed in a world which will bring out what is wanted and a world like the one he has to face. To see the personality the therapist must see the patient in all situations of life in which he is a part and countless new situations to bring out latent aspects of his personality.[82] The patient's reaction to symbolic situations may reveal to the therapist the deeper and less accessible aspects of his personality as they interact in specific life situations.

Closely related to this function of extending the field for the subject is the symbolic preparation which literature may afford for later traumatic situations. Burke alludes to works of art as strategies for encompassing situations.[18] Trilling speaks of the mithridate function of art by which tragedy is used as a small and controlled administration of pain to inure the reader or beholder to greater doses which life will force upon him.[111] Since frustration tolerance is crucial for adjustment, the use of literature as a kind of controlled shock therapy can be an important corollary to treatment. Rosenzweig points out that the mature personality is to be understood in terms of his ability to tolerate frustration, the protection having been built up gradually against inadequate responses to frustrating situations. During treatment by free association the patient has been encouraged to express frustration over and over without resorting to the ego defenses he employs in everyday life. The patient is thus constantly being frustrated instead of gratifying his self-protective tendencies. To consolidate the gains the therapist interposes interpretations which provide insight and prepare the ground for growth.[93] Carefully selected books not only might provide frustrating situations to be borne but also interpretations of such situations which permit the reader to rise above his own misfortunes and to accept philosophically his own limitations.

Freud's analysis of thinking is relevant to the function of extending experience.

> Thinking is an experimental dealing with small quantities of energy, just as a general moves miniature figures about over a map before setting his troops in motion. In this way, the ego anticipates the satisfaction of the questionable impulse, and enables it to reproduce the painful feelings which are attached to the beginning of the dreaded danger-situation.[41]

The ego in making use of an experimental cathexis, and by setting in motion by means of a danger signal the automatic pleasure-pain mechanism makes possible either a withdrawal from the objectionable excitation or the initiation of a counter-cathexis.[41] Or because the threat is symbolic and not real, the ego may become strengthened by its ability to anticipate frustrating situations in fantasy. Fenichel observes that such preparation consists economically in making ready amounts of counter-cathexis for the purpose of binding excitations to come. Unanticipated events are experienced more forcefully than those which are prepared for and therefore are likely to be the more traumatic.[33] Flugel remarks that there is little doubt that art has considerable value in providing a sort of mental gymnasium, in which, through suitable exercise, mental poise and stability can be achieved, difficult situations mastered, and disharmonies resolved:

> Imagination, by enabling us to foresee possible contingencies before they arise and to study hypothetical situations that are not actually present, provides us with a most potent means for dealing with reality. It becomes possible for us, without incurring danger and with a minimum expenditure of energy, to avoid errors and devise new methods of satisfying our desires.[34]

Since the therapeutic situation cannot provide an infinite number of identifications for the patient, books can be successfully used to complement and supplement the identification with the therapist.

TRANSFERENCE

Usually attributed to the transference are the most profound values and the most dire consequences of psychotherapy. How can bibliotherapy meet this challenge in such a way that the values are enhanced and the dangers minimized? It is the function of the transference to show the patient that he is reproducing something that happened long ago in his affection or ambivalence toward the physician.[38] As Jung describes the process, as long as we are unconscious of the self, it appears projected into the environment. With growing integration of the self, the projection is withdrawn. Hence it is the purpose of therapy to make the subject conscious of his projections. Projection is the first and inevitable step toward consciousness because everything of which one is unconscious is projected, and so it is through projection that one is confronted with his inner psychic content. But as long as the next step is not taken and the projection not withdrawn from the object into the subject, there is danger to psychic balance and stability. No true individuation can be achieved until the subject assimilates the contents of his unconscious and withdraws his projections. The latter is an act of self-recognition and the equivalent to becoming conscious.[54]

Through the study of the projections which the patient makes on the characters in a novel, the therapist can ascertain in a relatively short time the nature of the patient's irrational attitudes. If the patient invests upon a situation portrayed in a novel emotion of the same nature and intensity that he invested upon early traumatic experiences, it is clear that he is confusing reality with the social symbol.[19] This expression of the transference in reaction to characters in a book can give the patient insight into the manner in which he is re-living early experiences and feeling the same ambivalence that he did as a child without due regard for the fact that the situation is now changed and that what was appropriate emotion to the child is no longer appropriate for the adult.

One student, Marjorie, an elderly school teacher, in reacting to the mother in *Sons and Lovers,* was extremely ambivalent about the book. First she found it beautiful:

> I spent more time in thinking about it than in the actual reading. It aroused many memories of my early life. They came to me in the middle of the night, in the street car. Memories of my mother, of her death, of her punishment of me, of my brother's scorn of me.

Later she commented on not being able to bear reading it. Her final reaction to it was as follows:

> I never loved my mother. That is a dreadful thing to say, a dreadful thing to live through. I was happier when I was away from her. When I came home I was apt to be cross, sensitive, and unpleasant. My mother's spells of blues depressed me. Also she dominated me. I was ashamed of my attitude toward her so I never admitted it. . . . I was entirely too docile all my life, even submissive. That's why I hated the book even while I thought it beautiful. It made me see how many years of misery I caused myself. I didn't like to admit I had been so submissive. Also I didn't like to see my mother as she really was. Since her death I have idealized her. But now I know she wasn't mean like the mother in the book, nor spying and hypocritical. But she was efficient, too busy, ambitious, and brought up to believe in children's explicit obedience. I should wipe from my mind both the picture of a perfect mother and the lingering resentment toward her.

Another student, Anne, reacted in a similar fashion to *The Little Locksmith:*

> I raged at the author for leaving the book in the unfinished manner she chose. She left the van load of furniture—her mother's—dumped helter-skelter in an empty house. It left me angry, frustrated. Her callousness enraged me.
>
> Why did it matter to me? Why did I get so emotional about it?
>
> I know why it hurt with an almost physical hurt. I, too, had broken up a home. I never reassembled that one, nor made another. I have put down no roots. I am afraid of having them torn out again. Nearly twenty years later I read of a similar incident—and feel unreasoning anger.

Alexander and French have called attention to the dangers of the transference neurosis which represents the features of the original neurosis and which permits the conflictful elements to diminish and the gratification to increase, thus leading to inertia on the part of the patient and unnecessary prolongation of the treatment.[3] A dynamic reenactment of the pathogenic past is possible through identification with characters and situations in a book. The projections can be made manifest to the patient through the discussion of episodes in the book with the therapist. Time can be saved because the therapist may more forcefully and precipitately suggest to the patient that the father in the novel who is arousing such violent feelings in the patient is the patient's projection of his own father, that actually the father in the book does not have the exact attributes and faults which the patient has attributed to him. When the patient resists, the therapist may introduce evidence from the text which will be more convincing to the patient than would the therapist's interpretation without benefit of a common frame of reference. After admitting he has misread the text, the patient will then be forced to consider why he has misread it, and will ultimately be encouraged to accept the therapist's interpretation. The therapist, while being non-directive in his expression of opinion about the relationships in the patient's life, can be more directive concerning the relationships in a fictional character's life without threat to the patient. By discussing a character with the patient the therapist can test the patient's capacity for interpretation.

In the meantime the patient has been able to abreact a large amount of hostitility upon the character, and again it is less threatening to him to accept the therapist's interpretation of the transference to the character than it would have been to accept the same interpretation of his hostitlity to the therapist. This abreaction upon the characters can be continued with selected reading between interviews, thus saving the therapist's time and yet permitting the necessary venting of hostility. By this means, the transference, which is usually prolonged and attractive, may be made to successive characters in a book and thus serve a parallel function without the concomitant dangers. It is still necessary, of course, to allow the patient to handle conflictful emotional constellations and to experience a feeling of success in rehearsal in the therapeutic sessions. Again, properly directed reading can supplement the relationship by providing a sort of bridge between the private rehearsal in the therapist's office and the experimentation in real life situations with its inevitable penalties for wrong choices. The patient may try out vicariously several solutions to problems without paying the price of failure in the real world.

CATHARSIS

One of the most significant of the dynamic processes involved in the aesthetic experience is catharsis. Literature has the power to break through the subject's repression because, as Freud puts it, other men feel the same dissatisfaction as he with the renunciations demanded by reality and because this dissatisfaction, resulting from the displacement of the pleasure principle by the reality principle, is itself a part of reality.[38] In this way the artist helps the world to soften the impact with the reality principle because he is more skillful in the matter of averting a clash between desire and the harsh, external world:

> . . . he makes it possible for others, in their turn, to obtain solace and consolation ⸀or their own unconscious sources of gratification which had become inaccessible.[38]

Baudouin notes the similarity between analysis and aesthetic response:

> In its therapeutic capacity . . . analysis undertakes, among other things, to provoke beneficial discharges where repression has accumulated a pathogenic excess of emotions. In its aesthetic capacity, it observes that art provokes similar discharges in its own fashion. This common ground enables us to conjecture that in certain instances art may play the part of a true therapeutic agent in nervous disorders, a fact which is borne out by experience.[24]

One obvious reason for the therapeutic power of emotional involvement in a character is in its making unconscious impulses conscious or preconscious. As Freud observes, warded-off impulses lose connection with verbal expression, and by regaining verbalization, unconscious ideas become preconscious.[37] Since in therapeutic interpretations the patient is often unable to connect the words he hears from the therapist with his own emotional experience,[33] the use of literature as an adjunct to therapy permits a recapturing of the emotional experiences to which the subject may attach importance with a more economical expenditure of time than is often required in therapy. Schachtel analyzes the contribution of the writer to the recovery of past experiences:

> The lag, the discrepancy between experience and word is a productive force in man as long as he remains aware of it, as long as he knows and feels that his experience was in some way more than and different from what his concepts and words articulate. The awareness of this unexplored margin of experience, which may be its essential part, can turn into that productive energy which enables man to go one step closer to understanding and communicating his experience, and thus add to the scope of human insight. It is this awareness and the struggle and ability to narrow the gap between experience and words which make the writer and the poet. The danger of the schemata of language, and especially of the worn currency of conventional language in vogue at the moment when the attempt is made to understand and describe an experience, is that the person making this attempt will overlook the discrepancy between experience and language cliché or that he will not be persistent enough in his attempt to eliminate this discrepancy. Once the conventional schema has replaced the experience in his mind, the significant quality of the experience is condemned to oblivion.[99]

By providing the subject with a similar symbolic experience, the artist can help to bridge the gap between crucial experience itself and the conventional schematization he has given to the experience. The vigor and emotional impact of the artist's portrayal of childhood will often evoke recollection of repressed childhood memories, again in a fashion more economical than free association alone permits. Since the recall of early traumatic experiences must take place both from the standpoint of strengthening the ego and increasing the frustration tolerance of the subject and from the point of view of teaching him to discriminate between the past and the present,[3] the recall engendered by vicarious experience is a boon to the therapist. Moreover, since literature gives emphasis to the feelings, the recall is unlikely to be a mere intellectualized reconstruction of the past.

The catharsis that literature evokes does more than permit a rising to consciousness of dammed-up materials; it not only provides for the generation and release of tension but allows a channel for one's impulses, a link with reality for the withdrawn, a means of exorcism for the aggressive, and a means of expression for latent capacities for love and creation; and hence a premonition of what one might be. Erickson has observed that there is a tendency in modern man's ego to mechanize itself and be entirely free from "the very emotions without which no self regulating experience is possible."[30] Vicarious experience may provide a counter-irritant to this tendency. It is an empirical fact that sublimations, especially those that arise in childhood, depend upon the presence of models, a phenomenon which corroborates Freud's assumption that sublimation may be intimately related to identification.[33] Hence it is important to provide for the patient a large choice of identifications to extend his experience and provide a channel for his emotions. Since unconscious material under high pressure has for its sole aim, discharge, and since it is unburdened by the demands of reality, time, order, or logical considerations, it becomes condensed or displaced, following only the interests of increased possibility of discharge.[33] A derivative to this pushing toward motility is to displace its cathexis onto associated, connected ideas that are less objectionable to the conscious ego. Literature can provide such an acceptable outlet:

> Undoubtedly some of the pleasure in art form is due to the fact that we can realize in a world of unreality wishes and impulses that we otherwise would not desire to express or for whose realization the opportunity would never be offered. The wish is released and the sense of unreality relieves us of the necessity of rationalization . . . we are able to obtain in art the widest scope for the harmless play of those complex systems of impulses which the psychologists believe to constitute the ego.[67]

Tragedy, for example, as a synthesis of two moments which in real life exclude each other, enables one to live through his passions but leave behind the compulsion of his emotions.[21] Thus one's emotional life acquires greater strength and changes its form: passion is relieved of its encumbrance; "art gives us the motions of the soul in its depth and variety. We feel not a single emotional quality but continuous oscillation between opposite poles."[21]

> This means . . . even in the most morbid passages of a Leopardi or a Schopenhauer, that no matter how depressing the view presented, it can still fulfill something of the function of the primitive exorcism by naming life even as it is at its worst moments, and thus releasing us from fear of the unnamed and unknown . . . Lear, Oedipus, bring us back to love of life by deepened acceptance of men's constant desperate ruin, and, in the face of that, of man's heroic capacity for no less constant renewal.[76]

INSIGHT

In addition to the fact that imaginative literature facilitates identification and permits both a re-living of old experiences and a symbolic expression of forbidden or unused emotions, all of which are contributory to the progress of therapy, in exercising these necessary functions, it also contributes to the achievement of insight. In addition to understanding emotionally as well as intellectually one's own motivations and those of persons intimately connected with one, what does insight signify? It implies a *reeducation* of *one's emotions.* But when one understands that one is ambivalent toward one's mother because she has rejected one or that one is obsessively clean because of one's early toilet training or that one is fearful about sex experience because one was told as a child that sex was nasty, what indications are there that one's life will henceforward assume another direction more conducive to self fulfillment and happiness? As Fromm has observed, modern schools have too often merely "debunked," giving an understanding of motivations but substituting nothing new for the defenses that have been discarded. It is his conviction that there must be both psychological insight and philosophical values if the patient is to learn to live productively.[43] Likewise Schilder believes that mere emotional reenactment of previous conflicts is insufficient for therapy, that there must be a further educational synthetic process in order to direct the individual to a better adaptation of his freed emotions to further tasks and to encourage his inner drive toward the future.[100] The insight which literature fosters extends beyond mere re-living of traumatic experience and contributes to the development of the individual's ego integrative powers and to the achievement of direction and a sense of values.

A few assumptions concerning psychotherapy should be mentioned as a basis for the discussion of insight. Alexander and French conceive that the therapeutic relationship may constitute a situation in which the subject displays in his reactions to the therapist those rigid ways of perceiving and behaving which constitute his neurotic symptoms. These reactions may be utilized as the content for productive thinking.[3] Similarly the patient displays in his reactions to characters and situations in a book these same faulty and rigid perceptions, and these too may constitute the content for productive thinking. The therapeutic advantages in using these materials are twofold: first, the patient's accessibility is increased through his willingness to discuss a character like him rather than himself; second, insight may continue as he reads and thinks about what he reads during the gaps in interviews. Alexander and French believe that daily interviews tend to reduce the patient's emotional participation in the therapy; they tend to become routine and prevent the development of strong emotions by allowing the patient to verbalize his transference feelings as they emerge. Because analysis in which the emotional level is low must inevitably progress slowly, it is important to keep the emotional intensity as high as is commensurate with avoidance of threat to the patient's ego. At the same time the frequency of interviews should be curtailed so as to increase the emotional intensity and to safeguard against the patient's substitution of the safe analytic experience for life experiences.[3] If these assumptions are correct, directed reading would be especially useful to permit the continuance of productive thinking during gaps in interviews and to forbid too great reliance upon the therapist. Another principle of therapy, to place continually more responsibility upon the patient, can at the same time be served for he will have to continue to cope with his problems during his vicarious experiences with them. If it is the purpose of therapy to help patients "in neutrality, to re-experience and re-evaluate emotional reactions,"[44] properly structured approaches to imaginative literature enable the patient to be both participant and spectator, and in so doing, serve to develop his ego-integrative tendencies. He brings to bear on the situation in a novel his own predispositions, the congeries of circumstances in his own life, his unique perspective, and he must add them up in relation to what is given in the book. He must search for meaning and order, similarities among differences, differences among similarities, and hypotheses to account for both his own experiences and those portrayed in the book. This is productive thinking.

A young freshman boy, who had never done any reading before, commented as follows on Sherwood Anderson's *Winesburg, Ohio:* "The stories gave me a frightened doubt that I myself was being portrayed in an exaggerated fashion."

Another student, a woman in her middle forties who had been married four times and who had habitually overprotested her "perfect" adjustment, came to some significant conclusions about herself in her spontaneously written comments on *The Fountain.* After quoting a lengthy passage from the novel which ended with the phrase, "An intuitive resistance to an invasion of herself," she continues:

> Well, there you have it. That was why I pushed my present husband away, when I was seventeen, with such ferocity, such madness. I was almost out of my mind in my determination not to marry him, and not to see him. Well, now I know just what happened, after more than a quarter of a century. Why was I so violent about it, I have often asked myself. And then the payoff. Yes, I see it all now, plainly. After I got rid of him out of my life, my unconscious mind repudiated me, my self, the personality that I had given up my love to 'save.' That is why I became almost at once, from an individual who was fiercely individualistic, an almost completely selfless person. My—what? sub-subconscious—in turn repudiated the individuality which itself had repudiated love. My terrible temper, which used to flare up when I was a child and scorch everything around, completely disappeared after I no longer—as I thought—loved. For at least fifteen years I *never* felt anger, and put myself last out of all the world. Literally. There was just no "self" left. What I had fought to save just didn't exist any longer, "myself."
>
> What a strange thing to see everything so clearly at this late date. I think it is

because I have been too busy to think about myself. . . . My marriages too were obviously an attempt to punish myself for having killed my self. I married good men, and hated them as soon as the ring was on my finger. How many layers of 'us' there are!

Another relevant therapeutic assumption is that the personality represents an interdependent organization of dynamically related constituents. It is therefore impossible to change any constituent without affecting the whole, for the modification of any part entails reverberations throughout the rest. Thus it would matter relatively little if the approach were made from left to right, top or bottom, as long as a significant point were attacked; in the end, the initial effect would alter the total organization.[93] This theory suggests that the patient might well be permitted a certain amount of autonomy in the discussion of what a given book means to him and if he should begin with a discussion of philosophical theory or attitudes about life, as a defense against more affectively laden materials, or if he should be concerned with an analysis of the mother's motives rather than his own, his psychological field is changing and expanding nonetheless, and this alteration will produce subsequent alterations in his self concept. Hence whether the reading of books serves to bring about a rediscovery of the self, a more adequate understanding of others, an alteration in the concept of reality, or a changed concept of value, in any case the accomplishment of any one of these ends, and in whatever order, will contribute to the achievement of insight.

Insight has been equated with the development of the ego's integrative capacities, which, according to Alexander and French, is the prerequisite to productive perceiving and thinking and new ways of behavior.[3] By means of exposure to the mother prototype in a novel or play, the reader, to the extent that he is emotionally involved, will reenact his experiences with his own mother. In analyzing a fictional mother he may more accurately analyze his own mother. In so doing he must inevitably make a comparison between his own mother and the mother portrayed; this differentiation of the two mothers is a first step to integration. One cannot integrate without first having something to differentiate, and literature provides the means for differentiation. The therapeutic effect lies in the substitution of something conscious for what was unconscious.[38] Through the symbolic re-enactment of the old situation with the mother, and the perception of the differentiating features of the two mothers, there is an opportunity for conscious integration. The literary representation can facilitate this process thorugh the implicit meaning or interpretation the author has conveyed, the order he has given to the confusing fragments of experience. Since neurosis is resolved when the environment is no longer interpreted as symbolically threatening and conflictful,[75] it is important that ample opportunities for re-experiencing traumatic episodes be given to the patient. If as spectator he learns to view them as nonthreatening, through a flash of insight he may then recognize that even as participant he need not be threatened. The process of analysis as an interpersonal experience has a definite end: "That end is achieved when the patient has rediscovered his own self as an actively and interdependently functioning entity."[91]

Integrally related to self recognition is the capacity to penetrate beneath the individual Persona and discover who one is as distinguished from what people think one is or ought to be. The individual is prone to lose himself and his perception of what is real beneath the cultural overlays, the expectations of others, and the stereotypes. Here again it is the function of the artist to remove the veil. In presenting the concrete, the individual, and the particular, the artist necessarily blasts the stereotypes and reveals the person as he really is. Leaving conventional schemata about life behind, the writer presents the person in a human predicament and reveals him in his interaction with his fellow beings. He permits the reader to share his introspections, to overhear his conversations, and to accompany him on his adventures. In so doing the reader may perceive the interrelationships between the character's anxieties and his problems, the relationship between issues heretofore considered unrelated, and hence may reorganize his perception of himself and of reality. He may perceive that conflict and maladjustment occur in the presence of invalid, inconsistent or ambivalent attitudes which negate the principle of unification and self consistency.[110] Through the detachment which enables him to be a spectator in the life of a character in a novel, he may see how these inconsistent and invalid attitudes militate against the character's adjustment. Then it is only one further step to examine his own attitudes to test their validity.

Koestler calls this manner of integration a bisociative pattern of perception. Art provides the stimuli designed to elicit the integrative impulses in the reader and to canalize them in such a way as to lead them to satisfaction. The set of stimuli provided by art draws energy away from the tension-generating organic source and leads to catharsis, drawing on the reader's own reservoir of integrative energy:

> Whenever a narrative moving on a given field F1 is suddenly bisociated with a field of "higher value" F2, a specific mental experience occurs. It is an experience closely akin to what the contemplatives call 'spontaneous illumination,' and is the main source of aesthetic enjoyment. Its *intellectual* aspect is the sudden perception of the object in a new, brighter, and more relevant light, a new and deeper understanding of the objects of trivial experience, in short a eureka process which is the positive counterpart of the malicious eureka process of the joke. The *emotional* aspect is the result of the transfer of the integrative charge from the narrow associative meshwork F1 to the wider associative net of F2, with its greater emotion-absorbing capacity, in which it can suddenly expand—like water drained from a pipe into a wide system of irrigation channels. In this simultaneous occurrence of intellectual illumination and emotional expansion, which are but two aspects of the same bisociative process, lies the essence of the aesthetic experience.[63]

THE RELATION OF VALUES TO PSYCHOTHERAPY

Although the reliving of past experiences and the symbolic trying out of new experiences are necessary steps to increased consciousness and hence to the achievement of integration, psychotherapy need not stop at this point. After the subject has recognized his needs and becomes conscious of earlier frustrations, he no longer has need for compulsive fulfillment of infantile desires; for the first time he has some freedom of choice in his subsequent behavior. The psychological atom, according to Saul, is the traumatic infantile core in human nature. To split it is to free at last man's potential constructive and cooperative energies.[98] How shall he exercise this new prerogative? What choices shall he make? In what direction shall he move? What values shall he embrace? Alexander and French believe that a relationship which is optimal for the occurrence of reconstructive learning is one which, among other things, will center attention upon the dynamic potentialities of the subject's personality for healthy development rather than upon pathological mechanisms that are obstacles to treatment. Consistent with this end is the systematic effort to help him to determine the direction in which he must move to fulfill his potentialities.[3]

In order to provide this help the psychotherapist may well explore the possibilities for an empirical approach to values and determine his therapeutic goals in conformity to what is known of man's psychobiological nature and the nature of society, not as it is, but as it must be to permit man's fullest realization of himself. Saul regards evil in man as the persistent traumatic infantile; good, not as conformity to code but as productivity and the strength of maturity. Brotherly love represents man's efforts to grow up and achieve maturity.[98] Similarly Fromm suggests the meaning of adjustment. Freedom is not only the necessary condition of happiness but of virtue: "freedom not in the sense of the ability to make arbitrary choices and not freedom from necessity, but freedom to realize that which one potentially is, to fulfill the true nature of man according to the laws of his existence."[43] Psychoanalysis, Fromm believes, ignored the fact that the human personality cannot be understood unless we look at the totality of man, including man's need to find answers to the problem of the meaning of his existence:

> Our knowledge of human nature does not lead to ethical relativism but, on the contrary, to the conviction that the sources of norms for ethical conduct are to be found in man's nature itself; that moral norms are based upon man's inherent qualities, and that their violation results in mental and emotional disintegration.[43]

The key to productiveness lies in self-acceptance. Great destructiveness is not found in those who have little hostility against themselves. Also the life-destroying forces occur in inverse ratio to the life-furthering ones. Therefore, the degree of destructiveness is proportionate to the degree to which the unfolding of a person's capacity is blocked, to the blockage of the spontaneous expression of man's sensory, emotional, physical, and intellectual capacities, to the thwarting of his productivity. That man has an inherent drive for integration follows from the nature of man, from the principle that power to act creates a need to use this power, and failure to use it results in dysfunction and unhappiness.[43]

Since it is in the nature of man to move toward something larger than the individual self and participate in, and unite with, such large units,[7] the psychotherapist may help the subject not only to actualize himself but to strengthen his identification with a healthy subculture. In this perspective books may be used to help the patient to discover his potentialities, to achieve direction, and to formulate a philosophy consistent both with his own nature and the creation of the good society. It has already been noted that art acquaints man not only with his own nature but with that of others. In so doing it encourages both acceptance of self and a readiness to relate the self to other human beings on a mature basis. Literature may encourage further growth. Since it is implicitly a criticism and evaluation of human experience, it permits the reader to consider and weigh the relative satisfaction inherent in a diverse number of occupations and professions, and to evaluate a variety of ways and means of achieving "the good life." Beyond this, literature in relating all knowledge to human experience enables the reader to determine which values make for the happy and productive life. He may consider the multiple answers to the mysteries of human living in the pages of the novelists and dramatists. He may examine the joys that come from mature human relationships, from the enjoyment of nature and of the arts, from the explorations of science and philosophy, from the dedication to causes greater than the self. He may identify with lovers who are compatible, with artists who find joy in creation, or with those who foster justice, freedom, increased consciousness, and peace among men. Thus he may test out his own powers in imaginative participation and, thorough increased awareness of the manifold ways in which man may realize his fullest potentialities, make a choice consistent with his own needs and abilities. It is of the very essence of the artist's power to view life freshly, to penetrate the surfaces of things, to cut away the cultural overlays, to blast the stereotypes, "to see life steadily and to see it whole." The reader as emotional participant and collaborator in this process may move more surely in the direction of realizing his full capacities as a human being. The artist, as he fearlessly criticizes the existing order—its complacency, ignorance, and error—invites the reader to join with him in his repudiation of the forces of death. In accepting man's instincts as well as his intellect, in showing them to be the means with conscious direction for the fullest expression of man's nature, in presenting man as he loves and performs acts of courage and nobility, in viewing life not only as it is but as it might be and must be, the artist compels the reader to share in his affirmation of life.

REFERENCES

1. Alfred Adler, *The Practice and Theory of Individual Psychology.* (London: Kegan Paul, Trench, Trubner & Co., Ltd., 1946).

2. Sister Mary Agnes, "Bibliotherapy for Socially Maladjusted Children," *Catholic Education Review,* 44:8-16 (January, 1946).

3. Franz Alexander and Thomas French, *Psychoanalytic Therapy* (New York: The Ronald Press Company, 1946).

4. A. H. B. Allen, "A Psychological Theory of Aesthetic Value," *British Journal of Psychology,* 28:43-88 (July, 1937).

5. Gordon W. Allport, *Personality* (New York: Henry Holt & Co., 1937).

6. Gordon Allport, *The Use of Personal Documents in Psychological Science, Prepared for the Committee on Appraisal of Research,* Bulletin No. 49 (New York: Social Science Research Council, 1942).

7. Andrus Angyal, *Foundation for a Science of Personality* (New York: Oxford University Press, 1941).

8. Kenneth E. Appel, "Psychiatric Therapy," in *Personality and the Behavior Disorders,* II. J. McV. Hunt, ed. (New York: The Ronald Press Company, 1944).

9. Alice B. Auerbach, "Can Mental Hygiene Books Improve the Health? *Child Study,* 26:39-55 (Spring, 1949).

10. Edmund Bergler, "On a Clinical Approach to the Psychoanalysis of Writers," *The Psychoanalytic Review,* 31:40-70 (January, 1944).

11. Phyllis Blanchard, "Adolescent Experience in Relation to Personality and Behavior," in *Personality and the Behavior Disorders,* II. J. McV. Hunt, ed. (New York: The Ronald Press Company, 1944).

12. C. Bradley and E. S. Bosquet, "The Use of Books for Psychotherapy with Children," *American Journal of Orthopsychiatry,* 6:23-31 (January, 1936).

13. J. F. Brown, *The Psychodynamics of Abnormal Behavior* (New York: McGraw-Hill Book Co., 1940).

14. J. F. Brown, *Psychology and the Social Order* (New York: McGraw-Hill Book Co., 1936).

15. Alice I. Bryan, "Can There Be a Science of Bibliotherapy?" *The Library Journal,* 64:773-76 (October, 1939).

16. Alice I. Bryan, "Personality Adjustment through Reading," *The Library Journal,* 64:573-76 (August, 1939).

17. Alice I. Bryan, "The Psychology of the Reader," *The Library Journal,* 64:7-12 (January, 1939).

18. Kenneth Burke, *The Philosophy of Literary Form* (Baton Rouge: Louisiana State University Press, 1941).

19. Trigant Burrow, *The Biology of Human Conflict* (New York: The Macmillan Company, 1937).

20. S. H. Butcher, *Aristotle's Theory of Poetry and Fine Arts* (London: The Macmillan Company, 1923).

21. Ernst Cassirer, *An Essay on Man* (New Haven: Yale University Press, 1944).

22. Arthur W. Combs, "A Phenomenological Approach to Adjustment Theory," *Journal of Abnormal and Social Psychology*, 44:29-35 (January, 1949).

23. Elizabeth Creglow, "Therapeutic Value of Properly Selected Reading Matter," *U. S. Veterans Administration Medical Bulletin*, 7:1086-89 (November, 1931).

24. Roland Dalbiez, *Psychoanalytic Method and the Doctrine of Freud*, I and II (New York: Longmans, Green & Co., 1941).

25. Thomas De Quincey, "On Languages," in *The Collected Writings of Thomas De Quincey*, X. David Masson, ed. (London: A. and C. Black, 1897).

26. Irwin Edman, *Arts and the Man* (New York: W. W. Norton & Co., Inc., 1939).

27. T. S. Eliot, "Hamlet and His Problems," in *Critiques and Essays in Criticism.* Robert W. Stallman, ed. (New York: The Ronald Press Company, 1949).

28. Havelock Ellis, *The Dance of Life* (Boston: Houghton Mifflin Co., 1923).

29. Willis D. Ellis, ed., *A Source Book of Gestalt Psychology* (New York: Harcourt, Brace & Co., 1939).

30. Erik H. Erickson, "Childhood and Tradition in Two American Indian Tribes; with Some Reflections on the Contemporary American Scene," in *Personality in Nature, Society, and Culture.* Clyde Kluckholm and Henry A. Murray, eds. (New York: Alfred A. Knopf, 1948).

31. Milton H. Erickson, "A Study of an Experimental Neurosis Hypnotically Induced in a Case of Ejaculatio Praecox," *British Journal of Medical Psychology*, 15: Part I, 34-50 (April, 1935).

32. Stanley G. Estes, "Review of *Psychoanalytic Therapy* by Franz Alexander and Thomas Morton French, et al.," *Journal of Abnormal and Social Psychology*, 42:137-142 (January, 1947).

33. Otto Fenichel, *The Psychoanalytic Theory of Neuroses* (New York: W. W. Norton Co., 1945).

34. J. C. Flugel, *Man, Morals and Society* (New York: International University Press, 1945).

35. Lawrence K. Frank, *Projective Methods* (Springfield, Ill.: Charles C. Thomas, Publisher, 1948).

36. G. L. Freeman, *The Energetics of Human Behavior* (Ithaca: Cornell University Press, 1948).

37. Sigmund Freud, *Collected Papers,* IV (London: International Psychoanalytical Press, 1924).

38. Sigmund Freud, *A General Introduction to Psycho-Analysis* (New York: Liveright Publishing Co., 1935).

39. Sigmund Freud, *Group Psychology and the Analysis of the Ego* (New York: Boni and Liveright, 1922).

40. Sigmund Freud, *Introductory Lectures on Psycho-analysis* (London: G. Allen & Unwin, 1922).

41. Sigmund Freud, *New Introductory Lectures on Psycho-Analysis* (New York: W. W. Norton & Co., 1933).

42. Sigmund Freud, "Psychopathic Characters on the Stage," *Psychiatric Quarterly,* 11:459-464 (October, 1942).

43. Erich Fromm, *Man for Himself* (New York: Rinehart & Co., Inc., 1947).

44. Frieda Fromm-Reichman, "Recent Advances in Psychoanalytic Therapy," in *A Study of Interpersonal Relations.* Patrick Mullahy, ed. (New York: Hermitage Press, Inc., 1949).

45. S. Gagnon, "Is Reading Therapy?" *Diseases of the Nervous System,* 3:206-212 (July, 1942).

46. Kurt Goldstein, *The Organism* (New York: American Book Co., 1939).

47. Louis A. Gottschalk, "Bibliotherapy as an Adjuvant in Psychotherapy," *American Journal of Psychiatry,* 104:632-37 (April, 1948).

48. Ives Hendrick, *Facts and Theories of Psychoanalysis* (New York: Alfred A. Knopf, Inc., 1939).

49. S. Herbert, *The Unconscious in Life and Art* (London: George Allen & Unwin, Ltd., 1932).

50. Ernest Hilgaard, *Theories of Learning* (New York: Appleton-Century-Crofts, 1948).

51. Karen Horney, *Self-Analysis* (New York: W. W. Norton & Co., 1942).

52. Eliot D. Hutchinson, "Varieties of Insight in Humans," in *A Study of Interpersonal Relations.* Patrick Mullahy, ed. (New York: Hermitage Press, Inc., 1949).

53. Stanley Hyman, *The Armed Vision* (New York: Alfred A. Knopf, 1948).

54. Jolan Jacobi, *The Psychology of Jung* (New Haven: Yale University Press, 1948).

55. E. Kathleen Jones, *Hospital Libraries* (Chicago: American Library Association, 1923).

56. Ernest Jones, *Papers on Psychoanalysis* (New York: William Wood & Co., 1919).

57. Abram Kardiner, *The Individual and His Society* (New York: Columbia University Press, 1939).

58. Abram Kardiner, *The Psychological Frontiers of Society* (New York: Columbia University Press, 1945).

59. F. W. Kaufman and W. S. Taylor, "Literature as Adjustment," *Journal of Abnormal and Social Psychology*, 31:229-234 (July-September, 1936).

60. Hugh Kingsmill, *Samuel Johnson* (New York: The Viking Press, 1934).

61. Clara J. Kircher, *Character Formation through Books: A Bibliography* (Washington, D.C.: The Catholic University Press, 1945).

62. George S. Klein, "Clinical Perspective for Personality Research," *Journal of Abnormal and Social Psychology*, 44:42-49 (January, 1949).

63. Arthur Koestler, *Insight and Outlook* (New York: The Macmillan Company, 1949).

64. Kurt Koffka, *Principles of Gestalt Psychology* (New York: Harcourt, Brace & Co., 1935).

65. David Krech and Richard S. Crutchfield, *Theory and Problems of Social Psychology* (New York: McGraw-Hill Book Co., 1948).

66. Ernst Kris, "Approaches to Art," in *Psychoanalysis Today*. Sandor Lorand, ed. (New York: International University Press, 1944).

67. Herbert S. Langfeld, *The Aesthetic Attitude* (New York: Harcourt, Brace and Co., 1920).

68. Harold D. Lasswell, "Person, Personality, Group, Culture," in *A Study of Interpersonal Relations*. Patrick Mullahy, ed. (New York: Hermitage Press, Inc., 1949).

69. Kurt Lewin, *A Dynamic Theory of Personality* (New York: McGraw-Hill Book Co., Inc., 1935).

70. Kurt Lewin, *Principles of Topological Psychology* (New York: McGraw-Hill Book Co., Inc., 1936).

71. Donald W. MacKinnon, "Psychodiagnosis in Clinical Practice and Personality Theory," *Journal of Abnormal and Social Psychology*, 44:7-13 (January, 1949).

72. A. H. Maslow, et al., "A Clinically Designed Test for Measuring Psychological Security-Insecurity," *Journal of General Psychology*, 33:21-41 (July, 1945).

73. A. H. Maslow, "The Dynamics of Psychological Security-Insecurity," *Character and Personality*, 10:331-334 (June, 1942).

74. A. H. Maslow, "Problem Centering versus Means Centering in Science," *Philosophy of Science*, 13:326-331 (October, 1946).

75. Jules H. Masserman, *Principles of Dynamic Psychiatry* (Philadelphia: W. B. Saunders Co., 1946).

76. F. O. Matthieson, *From the Heart of Europe* (New York: Oxford University Press, 1948).

77. Karl A. Menninger, *The Human Mind* (New York: Alfred A. Knopf, 1937).

78. W. C. Menninger, "Bibliotherapy," *Bulletin of the Menninger Clinic*, 1:263-274 (November, 1937).

79. Thomas V. Moore, *The Nature and Treatment of Mental Disorders* (New York: Grune & Stratton, 1944).

80. Thomas V. Moore, "Bibliotherapy in Psychiatric Practice," in *Current Therapies of Personality Disorders*. Bernard Glueck, ed. (New York: Grune & Stratton, 1946).

81. Herbert J. Muller, *Science and Criticism* (New Haven: Yale University Press, 1943).

82. Gardner Murphy and Friedrich Jensen, *Approaches to Personality* (New York: Coward-McCann, Inc., 1932).

83. G. Murphy, L. B. Murphy and T. Newcomb, *Experimental Social Psychology* (New York: Harper and Brothers, 1937).

84. Gardner Murphy, *Personality* (New York: Harper and Brothers, 1947).

85. Henry A. Murray, *Explorations in Personality* (New York: Oxford University Press, 1938).

86. Jacob Panken, "Psychotherapeutic Value of Books in the Treatment and Prevention of Juvenile Delinquency." *American Journal of Psychotherapy*, 1:71-86 (January, 1947).

87. Stephen C. Pepper, "Emotional Distance in Art," *Journal of Aesthetics and Art Criticism*, 3:235-239 (June, 1946).

88. Mary D. Quint, "The Mental Hospital Library," *Mental Hygiene*, 28:263-272 (April, 1944).

89. David Rapaport, *Diagnostic Psychological Testing*, II (Chicago: The Year Book Publishers, Inc., 1946).

90. David Rapaport, *Emotions and Memory* (Baltimore: The Williams & Wilkins Co., 1942).

91. Janet M. Rioch, "Analytic Therapy," in *A Study of Interpersonal Relations*. Patrick Mullahy, ed. (New York: Hermitage Press, Inc., 1949).

92. Louise M. Rosenblatt, *Literature as Exploration* (New York: D. Appleton-Century Co., 1938).

93. Saul Rosenzweig, "A Dynamic Interpretation of Psychotherapy Oriented towards Research," in *Contemporary Psychopathology.* Silvan S. Tomkins, ed. (Cambridge, Mass.: Harvard University Press, 1946).

94. Joshua Rosett, *The Mechanism of Thought, Imagery, and Hallucination* (New York: Columbia University Press, 1939).

95. David H. Russell, "Reading Success and Personality Development," *Elementary English,* 25:73-82 (February, 1948).

96. Hanns Sachs, *The Creative Unconscious* (Cambridge, Mass.: Sci-Art Publishers, 1942).

97. Nevitt R. Sanford, Else Frenkel Brunswick and Daniel J. Levinson, Unpublished Manuscript (Berkeley, Calif.: University of California Public Opinion Study Research Staff).

98. Leon J. Saul, *Emotional Maturity* (Philadelphia: Lippincott, 1947).

99. Ernest G. Schachtel, "On Memory and Childhood Amnesia," in *A Study of Interpersonal Relations.* Patrick Mullahy, ed. (New York: Hermitage Press, Inc., 1949).

100. Paul Schilder, *Psychotherapy* (New York: W. W. Norton & Co., 1938).

101. Jerome M. Schneck, "Bibliotherapy for Neuropsychiatric Patients: Report on Two Cases," *Bulletin of the Menninger Clinic,* 10:71-86 (January, 1946).

102. Jerome M. Schneck, "Bibliotherapy and Hospital Library Activities for Neuropsychiatric Patients," *Psychiatry,* 8:207-228 (February, 1945).

103. Jerome M. Schneck, "Studies in Bibliotherapy in a Neuropsychiatric Hospital," *Occupational Therapy and Rehabilitation,* 23:316-23 (December, 1944).

104. Max Schoen, "Aesthetic Experience in the Light of Current Psychology," *Journal of Aesthetics and Art Criticism,* 1:23-33 (Spring, 1941).

105. John Shawcross, ed., *Shelley's Literary and Philosophical Criticism* (London: Humphrey Milford, 1932).

106. Muzafer Sherif and Hadley Cantril, *The Psychology of Ego-Involvements* (New York: John Wiley & Sons, Inc., 1947).

107. George V. Sheviakov, "Evaluation of Personal and Social Adjustment," in *Appraising Pupil Progress.* Eugene R. Smith and Ralph W. Tyler, eds. (New York: Harper & Bros., 1942).

108. Dora V. Smith, "Nature of the Reading Program to Meet Per-

sonal and Social Needs," in *Promoting Personal and Social Development through Reading*. William S. Gray, ed. Supplementary Educational Monograph No. 64 (Chicago: University of Chicago Press, 1947).

109. Richard Sterba, "The Problem of Art in Freud's Writings," *Psychoanalytic Quarterly*, 9:256-268 (April, 1940).

110. Frederick C. Thorne, "The Attitudinal Pathoses," *Journal of Clinical Psychology*, 5:1-21 (January, 1949).

111. Lionel Trilling, "The Legacy of Sigmund Freud: Literary and Aesthetic," *Kenyon Review*, 2:152-173 (Spring, 1940).

112. L. H. Twyeffort, "Therapy in Psychoneurosis," in *The Cyclopedia of Medicine, Surgery and Specialities*, Vol. 12. G. M. Piersol and E. L. Bortz, eds. (Philadelphia: F. A. Davis Co., 1945).

113. Frederic Wertham, "The Dreams that Heal," in *The World Within*. Mary Louise Aswell, ed. (New York: McGraw-Hill Book Co., Inc., 1947).

Suggestions for Further Reading

Alice I. Bryan, "Can There Be A Science of Bibliotherapy?" *Library Journal* 64:773-776 (October 1939).

Alice I. Bryan, "Personality Adjustment Through Reading," *Library Journal* 64:573-576 (August 1939).

Samuel McChord Crothers, "A Literary Clinic," *Atlantic Monthly* 118:291-301 (August 1916).

Salomon Gagnon, "Is Reading Therapy?" *Diseases of the Nervous System* 3:206-212 (July 1942).

Elizabeth Green and S. I. Schwab, "The Therapeutic Use of a Hospital Library," *The Hospital Social Service Quarterly* 1:147-157 (August 1919).

Evalene P. Jackson, "Effects of Reading Upon Attitudes Toward the Negro Race," *Library Quarterly* 14:47-54 (January 1944).

Josephine A. Jackson, "The Therapeutic Value of Books," *Modern Hospital* 25:50-51 (July 1925).

E. Kathleen Jones, *Hospital Libraries.* (Chicago: American Library Assn., 1939).

Thomas V. Moore, "Bibliotherapy in Psychiatric Practice," in Glueck, B. *Current Therapies for Personality Disorders,* (New York: Grune and Stratton, 1946).

Elizabeth Pomeroy, "Bibliotherapy—A Study in Results of Hospital Library Service," *Medical Bulletin of the Veterans' Administration* 13:360-364 (April 1937).

Ruth M. Tews, "Case Histories of Patients' Reading," *Library Journal* 69:484-487 (1944).

PART

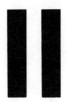

THE VIEW FROM
OTHER DISCIPLINES

Introductory Comments

The 1950s were a turning point in the social and behavioral sciences. Popular interest in psychology and in therapies of all types grew rapidly, and interest in bibliotherapy also expanded. About 200 articles were published between 1950 and 1958. Some 400 others have appeared since. Two-thirds of all the articles published on bibliotherapy between 1950 and 1960 appeared in journals outside the library field. This section presents papers from the fields of psychiatry, education, counseling, and occupational therapy.

Because psychotherapists have been prominent in bibliotherapy since the 1930s, their work is well-represented here. "Bibliotherapy in Psychiatry" by Fierman and Fierman is a review of the research and literature until 1952. They note that "While bibliotherapy, in one form or another, is firmly established as a useful adjuvant in the practice of psychiatry, there seems to be no well-established basic principle of bibliotherapy and practice." A decade later, Dr. Edwin Alston, in "Bibliotherapy and Psychotherapy," set forth some of these principles. He discusses personality development, psychopathology, mental health, and psychotherapy, and applies them all to the relevant uses of bibliotherapy. Although he is a strong supporter of bibliotherapy, he admits that "Bibliotherapy may be of great value for some patients. With others, bibliotherapy is simply not going to be applicable, or there will be preferred adjunctive measures."

It has usually been assumed that one such group of patients is the nonreader. But in Michael Shiryon's version of bibliotherapy, which he terms "literatherapy," the patient need not read—instead the therapist may tell stories or anecdotes to the patient as a basis for discussion and insight. Shiryon defines literatherapy as the "intentional planned use of literary writings and/or literary forms . . . to facilitate and enhance psychotherapy." He has presented a series of interesting speeches on the topic; unfortunately none of them has been published until now. "Literatherapy: Theory and Application" is presented here as an example of one version of bibliotherapy employed in psychotherapy.

Poetry therapy is another such variation. It is a form of bibliotherapy employing *only* poetry. Many articles and books have appeared on this therapy since its inception by Dr. Eli Greifer in 1963. A major difference in poetry therapy is its emphasis on writing, in addition to reading and discussing poetry for therapeutic purposes. Molly Harrower's article for *Current Psychiatric Therapies* is included here as it is an excellent survey of the field of poetry therapy.

Articles by two staff members of St. Elizabeths Hospital (in Washington, D.C.) exemplify descriptive pieces on bibliotherapy and psychotherapy. Dr. Kenneth Gorelick, a psychiatrist, uses bibliotherapy as a training technique with other psychiatrists. His paper, one of a series on bibliotherapy presented at the International Federation of Library Associations (IFLA) conference in 1974, stresses that "as a training experience, fictional literature has unique assets that live clinical experience lacks." Literature also has characteristics missing from institutional life. Daniel Sweeney, a psychologist at the same hospital, discusses his pioneering work with the withdrawn, institutionalized elderly and bibliotherapy.

Franklin Berry, a psychologist and researcher in Georgia, concentrates on systematizing the field and provides a new and very useful analysis. His conceptualization is designed to simplify further research in bibliotherapy by differentiating versions of bibliotherapy according to the receptive and expressive modes.

Although psychiatrists and psychologists have contributed much to the literature on bibliotherapy, over 80 percent of recent publications come from practitioners outside of medicine. Librarians comprise a large segment of this group, but the interest from other professionals is becoming increasingly evident in print. Inez Huntting, retired director of occupational therapy at a large psychiatric hospital, discusses the use of bibliotherapy in occupational therapy in her 1962 article. The definition of occupational therapy as "a program of selected activity conducted as treatment under medical direction for physical and psychological problems . . ." does demonstrate a marked similarity between the two disciplines. Huntting stresses the need for cooperation between occupational therapists and bibliotherapists. Archie L. Lejeune appeals for cooperation between school counselors and librarians. He discusses the relationship between counseling and guidance and bibliotherapy. "Bibliocounseling," he says, is "the clinical use of books in guidance and counseling situations that involve personal-social needs and/or problems of individuals or groups. . . ."

The educational context is the second most popular setting for bibliotherapy after hospitals, and much of the literature is concentrated in educational journals. A two-part article on "Contributions of Research in Bibliotherapy to the Language-Arts Program," originally published in 1950, has been reprinted here because it remains an excellent survey of both the theory and research in bibliotherapy as it relates to education. Russell and Shrodes aptly state that "Bibliotherapy may be conceived as an attempt to unite practices in education, in clinical work, and in mental hygiene." Harold Moses and Joseph Zaccaria in "Bibliotherapy in an Educational Context: Rationale and Principles" identify principles which combine mental health and education practices in bibliotherapy. This article was a precursor to their excellent book on bibliotherapy in education. The final paper from the field of education, "Using Books to Help Solve Children's Problems," provides an excellent discussion of the actual applications of bibliotherapy, and discussion of the values and processes involved.

Bibliotherapy in Psychiatry

By Louis B. Fierman
and Ella Yensen Fierman

Even in ancient times reading was prescribed for patients with apparently beneficial results.[30] In this century there has accumulated a sizeable number of publications on bibliotherapy, and several reviews as well as bibliographies on the subject have appeared.[7, 15, 31, 38, 54, 56, 58]

Most articles on bibliotherapy refer to its use in the field of psychiatry, especially in the practice of hospital or institutional psychiatry. Paradoxically, non-medical authors, librarians and occupational therapists far outnumber psychiatrists as contributors to this literature, and many standard textbooks on psychiatry do not refer to bibliotherapy at all. Articles on bibliotherapy vary a great deal in content and principle, and frequently the element of therapy is obscure. Topics range from the description of routine hospital library services[6] to the use of empirically recommended reading material for psychiatric patients.[2, 16, 24] Thus, while bibliotherapy, in one form or another, is firmly established as a useful adjuvant in the practice of psychiatry, there seem to be no well-established basic principles of bibliotherapy theory and practice. Such principles would be dependent on an understanding of reading behavior itself. We propose to review a number of studies and articles dealing with the determinants of reading, the effects of reading on behavior, and, the practice of bibliotherapy.

DETERMINANTS OF READING BEHAVIOR

Factors which determine and influence reading behavior of an individual may be grouped according to source; that is, the factors may be related to the individual, the reading material, or the environment.

Factors relating to the individual would include his psychological and physiological status, intelligence, education, past reading habits, social background, sex, age, and many other personal attributes. Mower[45] compared reading and other hobby activities of hospitalized psychiatric patients with those of hospital employees. He found that while the patients' choice of hobbies did not differ significantly from that of the employees, the patients were less active and less interested. He concluded that the amount of free psychic energy available was a crucial factor in reading and hobby development. Thus, a patient whose energy, attention, or concern is concentrated in his illness will have difficulty reading despite whatever potential therapeutic effects the reading might have. Appel,[2] reviewing the subject of psychiatric treatment, concluded that "the majority of nervously ill patients are unable to read because of the psychological disturbance inherent in their neuroses." Lazarsfeld[34] studied one aspect of the age factor as a reading determinant and demonstrated that her subjects, who were male and female non-patients of varying age, preferred plot-episodes involving characters nearest their own age. Other patient variables such as sex, nationality, socio-economic level and occupation have been cited also as influencing reading behavior.[10, 43, 54]

The concept of individual uniqueness and the need for awareness by bibliotherapists that reading will not have precisely the same significance for any two persons nor for the same person at different times has been emphasized by the Menningers.[41, 42]

Unconscious determinants of reading behavior have received little attention in the bulk of literature on bibliotherapy, although some authors do suggest that therapy should fit the patient's unconscious needs as well as his conscious interest and there are occasional references to the symbolic significance of books.[39, 41, 43] Psychoanalysts, however, have postulated some more-or-less universal unconscious factors inherent in reading. Strachey[57] proposed that independent of subject matter there was an extra element of gratification in the act of reading itself. This extra gratification he identified as being essentially oral, although scoptophilic and anal-erotic trends also seemed to be involved. Strachey equated pleasant easy reading with the first, or sucking, oral stage and the reading which "we have to get our teeth into and chew up before we can digest" with the second, or biting stage of oral libidinal development. Thus, an individual's pattern of libido distribution will influence the choice and manner of his reading.

The development of reading and talking are closely associated since everyone learns to read by first saying the written words aloud. However, reading involves oral incorporative mechanisms rather than the oral expulsive process used in speech. Strachey indicates that since reading "is a way of eating another person's words," reading difficulties may be expected where the reader is ambivalent about oral aggressive gratification. "If in such a situation the sublimation is unstable or incomplete there will be an immediate tendency to the release of a number of sadistic and destructive impulses" with "each word felt as an enemy that is being bitten up" and "that may in its turn become threatening and dangerous to the reader." This unconscious attitude may lead to obsessive rereading and reading aloud when there is unconscious doubt that the "enemy" as represented by the written words has truly been destroyed. Written words also may be perceived unconsciously as the excrement of the author, and reading may then involve coprophagic tendencies.

Other examples of instinctual gratification through reading are described by Fenichel.[18] He cites the common compulsion to read while sitting on the toilet as illustrative of the relationship between reading and anal-eroticism. "Material" regained by reading compensates for the loss of other material unconsciously treasured. The related impulse to read while eating is equated with "an attempt to distract attention from an oral-erotic excitement." Reading is further correlated with inquisitiveness which may be a substitute for gluttony.

Mower[45] in his study of hobby activities also concluded that the "oral intaking" character type finds reading more satisfactory as a hobby than do other character types.

Through mental mechanisms of symbolization and displacement reading may provide expression of oedipal conflictual strivings. Strachey explains that books and paper may be perceived unconsciously as female or mother symbols, and the printed words or author's thoughts may represent the male symbol. Reading then may express oral hostile destructive feelings towards one's father or feminine receptive wishes toward him. The hungry reader, so the parallel goes, enters the book or mother symbol; reads or devours the words or traces of the father; and is, in turn, fertilized by them. Scoptophilic impulses also utilize reading, according to Fenichel.[17] He cites a patient whose passion for reading was associated with an earlier phobia of picture-books. Looking and devouring were unconsciously equated, and scoptophilic impulses found expression in overcompensatory attempts "to know all about books" once the phobia of books had been removed.

The second group of factors determining reading behavior is related to reading material itself. This group of factors can be further divided into two groups: (a) the subject matter of reading material, and (b) the physical properties or structure of reading material.

Numerous studies have been made of patients' reading in terms of choice of rather arbitrarily classified subject matter.[23, 36, 49, 50] The usual design for these studies has been to attempt to correlate the standard psychiatric diagnoses of the patients studied with the conventional categories of the books they read, such as fiction, non-fiction, biography, science, and travel. That is, reading of "normals" is compared with that of "patients," and different diagnostic groups are similarly compared. Thus, fiction was reported by Pomeroy[49] to be the reading of choice among hospitalized psychiatric patients, although Lind[37] had reported opposite findings. Mayden[40] cites non-fiction as being preferred by hospitalized psychiatric patients but adds that fiction becomes more popular as patients improve. McFarland[39] concludes again that fiction is preferred. Such conflicting results highlight the limitations imposed by such broad and arbitrary classification schemes.

Papers dealing with the physical properties of books as determinants of reading choice include that of Lind[37] who reported that color of bindings and position on shelves were bases for selection of books by patients. Fleming[20] cites the significance of attractive book jackets in stimulating patient interest. McFarland[39] emphasizes the importance of reading material as structural objects capable of eliciting psychological responses. He indicates that factors such as size, shape, color, and weight of reading material arouse associations in people which influence and motivate them to select or reject any particular reading object. Similarly, the location of a book and its relationship to other books or objects in the physical environment may attract or distract the potential reader's attention and thereby facilitate or discourage the choice of that book.

Factors which are related to the environment and which influence reading behavior would include the entire milieu of an individual including the reading facilities available, the people within the environment and the relationship between them and the reader, and the physical and emotional setting in which reading may occur.

Pomeroy[48] emphasized the significance of the atmosphere of the hospital library on the reading of psychiatric patients. Davie[14] describes the physical features of a Menninger Foundation library which help make it attractive and comfortable for patients. McFarland[39] discusses the use of library book carts and the facilitation of social interaction among patients by using carts servicing at least two patients rather than one at a time.

That reading is a function of past and present relationships between the reader and other people is of central importance in understanding reading behavior and bibliotherapy. Strachey[57] writes that reading seems to be "the first intellectual activity that a child is systematically taught" and that "it is a subject of pride with the modern educator that he can teach children to read without tears." The teacher who is able to make learning to read a pleasant process or who can reduce the unpleasant aspects contributes to making reading an acceptable and pleasurable activity throughout the rest of the individual's life. Persons involved with the reading behavior of patients, such as librarians, ward personnel and therapists, will similarly affect the reader's attitude toward that activity. A psychotherapist who reads and enjoys books is more likely to influence his patients to therapeutic reading than one who does not. The reading recommendations of the therapist will be received by patients and modified according to the position the therapist occupies in the patient's mind.

The importance of transference phenomena is tremendous in any therapy.[21] The therapist who encourages reading when positive transference is strong in his patient is more likely to obtain compliance than when the patient is in a state of negative or strongly ambivalent transference. Fenichel[18] writes, "the mechanisms of transference improvements are identical with the mechanisms by which educators achieve their success." As part of the transference reaction, the patient thinks of his own behavior, including reading, as potentially eliciting reward or punishment from his therapist.

Thus, a patient may read to please his therapist or, conversely, to displease him. He may seek in books ways of competing with and defeating his therapist and, consequently, defeat his own treatment. Similarly, counter-transference attitudes in the therapist may influence his patient's reading behavior. The therapist may regard his patient's information gained from reading as a competition with his own therapeutic efforts and unconsciously discourage or belittle further independent reading by his patient. Bibliotherapy may be a tempting means for the therapist to express unconscious rejecting attitudes, that is, to send the patient via bibliotherapy to find the "answer" elsewhere.[19]

Similarly, the librarian and others distributing reading material to patients may reveal their own attitudes in the manner in which they handle and discuss their books and, in this way, can add to or detract from the patient's motivation to use reading. "Books improperly handled and serviced may become symbols of rejection in the mind of the patient".[39]

Associated with the influence of book distribution methods are the rules and restrictions of the library within the hospital. The patient's freedom to choose his own reading material may well affect the extent to which he will make use of the library facility. Restriction of the number or kind of books available to patients interferes with their freedom of choice and, in this way, limits the gratification the patient may obtain from reading and may even cause him to turn away from it.[39, 40]

EFFECTS OF READING ON BEHAVIOR

The basic assumption underlying bibliotherapy is that reading can and does influence behavior. From a common-sense point of view the assumption seems valid and confirmation hardly necessary. Reading is part of civilization and most literate people would probably attest to personal experience with some written communication which significantly impressed and patterned subsequent behavior. Yet, psychological theory and scientific methodology are never satisfied with the obvious and force us to search for contradictory factors and permit us to ask if the written word really does have such far-reaching effects on individual and mass behavior as is ascribed to it. Did *Uncle Tom's Cabin* truly provoke mass responses that would not have occurred if the book had not been written,[34] or did it serve as a contributing stimulus, or was it simply a symptom of the times? Do crime comics really provoke children into delinquent behavior,[59] or do they merely serve the disturbed response pattern already present in the children who read them? Are patients really helped or improved as a result of bibliotherapy or is reading behavior merely another manifestation of the patient's behavioral changes?

Some measure of validation of bibliotherapy theory can be deduced and interpolated from the fields of advertising, propaganda and education.[11] Reading has become almost prerequisite to educational achievement and social communication and interaction.

We have already reviewed articles indicating how reading can result in need gratification.[18, 43, 45, 57] That is to say, to a certain extent individual instinctual needs motivate reading, and some measure of instinctual gratification is achieved. More superficial levels of gratification by reading, such as reading for pleasure, information and recreation are listed by many writers.[2, 11, 41] There seems to be universal agreement that under suitable conditions reading can bring about reduction in psychophysiological tension and provide subjectively felt pleasure. This pleasure may be immediately experienced or felt subsequent to the actual reading, as in achieving recognition for subsequent reporting of knowledge gained through reading. Reading may provide temporary escape from personal conflicts; vicarious social experiences through identification with book characters; conscious and unconscious satisfaction through the symbolism of reading and conformity with social behavior; social approval and improved reality testing through identification with book characters; conscious and unconscious satisfaction through the symbolism of reading and conformity with social behavior; social approval and improved reality testing through identification with author and characters; problem-solving techniques and behavior guides learned from reading; modification of morals, ethics, and goals through the mechanism of identification.

Mayden[40] suggests that need gratification achieved through reading does not differentiate patients from non-patients and questions the value of the term bibliotherapy. She emphasizes that freedom to choose or reject reading material is especially important for psychiatric patients because of the already restricted limits on their freedom due to illness and hospitalization.

The gratification of unconscious needs in a patient by means of reading is described in a report by Allen.[1] The patient read a certain book from beginning to end and then expressed vehement criticism of it. Analysis of the patient's attitude plus a related dream indicated that those aspects of the book most vigorously criticized were also the most enjoyed by the patient unconsciously. Bibliotherapy may serve in gratifying and sublimating oral-libidinal drives and scoptophilic and analerotic tendencies.[17, 18, 57] Allen[1] suggests that bibliotherapy may facilitate sublimation of aggressive strivings and describes a case in point, a woman who reported in therapy, "Sometimes I feel like killing my husband but I read a detective story instead!"

Strachey[57] writes that "the facilities for reading offered to the whole population in modern life may, by providing the opportunity for a fargoing sublimation of some sadistic components, actually contribute to a diminution of unmodified brutality." This is in contrast to Wertham's thesis that the themes of crime and violence and sadism present in comic books, movies, television and radio stimulate, provoke and instruct children in imitative brutality.[59]

Fenichel[18] reviews Glover's[25] proposition that many psychotherapeutic effects result from the treatment providing the patient with artificial substitutes for his original symptoms. Improvement of the patient depends upon whether or not the substitute is: (a) compatible with the psychodynamic structure of the patient; (b) pleasurable by having secret sexual or power significance, and (c) far enough removed from the original instinctual meaning of the patient's symptom to avoid being recognized as a derivative of it. Incorrect but symptom-reducing interpretations, physical therapy cures of conversion reactions, and substitute rituals for compulsive patients are examples of the effectiveness of artificial substitutes for suitable patients. Thus, bibliotherapy may be expected to provide significant symptomatic improvement in selected obsessional patients.

Bibliotherapy has been recommended by Appel[2] and Allen[1] as a possible means of shifting patients' behavior in the direction of extraversion. The egocentrism of many psychiatric patients tends to be self-reinforcing and contributes to prolongation of illness. Reading may stimulate interest in things outside the self and so break the cycle. Banyai[5] describes the effects of bibliotherapy for patients hospitalized because of tuberculosis. Reading provides a link to the outside world and normalcy, and helps maintain optimism and adjustment to institutional life. Bibliotherapy as a means of maintaining and improving contact with reality for psychiatric patients has been reported by Gardner[24] and Menninger.[43]

The use of bibliotherapy as a means of achieving increased socialization and group activity is described by several authors. Bursinger and Kenyon[12] report successful group library activities conducted at the Tomah Veterans Administration Hospital. Group therapy for schizophrenic patients included reading aloud and discussing books; other library groups also formed to review and discuss literature; quizzes and film showings were conducted by librarians on locked wards. Hannigan[28] reported on a similar program at the Northport Veterans Administration Hospital. At that hospital group bibliotherapy was conducted by the librarian under the supervision of a staff psychiatrist who gave advice on the literature selection for individual patients. Blackman[8] reported on his experiences with a literary club in the group treatment of schizophrenia with subsequent improvement in their over-all hospital and social adjustment. Group therapy utilizing library facilities and activities has also been reported by Grossman.[26] The effects of book talks and selected reading assignments on groups of psychiatric patients was described by Lazell[35] who integrated bibliotherapy into a larger group therapy program. Heath[29] reported beneficial effects from reading in the group therapy of alcoholics. He described resistant patients whose motivation for treatment increased after reading literature on alcoholism. Schneck[52] combined group reading and role playing and reported the technique helpful in providing patients with insight into their own problems. Others have recommended combining bibliotherapy with recreation and hobby activities for patients.[44,45]

Therapeutic results have been ascribed to providing work experience to psychiatric patients within a library setting. Bursinger and Kenyon[12] emphasize the importance of the relationships between library and hospital staff and those patients working in the library. Activities such as managing book carts; working at circulation desks; shelving and filing books; checking overdue dates; and writing book reviews and book reports for hospital newspapers have all been reported and related to the general practice of bibliotherapy.[6, 13, 32, 52] McFarland[39] recommends pasting book reviews by patients inside books to personalize the transaction between reviewer and other patients.

Thus, it appears that many of the articles reporting on the beneficial effects of bibliotherapy, particularly in regard to groups of patients, treat as central to the experience the aspects of improved relationships, increased socialization, and evolution of healthier work and play patterns. Bibliotherapy thus regarded becomes more understandable as one aspect of milieu therapy[51] rather than as a specific separate therapeutic entity. In this context, bibliotherapy can be conceptualized as an additional technique in hospital milieu therapy for psychiatric patients, aimed at increasing social interaction, encouraging participation and sharing in human interests and activity, stimulating healthier identifications, and providing opportunities for experimentation in social roles.

The use of reading material in individual psychotherapy as a means of confrontation and interpretation with insight as a goal has been reported by several authors. Lazarsfeld[34] proposes that insight may result from a patient's reading rather than from the therapist's interpretations in situations where the patient regards the author as more "neutral" than his therapist. Transference resistance thus might be circumvented through bibliotherapy. Appel[2] believed bibliotherapy permitted the patient to discover insights for himself by removing the "personal factor." Others recommend bibliotherapy as a means of focusing the content of the patient's productions in the psychotherapeutic interview. Schneck[55] describes two patients with whom bibliotherapy was employed to stimulate more meaningful discussions of their problems and increase production of conflict material.

Lazarsfeld[34] found conflict material more accessible in her patients when she inquired into their reading preferences and the reading and characters with whom they identified. Kirchner[33] has reported therapeutic abreaction and improved identifications as a result of prescribed reading for children with behavior disorders.

Baker[3] sounds a warning note to those who adhere to the theory that bibliotherapy may function through the mechanism of imitation and identification. She suggests that personal experience books written by chronically ill or handicapped patients may set impossible goals of achievement for readers who are ill and aggravate reactions of frustration due to unrealistic identification.

THE PRACTICE OF BIBLIOTHERAPY

Bibliotherapy has been reported in psychiatric practice in private psychotherapy,[14, 28] hospital psychiatry,[14, 28] child psychiatry,[9, 33] and marital counselling.[46] Appel[2] observed that psychotherapy seemed to progress faster for patients utilizing bibliotherapy than for those who did not. Similarly, bibliotherapy provides a means of maintaining the doctor-patient relationship between interviews and after termination of therapy or after discharge from the hospital.[2, 55]

Timing bibliotherapy in psychotherapy is also a matter of concern. When the patient of his own accord requests reading matter is certainly an advantageous time for bibliotherapy.[2] The request suggests that the patient already perceives reading as a source of gratification and is, therefore, motivated to read. However, there are some patients who are motivated to read but, for one reason or another, do not make the request. Other patients who are able to benefit from reading can be motivated to do so by the therapist or other factors in the environment. It seems crucial that the psychology of the individual patient be the primary consideration in determining when and if reading is recommended, what is recommended, and how the recommendation is made.[2, 41, 43]

Some authors suggest specific types of reading matter for certain kinds of patients, for example, "impersonal" reading is recommended for paranoid and depressed patients.[24] Others employ a relatively specific sequence of books but vary this and the use of reading in accordance with the psychology of the individual patient.[2] Lazarsfeld[34] makes no recommendations but uses reading material that the patient remembers from his past.

The titles and use of particular books employed in bibliotherapy can be found in the reports of Appel,[2] Ebaugh,[16] Schneck,[55] Ball,[4] and Hannigan;[28] Kirchner[33] and Hall[27] have compiled bibliographies of books suitable for bibliotherapy with children.

The use of reading material for therapeutic purposes is still far from being an exact science. We agree with Allen[1] that although it may always remain more of an art than a science, that does not preclude the development of standards and methods. Bryan[10] and Oathout[47] have focused on the problem of establishing basic principles for the theory and practice of bibliotherapy and have condemned the perpetuation of principles and techniques based on untested assumptions. Oathout urges research which would provide detailed information on the reactions of particular kinds of patients to particular types of reading, using classifications determined by actual findings and repeatedly revised as succeeding hypotheses are systematically tested. More detailed case reports of the kind advocated by Schneck[54] also would be worthwhile. Similarly, there is need for systematic investigation of patient reaction from the viewpoint of unconscious factors involved in both the process of reading and the content of the reading material.

In view of the relatively limited conclusive data on the subject, it would seem wise for bibliotherapists to maintain a flexible open-minded attitude. It is an important fact that one's own reaction to a book is not always a valid basis for judging the emotional impact that book will have on others.[40] The unfortunate results of prescribing literature on the basis of faulty preconceptions in the therapist rather than on the basis of the psychology of the individual patient are well pointed out by Bryan.[10]

In regard to prohibitions, there seems to be little valid evidence to substantiate such censorship, at least in the case of psychiatric patients. The value of the freedom to make one's own selections as well as the sublimation possibilities in reading argue against restriction and censorship. For the present, the therapeutic value of prescribed reading seems to rest upon the skill and acuity of the therapist in understanding the psychodynamics of the individual patient and in relating reading to this.

The problems of research in bibliotherapy are inseparable from those of psychotherapy and social interaction. Ultimate understanding and development of bibliotherapy must, therefore, depend upon the evolution of methods and techniques of assessing and evaluating behavioral change and the process and effects of psychotherapy.

REFERENCES

1. E. B. Allen, "Books Help Neuropsychiatric Patients," *Library J.* 71:1671 (19-16).

2. K. E. Appel in J. Hunt, *Personality and the Behavior Disorders* (New York, 1944).

3. L. Baker, "Personal Experience Books," *Hospital Book Guide* 13:32 (1952).

4. R. C. Ball, "Prescription Books," *Am. Library A. Bull.* 145 (1945).

5. A. L. Banyai in W. R. Dunton and S. Licht, *Occupational Therapy* (Springfield, 1950).

6. E. M. Barber, "Library Activities in a Hospital for Neuropsychiatric Patients," *U. S. Veterans Bureau Medical Bull.* 7:180 (1931).

7. W. J. Bishop, "Hospital Library and Bibliotherapy," *Library A. Rec.* 1:198, 231, 274 (1931).

8. N. Blackman, "Experiences with a Literary Club in the Group Treatment of Schizophrenia," *Occup. Therapy* 19:293 (1940).

9. C. Bradley and E. S. Bosquet, "Use of Books for Psychotherapy with Children," *Am. J. Orthopsychiat.* 6:23 (1936).

10. A. I. Bryan, "The Psychology of the Reader," *Library Journal* 64:7 (1939).

11. A. I. Bryan, "Can There Be a Science of Bibliotherapy?" *Library J.* 64:773 (1939).

12. B. C. Bursinger and X. Kenyon, "Neuropsychiatric Hospital Library," *Library J.* 79:20 (1954).

13. L. Condell, "Library as a Road to Re-education in Responsibility for Neuropsychiatric Patients," *Med. Bull. Vet. Administration* 13:77 (1936).

14. L. Davis, "The Function of a Patient's Library in a Psychiatric Hospital," *Bull. Menninger Clin.* 4:124 (1940).

15. S. P. Delaney, "Bibliography on Bibliotherapy," *Bulletin of Bibliography* 20:135 (1951).

16. F. G. Ebaugh, "Library Facilities for Mental Patients," *Am. Library A. Bull* 29:619 (1935).

17. O. Fenichel, "The Scoptophilic Instinct and Identification," *Internat. J. Psychoanaly* 18:6 (1937).

18. O. Fenichel, *The Psychoanalytic Theory of Neurosis* (New York, 1945).

19. L. B. Fierman, *Proceedings, Area One Chief Librarians Meeting, Veterans Administration* (West Haven, 1954).

20. M. Fleming, "Our Library Circulation," *Washington Bulletin* 3:30 (1940).

21. S. Freud, "The Dynamics of Transference" in E. Jones, *Collected Papers of Sigmund Freud* (London, 1950).

22. S. Gagnon, "Organization and Physical Set-Up of the Mental Hospital Library," *Diseases of the Nervous System* 3:149 (1942).

23. S. Gagnon, "Is Reading Therapy?" *Diseases of the Nervous System* 3:206 (1942).

24. W. P. Gardner, "A Psychiatric Hospital Library," *Minnesota Library Notes and News* 12:179 (1938).

25. E. Glover, "The Therapeutic Effect of Inexact Interpretation," *Internat. J. Psychoanaly.* 12 (1931).

26. M. Grossman, "Group Therapy Program in a Neuropsychiatric Hospital," *Med. Bull. Vet. Administration* 21:149 (1944).

27. E. Hall, *Personal Problems of Children* (Boston, 1953).

28. M. C. Hannigan, "An Experience in Group Bibliotherapy," *Am. Library A. Bull.* 148 (1954).

29. R. G. Heath, "Group Psychotherapy of Alcoholic Addiction," *Quart. J. Studies on Alcohol* 5:55 (1945).

30. G. W. Henry, *Essentials of Psychiatry* (Baltimore, 1938).

31. E. K. Jones, *Hospital Libraries* (Chicago, 1939).

32. P. Jones, "Hospital Libraries in the State Hospitals of Minnesota," *Bull. Am. Hosp. A.* 3:433 (1929).

33. C. J. Kirchner, *Character Formation Through Books: A Bibliography* (Washington, 1952).

34. S. Lazarsfeld, "Use of Fiction in Psychotherapy," *Am. J. Psychotherapy.* 3:25 (1939).

35. E. W. Lazell, "Group Treatment of Dementia Praecox," *Psychoanalyt. Rev.* 8:168 (1921).

36. F. Leslie, "Choice of Reading Matter by Neuropsychiatric Patients," *U.S. Vet. Administration Med. Bull.* 7:779 (1931).

37. J. E. Lind, "The Mental Patient and the Library," *Bookman* 65:138 (1927).

38. A. M. Macrum, "Hospital Libraries for Patients," *Library Journal* 58:78 (1933).

39. J. H. McFarland, "A Method of Bibliotherapy," *Am. J. Occup. Therapy* 6:66 (1952).

40. P. M. Mayden, "What Shall the Psychiatric Patient Read?" *Am. J. Nursing* 52:192 (1952).

41. K. A. Menninger, "Psychoanalytic Psychiatry," *Bull. Menninger Clin.* 4:105 (1940).

42. W. C. Menninger, "Bibliotherapy," *Bull. Menninger Clin.* 1:263 (1937).

43. W. C. Menninger, "Bibliotherapy," *Ment. Hyg.* 4:28 (1938).

44. F. G. Millar, "Patients Ply Their Hobby in the Hospital Library," *Occup. Therapy* 14:121 (1935).

45. J. W. Mower, "A Comparative Study of Hobby Activities," *Bull. Menninger Clin.* 4 (1940).

46. E. H. Mudd and J. L. Whitehill, "The Use and Misuse of Books in Counseling," *Parent Education* 14:2 (1938).

47. M. C. Oathout, "Books and Mental Patients," *Library J.* 79:405 (1954).

48. E. Pomeroy, "Veterans' Hospital Librarians Meet in Washington," *U.S. Vet. Administration Med. Bull.* 5:637 (1929).

49. E. Pomeroy, "Hospital Libraries," *Med Bull. Vet. Administration,* 7:986 (1931).

50. M. D. Quint, "The Mental-Hospital Library," *Ment. Hyg.,* 28-263 (1944).

51. D. Rioch and A. Stanton, "Milieu Therapy," *Proc. A. Res. Nerv & Ment. Dis.* (Baltimore 1953).

52. J. M. Schneck, "Studies in Bibliotherapy in a Neuropsychiatric Hospital," *Occupational Therapy and Rehabilitation* 23:316 (1944).

53. J. M. Schneck, "Bibliotherapy," *Psychiatry* 8:207 (1945).

54. J. M. Schneck, "A Bibliography on Bibliotherapy," *Bull. Med Library A.* 33:341 (1945).

55. J. M. Schneck, "Bibliotherapy for Neuropsychiatric Patients," *Bull. Menninger Clinic* 10:18 (1946).

56. J. M. Schneck, "Bibliotherapy in Neuropsychiatry," in W. R. Dunton and S. Licht, *Occupational Therapy* (Springfield, 1950).

57. J. Strachey, "Some Unconscious Factors in Reading," *Internat. J. Psychoanaly.* 11 (1930).

58. U.S. Veterans Administration, *Bibliotherapy* (Washington, 1952).

59. F. Wertham, *Seduction of the Innocent* (New York, 1953).

Bibliotherapy and Psychotherapy

by Edwin F. Alston

This paper has to do with the possible uses and values of bibliotherapy in the treatment of emotional and mental illness. The discussion will be introduced with brief considerations of personality development, psychopathology, concepts of mental and emotional health, and psychotherapy from standpoints of goals, principles, techniques, and problems. We shall also want to review the rationale for thinking of bibliotherapy in connection with the treatment of the mentally ill. Such a background is necessary before we can see clearly the possible roles of bibliotherapy in the present treatment of psychological disorders.

The development of a human personality is an extremely complicated process. Here we shall not attempt to describe the details; rather we shall emphasize the diversity of factors that are involved in the growth and development of a human personality. At birth the individual exists largely as a potential. His very survival is dependent upon those who care for him; his future development is shaped first by the start they give him and subsequently by all of the experiences which he has on his way to adulthood. Physically and psychologically the individual will go through different phases of growth and development.[1,2] In each phase different needs and activities are prepotent. For instance, in the earliest months, eating, eliminating, and sleeping are dominant activities. Subsequently different periods are characterized by the special prominence of learning to walk, talk, control sphincters. As the years go by, at different stages, the individual will be especially involved in developing the nature of his relationships with people, of acquiring basic knowledge and skills. His sexual interest, curiosity, and activity will go through complex phases of development.

For optimal physical development, the individual requires adequate food, shelter, clothing, sleep, exercise, and protection from

"Bibliotherapy and Psychotherapy" by Edwin F. Alston reproduced with special permission from the publisher, *Library Trends* 11:159-176 (October 1962).

adverse elements such as disease. Likewise, for psychological development, there are basic requirements: adequate contacts with people,
example and instruction, help from others, and independent activity.
However, it is not sufficient simply to list the needs and activities
essential for growth and development. The quality, intensity, timing,
order of prominence, sequence, and associated experiences all relative
to his stage of development will be important factors in determining
the formation of the individual's personality structure. The point to be
emphasized here is that orderly growth and development is not
assured by any means, but rather is dependent upon a great number of
variables. The successes and failures, the gratifications and frustrations
which the individual meets in each stage of development will determine how well he is prepared to handle subsequent stages. Anywhere
along the line, the individual may become stuck or fixed either because of failure or because of excessive gratification.

The outcome of growth and development in the human being
usually leaves much to be desired. There is always some psychopathology. This fact is easy to understand when one considers the
complex processes of growth already referred to. Specific deficiencies
occurring in the growth process may be very subtle and not directly
observable. They are likely to occur throughout the course of development despite the wisest efforts and best intentions of everyone concerned. These deficiencies will be manifest in the failure to develop the
capacity for global integration of the personality. A chain is no
stronger than its weakest link. In order for one to evaluate the
integrity and health of a personality, it is necessary to consider its
weakness and dissociations as well as its strengths. The inevitability of
psychopathology may be clearly seen in terms of an analogy cited by
Salter: "Parents, and everyone else, are doing the best they know, but
just as there is only one way for a wrist watch to run correctly, and
hundreds of ways for it to get out of order, so is there only one way for
children to be psychologically sound and a multitude of ways for them
to develop psychological troubles. Consequently, probability is
against mental health, all of which is deplorable, but quite patent."[3]

Psychopathology may be described in terms of "disability, distress,
and dread," to use the terms of Whitehorn or "stupidity, misery, and
symptoms," to quote Dollard and Miller. It is manifest in physical
complaints, mood disturbances, defects in motivation, unrealistic self
attitudes, disturbances in relationships with other people, or
diminished capacity for gratification. Anxiety and tension of mild or
great degree and reactions to them are present in all psychopathology.
Psychopathology can be viewed as unstable, fragmented, fixed, and
maladaptive personality structure. The essence of psychological illness
is conflict or disassociation of various tendencies within the individual
and conflict between the individual and the world outside himself. It
can be conceptualized as incomplete development or as regression
resulting from undue stress or lack of essential maintenance. It

appears in all degrees of severity from that of personality structure which is extremely disorganized and conflicted to that which is barely evident. The most severe and disabling disorders are usually seen in psychoses; less crippling are the neuroses, as a rule; and least noticeable is the psychopathology occurring in so-called normals. When one considers the multiple ingredients that go into the development of the human personality, it is not difficult to understand that some psychopathology is present in every one. No one is perfect.

Because psychopathology is seen in palpable reality while mental health is more of a concept and cannot be demonstrated for all to see, psychopathology is easier to see, define, and understand than is mental health. Ideas of mental health will differ from one person to another. It has been conceptualized in a variety of ways. It can be defined in terms of freedom from symptoms, or as statistical normality; it is sometimes thought of as being related to a sense of well being. Jahoda has summarized a number of dimensions referred to by most writers on the subject as criteria for evaluating mental health. These include capacities for self-awareness, self-actualization, integration, autonomy, reality perception, and reality mastery.

Having referred to some of the qualities of psychopathology and a few of the concepts of mental health, we can recognize that the possible goals of psychotherapy are numerous and varied. The goals may be very explicit, or they may be very vague; they may be modest or extremely ambitious. The goal in any particular therapeutic program will, of course, depend upon considerations of time and money. In addition, the goal in therapy will be determined by the patient's psychopathology, psychological mindedness, motivation, age, intelligence, behavior and affect states; the goal will also be influenced by the therapist's experience, skill, philosophy, and various personal factors. Some categories of goals are (1) custodial care, (2) long-term support, (3) relief of symptomatology, (4) management through situational stress, (5) recovery of premorbid personality state, and (6) total reconstruction of the personality through the development of insight and reeducation. The goal, of course, will determine the form of treatment to be applied.

Psychotherapy involves, above all, a relationship between the therapist and the patient (or group of patients). Important categories of influence in all therapies include the therapist's personal impact (direct and transference) upon the patient and the approach to and content of the material dealt with. Within limits, what is said is of secondary importance to the interest, integrity, authority, and confidence which the patient sees in the therapist. In other words, the intense experience of a developing interpersonal relationship, perhaps very different from any other that the patient has known, seems to be the *sine qua non* of progress in therapy. This is evident in the fact that skillful therapists of diverse theoretical orientations employing widely different approaches seem to secure comparable results.

Depending upon the goal of therapy, the character and content of treatment can assume various forms. Therapy may be primarily reinforcement and support. This form means that the therapist will listen to the patient's problems, give him reassurance and support, and offer occasional advice or suggestions. This form of therapy is sometimes indicated in situations of acute stress or in cases where the patient is so fragile that this is all that he can tolerate. Otherwise this form of therapy is likely to be insipid and endless. If and when it is terminated, the patient is probably no better off than he was when he started. Another form of therapy has to do with reeducation and training. Here the therapist acts as something of a pedagog and attempts to impart new attitudes and skills to the patient. The trouble with it is that it may leave untouched or even enhance the opposing trends within the patient. This is a sort of patch work, and yet it may have a real value when there is not the need, indication, or realistic possibility of an all-out reconstructive effort. The third major form of psychotherapy is so-called deep therapy or insight therapy, represented primarily by psychoanalysis. Here the emphasis is upon a process devoted to the patient's actually *experiencing* the fullest possible knowledge of himself. This is hardly possible except in an appropriate relationship to another person, since it is all but inevitable that every person is going to have blind spots with respect to himself. It is a profoundly pertinent observation that "the problem of self-analysis is the counter-transference." Exhaustive self-knowledge is an essential condition for total personality synthesis when some trends of feelings, thoughts, and actions have failed to become incorporated into a global personality structure or have become dissociated from one another. It is not until the individual becomes capable of a wholeness within himself that he can achieve an occasional oneness with the world and some of the people outside himself with maximal chances for effectiveness and gratification with them.

Irrespective of the form of psychotherapy, there are a number of therapeutic instruments which may be used. In various forms, they will be used with different combinations, emphasis, and purpose. Therapeutic instruments may be used either for "curative" effect or for "technical" purposes in service of the total therapeutic process. Common to all psychotherapy is *respectful listening* to the patient's description of his problems, feelings, thoughts, and behavior. Such attention, of course, is essential not only to understanding the patient, but also to establishing contact with the patient. For the patient, the very act of attempting to communicate with another person about matters of personal concern may help him toward greater clarity and psychological expansion by improving his powers of association, discrimination, and synthesis. The description of personal experience in public language may provide him with some leverage against inner fixations. The feeling that another person has listened, understood, and tolerated may diminish the patient's sense of loneliness and isolation. Thus, listening without any other intervention may itself have considerable therapeutic value.

A second type of therapeutic intervention is that of *suggestion* which in a broad sense includes advice, counseling, guidance, instruction. It can be said that the effect of suggestion is always present in any therapeutic relationship whether or not it is recognized or used directly as such. Suggestion of a general character is more likely to have enduring value than concrete specific suggestion. The latter is likely to have a deceptive value in providing an immediate solution while neglecting increase of the patient's spontaneity and self-sufficiency. Two major dangers of suggestion include introducing something foreign to the patient's personality (making even more difficult the task of synthesis) and increasing the patient's dependency.

Manipulation involves nonverbal or indirect handling of the patient's problems. It may involve manipulating aspects of the milieu in which the patient lives; it may be directed specifically toward the patient. In manipulation the patient is relatively passive and the therapist is more active. As a therapeutic vehicle, it shares some of the values and limitations of suggestion.

Clarification has to do with restructuring the material offered by the patient. In clarification per se there is little emphasis upon "digging" more deeply but more upon dealing with what is at hand in terms of comparison, discrimination, and organization.

Interpretation is directed toward bringing into awareness a conscious knowledge of feelings, ideas, wishes, or memories which have been repressed and split off from consciousness. By bringing repressed material into awareness, interpretation offers the first step by which repressed material can be blended or fused with other contents of consciousness. If successful, interpretation leads alternately to a greater unity of the personality. Interpretation, of course, is inferential, based upon the therapist's general information and experience and his knowledge of the patient. It is subject to error in form, content, and timing, and in this sense it has some of the liabilities of suggestion and manipulation. One difficulty with interpretation resides in the fact that the same mechanisms responsible for repression in the first place will also stand against the return of the repressed material into consciousness. For this reason, attention has to be directed first toward the repressing mechanisms, the patient's defenses and resistances. When repressed material is successfully brought into consciousness, there will be a resulting anxiety which, if severe, may again evoke the repressing forces or lead to acting out. Accordingly it is necessary to anticipate the amount of anxiety the patient can tolerate and to make interpretations in such a way as to avoid crippling anxiety.

In psychoanalysis one uses all of the therapeutic instruments referred to above. Interpretation, however, is the ultimate vehicle of psychoanalysis, and all of the other instruments are used not for their curative value so much as for leading up to and otherwise serving the process of interpretation. By contrast to psychoanalysis, Rogers' client centered therapy places major emphasis upon reflection and clarification, minimizing the other techniques. More eclectic therapies will use all of the therapeutic instruments for curative as well as technical value. It should be said that when suggestion and manipulation are used for curative purposes, the field becomes clouded and the opportunity for clear, effective interpretation is minimized.

In addition to the use of the therapeutic instruments mentioned above in psychotherapy proper, adjunctive activities may be prescribed. These include occupational therapy, art therapy, music therapy, bibliotherapy, etc. Ordinarily such activities are not prescribed for the patient in psychoanalysis. Rather, efforts are largely confined to interpretative activity, and otherwise the patient is left to his own devices. The adjunctive therapies are utilized largely to provide the patient with interest, activity, outlets, structure; to develop new attitudes and skills; and to occupy the patient's time. They are used mostly with hospitalized patients.

Having considered the therapeutic devices used by the therapist, one may refer to the role of the patient in the therapeutic process. In a broad sense, the patient must think, feel, and act. In the therapy he must give and receive, and he must put into action the understanding, skills, and attitudes which he has developed. It is not enough for the patient and therapist to be talking in the same room. Each must strive for a meaningful encounter with the other. The patient must be able to postpone gratification, to endure frustration and tension which are inevitable accompaniments of growth and development. If he has to leave the field of therapy because of inevitable frustration and anxiety, he will obviously forsake any possibility of benefit from it. As stated above, it is not sufficient for the patient to acquire new knowledge, understanding, and attitudes. To obtain a firm grasp and value he must be able to apply these acquisitions in daily living. The patient has to be prepared to tolerate initial ineptness, failure, and adverse reactions and to persist until he has developed mastery, effectiveness, and gratification.

Psychotherapy, old as humanity itself, is nevertheless relatively stagnant as an art and science. In all the centuries of human history, few really important advances have been made. Psychoanalysis is a major exception to this statement, but even so, it has to be said that there simply are not innovations in psychoanalysis whose breadth and magnitude and effectiveness compare with innovations in other fields of medicine, education, art, and science. Failure of development probably has to do with the intensity of feeling that human beings have about the behavior of human beings, a feeling that constitutes a powerful resistance to experimentation and change. Major problems and challenges facing psychotherapy have to do with the effectiveness and breadth of application.

With respect to effectiveness there are not only problems of increasing effectiveness, but also problems of defining and evaluating effectiveness. Psychoanalysis, client centered therapy, hypnotherapy, "eclectic" psychotherapy, reciprocal inhibition therapy, experimental therapy, personal construct therapy, assertion-structured therapy, Gestalt therapy, and the other therapies too numerous to mention here, make their claims for success but have to admit their failures and inability really to predict the probability of success. There is no way yet really to evaluate success. No therapy today helps as much as must be possible. For comparable time and effort there may not be much real difference between one approach and another. The chances are that improvements or innovations in psychotherapy necessary to bring about significant measurable changes in effectiveness will have to be really drastic in nature. There is also little doubt that drastic innovations, if and when they are made, will meet with the same—or greater—abhorrence and opposition that originally confronted psychoanalysis and still does to some extent. Psychotherapy probably remains relatively ineffective because it is still limited to half measures. The breadth of applicability of psychotherapy, at present, is probably a secondary matter. If a really effective psychotherapy is ever developed, then will be the time to devise the means of making it more widely applicable. As it stands, the current psychotherapies are for the most part expensive and time consuming. Therapists are few in relationship to the needs. And the existing therapies are of little value for the most disturbed patients; they have their greatest value for those whose need is least.

There are many reasons for thinking that bibliotherapy might be of some value in the treatment of patients with psychological disturbances.[13, 14] Throughout centuries of history, the written word has acquired an increasing, fantastic time-and-space-binding significance for man. Man, in papers, pamphlets, and books, has recorded something, at least, about every conceivable aspect of his existence—his interests, aspirations, and activities. For information, instruction, inspiration, understanding, and entertainment, an individual today need not rely only upon his own life experience nor upon that of those immediately around him. In the poetry, fiction, or non-fiction of the world, a person can find broad coverage of the individual human situation in all times and places; he has immediate access to the recorded feelings, knowledge, ideas, desires, and activities of all kinds of men and women. In the world literature there is plenty to meet every need and taste. It is easily and widely available, to everyone, at relatively little cost. A helpful or favorite book, unlike a passing conversation, relationship, or experience, can be referred to time and again in the full and original form it had for the reader. The written word, which one can take or leave, is not as intrusive as the spoken word, nor is the written word likely to have been as associated with demands and prohibitions and other anxiety-provoking experiences as the spoken word.[15] Accordingly, many people can approach a book with minimal defensiveness and maximal accessibility. For many people, the written word has an exceptional authority and authenticity. Finally, in actuality, many if not most literate people can mention at least one or two books which have affected them profoundly, opening up new vistas, new directions for growth and development.

A striking example of the extent to which people in general look to books and pamphlets for help with personal problems is seen in the experience of the Metropolitan Life Insurance Company over the last decade with its educational pamphlets. Since 1947, this company has been issuing booklets on various aspects of physical and emotional illness. The response of the public gives an indication not only of the need and demand for help with personal problems but also of the interest and hope invested in the written word. In a personal communication, George M. Wheatley, Medical Director, writes:

> Perhaps some indication of the interest in our booklets relating to mental health can be gauged by the following figures. For example, from 1958 to 1961, our booklet, *6 to 8 — Years of Discovery*, was requested by 1,689,514 persons; there were 906,450 requests for *Nine to Twelve* in 1961; 6,640,190 requests for *Understanding Your Young Child* from 1947 to 1961; 4,227,150 requests for *Understanding Your Teen-Ager* from 1953 to 1961; 3,500,000 requests for *Emotions and Physical Health* from 1954 to 1961 and 2,200,000 requests for *Stress and What It Means to You* from 1958 to 1961. We have had numerous letters from individuals, PTA's, child study groups, physicians and others, telling us how useful our materials are to them, and how glad they are to receive them.[16]

Dr. Wheatley also makes reference to a film: "Since its release in 1956, our film on mental health, *Mr. Finley's Feelings*, has had a total attendance of 21,215,128. The purpose of the film was to stimulate questions and comments and provoke an exchange of ideas about the ways of meeting stress situations and handling day to day relationships with people. Through the response we have had, as well as the requests for further reading materials, we feel confident that *Mr. Finley's Feelings* is fulfilling its purpose."[16] Hardly any statement could exemplify more clearly the extent to which people look to written material for help in the solution of personal problems and concerns, the tremendous demand for such help, and the response that occurs when specific universal problems are discussed and the material is made easily and widely available.

Some people, perhaps quite a few people, are profoundly influenced by books where they find not only amusement and instruction but also understanding and inspiration. This basic fact lends hope to the idea that books may be useful in the treatment of psychiatric patients. But the matter is not as simple as it seems. While it is undoubtedly true that a few people can and do find in books a powerful stimulus for problem solving and further development, a probable fact is that most people are not so deeply affected. Some people simply do not read; others do not get much out of what they read.

As discussed above, really significant change in a person requires not simply a powerful incitement, but the incitement must be of appropriate form and content and has to develop in a proper order from initial contact to a peak of significance. It is difficult to imagine how such a process can be organized primarily around the reading of books. Books are not written with the individual patient in mind, and certainly no book will completely fit any one patient. By its very nature, the patient's psychological illness may preclude his discrimination between what applies to him and what does not; and his psychological illness may make it impossible for him to integrate effectively into his own particular situation what he has learned and felt. Activity is an absolutely essential condition to growth. Reading without active, critical participation and application can hardly be expected to have any significant effect. Finally, there is no book that can possibly substitute completely for a vital, give-and-take exchange between two people. Unless such a relationship is somewhere in the background, whole libraries of books will be of no avail. For those of us who are interested in bibliotherapy, it may be well to keep these reservations in mind, lest we be carried so far away by our enthusiasm that we seek more than it has to offer and derive from it less than what is possible.

The various purposes for which reading can be used by the patient and the physician have been treated quite extensively in the literature.[13, 14, 17-25] It is relevant to summarize some of them here. Obviously books may be of value for information and instruction, as guides in the development of new skills. Often patients will find courage to enter therapy or discuss a particular problem after reading about it. Occasionally a patient will be able to discuss something that he has read when he cannot at the moment talk about the same matter as it applies directly to himself. Thus, the discussion of a book is sometimes helpful as an introduction to more personal topics. Books may be used to help the patient obtain greater insight into his problems or to acquire language and ideas with which to communicate his problems.

They may help the patient focus attention outside himself and to find new interests. The reading of books may assist the patient in the processes of socialization by providing him something which he can share and talk about with other people. Often people can find new directions and attitudes in books. The knowledge to be acquired from books that other people have similar problems may give the patient greater courage to face his own problems, and a lesser sense of isolation and loneliness. Finally, although too much should not be made of it, there is the therapeutic value of relaxation and diversion to be found in books. Books may be and often are used for escape purposes, but this use should not cause us to overlook the possibilities of having our worries, concerns, and problems too much with us. Books may be used by the patient to take his mind off his problems for a bit so that he can eventually return to them with refreshed and new points of view.

Patients may derive from reading some definite therapeutic gains such as those listed above, but reading and its results may also become deterrents to therapeutic progress. It is possible to acquire erroneous information and misunderstanding from books. Reading may be used as a way of avoiding the personal issues of therapy or of achieving further withdrawal and isolation. False hopes and expectations may be engendered, or the patient may be discouraged, or depressive trends may be enhanced. In response to reading, the patient may attempt to use ideas and facts that do not apply to him. Some patients become overwhelmed or especially anxious from reading. Obsessive-compulsive tendencies may be enhanced. In short, reading may become a resistance to therapy, especially if the reading is not accompanied by appropriate critical discussion. Some writers on bibliotherapy suggest general contraindications to some types of reading for patients belonging to certain diagnostic categories. For instance, remarks are sometimes made about what a depressed or obsessive-compulsive patient should be allowed to read or prevented from reading. While these may be some fairly useful rules of thumb, one might also question any prescription of reading based upon Kraeplinian diagnostic categories. The indications and contraindications for bibliotherapy and the material recommended should be based upon an estimate of what the patient needs for therapeutic purposes at the moment and upon expectations of how he will use and respond to the material being considered.

The therapist may use the patient's interest and responsiveness to books in several different ways. He may use reports that the patient makes about his reading to further analyze and understand the patient. By and large, in insight therapy, it is seldom that a book is actually prescribed for a patient. The emphasis is more upon the patient's learning directly and specifically about himself. But when the patient reports that he has read a particular book, valuable insights may develop from analyzing his choice, what he got out of the book, his responses, etc. Whereas books are seldom prescribed in analytic therapy, probably most analytic therapists are quite attentive to what the patient reports about his reading and his attempt to relate this to other material which the patient is producing. In analysis as well as in other forms of therapy, the patient very often refers to his reading and very often reports having gained from it.[13] A quick review of this writer's patients now in therapy shows that about seventeen out of twenty-one patients have not only reported their reading of books, but have also made assertions about increased understanding, new points of view, etc. Also in analytic therapy, there is often a tendency on the part of the patient to choose and discuss books as a way of avoiding more direct discussion of himself. However, even this tendency can be used for the purposes of therapy when it can be pointed out that the patient is reading to divert himself from the work of analysis and when attempts can be made to infer what the patient is trying to avoid.

Reading of books, pamphlets, and articles can also be definitely prescribed for the patient. In such an instance, of course, the therapist as a rule will have a definite purpose in mind, tailored to the individual at the time he makes the prescription. He will probably encourage the patient to discuss what he has read and examine the ways in which this applies to the patient's situation. This essentially is the use that has been made of bibliotherapy in the two cases reported by Schneck,[26] and in "Objective Psychotherapy" described by Karpman.[27] Prescribed reading may be for any of the therapeutic purposes outlined above and may make use of fiction or nonfiction. When the therapist prescribes a book in this way, he should not only know what he is attempting to accomplish, but he should also be fairly sure of what is in the book in order to know that it is suited to his purpose. Very probably, any therapist who intends to recommend books should have in mind a small number which he can use for definite purposes and which he himself can know quite thoroughly. It is probably a futile gesture for the therapist to recommend books when he does not have a relatively fresh and recent knowledge. No one can keep fully in mind a large number of books sufficient for therapeutic purposes, and a busy therapist will seldom have time to examine many books for their therapeutic potentiality. A therapist who intends to make extensive systematic use of bibliotherapy would be well advised, therefore, not only to have his own list of well known reliable books but also to have the collaboration of someone such as a librarian who is able to pay more attention to books for therapeutic purposes.

There is another manner in which bibliotherapy can be employed. There is the possibility of designing a course of therapy using books as the principal focus and starting point of therapy and discussion. Powell, Stone, and Frank[28] experimented with having patients in two groups, one therapeutic and the other for discussion of a prescribed reading list. (They chose *Declaration of Independence*, Benedict's *Patterns of Culture*, Epictetus' *Discourse*, Farrell's *Young Lonigan*, Wolfe's *Look Homeward Angel*, Augustine's *Confessions*, and Plato's *Republic*.) They found that their therapy and reading groups offered different opportunities to different patients. In some patients the reading may afford a means of diminishing anxiety, of increasing self-esteem to the point of being able to function more freely in the therapeutic group. They also found that a given patient's success in either the therapeutic or reading group significantly enhanced his ability to make full use of the other group.

Wilson[29] has reported on a single case for whom twelve books were selected and prescribed over a period of more than two years. Several prolonged conferences and about eight report conferences were held with the patient. In the report conferences, the discussions were centered primarily around what the patient had read and how it pertained to him. At the end of each conference, after a book had been prescribed, it was left up to the patient as to when the next meeting would occur. There were intervals of many months between conferences.

Wilson had the patient tested before and after the course of bibliotherapy and concluded that the patient had made substantial gains. The
patient reported being satisfied with what he had achieved. Wilson
feels that such bibliotherapy is useful when time is at a premium and is
more especially useful in problems of attitude.

Reading material has also been put to use in "remotivation," a
technique developed by Dorothy Hoskins Smith, and widely used in
State and Veterans Administration Hospitals.[30, 31] Training and demonstration of this technique across the country have been supported
by a grant from Smith, Kline, and French Laboratories and sponsored
by the American Psychiatric Association. The technique consists of
twelve meetings of patients under the leadership of a trained remotivation therapist. After the therapist has helped to create an "atmosphere
of acceptance" the next step consists of reading a poem. A basic concept underlying the technique is that even very withdrawn people can
be aroused into talking about subjects outside their emotional tensions. However, "definitely barred are sex and marriage problems,
financial worries, racial questions, and matters concerning religion
and politics."[30] A poem or other piece of literature presenting rhythm
and evocative images of perception and motion is likely to attract the
attention of withdrawn people and provide the nucleus around which
more nearly normal conversations can be developed in the group.
Having awakened interest in the patients by reading of literature, the
remotivation sessions continue with stages referred to as "sharing the
world we live in," "appreciation of the work of the world," "the climate of appreciation." These different steps have to do with the
introduction into group discussion of different subjects having concrete interest chosen for variety, the elicitation of personal interests
from patients, and eventually the expressions of thanks to the patients
for their participation. It is said that "a mere series of 12 group conversations about such objective topics as fishing, railroads, cotton, rock
gardens, or cooking, conducted in an atmosphere of friendliness and
approval, can give mental patients a strong thrust toward recovery."[32]

Obviously, the use of bibliotherapy in private practice is going to
be very much different from that which is possible in a hospital setting.
Only rarely in private practice will there be the possibility of a sufficiently close working relationship between the therapist and a librarian to provide the basis for a team approach to bibliotherapy. It is
questionable whether or not such a team approach would justify the
difficulties of setting it up, especially if it required preference over
other therapeutic approaches. If a private therapist were to set up a
course of therapy with bibliotherapy as the central point of departure,
as in the work of Wilson, he might well request consultations with a librarian and other experts to develop an appropriate reading list. For
the most part, however, the main use to be made of bibliotherapy by
therapists in private practice will probably continue to be examination
of the patient's various reactions to books which he reports having

read. It will undoubtedly include occasional suggestions on the part of the therapist that a patient read some special book. The basis of the selection here will probably be books that are quite familiar to the therapist and which he feels will be of help to the patient at the moment in furthering the course of his understanding and therapy.

In the hospital setting there is, of course, opportunity for a much closer working relationship between the therapist and librarian, and the facilities are often such that more extensive use can be made of bibliotherapy.[33, 34] The physician and librarian can collaborate in the development of reading programs for any given patient, and they can confer with one another about their observations for evaluation and for determination of the succeeding steps. The physician and librarian will each have his own contributions to make to such a program. The physician may impart to the librarian something about what he hopes to achieve by prescribed reading for a patient. It may be helpful to the librarian if the therapist can summarize some of the patient's basic psychological mechanisms and indicate the type of books and subject matter that he has in mind for the patient. The physician may also wish to indicate what would be contraindicated for the patient in his therapy. The physician will doubtless want to follow up on his recommendations with discussions and observations of the patient's reactions. The librarian will probably want to have available a relatively limited list of books which might be used more frequently in bibliotherapy and a readily available knowledge of the contents, plots, problems treated, etc. From these the librarian should be able to make recommendations that would fulfill the physician's prescriptions. The librarian's interest and enthusiasm can be an additional and very important personal contact for the patient, and his observations about the conduct and reactions of the patient may be of considerable value to the therapist.

In summary, books may be of great value for some patients. With others, bibliotherapy is simply not going to be applicable, or there will be other preferred adjunctive measures. Bibliotherapy is likely to be more useful in psychotherapy oriented toward support re-education and training, and of much less value in analytic or insight therapies. It may be that a relatively systematic program of bibliotherapy along the lines indicated by Wilson, Karpman, and others can be developed to have some positive but limited value for some patients. This is an area for further investigation and development, although perhaps not one of top priority. Short of such a procedure, bibliotherapy is always likely to be adjunctive in nature to a broader program of therapy, and being adjunctive it may not be susceptible to standardization and precise evaluation. The use of bibliotherapy will always be more helpful for some than for others. To some it is doubtful that a highly standardized, precise form of generally applicable bibliotherapy can ever be developed. On the other hand, for any given therapist-patient situation, there may be times when the examination of a patient's reactions to a book or the recommendation that a patient read a book will be of real value in the overall program. This will probably have to remain an individual affair of the moment dependent upon the patient and the therapist. It is probable that bibliotherapy will remain a science and an art as applicable to the individual patient rather than to the patient population. Some therapists will always make more use of books than others; some patients will respond more to books than others. There are times that contact or understanding may be accomplished by way of a book as the vehicle. The science and art of bibliotherapy will be the matching of the therapist, patient, moment, and content, where a book is likely to be of more value than anything else.

REFERENCES

1. Otto Fenichel, *The Psychoanalytic Theory of Neurosis* (New York: W. W. Norton and Company, 1945), pp. 33-117.

2. Erik H. Erickson, *Childhood and Society* (1st ed; New York: W. W. Norton and Company, 1950).

3. Andrew Salter, *Conditioned Reflex Therapy* (New York: Capricorn Books, 1961), p. 40.

4. John C. Whitehorn, "Goals of Psychotherapy," in Eli Rubinstein and Morris B. Paroff, eds., *Research in Psychotherapy* (Washington, D.C.: American Psychological Association, 1959).

5. John Dollard and Neal E. Miller, *Personality and Psychotherapy* (New York: McGraw-Hill Book Company, 1950).

6. Marie Jahoda, *Current Concepts of Positive Mental Health* (New York: Basic Books, 1958).

7. Jerome Frank, *Persuasion and Healing, A Comparative Study of Psychotherapy,* (Baltimore: The Johns Hopkins Press, 1961).

8. Eduard Bibring, "Psychoanalysis and the Dynamic Psychotherapies," *Journal of American Psychiatric Association* 2:745-771 (1954).

9. Carl R. Rogers, *Client Centered Therapy: Its Current Practice, Implications, and Theory* (Boston: Houghton-Mifflin, 1951).

10. Frederick C. Thorne, *Principles of Personality Counseling* (Brandon, Vt.: Journal of Clinical Psychology, 1950).

11. Allen Wheelis, "The Place of Action in Personality Change," *Psychiatry* 13:135-148, (1950).

12. Robert Harper, *Psychoanalysis and Psychotherapy; 36 Systems* (Englewood Cliffs, New Jersey: Prentice-Hall, 1959).

13. William C. Menninger, "Bibliotherapy," *Bulletin of the Menninger Clinic* 1:263-274, (November 1937).

14. Jerome M. Schneck, "Bibliotherapy and Hospital Library Activities for Neuropsychiatric Patients: A Review of the Literature with Comments on Trends," *Psychiatry* 8:207-228, (May 1945).

15. Edwin F. Alston, "Psychoanalytic Psychotherapy Conducted by Correspondence," *International Journal of Psychoanalysis* 38:32-50 (1957).

16. George M. Wheatley, Medical Director, Metropolitan Life Insurance Company, Personal Communication (March 27, 1962).

17. K. E. Appel, "Psychiatric Therapy," in J. McV. Hunt, ed., *Personality and the Behavior Disorders*, vol. 2 (New York: The Ronald Press Company), p. 1107.

18. Daniel Brower, "Bibliotherapy in Progress." in Daniel Brower and Lawrence E. Abt, eds., *Progress in Clinical Psychology*, vol. 2 (New York: Grune and Stratton, 1956), pp. 212-213.

19. Alice I. Bryan, "Can There Be a Science of Bibliotherapy?" *Library Journal* 64:773-776 (October 15, 1939).

20. Alice I. Bryan, "Toward a Science of Bibliotherapy," in George Lawton, ed., *New Goals for Old Age* (New York: Columbia University Press, 1943).

21. Louis A. Gottschalk, "Bibliotherapy as an Adjuvant in Psychotherapy," *American Journal of Psychiatry*, 104:632-637 (April 1948).

22. Leland E. Hinsie and Robert Jean Campbell, eds., *Psychiatric Dictionary* (New York: Oxford University Press, 1960), p. 95.

23. Sofie Lazarsfeld, "Use of Fiction in Psychotherapy (A Contribution to Bibliotherapy)," *American Journal of Psychotherapy* 3:26-33 (January 1949).

24. Maurice Levine, *Psychotherapy in Medical Practice* (New York: The Macmillan Company, 1946), pp. 107-108.

25. Caroline Shrodes, "Bibliotherapy: An Application of Psychoanalytic Theory," *American Imago* 17:311-319 (1960).

26. Jerome M. Schneck, "Bibliotherapy for Neuropsychiatric Patients," *Bulletin of the Menninger Clinic* 10:18-25 (January 1946).

27. Ben Karpman, "Objective Psychotherapy, Principles, Methods, and Results," *Journal of Clinical Psychology* (Monograph Supplement, No. 6, July 1948).

28. J. W. Powell et al., "Group Reading and Group Therapy," *Psychiatry* 15:33-51 (February 1952).

29. J. Watson Wilson, "The Treatment of an Attitudinal Pathosis by Bibliotherapy: A Case Study," *Journal of Clinical Psychology* 7:345-351 (October 1951).

30. Elsie McCormick, "They Can Be Talked Back to Sanity," *Today's Health* 40:44 (March 1962).

31. Alice M. Robinson, *Remotivation Technique* (Manual Available from APA—Smith, Kline, and French Laboratories, Remotivation Project, Box 7929, Philadelphia, Pa.).

32. McCormick, "They Can Be Talked Back to Sanity," p. 45.

33. Ruth M. Tews, "Case Histories of Patients' Reading," *Library Journal* 69:484-487 (June 1, 1944).

34. Ruth M. Tews, "The Patients' Library," in Thomas E. Keys, *Applied Medical Library Practice* (Springfield, Ill.: Charles C. Thomas, 1958), pp. 57-134.

Literatherapy:
Theory and Application

by Michael Shiryon

The term "Literatherapy" (combining LITERAture and psycho-THERAPY) refers to the intentional planned use of literary writings and/or literary forms (metaphors, similes, allegories, etc.) to facilitate and enhance psychotherapy. As in any undertaking of psychotherapy, the person should, of course, be a well qualified psychotherapist. Therefore, I shall not dwell on the specifics of psychotherapy, but rather, I shall focus mainly on those aspects that are directly related to Literatherapy (Litt.).

When a person says to another person, "I see!", this phrase does not necessarily refer to the direct visual act of perceiving. Instead it may, at times, have a much broader and deeper connotation. It may mean a mental reflection, an understanding, an imaginative perception, an insight, a sudden realization, which may even be accompanied by a corrective emotional experience. In this broad and encompassing sense, psychotherapy could be loosely defined as "taking a second look." Taking a second look at learned ideas, beliefs, prejudices and values; taking a second look at memories (remembered ones and forgotten ones as well), at significant persons in one's life, at one's own image of oneself; taking a second look at one's attitudes; one's emotional reactions, one's dreams (of night and daytime), one's hopes and one's fears.

However, "taking a second look" involves risk and fear. It involves risk and fear of what one may find within oneself; risk and fear of change; risk and fear of the unknown. This fear interferes with the process of "taking a second look," the process of psychotherapy, by forming resistances and raising defenses, which, after all, are natural and healthy reactions to threat and attack.

Yet, the binding of much energy in defenses may interfere with the regular necessary functioning, and cause disturbances, problems and ill-being (as opposed to well-being). The image of a city which is threatened by an enemy could serve as a helpful illustration. Most of its people are mobilized to guard its wall and gates and strengthen its defenses against the feared attack. Meanwhile, with most of the workers, storekeepers, administrators etc. mobilized, the regular functions, which sustain the city in its everyday life, may come to a stand-still or even break down. Perhaps for a while the city could manage to keep up the most vital services with minimal manpower. But in the long run this emergency situation will have to be changed.

In the case of the city, relief may come when the people recognize that their walls are strong enough to provide protection against the enemy; or when they find out that there is no threat of attack; or when they realize that a small number of guards will provide sufficient warning in case of approaching danger. Thus, all the other people can return to their daily work and the city can go on functioning and developing as usual.

In the case of an individual, the ability to relax, to feel safe, will allow the person to relax his resistance, to lower his defenses and, in doing so, release his energies, strengths and abilities for constructive functioning and further growth. Within the framework of psychotherapy, this relaxing of resistance and defenses will allow and enable the person the further "taking of a second look," thus furthering the therapeutic process.

The ability to relax one's defenses will depend on the person's experiencing safety rather than threat. This approach would therefore question the popular image of "breaking through resistance" and "cutting down defenses," (perhaps even the more benevolent "interpreting them away!").

Support for this conceptualization is gained from recent publications of the findings of an ongoing, meticulous study of the process of psychotherapy. In these papers[3, 12, 13] the therapeutic process is seen as enabling "the unconscious ego to experience safety and to choose to lift a defense."[3] In other words, the emerging repressed contents does not break through the defenses in the process of psychoanalytic therapy, but the defenses are relaxed or lifted to allow its emergence, following the experiencing of safety (see also Sandler 1960,[4] Sandler and Joffe 1969,[5] for the central role of safety in psychotherapy).

A similar conceptualization of the process of psychotherapy, viewed from the therapist's angle, was presented in a paper on group Literatherapy (Litt.),[6] using the following folktale.

The wind and the sun argued as to which of them was the stronger one. Since they could reach no agreement, they decided to have a contest. They saw a man walking on the road, and the wind tried to rip off this man's hat and to tear off his coat but did not succeed. Finally, the wind had to give up and let the sun take its turn. As soon as the sun sent down a couple of its warm rays, the man took off his hat, took off his coat, and even unbuttoned his shirt. . .

With all of this in mind, let us turn now to see how Litt. may satisfy and facilitate the afore outlined approach.

In discussing the broader connotations of "taking a second look," three major avenues of perception may be distinguished: 1) The use of logic—the reasoning one; 2) The use of fantasy—the imaginative one;

3) The emotional reaction—the experiential one. Most, perhaps all methods of psychotherapy focus on one or two of these avenues as their main emphasis in therapy. The patient or client is compelled to accept the offered focus and to adjust to the particular method. (This is not to imply that the different therapists may not be sensitive to the patient's individual needs and may not adjust their method to these needs). Litt., in its use of the metaphor and the story, combines all three avenues (reason, imagery, experiencing). It further allows the patient to choose the proportions and focus with which he may be most comfortable, while still exposing him to all three.

In terms of the issue of feeling safe and able to relax one's defenses, the problem can be stated as the span between distancing and close involvement. The person needs an optimal distance to feel safe, and yet a maximal closeness to try on the new interpretation or experience. Folklore has recognized the need for both in the story about the woman who came to consult a Rabbi about some intimate problem. Being very shy, she told the Rabbi that she was doing this for a friend. The Rabbi thought that the problem was a very delicate one, and suggested that her friend should come to see him in person. "Oh, no!" protested the woman, "she will be too embarrassed to come in herself." "This is no problem," replied the Rabbi, "she can say that she is doing it for a friend."

A story allows a person both the distance and the involvement at the same time. As reader or listener to a tale, one can see himself as an outsider, as an observer, and feel free to observe and weigh the issues and even make relatively objective judgements. He is not as involved in being defensive and desperately searching for rationalizations as he may be when he is confronted with personal issues of his own.

Nathan, the prophet, understood this psychological problem when he wanted to confront King David about the Bath Sheba affair. Nathan wanted to help the king gain insight into the meaning of what he had done. Being a natural literatherapist, Nathan realized that if he were to confront the king directly, the natural reaction would be defensiveness. Nathan did not want to raise the king's defenses, but rather to relax them, so that the king would be able to "take a second look" at what he had done. To achieve this, Nathan told David the story about the rich man who took away the poor man's one and only sheep. This enabled David to pass judgement, and to react with full emotional outrage at the moral wrong that was committed by that distant "rich man." All that was then left for Nathan to do to bring the issue home, was to point out the connection, which he did, saying "You are this man!"

The fact that it is "just a story," provides the necessary distancing. Yet this very same safe distance, allows involvement through projection, identification, emotional reactions to the vivid issues, and vicarious experiencing of the situation described. The story provides a chance for "safe risk taking," since "it ain't necessarily you" who is seen as being involved in the happenings and relations of the story, and yet, indirectly, it is you.

This indirect, non-threatening approach to a person's problems, reflects more than a mere technique of psychotherapy. It respects the person and allows him more responsibility and decision making, without denying him the assistance of the professional therapist. It recognizes and respects his anxieties and fears, his embarrassment and his wish and right to maintain self-respect.

At the same time, it allows the therapist a great variety of options in terms of levels of interpretation and trial-interpretations, which the patient may accept or reject with little anxiety and guilt. Thus, even if he rejects it, the patient is not compelled to build up resistance or repress the indirect interpretation, but can continue to consider it until he is ready to accept it as valid (if indeed, it is valid).

All this should not imply that the therapist who uses litt. keeps telling his patient anecdotes and stories throughout the session. It only means a clear awareness and ongoing training in the use of the litt. techniques whenever and in whatever way that they may be useful to the person in treatment.

In group litt., the story becomes a systematic, integral part of each session. As conducted at Agnews State Hospital[10, 11] a typical session would run as follows. It would start with a short story (10-15 minutes), which was read out loud to the group. Then the participants were encouraged to react to the story as a life situation in any way they chose. (This differs from a literary analysis, since in group litt. the person who reacts to the story is the focus and aim of discussion, and not the story itself.) The pattern that took place in almost every one of the hundreds of sessions, which were conducted at Agnews, was the same. At first there came comments and reactions to various aspects of the story itself. Little by little the discussion would focus on a certain issue or problem that was brought up, either in the story or related to it. Finally the issues discussed were related, by the free choice of a participant, to an issue or a problem in his own life experience.

The important effects of litt. with the hospitalized patients, were not limited to therapy and the solution of specific personal problems. Litt. did not only help the patient leave the hospital, it also helped in preparing the patient to live in the outside world. Dealing through the stories with a variety of life situations and interpersonal relations, provided the participants with badly needed life experience, even if it was a vicarious one. Furthermore, it provided them with a means of further exploring the experiences of others as well as of themselves through the use of litt. Just as dreams serve as an ongoing self-therapy during our sleep (using, by the way, the principles of litt.), so can the litt. method serve as an ongoing self-therapy in our waking hours.

This applies not only to patient populations. As psychotherapy becomes more available to the classes who could not afford its price before; as sophistication about psychotherapy lessens its stigma; as it is more and more recognized for its usefulness in a person's handling of everyday problems, as well as planning his life and developing his human potentials; as hundreds of thousands or rather millions start asking, directly or indirectly, for assistance and guidance with the growing pressures of modern life; as all this and much more is happening (and it *has* been happening for quite some time, already), the value of litt. should be even more evident. Its role in therapy-preparatory functions, its great flexibility in allowing a gradual entry into deeper therapeutic issues, and its educative and training possibilities are almost unparalleled.

In a course in litt.[8] one of the students conducted a litt. session with office-workers at a financial company. The enthusiastic reactions and thoughtful comments raised the issue of lack of—and dire need for—any intellectual and/or emotional stimulation for masses of people in routine type jobs. The possibilities offered by litt. seem invaluable—if only for constructive exploration of the problems involved. The same may hold for growing concern with issues like boredom on the job,[1, 2] the plight of senior citizens, growing problems of leisure time, etc.

In community wide efforts, alongside the variety of health guidance centers, there is the urgent need for mental health guidance facilities. These should be able to provide a service combining education, prevention and at least to some extent therapy. All this will have to be done in a non-threatening fashion and in a method easy to comprehend and accept. What will communicate better across barriers of age, culture, education, class, etc., than the ancient yet always effective story, tale, anecdote, in short litt.? To paraphrase an ancient saying, "one story is worth a thousand words."

The idea of litt. is not a new invention. Librarians, especially in hospitals and institutions, have been involved in bibliotherapy since the turn of the century. Physicians and psychiatrists praised its value and some even used it. Other psychotherapists also write occasionally about various aspects of litt. without calling it by the same name and without recognizing its wide possibilities of application.[7]

In recent years there is also a noticeable growing trend of the use of bibliotherapy in school-counseling, in education, and in related fields.[9]

It would seem high time for professional psychotherapists to give such a rich and promising method as literatherapy more than just fleeting interest. It would seem worthwhile to develop systematic training programs and evaluations, and to start realizing its great promise.

REFERENCES

1. "Bored on the Job," *Life*, vol. 73, no. 9 (September 1, 1972).
2. "Who Wants to Work?—Boredom on the Job," *Newsweek* (March 26, 1973).

3. H. Sampson, J. Weiss, L. Mldonsky and E. Hause, "Defense Analysis and the Emergence of Warded Off Mental Contents: An Empirical Study," *Archives of General Psychiatry* (1972).

4. J. Sandler, "The Background of Safety," *The International Journal of Psycho-Analysis* 41 (1960).

5. J. Sandler and W. G. Joffe, "Towards a Basic Psychoanalytic Model," *The International Journal of Psycho-Analysis* 50 (1969).

6. M. Shiryon, "Group Literatherapy—A Bibliotherapeutic Approach," Presented at the Golden Gate Group Psychotherapy Society, Thirteenth Annual Scientific Conference, San Francisco (June 1970).

7. M. Shiryon, "25 Years of Bibliotherapy," Tutorial, presented at the California State Psychological Association—Twenty-fifth Annual Convention, Los Angeles, California (January 28, 1972).

8. M. Shiryon, "Litheratherapy: The Direct Use of Literature in Therapy and Counseling," X 412 (3). Course given at the University Extension, University of California, Berkeley (Summer 1972).

9. M. Shiryon, "From Bibliotherapy to Literatherapy: The Next Twenty-five Years," Tutorial, presented at the California State Psychological Association Twenty-sixth Annual Convention, Oakland, California (January 26, 1973).

10. E. Steffens and T. T. Tennant, Bibliotherapy Project, 1968-1969, final report. Patients' Library, Agnews State Hospital, San Jose, California (June 1969).

11. E. Steffens, C. Lack, B. Bettencourt and L. Leuschner, Bibliotherapy Project, final report. Patients' Library, Agnews State Hospital, San Jose, California (March 1972).

12. J. Weiss, "The Emergence of New Themes: A Contribution to the Psychoanalytic Theory of Therapy," *The International Journal of Psycho-Analysis* 52 (1971).

13. J. Weiss, "Continuing Research: The Modification of Defenses in Psychoanalysis," *Journal of the American Psychoanalytic Association* 20 (1972).

The Therapy of Poetry

by Molly Harrower

When the learned professors explained to Monsieur Jourdain, in Moliere's *Le Bourgeois Gentilhomme,* the difference between prose and poetry, he discovered to his surprise that he had been speaking prose all his life! In somewhat the same way, therapists have discovered that, perhaps unbeknownst, they have been using the now-called "poetry therapy" most of their professional lives. For once a procedure has acquired a name, many spontaneous and unsystematic activities suddenly take on new significance. Once a procedure has acquired a name it can become a technique to be taught, a bandwagon to be jumped on, an idea whose time has come. It can be advocated, researched, criticized.

The first systematic presentation of the use of poetry in therapeutic sessions, of the use of poetry as a means of communicating between therapist and patient, appeared in 1969, edited by J. J. Leedy.[1] From this collection of essays it appeared that the use of poetry was quite widespread, having grown up sporadically over many years. The first recorded use was in Pennsylvania Hospital nearly 200 years ago.[2]

The contributors to that volume had widely different backgrounds and theoretical orientation; in addition to psychiatrists and psychologists there was a college president, a poet, a professor of English, a rabbi, a clinical director of a large hospital, an instructor in remedial English, and a consultant to the Police Athletic League. The locales of established poetry therapy programs included state and private mental hospitals, mental health centers, college campuses, and a school, among others. Poetry therapy had been used with schizophrenic patients, disturbed adolescents, college students, and had progressed to a stage where research had been attempted to assess its value as a therapeutic agent. A proposed curriculum for training poetry therapists was included. Leedy's second anthology,[3] published in 1973, shows that the canvas had broadened to include such unexpected areas as successful work with poetry and the deaf, and such timely areas as work with drug addicts and prison inmates.

The most recent survey, as yet unpublished, is contained in the

Reprinted by permission of Grune & Stratton, Inc. and Molly Harrower, Ph.D.

work of Gilbert Schloss,[4] who sent out 1500 questionnaires to persons in the United States, Canada, and Europe whom he believed were using poetry in some therapeutic context. He asked questions concerning the type of poems used to evoke particular moods, and which poems were recommended as being specifically helpful to those in states of depression, anxiety, rage, etc. His third question related to whether poems were prescribed for various diagnostic categories: that is, were special poems used for schizophrenic, character disorder, or neurotic difficulties? Of the 250 replies to date, the majority of persons using this modality appear to be psychotherapists in private practice. However, other professionals included psychiatric nurses, educators, recreational therapists, and poets. Few described themselves as strictly "poetry therapists." The settings overlapped with those already represented: namely, clinics, drug centers, schools, and various institutions, medical hospitals, mental hospitals, and prisons.

Schloss broke down his returned questionnaires into four groups reflecting different uses of poetry. The majority of therapists utilized well-known poems to evoke or relate to specific moods, such as those referred to in the questionnaire itself. A second category used primarily poems that the therapist himself had written, at appropriate moments in the therapist-patient experience. A third group used poems written by their clients or patients, while a fourth group did not consider themselves therapists in any sense, but wrote attesting to the therapeutic value of poetry drawn from their own personal experience. This group included poets, teachers, and other persons who had incorporated poetry as part of their own growth experience.

RATIONALE

Poetry is of course seen differently by different therapists and authors. One facet that strikes many writers is that it is a means of communication for those who are psychologically isolated; another commonly expressed facet is that it allows the patient to objectify his feelings. The symbolism of poetry is seen as a lever to "release feelings and bring about catharsis and insight." Poetry is defined as the "most concentrated and vivid language of both the pulmonary and nervous systems; poetry is a challenging outcry from those who refuse to conform and who are in eternal revolt against the status quo. Poetry seeks for meanings under meanings. Poetry insists on finding a way of saying what is forbidden or impossible."

Poetry is seen by some as "the resolution of the disease within," "the facing of a conflict." It is seen as "encouraging the winds of creativity." It is seen as bestowing on an individual the sense of his having been "the most impersonal bearer of a message from the beyond-within, from the ocean of the unconscious on which our conscious selves sail." Through poetry, some feel, "unconscious strength can be converted into conscious use."

Aspects of poetry other than its content or symbolism have been emphasized by therapists. Meerloo,[5] for example, feels that at the most basic level poetry is related to biological rhythms: "The first clock the infant hears is the maternal heart beat," and Leedy finds that poems "with regular rhythms that most nearly approximate the beat of the human heart, affect many patients deeply."[1] Meerloo also speaks of the head banging of autistic children as a need to establish some rhythm, and asserts that this distorted need can be interrupted by reciting to them nursery rhymes and folk songs with strong rhythmic beats.

MODALITIES

Two different activities have to date been subsumed under the classification of poetry therapy. Failure to make a distinction between the two uses by writers in the field has blurred some of the issues, and has led to some justifiable criticism.

Poetry therapy on the one hand has been used to describe the reading of well-known classic poems by the therapist to the patient, on occasions, and with all-important timing in relation to his progress in treatment. In a somewhat similar manner it refers to the reading of poems, of a classical and established literary value, to groups of patients to elicit reactions or evoke certain moods. From a survey of the literature it would seem that it is therapists of long standing who have used this procedure as part of a larger therapeutic armamentarium, and on specific occasions.

Poetry therapy has also been used to describe the writing of "poems" in individual or group therapy by the patients themselves. This technique is now in full swing, and would appear to be more an outgrowth of the recognition of the value of creative self-expression than concern with poetry in the accepted literary sense of the word.

POETRY READ

Theodor Reik,[6] Smiley Blanton,[7] Milton M. Berger,[8] and Morris Robert Morrison[9] all give graphic accounts of how specific poems pierced the protective armor of particular patients with whom they were working. Often the poem's more direct emotional expression may enable a patient to tolerate within himself previously unacceptable or unrecognized desires or conflicts. The poem can become a bridge which the patient can use to reach new areas of himself. The poem gives an all important sanction to the expression of feelings which may have been severely repressed. Or the poem may show desires and longings about which the patient may have felt guilty to be universal, and therefore legitimate. The carefully selected poem may touch on deeply buried material.

The reading of classical poetry to groups of patients obviously has a somewhat different goal. The therapist cannot hope to touch on repressed areas that are pertinent for the group as a whole. Poems read to groups seem to be utilized in a way more akin to projective material. Individuals will respond to poetry with widely different perceptions and associations in a way similar to responses to a Rorschach inkblot or a TAT picture.

It is clear that the therapist who wishes to use poetry in this way, particularly with the flexibility needed to relate to an individual patient's momentary dilemma, must have a rich literary background. As a result of therapeutic experience he must enlarge his initial selections and must possess a wide variety of poems which come quickly to mind and which relate to moods of frustration, anxiety, fear, panic, and loneliness on the one hand, and joy, achievement, insight, and inner peace on the other.

There are a few poets who are also therapists, or, perhaps more acceptably stated, a few therapists who have published volumes of poetry. For such persons a rather unusual variation of poetry therapy is possible. The therapist can draw on his or her own poems to relate to the patient's experiences. A poem by the therapist, even if its authorship is not known at the time of its introduction into the therapeutic dialogue, can provide an unusual bond between patient and poet. It may become pertinent at a later date to discuss the steps taken by a writer toward greater objectivity and distancing from a powerful emotional experience. It is also clear that the "you are not alone, I have been there too" motive can be developed when appropriate.

POETRY WRITTEN

In separating what seem to be two clearly distinct activities, the value of fostering free-flowing expression among patients and clients is not questioned. An acceptable term is needed to describe the often extraordinary productions elicited under the instruction to "write poetry." Prisoners, drug addicts, minimally educated adolescents, deaf persons, and young children do produce moving verbalizations of their often long pent-up feelings. Of vital importance in obtaining these is encouragement by the therapist. It may well be that there is a certain mystique to the instructions to write poetry which may even be necessary in mobilizing the energies and feelings of the group. But there should be some concern lest therapists lower their standards of acceptable literary work to a point where there ceases to be a distinction between the often moving ventilation of personal problems and a universally accepted work of art.

True poetry can have its beginnings in what may be described as an exercise in verbalization during a therapeutic hour, but the chances of producing instant poets as a result of encouraging disturbed persons to express pent-up feelings seems unlikely. What is needed is some universally accepted distinctive term to describe these moving verbalizations which will allow poetry to retain its standards of excellence. With this as a proviso, the therapeutic value of this form of treatment can be examined.

EVALUATIONS

Therapists who write about the productions of deeply disturbed patients, drug addicts, prisoners, and malfunctioning adolescents all have in common a belief in and an enthusiasm for this mode of treatment.

Barley[10] states "Poetry therapy is not only possible, but the most important adjunct to the other psychiatric treatments offered in a correctional setting." Speaking of the residents of a correctional institution he adds: "In attempting to express himself poetically he will be hesitant for fear of making mistakes in spelling, punctuation, or even poetic style. These are unimportant. The important fact is that the individual speaks, expresses, goes on record and communicates his innermost feelings and hopes through the medium of poetry."

Schechter,[11] working in the treatment of drug abuse, is equally positive when describing her assignment to the group to write about the "unspeakable." "As the program developed, poetry therapy proved to be a curative bridge demonstrating that a poem can snap the lights on, offering clues for preventive medicine [and] hastening self-discovery." She states further, "Although early poems reflected self involvement and pity, after a process of more writing, negative poems moved outward, fostering new attitudes and behavior. Poetry offered constructive insights and solutions to human needs, fears and aspirations."

Miller's[12] work with adolescent girls shows an interesting variation, in that she prescribed the form to be employed when the girls wrote about themselves, the other members of the group, and the group as a whole. This would seem to have a highly instructional element, and relate personal problems to more objective demands of creative writing. Far from inhibiting the youngsters, this additional instruction seems to have yielded equally revealing productions with some literary merit. A few examples are given here:

> The Group
>   questioning, seeking—
>   loving, troubled, caring,
>   trying to help,
>   trying to reach out to one another.
> The Group
>   aware, painful—
>   struggling, sharing, probing,
>   discovering, mutual feelings.
> The Group
>   intent, serious—
>   searching, seeking, learning,
>   reaching to awareness,
>   insight.
> The Group
>   oneness, manyness—

    alone, together
    searching, finding, unfolding
    light.
The Group
    giving, receiving
    trusting, doubting, caring,
    helping one another help herself.
The Group
    friends, alike but different
    giving, listening, examining.
    a room of unhappy thoughts,
    a room of hopefully happy futures!

CAN POETRY THERAPY BE TAUGHT?

Lerner[13] has aptly stated that poetry therapy is a tool, not a school. Nonetheless, we can ask whether the would-be poetry therapist can receive instruction, and what techniques are employed to develop the required sensitivity in this field. Therapists who themselves utilize poetry in therapeutic sessions proceed on the assumption that the technique can be taught. Courses and demonstration workshops are available in several universities and independent centers in this country.

Leedy[3] writes that at the Poetry Therapy Center in New York City selected students, psychologists, teachers, nurses, social workers, and occupational therapists work as poetry interns. Such students are taught the principles and techniques of poetry therapy, and are given the opportunity to use their skills with patients, acting as co-therapists. Classes are also given at the New School for Social Research and at Dowling College. The first World Poetry Therapy Conference, held at Cumberland Hospital in Brooklyn, drew representatives from nine countries.

On the West Coast Lerner is active in the development of the Poetry Therapy Institute, and extension courses are given here in conjunction with the University of California at Los Angeles. One such course entitled "Poetry and the Therapeutic Experience" is described as "Poetry in relation to mental health, as a distinct aspect of educational and rehabilitation programs. Exploratory lecture-demonstration-discussion class designed for laymen, classroom teachers, psychologists, and other concerned professionals interested in the use of poetry as a valid tool in dealing with problems of mental health."

At Northeastern Illinois University, Vin Rosenthal offers a course on psychotherapy and poetry within the department of psychology: "This seminar explores the ramifications of the assertion that Poetry can be Therapy . . . utilizing the group experience as a source of stimulation, seminar participants write poems and share them with the group . . . their poems are used to help participants explore themselves as individuals, and develop concepts illuminating the relationship between poetry and psychotherapy." In a further description of this seminar[11] the distinction is made between poetic expression and the creating of poetry."

Lerner has asked what makes a good poetry therapist and suggests, "I believe that it is most important that the poetry therapist be authentic in his use of poetry with others. He must know his limitations as well as his potential, and be able to admit when he does not know something or when he feels uncomfortable. Honesty has a way of becoming evident in therapy. Being authentic also means recognizing one's blind spots so that the other person's authenticity and growth are not affected. The poetry therapist must be acquainted with a wide variety of poems, for the poem selected for therapeutic purposes ought to be powerful enough to suggest positive avenues of communication. The ability to write poetry is not, however, necessary; what is important is that the therapist has a genuine concern for people and a love of poetry . . . he tends to become sensitive to poems which are effective through experience."[13]

A CRITICISM OF POETRY THERAPY

W. H. Auden's criticism of poetry therapy rested on his own definition of poetry, namely, "The aim of writing is to enable people a little better to enjoy life or a little better to endure it."[14] This he feels cannot be considered a therapeutic task. Strangely enough, however, as Morrison[15] points out, there are definitions of the goals of psychotherapy which are remarkably similar to Auden's definition of poetry. For example Goldenson's[16] statement that the aims of psychotherapy could be thought of as "the resolution of handicapping or disabling conflicts and the opening of a pathway to a more meaningful existence." Thus, again to quote Morrison, "in the act of denial Auden has unwittingly reaffirmed how germane are the concerns of poet and therapist."

Poetry therapy, it would seem, is here to stay. It most certainly is not a panacea for all psychic ills; it is not sufficient in and of itself. Rather it is one of many ways in which insight can be reached, and inner growth achieved. "Poetry therapy is a new comer, but long before there were therapists there were poets, and from time immemorial man has struggled to cope with his inevitable inner turmoil. One way of coping has been the ballad, the song, the poem. Once crystallized into words, the all-engulfing feelings become manageable, and once challenged into explicitness the burden of the incommunicable becomes less heavy. The very act of creating is a self-sustaining experience."[17]

REFERENCES

1. J. J. Leedy, ed., *Poetry Therapy: The Use of Poetry in the Treatment of Emotional Disorders*, (Philadelphia: Lippincott, 1969).

2. R. E. Jones, "The Treatment of a Psychotic Patient by Poetry Therapy," in J. J. Leedy, ed., *Poetry Therapy* (Philadelphia: Lippincott, 1969).

3. J. J. Leedy, ed., *Poetry the Healer,* (Philadelphia: Lippincott, 1973).

4. G. Schloss, *Tongues of Wood: An Introduction to Poetry Therapy* (New York: Grosset & Dunlap [in press]).

5. J. A. M. Meerloo, *The Universal Language of Rhythm in Poetry Therapy,* (Philadelphia: Lippincott, 1969).

6. T. Reik, Foreword to *Poetry Therapy,* J. J. Leedy, ed. (Philadelphia: Lippincott, 1969).

7. S. Blanton, "The Use of Poetry in Individual Therapy," in J. J. Leedy, ed., *Poetry Therapy* (Philadelphia: Lippincott, 1969).

8. M. M. Berger, "Poetry as Therapy and Therapy as Poetry." in J. J. Leedy, ed., *Poetry Therapy* (Philadelphia: Lippincott, 1969).

9. M. R. Morrison, "Poetry Therapy with Disturbed Adolescents," in J. J. Leedy, ed., *Poetry Therapy* (Philadelphia: Lippincott, 1969).

10. B. J. Barkley, "Poetry in Cage," in J. J. Leedy, ed., *Poetry the Healer* (Philadelphia: Lippincott, 1973).

11. R. L. Schechter, "Poetry: A Therapeutic Tool in the Treatment of Drug Abuse," in J. J. Leedy, ed., *Poetry the Healer* (Philadelphia: Lippincott, 1973).

12. A. H. Miller, "The Spontaneous Use of Poetry in an Adolescent Girls' Group," *Inter Group Psychoth* 23:2 (April 1973).

13. A. Lerner, "Poetry Therapy," *Amer J. Nurs.* 73:8 (August 1973), p. 1336.

14. W. H. Auden, *New York Times,* 16 December, 1970, p. 49.

15. M. R. Morrison, "A Defense of Poetry Therapy," in J. J. Leedy, ed., *Poetry the Healer* (Philadelphia: Lippincott, 1973).

16. R. M. Goldenson, *The Encyclopedia of Human Development,* 1970, vol 2, p. 1082.

17. M. Harrower, *The Therapy of Poetry* (Springfield, Ill: Thomas, 1972).

"Great" Literature as a Teaching Tool in the Education of Mental Health Professionals

by Kenneth Gorelick

THE USES OF LITERATURE

As a training experience, fictional literature has unique assets that live clinical experience lacks. Thus it nicely complements the latter in educating helping professionals who will utilize a knowledge of depth psychology and the human relationship as the helping instrument.

The interaction of reader with writing is a two-party interaction that is a paradigm of the one-to-one therapeutic relationship, but with significant differences. (1) For example, the reader, as receiver of the communication, does not and cannot react upon the communicator or the communication, which is fixed in print. This is a valuable constraint on the beginner, whose anxiety about listening understandingly often leads him to speak prematurely. Most of us have been the caricature of the novice firing questions at a harassed patient as quickly as we can read them from the lists our teachers have provided, lest the silences put us in touch with our sense of doubt, insecurity, inexperience and ignorance. The written page is proof against this sort of abuse and helps the novice cultivate a comfortable listening attitude.

While the communication and communicator are fixed, the meanings received are by no means set. As one reads and rereads with varying perceptions, associations and moods, meaning alters. Here is an excellent paradigm to reinforce the idea that meaning depends much on the receiver's subjectivity. This cardinal point, which cannot be overemphasized, is further highlighted in the group analytic method to be discussed later. But in just comparing his own responses over time, the learner who has not yet confronted his subjectivity in personal therapy, nor yet realized the importance of so doing, begins to appreciate the importance of knowing and calibrating himself as the instrument of his craft.

Reprinted with permission from *Libri* 25(2):138-143. Copyright © 1975 by Danmarks Biblioteksskole.

Another advantage of literature over live experience is this: not only is the communicator immune from assault by the trainee, the trainee too is protected. Unlike a live patient, a literary piece does not overwhelm with speed and directness. Instead it affords an opportunity to review and reflect. (2) Not having to put energy into keeping defenses high, the trainee can put more into learning to listen artfully. (3)

Though fixed on the page, literature has something of teeming life about it, or else it would hold no interest. After all, it is the product of the creative processes of a highly intelligent, sensitive, insightful, and intuitive human being grappling with his life. The created product captures and emits these qualities. Literature can present as living actuality that which the textbook petrifies in jargon. What textbook teaches, what student is taught, descriptions of this quality:

> "He stood with arms akimbo . . . He looked as if he had been cuffed, kicked, rolled in the mud . . . and he smiled with a sense of security at the faces around. His ears were bending down under the weight of his battered felt hat. The torn tails of his black coat flapped in fringes about the calves of his legs. He unbuttoned the only two buttons that remained and everyone saw that he had no shirt under it. It was his deserved misfortune that those rags which nobody could possibly be supposed to own looked on him as if they had been stolen. His neck was long and thin; his eyelids were red; rare hairs hung about his jaws; his shoulders were peaked and drooped like the broken wings of a bird . . ."?[3]

Or what chapter on alcoholism conveys this understanding:

> "At the same time he first realized that he was drunk. He was bitterly ashamed of himself, drunk at this time, at his father's very deathbed, when his mother needed him so bad as never before, and when he knew, for he had learned by now to take people's word for it, that he was really good for nothing when he was drunk. And then to feel so thirsty on top of that . . .
>
> . . . the voices of the women, soothing him, trying to quiet him, only added to his tears, the richness of his emotions, and his verbosity, and before long he had realized that this too was useful, and was using it."?[4]

Certainly literature has a vivid three-dimensional quality that textbooks lack. (4)

The next relevant attribute of literature is its completeness. It represents the completed working out of a set of problems in a human life. Weeks, months and years of living and writing are condensed into hours of reading. A comparable unfolding is accessible clinically only with a long-term therapy experience. If the trainee does have time and chance to work with a patient at length, he could well emulate the writer's skill in producing a summary narrative. Conversely, we also wish the trainee to extrapolate intuitively from a limited experience with someone to the whole person, the whole life. This faculty will be sharpened on the student's repeated experience of observing how details and fragments of a story foreshadow the whole. This is beautifully illustrated in Kovel's analysis of *Madame Bovary*.[5]

In a related vein: a piece of fiction deals with growth, stress, change, challenge and confrontation. Such works as James Baldwin's *Go Tell It On the Mountain* and Mary Renault's *The King Must Die,* with their images of death and rebirth which touch at the core of mental healing, are manifestly on this subject. The teacher could compose an "epigenetic sequence" of readings to illustrate developmental crises in the life cycle. For example, Mark Twain is a mine of information about the latency age-pubescent boy; D. H. Lawrence is invaluable on intimacy; etc. Such an approach would emphasize "normative crises," with their progressive and regressive forces, of which clinical crises are but a subset. This normative emphasis would counterbalance the prevailing pathology-centered view.

Literature is a source of material for virtually any psychological school or theory of personality. It is a source of personality description, of intra- and interpersonal dynamics, of psychopathology. These do not exhaust the possibilites of the raw material, just as no cognitive framework can contain all the raw stuff of existence. Newer ways of looking at literature psychologically do not concentrate on the psychology of a single person as represented in a fictional personage. Rather, they treat the work as a whole, and examine the interplay of content (personages, actions) and form (imagery, symbols, tone, rhythm and other elements of style) to arrive at the central theme of what it is all about, what is the "personality" of the literary piece.[7] All these elements are analyzed and resynthesized into an image of the issues the author is grappling with in that piece.[8] The process of using all available clues—the totality of the communication—to reconstruct a pattern of meaningful understanding is analogous to the clinical reconstruction that is our ultimate goal.

The foregoing by no means exhausts what literature is nor how it can be used. Certainly its ability to involve the reader with his powers of intellect, feeling and imagination is important here. Another interesting attribute is its intermediate position between the person of the reader and the person of the author, between inner reality and outer reality, between symbol and thing. Applying an understanding of this special form of existence—technically called "transitional"—can add to our understanding of who writer and reader are, of why the writer writes, of why the reader reads.[9]

THE SMALL-GROUP ANALYTIC METHOD

> The ability to help a client know some of his more subtle messages, moods and feelings I think is determined by two factors. First is practice, practice at labeling feelings, especially interpersonal fears—finding words for the basic dimensions, the basic shapes, the general characteristics of gut level emotion. Second, and perhaps even more important, is the ability to overcome your own resistances to becoming involved in a psychologically intimate and meaningful way with another human being . . .[2]

The small group setting actualizes the assets of literature discussed in the first section. The small group—six to twelve members—has been emerging as a significant social unit of our day, both inside and outside psychology and psychiatry. This unit seems to provide just the right blend of qualities for our current needs: it is a shelter offering support and protection and yet a platform for taking bold risks; it permits intimacy and yet anonymity.[10] As an example of the method in practice, I will discuss my work with fourth-year medical students spending four weeks at our psychiatric hospital.

Each week prior to the meeting they will have read a fiction or nonfiction piece—of manageable length (an important criterion!)— which I have chosen for its richness and aesthetic appeal. My taste bias is toward the acknowledged "great" writers. But one could effectively use any writer and any literary genre if one knew how to be creative with it. I once heard Dr. Roland Fischer make brilliant use of an inspired comic book!

The four pieces form a coherent sequence. One such is as follows:

1. "Case of a Neurologic Crisis in a Small Boy: Sam."[6] This illustrates the "total field" concept, the boxes-within-boxes of a problem: the individual in whom the problem lodges and the ever-widening force fields of family, neighbors, society, culture, history etc. This reading also illustrates the concept of multi-determination of a behavior, the interpenetration of psyche and soma, the vicissitudes of a problem over time, and the strategy of psychoanalytically oriented therapy.

2. "Loneliness of the Long Distance Runner"[11] amplifies several of the preceding issues, especially that of the impact of membership in the out-group. Also, since this story deals with a non-patient, it conveys the universality of the concepts learned. We also see here the "action at a distance" of the psyche, i.e. the effect on current behavior of memories and feelings long repressed.

3. "The Death of Ivan Ilych"[12] is about a medical patient and raises important issues for the student doctors. This story too illustrates the correspondences between bodily action and psychic meaning ("He died as he had lived."). This is an exercise in oscillating between manifest meaning (the illness) and latent meaning (Ivan's existential feelings).

4. We conclude with the "Autobiography of a Schizophrenic's Experience,"[13] an unusually lucid account of the psychopathology and psychodynamics of the experience as lived by someone who was there and mastered it. This places that most terrible of terms, schizophrenia, back within the family of human individuation experiences.

The group process is a free discussion which taps the flowing conscious and unconscious associations of all the members. The story content is a starting point to stimulate their own questions, concerns, feelings and attitudes. Fundamental and sophisticated questions such as "What is mental illness?" are raised. Differences among the members are especially important as the discussion of differences gives the student some objectivity about himself.[14] Much of this occurs, though, without our being a therapy or sensitivity group. A student may see that he is overly sensitive, or overly callous; that he is too skeptical or too gullible; that he demands too much certainty or too much ambiguity. In general, these students, struggling to master the medical model and using it as a bulwark against anxiety, need to be encouraged to tolerate ambiguity and uncertainty and to maintain the inquiring attitude. Their active participation and involvement in discussion contrasts with the dumb, passive expressions often seen in the lecture hall.

My function as leader is to promote participation, interaction, to center the discussion on key issues, and to be didactic—this includes being didactic about the group process itself, such as pointing out when the subject is changed to avoid a charged issue. What occurs is "education" in the sense of drawing upon and drawing out what is already there in the form of natural endowment and the accumulated wisdom of years of living. Thereby, what Kagan has insightfully noted as the "feigning of clinical naivete"[2] is diminished. In the capacity I have mentioned, my role as a teacher closely parallels my role as psychotherapist ("the medium is the message"). The students have me as a model (and as a target!).

At the end of the session each group-as-a-whole has created its own unique interpretation of the work-as-a-whole. Each portrait is different, though with traits in common that I have supplied. The work-as-a-whole within the group-as-a-whole follows the model of a box-within-a-box. This structure is built of interlocking units of experiencing-and-examining and is cemented by feelings of working together in creative activity. The four weeks taken together are the next level in what I hope is an ever-amplifying harmonic of learning.

I wish to express thanks to Dr. John Nemiah and Dr. Julius Silberger, who were early models; and to Dr. Daniel Cowell, who has given latitude and encouragement.

REFERENCES

1. F. W. Barnes, G. E. Vaillant, L. L. Havens, et al. "A New Approach to the Study of Psychogenic Disturbances" *New England Journal of Medicine*, 283:959-963 (1970).

2. Norman Kagan, "Influencing Human Interaction—Eleven Years with Interpersonal Process Recall (IPR)," Unpublished manuscript. Michigan State University (1973).

3. Joseph Conrad, "The Nigger of the Narcissus," in *Three Great Tales*, Vintage Books (New York), p. 8.

4. James Agee, *A Death in the Family* (New York: Bantam Books, 1969), pp. 68-69.

5. Joel Kovel, "On Reading *Madame Bovary* Psychoanalytically," in

Paul G. Myerson, ed., *Psychiatry and Literature,* Grune and Stratton, August, 1973, pp. 331-345.

6. Erik H. Erikson, *Childhood and Society* (New York: W. W. Norton, 1963).

7. Norman N. Holland, *The Dynamics of Literary Response* (New York: Oxford University Press, 1968).

8. Kenneth Gorelick, "Kafka's 'Metamorphosis': A Psycholiterary Analysis," Unpublished manuscript (1973).

9. Arnold H. Modell, *Object Love and Reality* (New York: International Universities Press, 1968), pp. 10-18, 28-40.

10. Max Day, "The Therapeutic Envelope," Unpublished manuscript, Massachusetts Mental Health Center, Boston.

11. Alan Sillitoe, "The Loneliness of the Long Distance Runner," in Alan Casty, ed., *The Shape of Fiction* (Boston: D. C. Heath and Co., 1967), pp. 203-231.

12. Leo Tolstoy, "The Death of Ivan Ilych," Signet Classic (New York: 1960).

13. Anonymous, "An Autobiography of a Schizophrenic Experience," *Journal of Abnormal and Social Psychology,* 51:677-689, 195.

14. Julius Silberger, "Using Literary Materials to Teach Psychiatry," in Paul G. Myerson, ed., *Psychiatry and Literature,* pp. 275-285.

FOOTNOTES

1. Other paradigms have been used. Students have read, then witnessed, the performance of plays.[1] Professional actors have been used for role-playing. The trainees too have done role-playing, with and without sophisticated videotape techniques.[2]

2. Videotape is another way to review at an emotional distance. With this technique one can split off a part of himself. Video is a very congenial medium for the generation weaned on television. It is an important teaching tool complementary to literature, especially for displaying nonverbal communication.

   Literature, too, sends its taproots into early experience: the bedtime story, the fairy tale, etc.

3. Literature is intended to complement, not replace, experience with live persons. Two sorts of the latter are available to the trainee. He can observe clinical demonstrations, which often leave him too detached. Or he can have his own patient. This is a *must,* though it stirs high anxiety.

4. The late Dr. Ives Hendrick long ago recognized that the text could impede learning by offering formulae. He urged that psychiatry trainees take the patient as text.

Bibliotherapy and the Elderly

by Daniel Sweeney

I wonder how many of you know what isinglass is. Do you know the many uses to which suet can be put? Or perhaps I should ask do you know what suet is? Do you know that Christmas at a mental institution is one of the saddest times of the year and yet often enough it is not acknowledged as such? Do you know how to make herb tea? How many of us know the wisdom of some of the folk remedies that were used in homes years ago? Have you ever made wine or beer? Do you know who Fats Wallace is? Have you known anyone who grew up in Washington at the turn of the century and who remembers Anacostia when it was still farmland? Have you ever experienced life on a farm?

These are just a sampling of the disparate topics which have been discussed in a Bibliotherapy group which has been in progress for the past 14 months at St. Elizabeths Hospital. The members of the group are elderly ranging in age from the late 50's to 90 years. The diagnoses include schizophrenia, senility (also called chronic brain syndrome), and Alzheimer's disease (also called pre-senile dementia).

When patients are discussed it is common enough to differentiate them into two basic categories: those who are functionally ill and those who are organic. The former are those who experience "problems in living" or whose difficulties are thought to be primarily emotional or disturbances of personality development. These include the better-known psychoses (the schizophrenias and the manic-depressive psychoses), the neuroses, the character disorders, drug addiction, and alcoholism. They may be of any age. The organics are those who suffer a physical deterioration of cells in the brain. The therapeutic attitude of most staff at hospitals, whether explicit or more usually implicit, is that those who are functionally ill can still be helped but the "organics" are hopeless. Many of the "organics" are the elderly—those who are senile or suffering chronic brain syndrome. This group of people, the elderly, are perhaps the most neglected and poorly cared for population of persons which exists at most mental hospitals. They comprise at least 25 percent of the patients at St. Elizabeths and I would guess this is true of most state hospitals. What I am leading up to is a very simple statement, one that I think should be obvious, but one which needs to be stressed. Bibliotherapy can be used with one of the most difficult patient populations to be found in hospitals: the elderly, and even those who have experienced some organic impairment.

I do not think that many would debate the efficacy of bibliotherapy with the YAVIS group of institutionalized persons: the Young, Attractive, Verbal, Intelligent, and Sophisticated. However, there may be a tendency to avoid using it with the elderly and with other particularly difficult patient groups. I would like to tell you about our experiences with our group and to stress the principles which I believe underlie the use of bibliotherapy with any group of people but especially with the institutionalized elderly.

Bibliotherapy as we used it was primarily the use of poetry. But it also included music, slides, flowers, snow, etc. The essential difference between bibliotherapy and other therapies as I have seen them employed is that bibliotherapy addresses itself directly and consistently to healthy, progressive aspects of the person's character. Erich Fromm has a beautiful concept which constitutes one of the cornerstones of his theory of man. He talks of a dimension of the human person called biophilia. Biophilia means love of life and the biophilic person is the one who can derive joy from living, who is open to new experience, is spontaneous and alive, able to accept and embrace the beauty, sadness, harmony, and discord in the world about. The first principle that I would like to state is that bibliotherapy is, by and large, biophilic; it seeks to tap a person's capacity to experience joy in his life. Most therapies by their very nature tend to address what is pathological in the person while bibliotherapy begins with a thing of beauty (a poem, music, a picture) and seeks to elicit the person's responses to that object. Of course, the response need not be one of joy and acceptance. Quite often it elicits sadness and anger. But these emotions are perfectly appropriate and acceptable. In my experience what bibliotherapy has not elicited is depression, free-floating anxiety, or psychotic symptoms such as delusions or hallucinations. Bibliotherapy in our group has been essentially a healthy and progressive experience for patients and therapists alike.

Before Arleen Hynes and I began the bibliotherapy group we discussed our philosophies of what we thought should constitute the basis of what we would be doing. Arleen was particularly influenced by a concept proposed by Jerome Frank, M.D. It was the concept of the restoration of morale. It is Frank's contention that "the chief problem of all patients who come to psychotherapy is demoralization and that the effectiveness of all psychotherapeutic schools lies in their ability to restore patients' morale." Demoralization is in my experience one of the most pervasive characteristics of persons at St. Elizabeths Hospital, and it is particularly so among the elderly. Frank states that the demoralized person feels impotent, isolated and despairing. His "self-esteem is damaged and he feels rejected by others because of his failure to meet their expectations." Finally he states "the most frequent symptoms of patients in psychotherapy—anxiety and depression—are direct expressions of demoralization." Let us look for a moment at the elderly and address some of the symptoms Frank lists. *Impotence—* almost any person who is institutionalized is a dependent and impotent individual. They must rely on others to provide their food, to provide them with shelter, their clothing, a bed. The institution controls when they rise, when and what they eat, what they do during the day, when they retire. For the elderly who often are even more physically disabled than other patients they are even more at the mercy of others: impotent to care for their own most fundamental needs. I would add to Frank's list of characteristics of demoralization the feeling of anger. So often the anger is intense but it must be kept under wraps lest the person alienate those in the institution who provide for them. How fearful it must be to wonder and worry whether you will get your next meal. Believe me the individual may be meek and undemanding on the surface but beneath you can usually find an intense core of anger and it too must be addressed.

Let's look for a moment at isolation. To a large extent each of the members of our group was virtually alone in the world. Though some had relatives, they were often left weeks at a time without visitors. The experience of being alone and apart from those one loves and depends on for support is one of great isolation. Too, many had experienced the death of a spouse, children and friends which added to their feelings of abandonment. One 90-year-old patient who was 40 years in the hospital remembered visits from her family long ago and stated the only people she had left were her 86-year-old sister-in-law and niece, neither of whom were able or, perhaps, willing to visit. Basic principle number two therefore was that we saw a bibliotherapy group as an instrument for restoring morale. We sought to address the feelings of impotence, to alleviate their experience of isolation, and to replace feelings of despair with hope and confidence.

My own philosophy of the group sprang from a concept similar to that of the restoration of morale and it was that the group should provide the person with the opportunity to actively relax, to recreate and to re-create herself. We saw that the way to re-create oneself was not to sit passively but to be active. I cannot emphasize this idea enough. We saw ourselves not as entertainers who came to present a show or put on a performance for the group but as individuals who would stimulate, direct and facilitate the active use of their minds, their bodies, their dormant memories, their untapped capacities for joy in their past and present lives. Basic principle number three therefore was that we would place demands upon the patients to be active in the very best sense of the word. We attempted to structure the group so that the individuals would have a focus for their thoughts, exchange their ideas with one another, and stay focused on the topic.

The fourth basic principle flows I believe from the three previously mentioned. It is that the group should tap and foster feelings of competence. It is a truism to say that institutionalized patients experience a pervasive feeling of being incompetent; once again because of their peculiar situations it is particularly true that the elderly feel this way. At the start I asked a series of questions. These were areas of competence for the members of our group. They emerged in the course of our discussions of poems, music and slides and brought the group in touch with experiences in their lives when they were active, when they were related to others, when they had skills and arts—in sum, when they were competent. When an individual can feel a measure of pride in what she has done in the past, or in what she has been, known or experienced, her self-esteem is bolstered and she becomes more confident and able to cope with the present. Though it may not be necessarily so in other groups with the elderly, much of our energy and time was spent in reminiscence.

For every person the past is of the utmost importance in their present lives. This is particularly true for the elderly. The tendency to look back, to dwell on past experience, to live the present and view the future in the light of the past is probably a universal experience. With this in mind we encouraged reminiscence. We saw this as an opportunity to relive basically happy times since the stimulus to remember was so often a benign one: a reference from poetry, a discussion of a favorite song or singer. To be sure painful memories too were rife and we not only allowed them to arise but gladly entertained them simply because sadness and anger are also valid and all too human emotions. But perhaps more than any others we welcomed those memories which brought laughter and joy, and not insignificantly, most of the memories elicited were benign, joyful and progressive. Reminiscence can have a cathartic effect. For individuals hospitalized for psychiatric reasons past conflicts and anxieties have not been resolved. For the elderly these conflicts continue to have an effect on their psychic and emotional lives. And to the extent that the recounting of the past can help in the resolution of present difficulties we fostered accounts of the past.

I would like to be a little more concrete now and describe the way in which we structured the group. In order to establish an atmosphere conducive to relaxation and calm we chose as our initial meeting place a room in the library which was characterized by space, air and light, comfortable chairs, plants and an excellent stereo system. Later we were forced to change the meeting place to one which was less pleasant, but we tried as far as possible to maintain a pleasing milieu. For example, we were able to purchase an excellent portable sound system for our new meeting room (and in a large institution this is no small accomplishment).

Eating and drinking and their intrinsic sense of sharing together were also chosen as integral parts of the group. It is difficult to describe how important eating and drinking can be to individuals who live their lives in institutions. Coffee, tea, cookies or cake were served at each group meeting or in place of them we provided wine. This was done in a spirit of people joining together to eat, to drink, to talk and indulge in serious and light conversation. In an atmosphere which would encourage a sense of relaxation and a feeling of recreating oneself we hoped to reduce the anxiety and tension which so often accompanies group meetings not only for elderly people but for so many hospitalized psychiatric persons. To this end the leaders consciously attempted to build into the group a feeling of sharing, a sense of specialness and uniqueness that we hoped would eventuate in a group identity characterized by comraderie, friendliness and quite simply joy at being with one another.

We began each group with coffee and cookies and then read and discussed poems. Poetry with its intrinsic sensitivity to life and death issues was a particularly good way to introduce the ultimate future of each of us: aging and death. The elderly are quite aware either consciously or unconsciously of their mortality. Their bodies, their diets, their physical changes (hair color, wrinkles, dentures) are ever present reminders. We welcomed consideration of the theme of aging and death as a natural phenomenon — the leaves of autumn, the barrenness of winter, the death of Louis Armstrong, the age of Kate Smith, the Lindbergh kidnapping in the 20's which some of our members so vividly recalled. As in any such discussion there were tendencies to deny and avoid, to feel a sense of depression and fear and we were sensitive to force consideration gently but insistently at times and at others simply to touch upon the theme and then back off from it, aware that it would arise again. Arleen chose the poems that we discussed. We structured, focused, and directed the discussion but we never tried to force a particular theme. We did not have a hidden agenda that we were determined to have the group discuss and this is a critical area for anyone who is involved in bibliotherapy. If one comes to the group determined to discuss a given topic then one is likely to block the spontaneity and independence of the group. It becomes an exercise rather than an experience, a didactic episode rather than a sharing of thoughts, opinions, and feelings.

Conducting a group for the elderly and especially for those who have suffered some brain damage necessitates that the leaders be extremely active. Memories for recent events are seriously impaired with some patients, there is a tendency to perseverate: to repeat one idea or statement over and over and over and over and over. There is a tendency not to be able to listen to one another — speech is distorted, hearing fades, eyesight prevents one from realizing who is present, to whom others are speaking, etc. It becomes the task of the leaders to stop those who repeat, to facilitate the communication between members by restating questions and pointing out to patient A that patient B is talking to her. There is a tendency also to lose focus, to begin to ramble and to go so far afield that the poem is lost. It is the task of the leaders to bring the group back to the poem when discussion begins to be unproductive. This calls for authoritative, firm but gentle intervention. If the group was to be more than seven or eight people talking aloud with no one hearing the others we found that we had to take an active part in stopping the conversation and specifically asking quieter members direct questions. At times we went around the group, member by member, repeating the question and eliciting answers. We found we had good results when structure and limits were supplied by taking poems stanza by stanza and even line by line, asking the meaning of the words or how the person thought and felt about what was read.

We had to deal (and quite often anyone who attempts to conduct a group in a mental hospital will experience the same) with intense resistance initially. There is a great reluctance and refusal often on the part of psychiatric patients to get involved in therapy of any kind. Some members stated that it was all right once or twice but not on a regular basis or as one put it "take somebody else, take the younger people, I don't need it." The first elements in the solution of the resistance consisted of a gentle but firm and uncompromising insistence on our part that the person come to group; a quasi obsessive-religious adherence to holding sessions, so that the days and times became etched in the minds of those who attended—this consistency, constancy and structure are essential in working with such groups; the presence of a known and familiar member of the nursing staff who accompanied the persons to the group.

We found that after a few months all members of the group perhaps with one exception eagerly attended the groups. This in itself is remarkable in my opinion. Some members of the group took pride in getting to sessions on time by themselves. Others needed to be accompanied to the group. But even this was part of the therapy. For some it represented a personal invitation to come and share and was perhaps a measure of how much we cared for her.

Most people in the group now recognize one another and there is warmth in greetings, in going to and from the meeting room. Names still are a problem. After 14 months of meeting twice weekly with them most still do not know our names! However, there is a group identity, and I believe some of the isolation and loneliness of their lives has been dissipated. Members of the group now have a forum in which to speak their minds. Patients often express their anger and concerns about life in the hospital, ward injustices on the part of the other patients or staff, concerns about going to foster homes, resentment about their children whom they feel have abandoned them or treated them unjustly. But happy topics are also discussed. As a result of one group discussion we arranged a trip to the race track. We've discussed women's lib, male-female relationships, the Bible, how to make biscuits, how to make soap, we've danced, joked and argued. In summary, it is a demanding and hard group but one that quite simply is fun and a joy!

Contemporary Bibliotherapy: Systematizing the Field

by Franklin M. Berry

In the first part of this paper an attempt is made to analyze the field of contemporary bibliotherapy. Clinical bibliotherapy is distinguished from educational bibliotherapy. In the second part of the paper an attempt is made to analyze the bibliotherapy situation itself. Different versions of individual and group bibliotherapy are identified operationally using such dimensions as emphasis on receptive language mechanisms (e.g., participant reads or listens to pre-existing literature) vs. emphasis on expressive language mechanisms (e.g., participants create literature, orally or in writing).

THE CLINICAL BIBLIOTHERAPY VS. EDUCATIONAL/ HUMANISTIC BIBLIOTHERAPY DISTINCTION

At the fourth Bibliotherapy Round Table held in Washington, D.C., in January, 1977, I suggested that the field of bibliotherapy consists of two major branches, namely, clinical bibliotherapy and educational/humanistic bibliotherapy. The clinical version of bibliotherapy is a form of psychotherapy; it is practiced by a wide range of mental health professionals including psychiatrists, psychologists, social workers, counselors, ministers, nurses, art therapists and so on. It is a special purpose technique for some (e.g., see Leedy[4]) and a full or complete method of psychotherapy for others (e.g., see Lerner[5]). The educational or humanistic version of bibliotherapy is also practiced by mental health professionals, especially counselors, working in educational settings (e.g., see Zaccaria & Moses[11]). It is important to note, however, this version of bibliotherapy is also practiced by educators, working in either educational settings (e.g., see Schulteis,[9] Brown[3]) or special purpose settings like nursing homes (e.g., see Kaminsky,[7] Koch[8]). In such settings the goals of the bibliotherapeutic process may be to attain some specific instructional objective, say, of increasing the rate of creative self-expression in writing or of increasing empathetic

This article is based, in part, on two prior papers, Berry (1976; 1977).

understanding for minority groups. Still other uses of the technique are concerned with the more general goals of "adjustment," self-discovery, self-actualization or attaining "emotional maturity."

At this point, it may prove useful to make some specific comparisons between clinical bibliotherapy and educational/humanistic bibliotherapy. I am referring here to operations which define these two versions of bibliotherapy.

Consider the following operational definition of contemporary bibliotherapy:

> Bibliotherapy is a family of techniques for structuring an interaction between a *facilitator* and a *participant*, an interaction which is in some way based on their mutual sharing of *literature* in the broadest sense possible.

Given this definition, it becomes apparent that the principal ingredients of bibliotherapy consist of (1) the bibliotherapist-facilitator, (2) the bibliotherapy-participant or participants and (3) the literature that they in some sense share or mutually experience. It is important to note that the phrase "their mutual sharing of literature in the broadest sense possible" encompasses all possible literary forms, from poems to short stories to autobiographical novels and to personal diaries, life histories and so on. The phrase also encompasses those literary productions existing in the world's literature, those created by the facilitator or bibliotherapy-participants, and those transmitted in a non-textual form like films, videotapes, tape recordings and so on.

Given these specifics, I believe that it will become clear that the features which distinguish clinical vs. educational/humanistic bibliotherapy are:

(a) the different facilitator roles and functions, i.e., therapist vs. general group leader/manager/discussant)

(b) the different characteristics of the participants ("sick" vs. "well" or patients or clients vs. students or volunteers);

(c) the different goals of the bibliotherapeutic process ("getting well" vs. self-actualization or attainment of some educational goal).

In concluding this section it ought to be emphasized that the *same* literary form can be used in either version of bibliotherapy and that the literature which is shared does not differentiate bibliotherapy-as-psychotherapy (clinical bibliotherapy) from bibliotherapy-as-education/growth (educational/humanistic bibliotherapy).

ANALYZING THE BIBLIOTHERAPY SITUATION*

As we have seen, any bibliotherapy situation must consist of a participant, a facilitator and some literature that they in some sense share. As many have pointed out before, it is possible to structure the bibliotherapy situation as a one-to-one encounter, so-called individual bibliotherapy, or it may be a one-to-many encounter, with one facilitator

---

*The analysis offered here is believed to be equally applicable to either clinical or educational/humanistic bibliotherapy.

and several participants, so-called group bibliotherapy. It is of course also possible to vary the number of facilitators; two facilitators might work together as "co-therapists." These various ways of structuring the bibliotherapy situation are undoubtably important since they are highly likely to influence the manner in which the literature involved is experienced. For example, in the individual bibliotherapy situation only two persons' perceptions of a given literary work are shared; while in group bibliotherapy, there are as many perceptions shared as there are participants and facilitators. Likewise, the group situation may involve participant: participant sharing which is by definition excluded from the individual bibliotherapy situation. In a similar vein one could enumerate a number of different ways of structuring the group bibliotherapy situation: "open" vs. "closed" group; homogeneous vs. heterogeneous group composition; supportive vs. attacking group atmosphere and so on. Again these differences would be expected to influence how the sharing of literature is accomplished.

While these different ways of varying the bibliotherapy situation are important they do not seem as basic to the bibliotherapeutic process as those involving the direct experiencing of the literature itself by the participant(s). Importantly, the facilitator may be presenting the literature for sharing, or it may be the participant who is presenting it. Also, importantly, the literature presented may be the literature-of-others or the literature-of-self. Finally, the experiencing of the literature itself may take place within the bibliotherapy session (especially with short pieces) or it may be experienced outside of the bibliotherapy session, but shared within a session. It is the present writer's contention that those operations which determine how the participant directly experiences the literature used in bibliotherapy constitute the single most important class of parameters of the bibliotherapy situation under consideration here. This is so because such operations seem to go to the heart of the bibliotherapy process. The remainder of this preliminary analysis will be devoted to this issue.

Figure 1 is an attempt to summarize some of the different ways that literature can be experienced by a participant. The receptive vs. expressive language dimension emphasizes the differential processing of the literature-of-others (Cells A and B) vs. the literature-of-self (Cells C and D). The former is experienced as an "input" while the latter is experienced as an "output" (at least initially). It is possible of course that bibliotherapy which is based mainly on receptive language mechanisms does not produce beneficial effects for the same reasons as bibliotherapy based mainly on expressive language mechanisms. For example, there may be certain therapeutic benefit derived from the act of self-expression itself (possible only in Cells C and D).

The written vs. oral literature dimension emphasizes the fact that both preexisting literature (the world's literature) and participant-generated literature can be expressed and/or created in oral or written form. Shiryon (1970) has argued for the use of oral literature, folktales,

FIGURE 1

**NATURE OF PARTICIPANT'S
LINGUISTIC RESPONSE**

NATURE OF THE LITERATURE		Receptive Language (Input)	Expressive Language (Output)
	Written	A	C
	Oral	B	D

A - Traditional Bibliotherapy (Participant reads literature himself/herself; written literature is read to participant.)

B - Literatherapy as defined by Shiryon (1972). (Oral literature is communicated to the participant.)

C - Creative Writing Therapy (Participant creates literary products, poems, short stories, diary entries, life history recollections etc.; they are written works.)

D - "Creative Orating Therapy" (Participant creates literary products orally, e.g., a poem or short story or an oral diary or an oral life history etc.; they are oral works.)

Proposed Systematization: Cells A, B, C and D are all variants of bibliotherapy; each cell represents a uniquely different literary experience for the participant. The nature of the literature presented to the participant whether existing in written or oral form, or the type of literature created by the participant whether written or spoken, affect how the literature is experienced by the participant.

Figure 1. A systematization of contemporary bibliotherapy. (It should be noted that Cells A - D constitute four different means of structuring the bibliotherapy situation for any given literary genre; Cells A - D could involve the genre of poetry or the genre of short story and so on.)

fables etc. in bibliotherapy (Cell B); Leuner (1969) has reported requiring participants in psychotherapy to create spoken stories (Cell D). The written vs. oral literature tradition obviously emphasizes different components of the participant's receptive language mechanisms: (a) with written literature (Cell A), visual information-processing is emphasized; (b) with oral literature (Cell B), auditory information processing is emphasized. It seems reasonable to expect that bibliotherapy based on an emphasis on visual information processing mechanisms may be differentially effective from bibliotherapy based on an emphasis on auditory processing mechanisms. At present, however, such comparisons have not been made.

In a similar vein it seems reasonable to expect that creating written literary products (Cell C) would emphasize different information processing mechanisms than creating spoken literary products (Cell D). That is to say, it seems reasonable to expect that the written vs. oral literature dimension also emphasizes different components of the participant's expressive language mechanisms: (a) with written creative products, certain processing mechanisms would be called into play; (b) with orally created products, certain other processing mechanisms would be called into play. To be quite specific, asking participants to write poems, short stories and so on may have decidedly different implications for the bibliotherapeutic process than asking them to create such products orally. This would seem especially true when the creation of the literary product by the participant occurs within the bibliotherapy session. For example, the participant might be more likely to reveal his/her significant concerns in an orally created story — one that could not be erased, or revised or discarded. Indeed, much work with projective tests like the Thematic Apperception Test, in which people make up stories about pictures, seems closely related to bibliotherapy based on creating aloud (Cell D of Figure 1).

Finally, it is interesting to note that each Cell of Figure 1 can take place within a bibliotherapy session or outside one. A participant could read or listen to written literature on his or her own or in the presence of a facilitator (Cell A). A participant could listen to an oral literature selection alone or with the facilitator (Cell B). A participant could create a written literary product on his or her own or in the presence of a facilitator (Cell C). A participant could create an oral literary product alone (say, using a tape recorder) or with the facilitator (Cell D).

In closing, I would like to point out that I believe that a conceptual analysis of contemporary bibliotherapy must precede an empirical attack on this field. It is hoped that these preliminary comments will help pave the way for an empirical study of the bibliotherapeutic process itself.

REFERENCES

1. F. M. Berry, "Analysis of Processes in Bibliotherapy." Paper presented at the Fourth Bibliotherapy Round Table, Co-Sponsored by the National Council on the Aging, Inc., Washington, D. C. (1977).

2. F. M. Berry, "Toward a Conceptualization of Literature-Based Therapies." Paper presented at the Third Bibliotherapy Round Table, Atlanta (1976).

3. E. F. Brown, *Bibliotherapy and Its Widening Applications* (Metuchen, New Jersey: The Scarecrow Press, 1975).

4. J. J. Leedy, *Poetry Therapy* (Philadelphia: J. B. Lippincott Company, 1969).

5. A. Lerner, "Poetry Therapy: A Healing Art." *The Study of English* (January 1, 1974), p. 22-27.

6. H. Leuner, "Guided Effective Imagery (GAI): A Method of Intensive Psychotherapy." *American Journal of Psychotherapy* 23:4-22 (1969).

7. M. Kaminsky, *What's Inside of You It Shines Out of You.* (New York: Horizon, 1974).

8. Kenneth Koch, *I Never Told Anybody: Teaching Poetry Writing In A Nursing Home.* (New York: Random House, 1977).

9. Sister Miriam Schultheis, *A Guidebook for Bibliotherapy* (Glenview, Illinois: Psychotechnics, Inc., 1972).

10. M. Shiryon, *Twenty-Five Years of Bibliotherapy.* Paper presented at the 25th Annual Convention of the California State Psychological Association, Los Angeles (1972).

11. J. S. Zaccaria & H. A. Moses, *Facilitating Human Development Through Reading: The Use of Bibliotherapy in Teaching and Counseling.* (Champaign, Illinois: Stipes Publishing Co., 1968).

The Role of the Occupational Therapist as Related to Bibliotherapy

By Inez Huntting

From experience and from a survey of the literature one might recognize the role of the occupational therapist in relation to that of the bibliotherapist as comparable to that of an elder sibling as well as that of a fellow clinician. Both disciplines are concerned with the welding of the art and the science of treatment; the emphasis in each is upon helping people to help themselves.

The changes that have taken place in the United States during this century have affected every aspect of life, including the procedures and methods used in caring for the physically and mentally ill. In some instances, a procedure has been recognized, used, discarded, and brought back with improvements, or in a new form. In his book *American Notes,* Charles Dickens describes his visit to an insane asylum and notes his observations of patients performing tasks, participating in recreational pursuits, and reading.[1] During the nineteenth century these activities seemed a part of the institutional atmosphere; however today such are considered a part of the patient's treatment. The patient's involvement in a part or all of these facilities is planned for him individually with concern for the rehabilitative effects; this planning has been termed occupational therapy and bibliotherapy.

As medical science has extended the life of the human being and brought about what seems to be miraculous cures for bodily ills, the emotional suffering of man has become more obvious. It is from this awareness and the desire to alleviate this suffering that occupational therapy and bibliotherapy came into being. Gradually we have learned that the art of medicine includes treating man's ego as well as his body; that a strong ego must fulfill the need to create (to produce) and the need to expand intellectually (to learn). Just as the patient with a maimed body needs the assistance of medically trained persons in regaining the functions of the body, so his ego needs the aid of understanding and psychiatrically trained people to help the patient to regain his desire to learn and create.

Since 1900 many medical and library journals have carried papers and articles about the use of literature in treating the acutely or chronically handicapped person. The subject matter includes descriptions of the personality type most effective as a patient librarian, the physical plant of a patient library, the structuring of services, and the method of book selection. Librarians and others have written of their fruitful experiences in serving hospitalized patients through books. Individual physicians, occupational therapists, chaplains, nurses, and psychologists have supported, and do support, the hospital librarian in pointing out the need of this service for the patient. In most hospitals, administrations have provided library space and have included salaries for librarians in the budget, as well as a fund to maintain the patient library.

Since the need for bibliotherapy is recognized and to a greater or lesser degree (depending upon the financial condition of the institution) is provided for, why does the bibliotherapist often experience considerable difficulty in establishing a program? Occupational therapy as a profession is older than bibliotherapy; yet, frequently it too has difficulty in becoming established as an integral part of treatment. Occupational therapists have recognized a number of reasons for this, the most common and perhaps most superficial of which is that of the profession's youth. Since bibliotherapy is experiencing some of the same struggles, the occupational therapist may be of some assistance to this even newer profession.

By definition, occupational therapy is "a program of selected activity conducted as treatment under medical direction for physical and psychological problems. The occupational therapist is professionally skilled by selection and education to administer the program to meet prescribed objectives. The activity undertaken by the patient, the atmosphere in which he performs, and his relationship with the professional staff are the dynamic factors in occupational therapy."[2] In the absence of a patient library service and by the nature of the definition of the profession, the occupational therapist has often had the patient library delegated to his department. This responsibility may mean providing library service through acquiring reading materials (often by soliciting donations), setting up and maintaining a simple book loan service, providing book cart service to confined patients, or procuring specific books for individuals either by request from the patient or from his physician. Upon occasion the occupational therapist may, through knowledge of the patient's illness and his individual needs, use literature as a treatment medium.

As the number of librarians working directly in the hospital increases, the occupational therapist finds not only that he is relieved of providing a service that he is not satisfactorily equipped to handle but also that a professional person with similar interests and concerns has been added. In fact, he has a new associate. This increase is very important; in the hospital community many clinical services have limited personnel. Departments that have common functions and problems often improve their forces by combining some facets of their programs. The two services that we are primarily concerned with at this time may work together on a referral basis by sharing specific sessions and through supplying particular materials that assist the other discipline.

When the physically handicapped person gains in strength, his total energy is no longer needed for fighting pain or disease; the hours between treatments become a burden to him and the need for interest stimulation becomes evident. The occupational therapist is frequently the first person to be cognizant of this need since his treatment medium creates intensification of the patient's interest outside himself. It is at this point that the patient is fortunate who is in a setting where there is good relationship between the library and the occupational therapy department personnel, for the latter will help facilitate the service of the librarian as early as possible. The occupational therapist also may be of help to the patient and the librarian by supplying reading devices[3] designed to provide therapeutic aid for the individual patient.

Much of the procedure in occupational therapy which is necessary for the patient may be in itself uninteresting to him. The therapist may not be able to engage the patient's interest in the activity medium required, and thus the curative effect of treatment may be diluted. The service of the librarian is of great consequence through its ability to stimulate and broaden the patient's interest in literature or study. An example of such cooperation is shown in the instance of a patient who needed sustaining finger and wrist exercises which could best be obtained by molding clay. The patient did not like the damp, sticky substance and felt sure that he could not produce an acceptable product. However, accomplishment was very important to him. The hospital librarian was able to draw this man into reading and learning about clay, the various methods of creating shapes and forms, and the part which ceramics has played in history. Not only did she enrich the patient's life through helping him to develop a new interest, but she also aided in the treatment of alleviating his frustrations and resistance.

The authors of the literature concerning bibliotherapy directly or by implication indicate that it falls into the category of psychological medicine. With this in mind, let us look at some possibilities for cooperative work between the bibliotherapist and the occupational therapist in the field of psychiatry.

Again turning to published papers on the therapeutic use of literature, we find several references to the values of group reading.[4] One of the purposes of such is that it provides a means of assisting patients to

interact more easily and become a basis upon which to form relationships. The bibliotherapist usually takes an active role in this group
reading and participates freely. An occupational therapist who is
trained in making clinical observations is the logical choice as the
observer for such a group. In addition to knowing how to observe and
report observation of patient performance, he is familiar with or can
quickly become familiar with the bibliotherapist's techniques; he is understanding of and sympathetic with the goals of achievement. If the
same group of patients receive treatment from both disciplines and the
bibliotherapist and occupational therapist collaborate by comparing
individual patient reactions and performances, their reports can be of
assistance in determining further treatment and/or discharge planning.

Frequently the occupational therapist may have a permanent
treatment area adjacent to the patient quarters while the librarian may
work from a central unit that is some distance from the patient areas.
When such is the case, the two disciplines can advantageously plan a
combined group program using the occupational therapy facilities.

One plan of this nature was worked out by a hospital librarian and
an occupational therapist in the following manner. The librarian spent
one and half days in a psychiatric section that had a 40-bed capacity.
She spent the half day taking the book cart to patients in their rooms,
visiting with them, and later comparing impressions of individual patient needs with the occupational therapist. The full day visit consisted
of two group sessions and an issuing of books from a central location in
the occupational therapy clinic.

The first, or morning, session was held for patients who received
daily psychotherapy and occupational therapy. This was a discussion
meeting with the topic of discussion based upon reading that the
group had chosen the previous week. The librarian acted as a leader-
moderator. Frequently members of the medical staff joined the group.
At times one or more of the members would, because his or her doctor
was present, attempt to change the focus of the discussion, usually trying to use this time as an opportunity for a "gripe" session. The librarian contrived to give the spokesman some freedom, but would steer the
discussion back to the original subject. To create a relaxed climate and
an atmosphere of easy friendliness, the group would set a buffet table
with coffee and cookies. Patients from the group were responsible for
this preparation; the food had been baked in occupational therapy the
previous day.

The second, or afternoon, session was held for patients who were
receiving occupational therapy daily as well as electric shock therapy
or drug therapy. The approach used by the librarian and the therapist
differed considerably for this group. In order to help the patient to
become oriented to the change in pace, the program was much more
formalized. As the group entered the occupational therapy area one of
the patients presided at a tea table serving tea, coffee, or some seasonal

beverage. Usually the hostess was the individual who had baked the cake or cookies that were served at the large table where members of the group gathered after receiving their beverages. While the group was eating, the librarian started to read aloud. The subject matter for reading had been chosen the previous day so that it would be appropriate for the mood of the majority of those present. The librarian found that travel and human interest stories of a historical nature were usually the most meaningful to the majority of patients. Following a twenty-minute to a half-hour reading session, the group briefly discussed the content of the story and then talked of their own experiences that the reading helped them to recall. Before leaving the area, the patients checked out books from the book cart, which was left near the door, or requested the librarian to bring specific books on her next visit.

In both groups the value of these sessions was not so much the food, either for mind or body, but that of having a time that was clearly set aside for open discussion around a central theme where the patients were respected as individuals for their opinions and contributions. The success was due not so much to the material presented but to the manner in which the session was handled. Some of the important points were the regularity of the session—patients knew they could depend upon the meetings; the preparations the day before gave them something to look forward to; although the session was for all patients, attendance was elective; and most important was the easy way in which the librarian and the occupational therapist handled their roles. During the serving of food the librarian mingled with the patients, often letting them show her the work which they were doing during their occupational therapy sessions, or perhaps through conversation she would lead a shy person into an active circle while the occupational therapist was being a helper to the hostess or host. During the discussion period, the occupational therapist helped to draw individuals into the conversation or would perhaps instigate discussion by involving some member at the far end of the table. Patients of both groups usually were loathe to leave the area at the end of the session. Although the librarian and occupational therapist elected to clean up the serving table following the meeting, they always had ample voluntary assistance.

It was necessary to follow a general pattern for these sessions, but it was equally important that this pattern not be too highly structured so that all members were free to be themselves. By evaluating each session and comparing observations made of patient behavior, both participants were able to maintain objectivity, to learn in what areas patients needed specific assistance in regaining, or acquiring for the first time, better social attitudes. All of this was possible because the librarian and the occupational therapist had a common goal and were thus able to participate in a cooperative manner by melding their professions and personalities to that goal.

Another example of this cooperative approach might be that wherein the group reading hour is preceded by a luncheon prepared as a part of the occupational therapy homemaking training program. The library service would be involved more extensively in the project through assisting patients to use the library facilities in finding information concerning homemaking problems that could be solved in this kind of rehabilitation plan.

Earlier we have noted the assistance that the bibliotherapist can give in creating interest in the media necessary to occupational therapy for the physically disabled; such is also true in the treatment of the emotionally ill person. In a similar manner the bibliotherapist might receive assistance from the occupational therapist. The bibliotherapist may be attempting to channel a patient's fantasy into realistic avenues through educational media. The occupational therapist could assist in this attempt by offering the patient activities involving the same subject.

In the area of patient work assignments, the two disciplines have many opportunities to plan effective jobs in the library that will enable evaluation of a patient's readiness for community living or his need for a change in treatment, or to determine job training or educational possibilities for the patient upon his discharge.

The dependency of one discipline upon another was pointed out in 1944 by Dr. Jerome M. Schneck when he said to the Kansas Occupational Therapy Association, "rarely is one person sufficiently well versed in general literature and experience in psychiatric work to permit him to bear full responsibility in a program of bibliotherapy. A team of workers is more effective, consequently, in order to prescribe the most effective literature for the mental patient."[5] The term "team" as used by Dr. Schneck refers to the professional personnel of a hospital or hospital unit who are responsible for planning and carrying out treatment. The leader of the team is the physician who has final responsibility for the patient; the team members receive direction from him for carrying out their treatment procedures. The contribution made by each member is enhanced by a free flow of information between persons working with the patients and has led to regular planning and evaluation sessions commonly called "team meetings." The bibliotherapist and the occupational therapist who work together can be effective team members because they can give a detailed and clear picture of a patient's progress through the continuity of planned treatment. When working cooperatively, they can more readily recognize the methods that they can use most beneficially for each patient and thus more quickly integrate their service into the overall treatment program for the patient.

Dr. John C. Whitehorn, Jr., in his *Guide to Interviewing and Clinical Personality Study* has pointed out man's need for directed activity.[6] There are many other such references in medical literature; yet both the bibliotherapist or librarian and the occupational therapist are frequently frustrated by the seeming lack of serious concern given to the service which they provide the patient. Too frequently they are aware that the attitude held by the medical staff is that of looking upon either discipline as one which offers a nice although nonessential service for the patient: it helps the patient to while away dull hours by giving him a book to read or something to do. As a result of this occupation of his time the uncomfortable patient is less likely to upset others and as a consequence does not present an administrative problem. Because there is daily proof that this contribution is rehabilitative in nature and because it is known that long before these professions were created, the curative values of reading and work were recognized, it seems logical that there should be some attempt to understand and solve this dilemma. Toward this end one might pose questions such as the following:

1. Is it not quite possible that because of the very fact that the acceptance is of such long standing, the value may be taken for granted?

2. Do we perhaps nurture the "occupy time" concept through our inability to be specific regarding the treatment aspects of the activity for the individual patient?

3. Do we concern ourselves with the medical, psychiatric, psychological, and cultural details of each patient whom we deal with as much as with the media which we use to contribute to his treatment?

4. The term "therapy" implies specific knowledge of medicine and curative agents. This term is, it seems, broadly used and has become less definitive than we may realize. Consequently, have we fallen into a trap wherein we assume that all our practices are therapy because patients seem to improve with our ministrations?

5. Do we know why the patient improves?

6. Can we repeat a procedure exactly with reasonable assurance of the outcome?

7. Have we determined what in our particular discipline is "service" and what is "treatment"?

Of the things they do both bibliotherapist and occupational therapists should be able to define clearly which ones are "service oriented" and which are "specific treatment."

Earlier in this paper it was noted that people from other disciplines, as well as librarians, have pointed out the rehabilitative effectiveness of a bibliotherapy program. Some writers have indicated what the bibliotherapist must know in addition to his knowledge of books. Dr. Thomas V. Moore has indicated that one must consider the type of hospital, the kind of patient to be served, and the kinds of problems that are presented. He feels that the use of bibliotherapy is "based upon the fact that the mind stores ideals and principles of conduct which in due season may have a great deal to do with conduct."[7] He points out the emotional overlap in illness; 50 to 75 per cent of all illnesses are complicated by or precipitated by emotional conflict. Such information alerts us to the fact that the bibliotherapists must be cognizant of and understand psychological as well as physical medicine if he is to be a member of the treatment team.

In the university the occupational therapist learns the fundamentals of the use of activity media in the treatment of people suffering from many physical and emotional illnesses. It is only through experience under good direction and continuous study that he becomes professionally proficient.

The bibliotherapist, too, must have this kind of background and experience in order truly to be a therapist. If through this work the individuals of these two disciplines learn how to augment the work of the other, they will surely recognize their common interests and goals. The greatest barrier to their working together is the tendency toward isolation. Both should seek means of assisting one another and of learning from each other.

When we as individuals have learned to use our media, have acquired medical knowledge, and finally have learned to use ourselves in the therapeutic process, we shall have become therapists.

REFERENCES

1. Charles Dickens, *American Notes for General Circulation* (London: Chapman and Hall, 1842) Vol. 1, pp. 106, 109.

2. American Occupational Therapy Association, *Occupational Therapy Reference Manual for Physicians* (Dubuque: William C. Brown Company, 1960), p. 3.

3. J. W. Powell, "Group Reading in Mental Hospitals," *Psychiatry,* 13:213-226 (May 1950).

4. Josephine C. Moore, "Reading Aids for Quadriplegic Patients," *American Journal of Occupational Therapy,* 10:119-120+ (May-June 1956).

5. Jerome M. Schneck, "Studies in Bibliotherapy in a Neuropsychiatric Hospital," *Occupational Therapy and Rehabilitation,* 23:316-323 (December 1944).

6. John C. Whitehorn, Jr.,"Guide to Interviewing and Personality Study," *Archives of Neurology and Psychiatry,* 52:197-216 (September 1944).

7. W. J. Coville, "Bibliotherapy: Some Practical Considerations (Part I)," *Hospital Progress,* 41:138-142 (April 1960).

ADDITIONAL REFERENCES

Helen Becker, "The Hospital Librarian Speaks to the Occupational Therapist," *American Journal of Occupational Therapy*, 1:354-357 (December 1947).

N. Blackman, "Experience with a Literary Club in the Group Treatment of Schizophrenia," *Occupational Therapy and Rehabilitation*, 19:293-303 (October 1940).

Florence Glaser, "The Library As a Tool in Re-education," *Top of the News*, 16:24-27 (May 1960).

Margaret C. Hannigan, "As the Librarian Sees It," *Top of the News*, 16:13-15 (March 1960).

R. E. Hart, "Paving the Road to Health with Books," *Occupational Therapy and Rehabilitation*, 22:228-233 (October 1943).

Clara E. Lucioli, "Full Partnership on the Educational and Therapeutic Team," *ALA Bulletin*, 55:313-314 (April 1961).

J. H. McFarland, "A Method of Bibliotherapy," *American Journal of Occupational Therapy*, 6:66-73+ (March-April 1962).

Edith M. Maeda, "The Link Between Hospital and Community," *Top of the News*, 17:48-49+ (October 1960).

Edna Pearl Moody, "Books Bring Hope," *Library Journal*, 77:387-392 (March 1, 1952).

Dallis Pratt, "Values—Their Dynamics in Behavior and Psychotherapy," *Journal of Pastoral Care*, 9:189-202 (1955).

Theresa E. Pratt, "Patients' Libraries and Musical Activities in a Mental Hospital," *Occupational Therapy and Rehabilitation*, 19:379-386 (December 1940).

Mary Jane Ryan, "Bibliotherapy and Psychiatry: Changing Concepts, 1937-1957," *Special Libraries*, 48:197-199 (May-June 1957).

E. Preston Sharp, "The Philadelphia Team—Free Library and Youth Study Center," *ALA Bulletin*, 55:324-328 (April 1961).

Joel Vernick, "The Use of the Library in a Psychiatric Setting," *Top of the News*, 16:27-30 (May 1960).

L. R. Wolberg, "Bibliotherapy," *The Technique of Psychotherapy* (New York: Grune and Stratton, 1954), pp. 578-582.

Bibliocounseling as a Guidance Technique

by Archie L. Lejeune

There are four main items around which my approach to bibliocounseling as a guidance technique will center; they include: first, a rationale of the guidance and counseling process; second, the power of books; third, the role and value of bibliocounseling, and, fourth, counselors and librarians working together.

A RATIONALE OF THE GUIDANCE AND COUNSELING PROCESS

It would seem necessary at the outset, to briefly explore and examine the origins and nature of guidance and counseling in American schools. First, however, may we preface all remarks that follow with a general statement regarding guidance: definitions of guidance are legion—and have been very profusely propounded in scores of volumes over the past half-century or more. For our purposes, we provide the following as a non-exclusive context of guidance: guidance is the process of helping individuals to achieve the self-understanding and self-direction necessary to make the maximum or optimum adjustment to school, home, and community or society. Gilbert Wrenn puts it this way: "Guidance in schools is an American phenomenon. No other country in the world devotes so much attention to the child as an individual—and to assisting children in the decisions they must make as they grow up. This is a point of fundamental significance. Schools in all societies are concerned with the transmission of cultural heritages and with the socialization of the child. But in the United States, as in any democracy, there is an additional emphasis on the individual and on his needs and desires."

Hence, guidance is a rather inclusive term implying a process implicit in which are multitudinous services and approaches. For example:

> Guidance means realizing that each pupil is an individual, not just one of 36 pupils in a geometry class.

Guidance means accepting each pupil as an independent personality.

Guidance means arranging the school environment in the interest of the individual student.

Guidance means making a systematic study of individuals who deviate from the average as well as those who are completely normal.

Guidance means helping the individual student to understand himself and to modify his ways of adjusting.

Guidance means helping each pupil to learn to live as a cooperating member of a family and of a community.

Guidance means helping each pupil learn to make the best use of his physical condition.

Guidance means helping each pupil make a realistic choice of career.

Ideally conceived, then, guidance enables each individual to understand his abilities and interests, to develop them as well as possible, to relate them to life goals, and finally to reach a state of complete and mature self-guidance as a desirable citizen of a democratic social order.

Although the guidance movement began earlier in colleges and universities, most modern studies ascribe the beginning of the movement to its high school origins and more specifically to the work of Frank Parsons in Boston in 1908. Parsons established the Vocation Bureau of Boston in 1909. Its primary purpose was to assist young men to make vocational choices based upon their occupational aptitudes and interests. The Bureau was to later become part of Harvard University. Parsons also established the first counselor training program in America. His book *Choosing a Vocation* was published in 1909 and was regarded as a guidance "bible" for years to come. Thus, the year 1969 may rightfully be regarded as the 60th anniversary of guidance in the United States. Basically, the theme of Parson's book was that "vocational choice" was true reasoning based upon accurate information about oneself and the requirements of the vocation considered.

Implementation of guidance services in schools, as could be expected, has undergone a considerably evolutionary process. The key person in any school's guidance program today is the counselor. Today's counselor is a true professional in every sense of the word. Because of our democratic origins, technological advances, educational research, and a variety of social and economic forces, the past half century has witnessed the growth of a new profession—counseling—which is deeply rooted in the traditional fields of psychology, sociology, and education, yet beginning to develop some unique characteristics of its own.

The counseling service is viewed here as that part of the guidance service that provides a one-to-one relationship between a student who seeks better understanding of self and/or his world and a professional counselor skilled in the attitudes and techniques necessary to help the pupil in the relationship achieve such an understanding.

The counseling service has been described by many as the "heart" of the guidance function. The central purpose of the counseling service in schools is generally viewed as assistance to pupils in understanding themselves and in making choices that are individually satisfying and socially effective. Counseling, then, must be focused upon the individual problems and needs of students in the school. "Most leaders in the field agree that the desired outcome of counseling is self-realization and self-direction on the part of the client."

With the above stated outcome as a context, let us consider for a moment a brief review of three of the major stages in the development of counseling which should serve as a basis (or to clarify) further our understanding of present-day concepts and practices in particular as it relates to the subject bibliocounseling:

The three stages identified in the developing of counseling are as follows: counseling as vocational guidance, counseling as psychotherapy, and counseling as social interaction in personality development.

Counseling as Vocational Guidance

As was indicated earlier, organized counseling began with major emphasis upon assisting the individual to inventory his assets and liabilities for the selection of, and training preparation for occupational adjustments. The emphasis continued until the 1940's.

Second, Counseling as Psychotherapy

A second stage in the evolution of modern concepts of counseling arose from the attempts of psychologists and others to apply to the treatment of emotional conflicts of the individual, the therapeutic techniques developed by Freud and his followers. The chief concern of the psychotherapists of the early 1940's was the origin of behavior to be found in the individual's ego attitudes or ego involvements. Needless to say, this stage had a most disruptive impact upon vocational guidance which, not infrequently, set the vocational guidance counselor against the psychotherapist in pitched battles (literally).

The prime criticism of this approach to counseling practice was that following the prototype of Freud, psychotherapy had developed as a one-to-one therapist-client relationship in social isolation deliberately set apart from the client's daily social context. In a word—therapy is best achieved when the client goes away temporarily from his social world.

Counseling as Social Interaction in Personality Development

The third and presently emerged stage in the development of modern counseling stems, in large part, from Kurt Lewin's attempts to understand man in his social context, that is, as a personality interacting with other personalities in a social culture. Lewin's research and work in this area formed the basis for his treatise of this subject that was published in 1948 under the title of *Resolving Social Conflicts.*

Today, emphasis in counseling is very definitely centered on the third stage and quite likely—perhaps—evolving towards a fourth stage: the self-image of the individual. According to writing and research relative to this concept, the self-image is the center of the child's private world—the core of his personality. Self-image sets the boundaries of individual accomplishments and it tells a person what he can and cannot do. All through life a person faces the persistent questions of "Who am I?", "What am I?", "Where am I going?", and "How do I get there?" Self identity is basic to self-concept. The child constantly strives to achieve and maintain this identity.

A Final Word on Counseling

Counselors in schools today employ one of three approaches or philosophies in their work with students: directive, nondirective, and eclectic. In essence, proponents of the directive philosophy are of the opinion that "the history of pedagogy, as well as that of therapy, indicates that some type of direct assistance from outside the individual's human capacities seems to be needed to achieve inner growth." ". . . that freedom of choice cannot be allowed students in our schools. The immature student is not always able to make the wisest, or even a wise decision."

According to the nondirective philosophy: The student decides for himself that he is in need of help, that he must seek that help, and that he must accept the responsibility for solving his problems. The counselor's role becomes one of structuring and reflecting feeling, creating an atmosphere of security in which the client is free to talk about his problems in his own way, at his own pace, and for his own purposes. As his feelings are reflected, the client learns to know his problems, to accept them to gain insight as to why he has them, and to evaluate accurately his needs and goals.

According to the "eclectic" approach, which is a more recent development among counselors who recognized values in both directive and nondirective approaches, counselors should be flexible enough to employ different counseling approaches. The approach to be used is determined by the nature and extent of the client's problem.

Many generalists in counseling feel, however, that counseling approaches or techniques should be viewed as falling on a scale or continuum ranging from the least directive approach to the most directive approach—rather than as three distinct types or approaches.

The implications for the counselor thus are quite clear: There is no shortcut to self-realization. It is a long-term process. It involves extensive experience, exploration, reading about occupations and the biographies of successful men and women; it involves trial and error and the chance to confer with well-informed and well-trained counselors. It is in this regard that bibliocounseling can be a very effective technique or tool in the guidance/counseling process.

THE POWER OF BOOKS

In this day and time of the impact of television and the other mass media of communication, there seemingly is a popular misconception which holds that books are futile objects, with very limited power and influence. That is, the idea seems to prevail widely that books are harmless, innocent, ineffective, full of theory, and of little significance for the practical man of affairs.

According to this notion, books have a place in education, they are appropriate for little children, invalids, and club women and perhaps they may have some value for recreational purposes. Otherwise, they are of slight consequence.

On the contrary, books are dynamic and vital, capable of changing the whole direction of events; sometimes for good, sometimes for evil. Throughout history, there is ample evidence that books are not inanimate, peaceful articles belonging to the cloistered shades and academic quiet of monasteries, universities, and other retreats from an evil, materialistic world.

The incidence of book burnings, banishment and murder of writers, and the suppression of ideas and opposition by dictators down through the ages to the present, bear mute testimony to the power — the explosive forces pent up in books.

Several years ago, I had the personal pleasure of hearing a most inspiring speech. The speaker was, most appropriately, a Dean of Library Administration and his topic dealt with the power of books in a most dramatic and eloquent manner. In his remarks, he depicted the effect that several well-known books had had on human thought and action in a rather large segment of the world. The books concerned did not include any well-known works in religion or philosophy — surprisingly enough — and excluded as well many great literary masterpieces of fiction, drama, and poetry primarily, in the speaker's opinion, because of the intangible nature of their influence and the difficulty in measuring their effect by objective, non-controversial standards.

The theme established by the speaker was that the books in question had such great impact on society because of the nature of their contents and the timing of release as related to conditions existing in the society or nation involved.

Consider for a moment some of his examples: *The Prince,* which has been a best seller for over 400 years, was written by Machiavelli for the express purpose of freeing his beloved Italy from foreign aggression; England was ready for a vast expansion of her commercial and industrial economy when Adam Smith wrote *The Wealth of Nations;* Thomas Paine's *Common Sense* triggered the American Revolution; Harriet Beecher Stowe's *Uncle Tom's Cabin* did likewise for the Civil

War; Karl Marx's *Das Kapital* described the capitalistic system as he found it in 19th-Century England and his doctrines propounded therein have long since had the official force of a religion in the Communist World; Henry David Thoreau's essay *On the Duty of Civil Disobedience* ultimately was to provide the inspiration and impetus for the non-violent resistance movements of Gandhi in India and Martin Luther King in the United States; and, last but by no means least, Adolph Hitler's *Mein Kampf* became the philosophy of millions of people in the late 1930's. Five million copies of Hitler's book were sold in Germany in 1939 and who knows how many copies of *Uncle Tom's Cabin* have been sold since its release!

Obviously, these books carried messages of a highly emotional nature, appealing to untold millions of people—sometimes the influence was beneficent and sometimes evil. Clearly, books can be forces for both good and bad—they are, as well, dynamic and powerful instruments, tools, or weapons.

Furthermore, as tools or weapons in the literary arsenal of the counselor, books may serve the following purposes in the lives of young people:

Locating information necessary to the solution of personal problems.

Identifying, extending, and intensifying their interests.

Giving young people an awareness of themselves and others.

Furnishing emotional release or satisfaction.

Inducing intellectual curiosity and reflective thinking.

Developing social insight through the reinforcement of challenging of attitudes.

Giving opportunity for re-examination of a sense of values.

Providing aesthetic experience.

Developing critical appreciation of books, magazines, and newspapers.

Giving a sense of belonging to the culture.

Furnishing recreation through pure enjoyment and entertainment.

Nothing the adolescent or child learns is likely to serve him so well as the love of books and the ability to use them.

THE ROLE AND VALUE OF BIBLIOCOUNSELING

Question

Can the best literature of man be used to encourage the development of a more mature personality which will result in more effective living in an age in which we find so many conflicting problems and ideologies? In a word, Yes! Bibliocounseling is viewed herein as the clinical use of books in guidance and counseling situations that involve personal-social needs and/or problems of individuals—or groups for that matter. Of course, bibliocounseling is synonymous with bibliotherapy in this context which, essentially, is the vehicle or means by which the former is effected.

Bibliotherapy has been described as a process of dynamic interaction between the personality of the reader and literature—interaction which may be utilized for personality assessment, adjustment, and growth. Adolescent identification with literary characters offers a means through which counselors may better understand student self-concepts and development.

We would stress at this juncture that counseling is not advising! Counseling is characterized by a permissive atmosphere in which the counselee or client is helped to interpret circumstances surrounding a problem or need; advising carries the connotation of supplying for the pupil ready-made solutions for his problems. In the utilization of bibliocounseling as a tool or technique, the counselor might employ any or all of the following types of assistance to a student:

Provide a good listening ear.

Reflect positive and negative feelings.

Interpret past experiences.

Provide a healthy dose of positive verbal reinforcement.

Provide appropriate social models for imitation.

Recommend desirable books or other reading matter that serve to provide the student with ego-strengthening and self-actualization experiences.

The effective counselor is cognizant of the fact that goals in counseling must be clarified before the means of obtaining them can be determined. Success or failure can only be evaluated if these goals are stated in observable behavioral terms. The goals must be directly related to the problem or problems stated by the counselee. It is the initial responsibility of the counselor to help the counselee clarify these problems and subsequent behavioral goals through such means as discussion of the feelings of the counselee and the facts surrounding specific problem situations. If the defined goals are within the bounds of the counselor's ethical standards as well as those of his profession, then means can be identified to bring about problem solution.

There are at least three sources from which information can be gathered to aid in identifying the counselee's problem. These sources are the diagnostic interview, observation, and psychometric evaluation.

The Diagnostic Interview

Utilizing this approach, the counselor isolates or pins down the problem of the counselee to such specific circumstances that enable the counselor to make better decisions regarding which techniques to use in order to help the counselee attack his behavioral goal.

Observation

Observations of the counselee are usually best when conducted systematically and when more than one observer is involved. Observation reports should indicate the conditions under which the counselee was observed.

Psychometric Evaluation

Interest or personality inventories, or ability scales can be of help to the counselor in understanding what the counselee is really trying to tell him. Results of such instruments can help the counselor as well to determine if he and the counselee are on the right track in identifying the problem.

If the goal of bibliocounseling is to bring about change in counselee behavior—and I submit that this is the goal of counseling—then the counselee's problem must be stated in terms of the specific behavior change that he would like to make.

The entire process of counseling for each counselee can be seen as a sequence of decision-making behaviors. Each decision culminates in a trial run providing new information for the next decision. In this way, the success of counseling can be evaluated quite easily in terms of observable actions of the individual

Major problem areas for which individuals frequently seek assistance from counselors include the following: (1) educational needs and problems; (2) vocational needs and problems; and (3) personal-social needs and problems.

The area of personal-social needs and problems is one in which the counselor needs to exercise a maximum degree of caution. Many parents tend to grumble when they discover that their children are being psychoanalyzed by school counselors. Many counselors are not sufficiently skillful to employ projective and other useful techniques for diagnosis of problems of a highly emotional character. The counselor should be cognizant of the fact that conditions do exist in many schools which tend to create personal-social problems for many pupils. Many of them, fortunately, are not serious emotional difficulties and may usually be prevented from becoming so if the counselor recognizes and meets them while they are still of an incipient nature.

Results of administering the Mooney Problem Check List reveal that adolescents rate quite heavily in positive answers on a list of three hundred problems that press them from day to day. In other words, any given adolescent testifies to the fact, when questioned on the standard form, that he is torn by a multitude of emotional problems.

First of all, there are family problems, such as subterranean discord and open bickering, poverty and drunkenness, and irresponsibility in economics and emotional support. For students confronted with a plethora of such problems, the counselor might recommend or expose to the adolescent the following types of literature: Galbraith, *Cheaper by the Dozen;* Van Druten, *I Remember Mama;* Skinner and Kimbrough, *Our Hearts Were Young and Gay.* In books such as these, we see revealed, if not what family life always is, a glimpse into that which it might be and might become with a little doing on the part of those involved.

Other problems of adolescents are social ones, sometimes magnified by teenagers beyond proper perspective, in the eyes of the adult who sees youth from a safe and remote distance. The teenagers worry about looks in general and about blemishes and rashes in particular — about not enough dates on the one hand and about too many dates on the other. Often they worry about the problems of shyness, which everyone actually possesses and inevitably manifests within a given situation. It is well for teens to learn, through reading, that the great actors and actresses, for example, beginning with the accentuated case of Garbo, are almost without exception shy people in their personal and private lives — and even in their public lives.

The teens, like their elders, worry about the degree of popularity which their lives will accord to them. Because it is merely a date to a prom that is at stake, it is no less imminent to them than are the economics of company production to adults. When youth read the right columns in such journals or periodicals as *Scholastic Magazine* or *Practical English* or *Seventeen* or *Ingenue* and others, they develop for themselves answers and speculations that come to grips with their fears and tensions. When, on the contrary, they read the highly contrived pat answers to be found in the likes of "Dear Abbie," etc., they only collide ultimately with a thudding despair. For there are few really pat answers to emotional problems in life and in literature (for the young in particular).

Thus, when the adolescent ponders on the questions of "Who am I" — Do I exist? — What is truth?" he knows full well that he will not find the answers among his peers or friends — he needs instead to build a reading structure — a background of information — as a foundation against "the gates of emotional confusion that prevail."

The adolescent reader — the one who is learning to read and who has not forever forsaken the things of imagination and romance and word adventure for the world of rent and taxes and installment payments on a cemetery lot — should read in order to see the relationship between himself and the human environment into which he has been cast. This is not to say that the basic purpose of reading should be purely or solely utilitarian — the basic purpose of reading should be and always is one of pleasure.

I repeat that one should read, basically, for one purpose — pleasure. And it is always a pleasure as human beings, one to another, to try to find out who in the world we are, and why.

Since books can provide a source of psychological relief from the various pressures and concerns that stem from things that happen to children, the counselor may use bibliocounseling in one of two ways:

First, he may attempt to solve an individual's actual and existing emotional problems and pressures by bringing him a similar experience vicariously through books. Recognition and understanding of a problem and its solution in literature provides the individual with insights into his own problems and presumably he is then able to take steps toward solving them.

Second, he may use literature for preventing a particular problem from becoming a "hard case." The theory being here that a child is able to make a satisfactory adjustment when a problem eventually arises in his own life because he met one similar to that which was depicted in the literature he read in the past. (This is somewhat analogous to that of inoculation to prevent a contagious disease.)

A word of caution here about the use of books for therapeutic purposes: Bibliocounseling is not an open-o-sesame or a panacea! The process by which the reading of a book affects a child should not be over-simplified—for the child is not quite so plastic a creature that he is easily changed by what he reads. Furthermore, the numerous variations and the factor of unexpectedness which is characteristic of human relationships prevents the automatic categorizing of children as specific psychological types.

Further, books that are used for therapeutic purposes should exemplify good literature and should be used in a manner that is based on sound educational and psychological principles. The characters in the books should be lifelike and complete—yet individual entities.

In recommending a book, knowing the individual is just as important as knowing the book.

Carefully selected and recommended books can play a very constructive role—especially in lives of those who are denied the simple pleasures due them by birthright.

Biographies, of course, are used extensively in bibliocounseling—and rightfully so—in addition to depicting the lives of successful persons, biographies are particularly helpful in showing failures in their true proportion.

The counselor should see to it that the reading of books is accompanied by follow-up activities such as interviews, projective techniques, and sociometric techniques. In this way, significant changes that occur in the individual may be identified and perhaps reinforced as well.

COUNSELORS AND LIBRARIANS WORKING TOGETHER

Reading serves many purposes in the lives of young people. Hence, schools of today, ideally, should place increasing emphasis on effecting closer ties or cooperation between the school guidance department and the school library. In light of the many changes that have occurred in recent years in the world of work and society (and undoubtedly will continue to occur), guidance programs and libraries serving young people must constantly re-examine and reassess their stock of materials and services.

In many schools, one of the functions of the library has logically come to be the implementation and extension of the school's guidance program. In these situations, the school librarian works in close cooperation with the counselor in regard to the school's collection of books, materials, and services. Where there is no guidance department, the librarian may actually undertake as much of a guidance program as time will allow. Further, the library in the school offers constant partnership with the classroom teacher in guiding the personal reading of students.

In some newly built schools of today, counselors are being provided with a library-type facility wherein the school's supply or stock of guidance materials and special reading materials is stored and made available to students. Students are permitted to browse in the facility and to check out materials they desire. Where counselors have no such facility, the librarian should consider the following as desirable cooperative endeavors with counselors in the guidance program: (These actually are examples of activities presently in operation in various schools throughout the country.)

Classes, groups, or individual pupils come to the library for reference and research on career projects.

Library instruction on career materials is given to groups and classes.

Lists, leaflets, or bulletins of occupational information available in the library are prepared for counselors, teachers, and students.

Displays and exhibits of educational and occupational material are set up in the library.

Material is provided for career clinics or career day programs. In some schools, programs are planned in part or entirely by the librarian.

Counselors and teachers are kept informed as to new books and/or materials that are added to the library.

Librarian arranges film programs during each school term for classes in occupations.

Bulletin board material such as book jackets, posters, charts, etc., are made available to teachers and counselors for displays.

Television shows on careers are presented.

Special sections on career and educational information are included in book fairs for seniors.

Obviously, an effectively cooperating team of counselor and librarian can be of inestimable value to a school.

It can truly be stated that one of society's most baffling concerns is better understanding of our greatest resource, man himself. Man loves, hates, reasons, creates his own values, and it is these that make him so completely unique.

Contributions of Research in Bibliotherapy to the Language-Arts Program I

by David H. Russell
and Caroline Shrodes

New ideas and procedures continually spring into action in an enterprise as vital as the school. The creative teacher and the interested group of children or adolescents compose a dynamic situation in which new practices either evolve or erupt. A fresh approach to the study of the community, an original story or play, novel insights in history or science, and other creative developments are always appearing in a good school.

Among the newer interests of some such schools today is the process of bibliotherapy. Teachers and children are increasingly using books, not simply to practice reading skills, but to influence total development. The influence of reading upon personalities is a current concern of an increasing number of librarians and language-arts teachers.

A THEORY OF BIBLIOTHERAPY

Bibliotherapy may be defined as a process of dynamic interaction between the personality of the reader and literature—interaction which may be utilized for personality assessment, adjustment, and growth. This definition suggests that bibliotherapy is not a strange, esoteric activity but one that lies within the province of every teacher of literature in working with every child in a group. "It does not assume that the teacher must be a skilled therapist, nor the child a seriously maladjusted individual needing clinical treatment." Rather, it conveys the idea that all teachers must be aware of the effects of reading upon children and must realize that, "through literature, most children can be helped to solve the developmental problems of adjustment which they face."

David H. Russell and Caroline Shrodes, "Contributions of Research in Bibliotherapy to the Language-Arts Program," *School Review* 58:335-342 (September 1950).

Lest, by this definition, bibliotherapy be made to seem too commonplace, it may be well to point out that the process is not involved every time a child or adolescent has a book in his hand. Many literature periods are still of the sort Henry Seidel Canby calls "cross-word-puzzle scholarship," with emphasis upon literary details rather than upon enjoyment and emotional response to a work of art. Even in the latter approach to literature, thoughtful teachers of the language arts are no longer sure that a particular selection or poem is a "good" one for all members of a class. They are realizing that the piece of literature which may have a profound effect on one child leaves another utterly unmoved. They are becoming aware that every story, poem, or selection is read by a specific individual who brings to it his own complex perceptions and reactions, based on his particular needs. The book that illustrates courage to one child may give hints on home decoration to another; the story that suddenly gives an adolescent insight into his own family situation may be utterly boring to his neighbor in the class. Interaction between the work of literature and the individual may or may not take place.

If there is a genuine therapeutic effect from reading, it may be explained theoretically in terms of *identification, catharsis,* and *insight,* terms originating in psychoanalytic literature but now more widely accepted by psychologists. In such terms, bibliotherapy becomes a process of identifying with another character or group so that feelings are released and the individual develops a greater awareness of his own motivations and rationalizations for his behavior.

Identification is the real or imagined affiliation of one's self (or sometimes a parent or a friend) with a character or group in the story read. It may be facilitated by various conditions.[54] It may augment self-esteem if the character is admired or increase feelings of belonging by reducing the sense of difference from others. It may increase understanding of the parent or friend, be productive of a more realistic attitude toward his limitations or strengths, and even reduce a sense of guilt which was a product of earlier difficulties with that parent or friend.

Thus, identification usually involves *catharsis.* The fact that the reader feels he is the character read about means that he shares the character's motivations and conflicts and experiences vicariously the character's emotions. As the reader puts himself in the place of others, he comes to understand the needs and aspirations of these others—and of himself. Reading may therefore provide a release of tension through symbolic gratification of socially unacceptable urges or substitute gratification of socially approved motives.

Finally, when the self-recognition in identification is borne out in reality, the identification represents *insight*—seeing one's self in the behavior of the character and thereby achieving an awareness of one's own motivations and needs. If his adjustments to life situations are maladaptive, the individual's recognition of himself in the character may help in breaking certain habits. On the other hand, if the character appears to work out a satisfactory solution to his problem, opportunity is provided for the reader to incorporate some of the character's behavior in his own methods of adjustment to a similar problem.

Identification does not always lead to insight, for it may consist simply in imputing one's own motives to others, in reading one's own interpretation into the behavior of the fictional character. One form of such identification is to seek a scapegoat and vent upon the chosen character a strong emotion felt in an earlier affective experience. In general, however, the close inter-relationships and interaction of identification, catharsis, and insight are apparent. Implicit in this discussion are other mechanisms of behavior such as projection, rationalization, repression, autism,[46] and compensation—all of which influence the degree and nature of any therapeutic process which may occur.

This summary of a theory of bibliotherapy is put largely in psychoanalytic terms. Although research in psychology and medicine has not yet identified all their implications, they are terms which have been incorporated into the work of many clinics and the writing of many psychologists.[60] At present they seem to give the best theoretical explanation of the process of bibliotherapy. As Shrodes[62] has pointed out, dynamic psychology, field theory, and the newer emphasis upon autism in perception and cognition, as well as psychoanalytic theory, may be shown to have congruent points of view in explaining the diagnostic and the adjustment values of bibliotherapy. The eclectic nature of the theory is further illustrated in some of the possible values of bibliotherapy stated in the literature on the subject.

VALUES OF BIBLIOTHERAPY

Divergent attitudes toward the values of reading include Plato's injunction that myths are not good for the morals of the young, Francis Bacon's assertion that "reading maketh a full man," and Adler's conviction that reading improves thinking.[1] In addition to the recreational and informational values usually attributed to reading, a number of therapeutic values have been stated. As might be expected, some of the first of these statements were medical. In his book *Fear,* Oliver says, "The right kind of book may be applied to a mental illness just as a definite drug is applied to some bodily need."[47] Menninger states:

> "The whole matter of bibliotherapy, of the relief of suffering by the psychological processes induced by reading, is a field in which we have little scientific knowledge. But our intuition and our experience tell us that books may indeed "minister to a mind diseased" and come to the aid of the doctor and even precede him."[43]

Other writers have mentioned more specific values of bibliotherapy. Although often stated from the clinical point of view, many of these have implications for the school's language-arts program. Appel[5] believes bibliotherapy can help the individual in six ways. It can help him (1) to acquire information and knowledge about the psychology and physiology of human behavior; (2) to live up to the injunction, "Know thyself"; (3) to become more extraverted and find interest in something outside himself; (4) to effect a controlled release of unconscious difficulties; (5) to use the opportunity for identification and compensation; and (6) to clarify difficulties and to acquire insight into his own behavior.

Bryan[11] believes that bibliotherapy can help develop maturity and nourish and sustain mental health. She states such specific values as giving the person the feeling that he is not the first to encounter the problem he is facing; permitting the reader to see that there is more than one solution to his problem or more than one choice to be made; helping the reader to see the basic motivation of people involved in situations such as his own; helping the reader to see values in experience in human, rather than material, terms; providing facts needed in solving a problem; and encouraging the reader to plan and execute a constructive course of action.

In addition to some of the points made above, Gottschalk[26] believes that reading may have therapeutic values by stimulating the patient to discuss problems which he ordinarily avoids because of fear, shame, or guilt; by helping the patient to analyze and synthesize further his attitudes and behavior patterns; by providing vicarious life experiences without exposing the person to the real dangers of actual experience; by reinforcing, through precept and example, acceptable social behavior and inhibiting infantile patterns of behavior; by stimulating the imagination; and by enlarging the individual's sphere of interests.

Smith and Twyeffort[66] regard the development of insight as the crucial factor in bibliotherapy. In addition to points made above, they believe reading may be a valuable adjunct to treatment in helping the patient achieve insight, defined as an emotional as well as an intellectual appreciation of the causes of his difficulties; may assist toward a better understanding of the manifold function of personality, especially the role of the emotions and the nature of complexes; may aid the patient in verbalizing and externalizing his problems; may help dispel a sense of isolation; may show how persons with the same personal liabilities tackled apparent failure with some success; may facilitate frank stock-taking of personal assets and liabilities; and may begin deeper changes in a person who is inclined to respond at a superficial level.

In an earlier book[51] and a recent chapter[50] Rosenblatt analyzes the contributions of imaginative literature less in medical terms and more in relation to the work of the teacher. She believes that prolonged contact with personalities in books may have such social effects as (1) leading to increased social sensitivity, enabling the reader to put himself in another's place; (2) developing the habit of interpreting the interactions of temperament upon temperament; (3) enabling one to feel the needs, sufferings, and aspirations of other people; (4) helping an individual to assimilate the cultural pattern by acquainting him with the attitudes and expectancies of his group; and (5) releasing the adolescent from provincialism by extending awareness beyond his own family, community, and national background. In addition, Rosenblatt gives a number of personal values in bibliotherapy, such as those stated by other authors. She further recognizes the preventive values of literature. She believes that literature may prevent the growth of neurotic tendencies through vicarious participation in other lives and that the guilt-possessed or rebellious adolescent may understand himself better even if his conduct is not prized in his environment. She states: "Frequently literature is the only means by which he can discover that his own inner life reflects a common experience of others in his society."[51]

These possible values of bibliotherapy help to extend the concept of the process. They indicate some of the newer possible uses of literature in the clinic or classroom with a group or an individual. Most of the writers quoted agree that bibliotherapy provides opportunity for catharsis and greater insight into one's own motivation and the behavior of others. They agree that in bibliotherapy some sort of integration of intellectual perception and emotional drive takes place.

An analysis of the formal research which illustrates in specific situations the theoretical values of bibliotherapy given in this article and a discussion of bibliotherapy in the schools will be presented in an article to follow.

(Bibliography follows next article.)

Contributions of Research in Bibliotherapy to the Language-Arts Program II

by David H. Russell
and Caroline Shrodes

A theory of bibliotherapy and its possible values and a bibliography of writings on the subject were presented in the first part of this article, which appeared in last month's issue of the *School Review*. Part II presents a digest of the research on bibliotherapy and suggests implications for practice and further research.

RESEARCH AND PROFESSIONAL LITERATURE ON BIBLIOTHERAPY

The scanty literature available on bibliotherapy gives theories of the process and leads for further research, but it contains few definitive answers for teachers, librarians, psychologists, and psychiatrists. Many of the articles have been written for and by librarians and others working with patients in general and mental hospitals, and these efforts are largely descriptive rather than experimental. In educational literature, studies of the relationships between reading difficulties and personality maladjustments have been summarized by Gates,[24] by Wilking,[73] and by Russell.[52] Russell points out that evidence of the positive effects of reading is largely lacking. Most of the writing summarized below deals with hypotheses about the process of bibliotherapy. A few illustrations of the use of bibliotherapy in case-study approaches to research in medical institutions, in libraries, and in schools can be given.

General summaries of research in bibliotherapy.—These studies are limited in scope and content. In a pioneer volume in 1923 Jones[30] discussed uses of books in hospital libraries and gave classified reading lists. Bryan later wrote a series of three articles[10, 11, 12] which developed a theory of bibliotherapy and gave steps needed to make it a

David H. Russell and Caroline Shrodes, "Contributions of Research in Bibliotherapy to the Language-Arts Program," *School Review* 58:411-420 (October 1950).

more exact science. While most writers use the term with reference to mental-hygiene literature and to books of a didactic nature concerned with adjustment, personality, child-rearing, and similar topics, Bryan includes the whole range of literature—novels, plays, poetry, reference, and scientific books—in the materials to be used in bibliotherapy. Schneck[58] gave one of the most complete lists of bibliographies for use in bibliotherapy, but he confined his account largely to materials for use in general hospitals and with neuropsychiatric patients. Other lists have been developed by Appel,[5] the Elliotts,[21] and Levine.[34] Tyson[69] reviewed some of the recent writing on bibliotherapy before analyzing the content of mental-hygiene textbooks, popular books, and a popular journal on personal adjustment. Shrodes[62] listed 113 items in her study developing a theory of bibliotherapy and applying it in case studies of college students.

General descriptions.—A number of studies related more or less closely to the field of bibliotherapy are also available. A pioneer investigation by Downey[18] attempted to divide readers into three main categories: persons who are detached, impersonal *spectators* as they read; persons who are *participants* as they read, becoming deeply involved in the emotions and situations of the story; and persons who become emotionally involved but *philosophers* about the story because their projections are not egocentric so much as mature reactions to the story.

In a summary of the first years of development of projective methods of studying personality, Sargent[56] includes some references on drama, story-telling, and language in relation to personality which have implications for bibliotherapy. Although not strictly research, Rosenblatt's exploratory work[51] contains many ideas fundamental to a theory of bibliotherapy. Waples and Others[71] have also studied the influences of reading upon people from a somewhat different point of view from the one expressed in the first part of this discussion. Gray[27] has summarized thirty studies dealing with the effects of reading on information and beliefs, attitudes and morale, public opinion, voting, crime, and antisocial behavior. Carlsen,[14] in a study of the influence of reading upon attitudes, found that white adolescents at the eleventh-grade level vary in their reactions to stories about Negroes in terms of their previous attitudes to Negroes. In a study somewhat more closely related to the present theme, Loban[36] reviews some of the previous work in bibliotherapy as background for his comparison of the responses to ten literary selections made by two groups of adolescents who were rated as extremely high and low in their capacity for sympathy. His study emphasizes the need of adolescents for a teacher's help in discussing the significant causes underlying behavior and events in a story.

Medical uses.—Medical explorations (rather than experiments) in bibliotherapy seem to be the most numerous group described in the literature. Schneck[57] has described the bibliotherapy project which has been operating at the Menninger Foundation in Topeka, Kansas, for several years. Earlier, Menninger[43] described briefly a few examples of bibliotherapy, and Schneck[59] has reported on two other cases from this clinic. Some early reports[16] on the use of bibliotherapy in United States Veterans Hospitals are available, and more information should be forthcoming from this source. Bradley and Bosquet[9] advised physicians on the use of books for children, suggested four therapeutic uses of literature, and attached a short bibliography of useful stories and books.

As a result of experience in using mental-hygiene literature, rather than imaginative literature, Gottschalk[26] believes that patients with mild psychoneurotic disturbances are more likely to be helped by supervised reading than are severely disturbed or psychotic patients. Gagnon[23] disagrees with Gottschalk and emphasizes the danger in furnishing early and mild cases of schizophrenia with books which might facilitate their flights from reality. However, he states that reading may have sedative effects on persons in moderate manic or excitable states. Smith and Twyeffort[66] believe that many maladjustments are due to ignorance or inaccurate knowledge and, therefore, recommend books with mental-hygiene content. Moore[45] describes work with adolescents. After giving early examples of bibliotherapy in hospitals and in the Delaware Human Relations classes, he describes two cases in which "the data . . . presented give us a glimpse of a technique of great, therapeutic importance."[45]

A number of the reports cited are of interest to librarians. These include the writings of Jones,[30] of Bryan[10, 11, 12] and of Schneck,[57, 59] mentioned above, and another article in which Quint[49] points out the values of reading in a total program of maintaining contact with reality. Although not research, librarians may be interested in anthologies, such as those of Shrodes, Van Gundy, and Husband[63] and of Strode,[68] which are collected for the purpose of giving psychological and sociological insights through literature. A few studies of the use of the library to influence specific attitudes are available, such as Jackson's investigation[29] of the attitudes of white children in Atlanta, Georgia, toward Negro children before and after reading material dealing with Negro children.

Educational Applications Studies dealing with the positive use of literature in school situations for therapy are likewise meager, although a beginning in experimentation is evident. In addition to Loban's work,[36] an early study by Lind[35] gives reports obtained through interview and written document of what thirty adults thought the four main values of reading were to them as children. Russell's more recent study[54] of 680 teachers' memories of books read as children found a variety of remembered effects, including identification with characters, enjoyment of humor and fantasy, enrichment of everyday experiences, imitation of activities as in dramatic play, and added knowledge of facts.

Articles by Sister Mary Agnes[40, 41] and the investigation by Sister Lorang[37] developed some hypotheses which require further investigation. Sister Mary Agnes found some improvement in the adjustments of four out of five children in the upper elementary grades after the reading of four or five books, although only one of the five children saw any connection between his own problems and those of the characters in the books. Sister Lorang used a questionnaire to get the opinions of 2,308 high-school students, in eight schools, about specific books and magazines that they had read and the effects of this reading on them. Fifty-three percent of the group said they had tried to act like a character in a book and 21 per cent like a character in a magazine.

A publication by Kircher,[32] influenced by the work of Moore,[45] emphasizes the dynamic character of the reading process and its help in emotional adjustment. Unlike some other writers, Kircher believes literature may produce a delayed response, that solutions contained in it may be utilized a considerable time after the reading. She also gives an annotated bibliography of children's stories and adds the principles or solutions which they may contain for children reading them.

Smith[67] reviewed some of the research on the personal and social influences of reading and reported a study in which teachers asked 502 children in Grades IV through VIII if they remembered any book, story, or poem which had changed their thinking in any way. About 60 per cent of the group reported changes in attitude, but only 9 per cent changes in behavior as a result of reading; 30 per cent told of changes in thinking as a result of new or enlarged concepts obtained through reading.

Another study of a different sort, based on the hypothesis that reading has direct influence on attitudes and adjustments of children, is that of Child and Others[15] who analyzed a group of third-grade textbooks in reading for the social ideas and stereotypes contained in them. The study offers no proof that children are affected by reading such textbooks, but it is useful in pointing out the middle-class backgrounds of the books and in listing some of the ideas implied which teachers often take for granted without examining them critically. Using a somewhat similar method, Wenzel[72] applied the ideas of Rosenblatt[51] and of Sample[55] in analyzing certain children's stories. The illustrations are useful examples of how a teacher, a librarian, or small groups may analyze fictional materials to find ideas implicit in them which may be more or less unconsciously absorbed into children's attitudes.

The values of literature in inducting the child into his culture have been investigated by the Shaftels,[61] who made an exploratory study of the use of problem stories based upon the developmental tasks of middle childhood. After reading and discussing the stories, the children were given opportunity to act out their solutions. Other references to psychodrama are given in the summary by Sargent.[56] The use of reading in conjunction with psychodrama and sociodrama to arrive at the solution of children's problems would seem to be a fruitful lead for further research and practice.

Although not conducted in the school situation, procedures used by Panken[48] seemed to show the usefulness of bibliotherapy with a group of juvenile delinquents for whom psychotherapy was unavailable. In children's letters to the judge—letters answered by him personally—there was some evidence that carefully selected books may stimulate healthy identifications, alter antisocial attitudes, and ameliorate the effects of a bad environment.

Not all the writing on bibliotherapy is as positive about its benefits as are the studies mentioned above. For example, Goldsmith[25] found that children are not usually able to draw inferences from fables. Therefore, the belief that fables are concrete examples of abstract truths, useful in character education, may be seriously questioned. Russell[53] suggests that literature can be expected to influence adjustments only if the children are able to read easily and well, if wide varieties of suitable materials are available, if a permissive reading environment exists, and if school and community experiences reinforce the reading. The importance of a permissive environment and of an opportunity to manipulate the elements of a reading situation toward several possible interpretations or reconstructions is suggested by Husband.[28] He also states:

> In the degree that a reading situation exerts a compulsion toward preciseness in interpretation, it tends to create a negative response, which diminishes with the progressive development of reading maturity or sophistication.[28]

In a study of the effects of reading a novel on a tenth-grade group, Meckel[42] is cautious of expecting positive effects automatically to follow reading. He states that his findings do not justify concluding that a pupil having tensions and anxieties may be given a novel which deals with the same tensions and anxieties and expecting therapeutic results to follow automatically. On the contrary, the data suggest that these anxieties, if they are serious, may tend to repress and to block the desired response to the very situations and ideas having potential therapeutic value.

Auerbach makes somewhat the same point in connection with mental-hygiene literature:

> Each book is read . . . by a specific individual who brings to the book he is reading his own complex reactions and biases, based on his particular needs. . . .
>
> The more mature the reader is, the more he will pick what he needs or distort what he reads to fit his emotional needs.[7]

The literature on bibliotherapy contains both research evidence and opinion which should act as a brake on undue claims for the process. Apparently, there is no guaranty that a particular piece of literature will influence a certain child or adolescent or that an influence, if it exists, will operate in the direction desired.

IMPLICATIONS FOR RESEARCH AND PRACTICE

Need for validation.—The positive values claimed for biblio-therapy in certain studies and the reservations about it raised in others point clearly to the necessity of validating the procedure experimentally. From at least the days of the Greeks, great teachers have always used literature in attempts to influence their pupils' attitudes and ideals. Nearly all the studies cited above claim some influence on the adjustments of the persons who have read prescribed books or stories, but these claims have not always been validated by study of the later behavior of the patient or pupil. One attempt to validate the process has been made by Tyson[69] who sought the opinions of authors, analysts, and college undergraduates regarding the value of biblio-therapy. Six of the eight psychoanalysts favored it as an adjunct to individual treatment. There was a general consensus that reading has value as a source of information and as reassurance for persons with mild personality disorders. Obviously, much more work in the validation of the process of bibliotherapy is needed.

Extension into schools.—Besides lack of validation, another limitation evident in the literature is the paucity of work with the average or the mildly disturbed person outside the clinic or hospital. Several writers suggest that bibliotherapy is more likely to be successful with younger people; several, that it is most applicable in cases of only mild disturbance. The implications for schools and colleges, with their facilities for recommending books and discussing them in group guidance situations, would seem to be fairly clear. In this practice, limitations, such as reading ability of pupils and home and community influences, must also be recognized. But work so far done in the field indicates the possibility that literature can be used most effectively not in institutions for the mentally ill but in schools where it is possible to influence the adjustment of the so-called "normal" child or youth.

Types of reading.—A third implication for research and practice concerns the values of imaginative versus didactic and factual literature. A number of analysts cited above prescribe factual books for their patients and, in truth, believe that these are best for the individual who needs more contact with reality. On the other hand, psychiatrists and psychologists admit that great artists are penetrating interpreters of the human personality. Since the great writer has the power to understand, describe, and project to the reader some phase of personality, he should be enlisted as an ally in diagnosis and therapy. There are some suggestions that admonitory, prescriptive reading is largely an intellectual exercise whereas the identification, projection, and other mechanisms involved in reading imaginative literature may incorporate into the reading situation the emotional behavior associated with most maladjustment. A further possibility is that both factual and fictional materials are useful, depending upon the particular needs of the individual, and, therefore, that the teacher's or librarian's task is to find some balance between these types of material.

Use of literature in appraising personality.—A fourth implication for research concerns the values of literature in assessment of personality or diagnosis of personality difficulties. Some skillful language-arts teachers study a pupil's reading interests. If they find that these deviate widely from the norm of the group in which the child or adolescent is found, they gain information about that pupil. The current interest in projective techniques suggests that research might go much further in using reactions to pieces of literature as one means of studying personality. If individual perception of ink blots or vague pictures can give such clues, reactions to selections from literature would seem to be a fruitful source of study of personality.

Bibliotherapy in clinical treatment.—A fifth implication for research concerns the use of bibliotherapy in clinical situations. There is some evidence that bibliotherapy makes for economy of time and effort in that an individual may be reading and thinking about his problems when he is away from the clinic or therapist. In view of present shortages of skilled clinical workers and the very recent establishment of such services by some school systems, research on bibliotherapy as a facilitation of treatment should be undertaken.

Relations between reading materials and the reader.—A final implication for research is of especial concern to school people. Bibliotherapy may be regarded as only one phase of a larger-scale study of relationships between reading materials and the reader. In the past, literature has been studied in terms of its own structure and in terms of the person producing it. The time is long overdue for comprehensive studies of the effects of literature upon the reader. In such studies, bibliotherapy will have an important place because certain characteristics and effects may be observed more easily in the somewhat extreme cases involved in bibliotherapy. Research on bibliotherapy should, therefore, prove fruitful of hypotheses to be tested with children and adolescents in ordinary classroom situations.

SUGGESTIONS FOR LIBRARIANS AND TEACHERS

In addition to the six implications for research, a number of suggestions arising out of the literature concern more directly the work of librarians and language-arts teachers.

Matching reading with the difficulty.—One problem is: What kind of story for what kind of difficulty? Should the adolescent with parent-child problems be advised to read a story of family conflict, or must he be approached more indirectly? Will the quiet, recessive boy profit by reading about a person like himself or an extroverted, popular adolescent? In one clinic Menninger[43] finds it impractical to prescribe books on the basis of one diagnostic category, of etiological factors, or of type of personality. Rather, the individual's present psychological status, his emotional state, the amount of his withdrawal from reality, and his ability to profit from reading are taken into account.

The answer for teachers or librarians, then, is not clear cut. The recommendation of pleasant, cheerful books instead of stories dealing with emotionally disturbed characters, morbid themes, or unhappy endings may seem to be a good beginning for a child or youth who is himself unhappy and disturbed, but at some later time, perhaps, he will need to read stories which deal more directly with his problem. Perhaps the child or adolescent who has already built fairly satisfactory psychological defenses should not be forced to tear these down because of a more direct discussion of his problems in literature. The teacher or librarian can, at best, work on an experimental basis, trying different sorts of stories and giving opportunities for discussing and restructuring these in the group situation, with perhaps deeper analysis in individual interviews.

Involvement of entire language-arts program. — This suggestion merges into the one given by Husband,[28] the Shaftels,[61] and others that children and youth need opportunities to discuss a character, to disagree with a solution, to dramatize or act out their own solutions. Thus, not only the literature period but the whole language-arts program is involved. The modern teacher uses the child's or adolescent's problems as one source of motivation for writing a personal letter or history for the teacher, not something shared with the whole group. Through this personal writing, the teacher's and pupil's insight into a problem may be increased. The teacher may become less concerned with split infinitives and more concerned with split personality; unity and coherence in the paragraph may become subordinated to unity and coherence of the self.

The teaching of reading. — There are also implications from bibliotherapy for the teaching of reading. A child or adolescent must be able to read rather easily the material presented to him if identification and positive emotional response are to develop, but the teaching of reading cannot stop at accurate word recognition or even at comprehension. Particularly in the upper-elementary and the secondary-school grades, the dynamic nature of the reading of literature must be considered by the teacher. The selective nature of perception and cognition, the fact that even young children may discover in reading what they want to discover needs further emphasis in the whole program of reading instruction. Crossen,[17] for example, has shown that a group of ninth- and tenth-grade pupils unfavorable to the Negro make lower scores on a critical reading test based on materials about Negroes than a similar group with indifferent (neither favorable nor unfavorable) attitudes toward the Negro.

The teaching of reading, at least beyond the initial learning stages, must be directed not only toward accuracy and objectivity but also toward positive emotional values. Children and adolescents need many opportunities to use their reading in creative ways for enrichment of their experience and better understanding of themselves and others.

Cautions for teachers. — A few writers and speakers have suggested recently that the language-arts teacher should not attempt bibliotherapy, that it is too difficult and dangerous a process to be tried out by untrained persons. The writers of this article have some sympathy for this point of view. They are aware that few teachers are trained therapists. They are equally aware, however, that most psychologists and psychotherapists have no final answers to problems of influencing human adjustment, that experimentation is needed in attempting to meet personal needs of children and adolescents as well as adults. It seems that bibliotherapy offers one such experimental approach, particularly when correlated with other procedures attempting to improve insight and adjustment. These two articles have emphasized, furthermore, the planned use of literature with the so-called "normal" child, the individual whose problems and tensions are the usual developmental ones rather than deep-seated conflicts. In such cases the dangers of using emotionally charged literature should be less.

But even to attempt bibliotherapy on this level, the teacher must have certain resources. In addition to those mentioned in previous statements, he must know a wide range of books — books which illustrate the ideas to be presented to the child or adolescent. Wide reading of stories for youth should be supplemented by knowledge of books about juvenile literature, such as Eaton's *Reading with Children,*[20] Duff's *Bequest of Wings,*[19] Arbuthnot's *Children and Books,*[6] Smith's chapter on "Guiding Individual Reading,"[64] and even Lenrow's *Reader's Guide to Prose Fiction.*[33] Teachers in both elementary and secondary schools will find particularly helpful the publications *Literature for Human Understanding*[3] and *Reading Ladders for Human Relations.*[4] A group of teachers may build similar lists to fit the needs and problems of youth in a particular community.

In addition to knowing books, the teacher must know the child or adolescent. He must be aware of the usual characteristics of children of the age level with which he is working and recognize any deviations from the usual shown by an individual or group. He will profit by knowing something of the individual's abilities and interests; by knowing the pattern of the child's reading interests in relation to the rest of his group; by having some personal reports from the pupil about his family, his activities, and his ambitions; by observing his behavior in classroom, in informal groups, or on the playground. As time and energy permit, the teacher must have informal interviews with the pupil, both before and after bibliotherapy is begun. In beginning the process, he will know enough about the child or adolescent to suggest a story in which identification is often pleasant and easy.

This knowledge of books, plus knowledge of children or adolescents, puts such a burden on the teacher that once again the process of bibliotherapy seems impossibly difficult. But what language-arts teacher can teach without knowing something about books and about children? The knowledge and understanding are there for any good teacher; it is simply a case of directing them along a channel leading to therapy through literature. Furthermore, in most schools the sole responsibility does not rest upon the teacher. The best approach to bibliotherapy is often a co-operative approach involving the teacher, the librarian, the school counselor or psychologist, and others who know the child well. An occasional case conference of such persons to discuss the individual and suggest reading and other therapeutic measures is desirable.

Finally, bibliotherapy may be conceived as an attempt to unite practices in education, in clinical work, and in mental hygiene. Teachers of the language arts and of psychology may use bibliotherapy to illustrate ideas common to both fields. Clinical workers may use it with economy for diagnosis, prognosis, and therapy. Mental-hygiene experts may include it in an expanding program of positive mental health and prevention of mental disorders. Research and practice are urgently needed in schools and other institutions if this new technique for human welfare is to become generally available.

BIBLIOGRAPHY

1. Mortimer Adler, *How To Read a Book* (New York: Simon & Schuster, 1940).
2. Franz Alexander and Thomas M. French, *Psychoanalytic Therapy* (New York: Ronald Press, 1946).
3. American Council on Education, Committee on Intergroup Education. *Literature for Human Understanding* (Washington: American Council on Education, 1948).
4. American Council on Education, Committee on Intergroup Education. *Reading Ladders for Human Relations* (Washington: American Council on Education, 1949, revised).
5. Kenneth E. Appel, "Psychiatric Therapy," *Personality and the Behavior Disorders*, II. Edited by J. McV. Hunt (New York: Ronald Press, 1944), pp. 1107-63.
6. May Hill Arbuthnot, *Children and Books* (Chicago: Scott, Foresman & Co., 1947).
7. Aline B. Auerbach, "Can Mental Hygiene Books Improve Mental Health?" *Child Study*, XXVI (Spring, 1949), 39-40.
8. Phyllis Blanchard, "Adolescent Experience in Relation to Personality and Behavior," *Personality and the Behavior Disorders*, II. Edited by J. McV. Hunt (New York: Ronald Press, 1944), pp. 691-713.
9. Charles Bradley and E. S. Bosquet, "Uses of Books for Psycho-

therapy with Children," *American Journal of Orthopsychiatry,* VI (January, 1936), 23-31.

10. Alice I. Bryan, "The Psychology of the Reader," *Library Journal,* LXIV (January, 1930), 7-12.

11. Alice I. Bryan, "Personality Adjustment through Reading," *Library Journal,* LXIV (August, 1939), 573-76.

12. Alice I. Bryan, "Can There Be a Science of Bibliotherapy?" *Library Journal,* LXIV (October, 1939), 773-76.

13. Dwight Burton, "Books To Meet Students' Personal Needs," *English Journal,* XXXVI (November, 1947), 469-73.

14. George R. Carlsen, "A Study of the Effect of Reading Literature about the Negro on the Racial Attitudes of a Group of Eleventh-Grade Students in Northern Schools." Unpublished Doctor's dissertation, University of Minnesota (1948).

15. Irvin L. Child, Elmer H. Potter and Estelle M. Levine, *Children's Textbooks and Personality Development: An Exploration in the Social Psychology of Education.* Psychological Monographs, Vol. LX, No. 3 (Evanston, Illinois: American Psychological Association, Northwestern University, 1946).

16. Elizabeth Creglow, "Therapeutic Value of Properly Selected Reading Matter," *U.S. Veterans Administration Medical Bulletin,* VII (November, 1931), 1086-89.

17. Helen J. Crossen, "Effects of the Attitudes of the Reader upon Critical Reading Ability," *Journal of Educational Research,* XLII (December, 1948), 289-98.

18. June E. Downey, "Literary Self-projection," *Psychological Review,* XIX (July, 1912), 299-311.

19. Annis Duff, *Bequests of Wings.* (New York: Viking Press, 1944).

20. Anne Thaxter Eaton, *Reading with Children* (New York: Viking Press, 1940).

21. H. S. Elliott and G. L. Elliott, *Solving Personal Problems* (New York: Henry Holt & Co., Inc., 1936).

22. Lawrence K. Frank, *Projective Methods* (Springfield, Illinois: Charles C. Thomas, 1948).

23. Salomon Gagnon, "Is Reading Therapy?" *Diseases of the Nervous System,* III (July, 1942), 206-12.

24. Arthur I. Gates, "The Role of Personality Maladjustment in Reading Disability," *Pedagogical Seminary and Journal of Genetic Psychology,* LIX (September, 1941), 77-83.

25. Sadie Goldsmith, "The Fable as a Medium for Character Education," *Elementary English Review,* XVI (October, 1939), 223-25, 228.

26. Louis A. Gottschalk, "Bibliotherapy as an Adjuvant in Psychotherapy," *American Journal of Psychiatry*, CIV (April, 1948), 632-37.

27. William S. Gray, "The Social Effects of Reading," *School Review*, LV (May, 1947), 269-77.

28. John D. Husband, "A Technique for the Evaluation of Growth in Certain Affective Phases of Reading among High School Pupils," *Journal of Educational Research*, XXXIX (December, 1945), 265-71.

29. Evalene P. Jackson, "Effects of Reading upon Attitudes toward the Negro Race," *Library Quarterly*, XIV (January, 1944), 47-54.

30. E. Kathleen Jones, ed. *The Hospital Library* (Chicago: American Library Association, 1923).

31. F. W. Kaufman and W. S. Taylor, "Literature as Adjustment," *Journal of Abnormal and Social Psychology*, XXXI (July, 1936), 229-34.

32. Clara J. Kircher, *Character Formation through Books: A Bibliography* (Washington: Catholic University of America Press, 1945).

33. Elbert Lenrow for the Commission on Secondary School Curriculum, Progressive Education Association. *Reader's Guide to Prose Fiction* (New York: D. Appleton—Century Co., Inc., 1940).

34. Maurice Levine, *Psychotherapy in Medical Practice* (New York: Macmillan Co., 1942).

35. Katherine Niles Lind, "The Social Psychology of Children's Reading," *American Journal of Sociology*, XLI (January, 1936), 451-469.

36. Walter Loban, "Adolescents of Varying Sensitivity and Their Responses to Literature Intended to Evoke Sympathy." Unpublished Doctor's dissertation, University of Minnesota (1949).

37. Sister Mary Corde Lorang, *The Effect of Reading upon Moral Conduct and Emotional Experience.* Studies in Psychology and Psychiatry, Vol. VI, No. 5 (Washington: Catholic University of America Press, 1945).

38. Robert L. McCaul, "The Effect of Attitudes on Reading Interpretation," *Journal of Educational Research*, XXXVII (February, 1944), 451-57.

39. Donald W. MacKinnon, "Psychodiagnosis in Clinical Practice and Personality Theory," *Journal of Abnormal and Social Psychology*, XLIV (January, 1949), 7-13.

40. Sister Mary Agnes, "Social Values in Children's Poetry," *Elementary English Review*, XXII (April, 1945), 133-38.

41. Sister Mary Agnes, "Bibliotherapy for Socially Maladjusted Children," *Catholic Education Review*, XLIV (January, 1946), 8-16.

42. Henry C. Meckel, "An Exploratory Study of Responses of Adolescent Pupils to Situations in a Novel." Unpublished Doctor's dissertation, University of Chicago (1946).

43. Karl A. Menninger, *Human Mind* (New York: Alfred A. Knopf, Inc., 1937), p. ix.

44. Thomas V. Moore, "Bibliotherapy in Psychiatric Practice," *Current Therapies of Personality Disorders*, Edited by Bernard Glueck (New York: Grune & Stratton, Inc., 1946), pp. 132-53.

45. Thomas V. Moore, *The Nature and Treatment of Mental Disorders* (New York: Grune & Stratton, Inc., 1943), p. 232.

46. Gardner Murphy, *Personality* (New York: Harper & Bros., 1947).

47. John R. Oliver, *Fear* (New York: Macmillian Co., 1928), p. 291.

48. Jacob Panken, "Psychotherapeutic Value of Books in the Treatment and Prevention of Juvenile Delinquency," *American Journal of Psychotherapy*, I (January, 1947), 71-86.

49. Mary D. Quint, "The Mental-Hospital Library," *Mental Hygiene*, XXVIII (April, 1944), 263-72.

50. Louise M. Rosenblatt, "The Enriching Values of Reading," *Reading in an Age of Mass Communication*, Edited by William S. Gray (New York: Appleton-Century-Crofts, Inc., 1949), pp. 19-38.

51. Louise M. Rosenblatt, *Literature as Exploration* (New York: D. Appleton—Century Co., Inc., 1938).

52. David H. Russell, "Reading Disabilities and Mental Health: A Review of Research," *Understanding the Child*, XVI (January, 1947), 24-32.

53. David H. Russell, "Reading Success and Personality Development," *Elementary English*, XXV (February, 1948), 73-82.

54. David H. Russell, "Identification through Literature," *Childhood Education*, XXV (May, 1949), 397-401.

55. Hazel Sample, *Pitfalls for Readers of Fiction* (Chicago: National Council of Teachers of English, 1940).

56. Helen Sargent, "Projective Methods: Their Origins, Theory and Application in Personality Research," *Psychological Bulletin*, XLII (May, 1945), 257-93.

57. Jerome M. Schneck, "Studies in Bibliotherapy in a Neuropsychiatric Hospital," *Occupational Therapy and Rehabilitation*, XXIII (December, 1944), 316-23.

58. Jerome M. Schneck, "Bibliotherapy and Hospital Library Activities for Neuropsychiatric Patients," *Psychiatry*, VIII (February, 1945), 207-28.

59. Jerome M. Schneck, "Bibliotherapy for Neuropsychiatric Pa-

tients: Report on Two Cases," *Bulletin of the Menninger Clinic,* X (January, 1946), 18-25.

60. Robert R. Sears, *Survey of Objective Studies of Psychoanalytic Concepts.* Social Science Research Council Bulletin No. 51 (New York: Social Science Research Council, 1943).

61. George Shaftel and Fannie R. Shaftel, "Report on the Use of a 'Practice Action Level' in the Stanford University Project for American Ideals," *Sociatry,* I (December, 1947), 57-245; II (March, 1948), 65-253.

62. Caroline Shrodes, "Bibliotherapy: A Theoretical and Clinical-Experimental Study." Unpublished Doctor's dissertation, University of California at Berkeley (1949).

63. Caroline Shrodes, Justine Van Gundy and R. W. Husband, *Psychology through Literature: An Anthology* (New York: Oxford University Press, 1943).

64. Dora V. Smith, "Guiding Individual Reading," *Reading in the High School and College,* pp. 180-205. Forty-seventh Yearbook of the National Society for the Study of Education, Part II (Chicago Press, 1948).

65. Dora V. Smith, "Nature of the Reading Program To Meet Personal and Social Needs," *Promoting Personal and Social Development through Reading,* edited by William S. Gray. Supplementary Educational Monographs, No. 64 (Chicago: University of Chicago Press, 1947), pp. 11-16.

66. Lauren H. Smith and Louis H. Twyeffort, "Psychoneuroses: Their Origin and Treatment," *The Cyclopedia of Medicine, Surgery and Specialities,* edited by G. M. Piersol and E. L. Bortz (Philadelphia: F. A. Davis Co., 1945), XII, 858-83.

67. Nila Banton Smith, "Personal and Social Values of Reading," *Elementary English,* XXV (December, 1948), 490-500.

68. Josephine Strode, *Social Insight through Short Stories* (New York: Harper & Bros., 1946).

69. Robert Tyson, "The Validation of Mental Hygiene Literature," *Journal of Clinical Psychology,* IV (July, 1948), 304-6.

70. Robert Tyson, "Content of Mental Hygiene Literature," *Journal of Clinical Psychology,* V (April, 1949), 109-14.

71. Douglas Waples, B. R. Berelson and F. R. Bradshaw, *What Reading Does to People* (Chicago: University of Chicago Press, 1940).

72. Evelyn Wenzel, "Children's Literature and Personality Development," *Elementary English,* XXV (January, 1948), 12-31.

73. S. Vincent Wilking, "Personality Maladjustment as a Causative Factor in Reading Disability," *Elementary School Journal,* XLII (December, 1941), 268-79.

Bibliotherapy in an Educational Context: Rationale and Principles

by Harold A. Moses
and Joseph S. Zaccaria

Reading materials have traditionally played an important role in both the instructional and guidance aspects of the educative process. In general, the emphasis has continued to be on the utilization of the printed word as a didactic (instructional) medium. It has been felt that textbooks, novels, anthologies, monographs, pamphlets, educational and occupational materials, and more recently—programmed instructional materials contain significant cognitive learnings which the student must master in order to be educated adequately, to solve a particular problem, or to make an important decision.

Historically, however, there has been a trend parallel to the above line of thought which has emphasized the use of reading materials to promote mental health by serving as media for enabling students to solve critical problems they encounter at various developmental stages in their lives. This use of books for therapeutic rather than instructional purposes is known as bibliotherapy. Bibliotherapy has been defined as a process of dynamic interaction between the personality of a reader and the literature he reads—interaction that can be used for personality assessment, adjustment, and growth. Thus, the practitioner (e.g., teacher, counselor) can use both instructional and imaginative literature as vehicles for mental health objectives.

Although books have been used for therapeutic purposes, literally for centuries, it has only been rather recently that the fundamental dynamics of bibliotherapy have been recognized. The bibliotherapeutic process consists of the following three general stages:

1. Identification: First the reader identifies himself with one of the major characters in the book.

2. Catharsis: As a result of this identification, catharsis occurs, i.e., a release of emotion or psychological tension.

Reprinted with permission from *High School Journal* 52:401-411 (1969). Copyright © 1969 by University of North Carolina Press.

3. Insight: Because of the release of tension the individual
                     can then achieve new insight into his problem
                     via the process of "working through."

A number of principles have evolved for the use of bibliotherapy,
some of which are summarized below:

Principle I: *Understand the nature and dynamics of bibliotherapy, in-
corporating the theoretical aspects of bibliotherapy into a functional theory.* As
professionals, teachers and counselors have a responsibility to be
aware of the relevant theory and research as they relate to the practitioner's role and function. A growing body of theory and empirical research is providing the practitioner with an increasingly more adequate basis for his work. These findings can be incorporated into a
well-articulated and operational frame of reference enabling the practitioner to develop goals and adequate means for achieving these goals.
The evidence is clear that bibliotherapy can be a useful technique for
the teacher or the counselor trying to achieve mental health goals.

Principle II: *Possess at least a general familiarity with the literature
which the student will use.* Although at first this principle may appear to
be axiomatic, in practice this principle has sometimes not been
followed. Some important factors to which the practitioner should be
sensitive include student characteristics, e.g., age, sex, type of problem, reading level, reading preferences, etc. and literature characteristics, e.g., type of literature, level of difficulty, plot, characters,
length, readability, style, etc. The inherent dangers in not being
familiar with the literature read by the student are obvious.

Principle III: *Bibliotherapeutic reading can be encouraged through the
use of prompting techniques.* Since the typical student does not think of
reading as a means for dealing with personal problems, the teacher or
counselor must introduce the possibility of using bibliotherapy as a
technique for resolving personal dilemmas and interpersonal conflicts.

Principle IV: *Readiness is an important factor to be kept in mind when
considering the utilization of bibliotherapeutic techniques.* In essence, bibliotherapy is both a therapy and a process of learning new attitudes
and values, and of developing more mature self insight. In general the
most favorable time for introducing bibliotherapy is when a working
relationship involving mutual trust has been developed, the student's
problem has been described and somewhat explored, and the student
is exhibiting personal involvement in grappling with his problem.

Principle V: *Books should be suggested rather than prescribed.*
Although some practitioners have achieved satisfactory results by
prescribing specific reading materials and other practitioners have
encouraged students to select their own reading without any assistance, most teachers and counselors suggest a number of alternative
selections from which the individual selects the actual piece of literature that he will read.

Principle VI: *The practitioner should be sensitive to physical handicaps
of the individual which may dictate the necessity of using special types of read-*

ing materials. Significant factors to be kept in mind for students with visual handicaps include the size of the type, the design of the type, the space between the lines, the size and type of illustrations used, etc. Two excellent bibliographies of books for the visually handicapped are listed below:

1. Haycraft, H. *Books for the Blind.* Washington, D.C.: Library of Congress, Division for the Blind (no date).

2. Nieman, D. E. (ed). *Reading Aids for the Handicapped.* Chicago: American Library Association, 1966.

Principle VII: *Bibliotherapy appears to be most effective with individuals of average and above-average reading ability.* While bibliotherapy has been used effectively with individuals within a wide range of reading ability, general intelligence, and personality characteristics, bibliotherapy is more useful and effective with students of average and above-average reading ability because these students are sufficiently proficient in reading and are more apt to feel comfortable in reading.

Principle VIII. *The reading of the literature by the individual should be accompanied or followed up by discussion and counseling.* The discussion or counseling which accompanies or follows the reading is a key step in the process of working the problem through to eventual insight and developing more effective coping behavior. The individual's reaction to the literature, how he agrees or disagrees with the decision or behavior of some character in the plot, insights gleaned from the reading, how the emotional experiences of the characters in the book provide an extension of the individual's own experience, the meaning of the literature for the individual, etc., constitute some of the commonly used themes for the discussion or counseling accompanying the reading.

Principle IX: *Bibliotherapy is an adjunct to other types of helping relationships.* Nowhere in the literature or research is it suggested that bibliotherapy is a complete form of treatment for student problems. Bibliotherapy is clearly ancillary or supplemental. It is used in conjunction with other techniques.

Principle X: *Although bibliotherapy is a useful technique it is not a panacea.* Bibliotherapy does not replace other techniques. It cannot be used indiscriminately and it cannot be used with all persons, in all settings, and for all purposes. Undoubtedly, bibliotherapy should be used as a technique only by certain teachers and counselors, for as in the case of all educational and therapeutic techniques it will be adopted, adapted, and utilized effectively by some practitioners and abhorred, criticized, and avoided by others.

SUMMARY

The value of the printed word in the solution of personal problems and the promotion of mental health has long been recognized but has been accorded little attention in the literature and has been neglected by most teachers and counselors. Although bibliotherapy, like all other techniques, does have its limitations and may even be detrimental if inappropriately used, it also has definite potential which should be capitalized on and exploited by those working in a helping relationship with others.

Since space limitations prohibit the listing of even a sample of books which may be used as bibliotherapeutic media in the many problem areas confronted by teachers and counselors, the interested reader is referred to *Principles of Practices of Bibliotherapy: A Resource Book for Teachers and Counselors.* Here he will find a comprehensive listing of books covering virtually all problems experienced by all types and ages of individuals.

As an example of imaginative and didactic books available for therapeutic use the following is a selected list of books appropriate for use with high school students and their parents in three common problem areas.

Home and Family Living

Wayne J. Anderson, *Design for Family Living* (Minneapolis: T. S. Denison and Co., 1964). A candid discussion of how individual and family needs can be met within the context of family life. Adolescent,* adult.

Zachary Ball, *Kep* (New York: Holiday House, 1961). Kep faces a difficult time when after his father's death he is sent to live with a family whose son had died. Adolescent.

Bianca Bradbury, *The Amethyst Summer* (New York: Ives Washburn, 1963). When her mother must leave to care for an ill relative, Bayley faces the responsibility of caring for the family. Juvenile.

Bianca Bradbury, *Goodness and Mercy Jenkins* (New York: Ives Washburn, 1963). A spirited girl revolts against her Puritan guardians and the marriage they arranged for her. Adolescent, adult.

Vivian Breck, *High Trail* (Garden City, New York: Doubleday and Co., 1958). Girl learns responsibility and perseverance when her father breaks his leg. Juvenile, adolescent.

Jean de la Brete, ed., *My Uncle and the Cure* (New York: Vanguard Press, 1958). The story of the struggles of a young orphaned girl. Adolescent.

Rebecca Caudill, *Free of Freedom* (New York: The Viking Press, 1949) Problems faced by a Kentucky frontier family and how they result in a strong sense of family solidarity. Juvenile.

Helen Daringer, *Stepsister Sally* (New York: Harcourt, Brace and World, 1952). Story of how one girl faced and solved the problems of adjusting to a new family after father's remarriage. Juvenile.

---

*Juvenile, grades 6-8; adolescent, grades 8-12.

Cateau DeLeeuw, *From This Day Forward* (Philadelphia: Macrae Smith Co., 1951). Girl learns that just because her parents are divorced, all marriages are not failures. Juvenile.

Marguerite Dickson, *Only Child* (New York: David McKay Co., 1952). An only child learns consideration of others. Juvenile, adolescent.

Mary Dolim, *The Bishop Pattern* (New York: William Morrow and Co., 1963). The story of the efforts of a homeless little girl to adjust to a strange family. Adolescent.

Gilbert Douglas, *Hardness* (New York: Thomas Y. Crowell Co., 1957). Dean resents being unfavorably compared with his more able older brother. Adolescent, adult.

Lois Duncan, *The Middle Sister* (New York: Dodd, Mead and Co., 1960). A girl has a difficult time competing with an older and a younger sister, each of whom is more talented and attractive than she. Adolescent.

Ann Falk, *Who is Erika?* (New York: Harcourt, Brace and World, 1963). Erika resents her new stepfather but learns to adjust when she takes a better look at herself. Juvenile, adolescent.

David Fletcher, *The King's Goblet* (New York: Pantheon Books, 1962). Depicts strife created by difference between adolescent and family values. Juvenile, adolescent.

Kathryn Forbes, *Mama's Bank Account* (New York: Harcourt, Brace and World, 1949). A story of family life which illustrates honesty, resourcefulness, and a sense of values. Adolescent.

Mary and Lawrence Frank, *Your Adolescent at Home and in School* (New York: The New American Library, 1959). A practical guidebook on how to help adolescents face and solve problems. Adolescent, adult.

Irene Hunt, *Up the Road Slowly* (Chicago: Follett Publishing Co., 1966). Julie is forced to live with a stern aunt after her mother's death. Juvenile, adolescent.

Bryna Ivens, ed., *Nineteen from Seventeen* (Philadelphia: J. B. Lippincott Co., 1955). Short stories about family life and teenage adjustment from *Seventeen* magazine. Juvenile, adolescent.

Jim Kjelgaard, *The Black Fawn* (New York: Dodd, Mead and Co., 1959). An orphaned boy learns to adjust to life on his grandfather's farm and finds out what it means to be loved. Juvenile.

Oscar Lewis, *The Children of Sanchez* (New York: Vintage Books, 1961). A good illustration of how individual differences in the perception of the same behavior can result in difficulties in interpersonal relationships.

Mina Lewiton, *Cup of Courage* (New York: David McKay Co., 1948). The story of the problems faced by a boy and girl whose mother is dead and whose father is a drunkard. Juvenile, adolescent.

Mina Lewiton, *The Divided Heart* (New York: David McKay Co., 1947). A 15-year-old girl adjusts to the divorce of her parents. Juvenile, adolescent.

Edith Neisser, *Mothers and Daughters* (New York: Harper and Row, 1967). Suggestions on how mothers and daughters may have a more meaningful relationship. Adolescent, adult.

Gene Olsen, *Tin Goose* (Philadelphia: Westminster Press, 1962). Sixteen-year-old Danny has some problems in getting along with his grandfather. Juvenile, adolescent.

John Reese, *Three Wild Ones* (Philadelphia: The Westminister Press, 1963). Boy tries running away to solve home problems with his mother and stepfather. Juvenile.

Ruth Sawyer, *Year of Jubilo* (New York: The Viking Press, 1940). A 14-year-old girl helps to keep the family together following the death of her father. Juvenile, adolescent.

Zoa Sherburne, *Almost April* (New York, William Morrow and Co., 1956). Karen experiences difficulty in overcoming her unwarranted jealousy of her stepmother. Juvenile.

Anna Warnlof, *The Boy Upstairs* (New York: Harcourt, Brace and World, 1963). Fredrika has a difficult time before she learns to accept her parents' divorce. Juvenile, adolescent.

Lenora Weber *Meet the Malones* (New York: Thomas Y. Crowell Co., 1943). Children learn to accept responsibility during their father's absence. Juvenile, adolescent.

Kathryn Worth, *They Loved to Laugh* (Garden City, New York: Doubleday and Co., 1959). An orphaned girl learns the joy of working and sharing after her adoption. Juvenile.

Johann Wyss, *Swiss Family Robinson* (Cleveland: The World Publishing Co., 1947). The story of how a Swiss family, shipwrecked on a deserted island, established a new home. Juvenile, adolescent.

Ethnic and Socio-Cultural Relationships

Margaret Anderson, *The Children of the South* (New York: Farrar, Straus and Giroux, 1958). A southern teacher illustrates the harmful effects of desegregation. Adolescent, adult.

Joe Archibald, *Outfield Orphan* (Philadelphia: Macrae Smith Co., 1961). A story of baseball and a Negro boy's growth to maturity. Juvenile, adolescent.

Dorothy Baruch, *Glass House of Prejudice* (New York: William Morrow and Co., 1946). A series of true incidents which illustrate the persecutions and sufferings endured by members of minority groups. Adolescent, adult.

Giorgio Bassani, *The Garden of the Finzi-Continis* (New York: Atheneum Publishers, 1965). A young Jewish couple in love experience prejudice and indignities in Fascist Italy. Adolescent, adult.

Claire Bishop, *Martin de Parres: Hero* (Boston: Houghton Mifflin Co., 1954). Martin was rejected as a child due to his mixed racial heritage but became a Dominican lay brother and served others. Juvenile.

Catherine Blanton, *Hold Fast to Your Dreams* (New York: Julian Messner, 1955). A Negro girl exercises perseverance in her ambition to become a ballet dancer. Juvenile, adolescent.

Frank Bonham, *Burma Rifles: A Story of Merrill's Marauders* (New York: Thomas Y. Crowell Co., 1960). A Japanese-American soldier overcomes prejudice while serving with Merrill's Marauders. Juvenile, adolescent.

Arna Bontemps, *We Have Tomorrow* (Boston: Houghton Mifflin Co., 1945). Inspirational biographies of Negroes who have succeeded in breaking the color barrier. Adolescent.

Hal Borland, *When the Legends Die* (Philadelphia: J. B. Lippincott Co., 1963). A Ute Indian finds himself rejected by both the whites and his own people. Adolescent, adult.

Pearl S. Buck, *The Big Wave* (New York: The John Day Co., 1948). The story of a Jewish family living in China and of the cultural conflicts. Adolescent, adult.

Pearl S. Buck, *The Hidden Flower* (New York: The John Day Co., 1952). The problems faced by a Japanese girl who marries an American soldier and finds that she is rejected by her mother-in-law. Adolescent, adult.

Dorothy Butters, *Heartbreak Street* (Philadelphia: Macrae Smith Co., 1958). The story of Kitty's struggles to overcome the limitations which she attributed to her immigrant background. Adolescent.

Betty Cavanna, *A Time for Tenderness* (New York: William Morrow and Co., 1962). Peggy falls in love with a Brazilian boy and they face the problems of adjusting to diverse cultures and backgrounds. Adolescent, adult.

Chung-Cheng Chow, *The Lotus Pool* (New York: Appleton-Century-Crofts, 1961). A Chinese girl is forced to fight tradition and her family in her quest for an education. Adolescent.

Robert Coles, *Children of Crisis* (Boston: Little, Brown, and Co., 1967). A study of the fear and tension in Negro children during racial strife in the South. Adolescent, adult.

Adele DeLeeuw, *The Barred Road* (New York: The Macmillan Co., 1954). Susan works to increase the group acceptance and understanding of a Negro girl. Juvenile, adolescent.

John Franklin, *Three Negro Classics: Up from Slavery; the Souls of Black Folk; the Autobiography of an Ex-Coloured Man* (New York: Avon Book Division, 1965). Three important Negro classics in one volume. Adolescent, adult.

Nathan Glazer and D. P. Moynihan, *Beyond the Melting Pot* (Cambridge, Mass.: The M.I.T. Press, 1968). A discussion of how culture has affected the achievement, political action and attitudes of five major ethnic groups in New York City. Adolescent, adult.

Dick Gregory and Robert Lipsyte, *Nigger: An Autobiography* (New York: E. P. Dutton and Co., 1964). An autobiography of the famous comedian. Adolescent, adult.

John H. Griffin, *Black Like Me* (New York: The New American Library, 1961). Story of a white man's account of what it is like to live as a Negro in the South. Adolescent, adult.

Lorraine Hansberry, *Raisin in the Sun* (New York: Random House 1959). A play depicting a South Chicago Negro family which struggles to escape from the ghetto. Adolescent, adult.

John Hersey, *The Wall* (New York: Alfred A. Knopf, 1950). An account of the inhumane treatment of Jews in a Warsaw ghetto by the Nazis. Adolescent, adult.

Jesse Jackson, *Anchor Man* (New York: Harper and Row, 1947). Charley faces the problem of doing what is right to his race and to his white friends. Juvenile.

Martin L. King, *Why We Can't Wait* (New York: The New American Library, 1964). Dr. King describes the problems and reasons for the Negro's quest for civil rights. Adolescent, adult.

Gerda Klein, *All But My Life* (New York: Hill and Wang, 1957). The story of a Polish girl's experiences in a German concentration camp. Adolescent.

Nora Kubie, *Joel* (New York: Harper and Row. 1952). A young Jewish refugee migrated to colonial America and found a new way of life. Adolescent, adult.

Harper Lee, *To Kill a Mockingbird* (Philadelphia: J. B. Lippincott Co., 1960). A Southern lawyer learns about prejudice when he defends an unjustly accused Negro. Adolescent, adult.

Oscar Lewis, *La Vida* (New York: Random House 1966). Disadvantaged Puerto Ricans tell of their problems and struggles. Adolescent, adult.

George Mardikian, *Song of America* (New York: McGraw-Hill Book Co., 1956). An immigrant boy who made good expresses his gratitude for the American way of life. Adolescent, adult.

Melissa Mather, *One Summer in Between* (New York: Harper and Row, 1967). A story of how a Southern Negro girl who spends a summer with a Northern white family gradually changes her perceptions. Adolescent, adult.

Florence Means, *The Moved Outers* (Boston: Houghton Mifflin Co., 1945). Story of the life of two children of Japanese-American parents in a relocation camp during World War II. Juvenile, adolescent.

Florence Means, *Reach for a Star* (Boston: Houghton Mifflin Co., 1957). A Negro girl develops a tolerance for others. Juvenile, adolescent.

Florence Means, *Teresita of the Valley* (Boston: Houghton Mifflin Co., 1943). A girl is somewhat ashamed of her Spanish name and changes it but after learning about her Spanish-American heritage she is proud of her ancestry and her Spanish name. Juvenile, adolescent.

C. Fayne Porter, *Our Indian Heritage: Profiles of Twelve Great Leaders* (Philadelphia: Chilton Co., 1964). Biographical stories of interesting but not widely known facts concerning 12 famous American Indians. Adolescent, adult.

Anna Rose, *The Gentle House* (Boston: Houghton Mifflin Co., 1954). A Latvian boy has difficulty in adjusting to his American foster home. Juvenile, adolescent.

Aimee Sommerfelt, *Miriam* (New York: Criterion Books, 1963). The story of the persecution of the Norwegian Jews during the German occupation of that country. Adolescent, adult.

Monica Sone, *Nisei Daughter* (Boston: Little, Brown and Co., 1953). A Japanese-American has divided loyalties between her Japanese parents and the American culture. Adolescent, adult.

Virginia Sorensen, *Plain Girl* (New York: Harcourt, Brace and Co., 1955). An Amish girl learns that one can be rich in spite of poverty and learns to overcome her bashfulness. Adolescent.

Dan Wakefield, *Island in the City: the World of Spanish Harlem* (New York: Citadel Press, 1960). A realistic portrayal of the problems faced by Puerto Ricans living in New York City. Adolescent, adult.

Keith Wheeler, *Peaceable Lane* (New York: New American Library, 1960). A novel about the resulting tensions when a Negro family moves into an all-white community. Juvenile, adolescent.

Jade Wong, *Fifth Chinese Daughter* (New York: Harper and Row, 1950). A Chinese-American girl has a conflict between her Chinese parents and the American culture. Adolescent, adult.

B. and Jan Young, *Across the Tracks* (New York: Julian Messner, 1958). Betty discovers that her Mexican ancestry is something of which she can be proud. Juvenile, adolescent.

Peer Relationships

Ethel Anderson, *High Apple on the Tree* (New York, Funk and Wagnalls Co., 1957). Helping a paralyzed friend helps a girl to consider others. Juvenile, adolescent.

May Becker, *Under Twenty* (New York: Harcourt, Brace and World, 1932). Short stories about problems girls face in growing up. Juvenile, adolescent.

Bernice Bryant, *Miss Behavior* (Indianapolis: Bobbs-Merrill Co., 1960). A teen-age girl develops her personality and popularity. Juvenile, adolescent.

Ardis Burton and Joseph Mersand, *Stories for Teen-Agers, Books 1 and 2* (New York: Globe Book Co., 1959 and 1960). Stories about common teen-age problems. Juvenile, adolescent.

Mayde Chastain, *Bright Days* (New York: Harcourt, Brace and World, 1952). Girl learns to accept others without being unduly influenced by them. Juvenile.

Richard T. Flood, *Fighting Southpaw* (Boston: Houghton Mifflin Co., 1949). A shy boy is an expert pianist, but wishes to become a baseball pitcher. Juvenile.

Bryna Ivens, ed., *Stories from Seventeen* (Philadelphia: J. B. Lippincott and Co., 1955). Fourteen short stories about young people and the problems they face. Juvenile, adolescent.

Jessica Wilcox, *Time to Grow Up* (New York: Harper and Row, 1962). A guide for girls on many of the problems faced by most adolescents. Juvenile, adolescent.

Catherine Woolley, *Cathy's Little Sister* (New York: William Morrow and Co., 1964). Cathy learns the value of making friends of her own age instead of trying to join her older sister's crowd. Juvenile.

REFERENCE

J. S. Zaccaria and H. A. Moses, *Principles and Practices of Bibliotheraphy: A Resource Book for Teachers and Counselors* (Champaign, Illinois: Stipes Publishing Co., 1968).

Using Books To Help Solve Children's Problems

by George D. Spache

"Into books good and wise men and women have put their best and wisest thoughts, and the young mind, reading, can shape itself to noble ends" (by Pearl S. Buck, as quoted by Russell.[8])

Even before the invention of the book as we know it, teachers used reading materials to help individuals solve their personal adjustment problems. In fact, during certain periods in the history of reading, the primary purpose of most American readers seemed to be the inculcation of desirable character traits and moral values. *The New England Primer,* one of the first and most widely used of all American schoolbooks, was replete with such admonitions as:

"He who ne'er learns his A,B,C,
    Forever will a Blockhead be;
But he who to his Book's inclined,
    Will soon a golden Treasure find."

In the latter part of the nineteenth century, the *McGuffey Readers* also exemplified this didactic approach to character training through books. In the 1930's and 1940's there was a tremendous outpouring of reading materials intended to foster inter-group and international understanding.

Modern educators have certainly recognized that reading may have an impact upon the reader. But their approach has been much more cautious and less confident that reading necessarily molds individuals. The process of using books in this fashion has come to be known as bibliotherapy or, literally, treatment through books. In their comprehensive review of the literature on bibliotherapy Russell and Shrodes[14] define it as a process of dynamic interaction between the personality of the reader and literature. Such a definition makes no assumptions about the inevitability of reading influencing the personality of the reader. As we shall see, many conditions are necessary in the reader as well as the materials before this interaction may take place.

VALUES OF BIBLIOTHERAPY

According to various authorities, the values of bibliotherapy include the opportunity to learn to know one's self better, to understand human behavior and to find interest outside the self. Literature may promote the mechanisms of identification, compensation and rationalization. Thus it may enable the reader to recognize that he is not the first to meet and solve his problem, and to find face-saving solutions that help him to meet life without feelings of inferiority, or guilt, fear or shame. Or the reading experience may bring to the forefront of the reader's consciousness problems he has as yet failed to recognize as his own and, subsequently, provide the insights needed for solution.

In addition to these personal values, bibliotherapy may contribute to the socialization of the individual. Reading may increase ability to understand others by giving social insights, promoting empathy and thus, for example, modifying racial attitudes. Appropriate literature may give an understanding and love of country which contributes to feelings of security and the sense of belonging. It can reinforce socially acceptable modes of behavior and clarify and strengthen the individual's concept of his own role in society. As the forefathers of American education believed, reading may certainly foster the development of social values and ideals.[11, 15, 16]

In the secondary school particularly, reading materials may serve to reflect the feelings, needs and emotions of pupils, as in the work of Dorothy Bratton.[1] Other potentialities are 1) teaching the apathetic the love of reading, 2) satisfying adolescent emotional and psychological needs, 3) throwing light on the problems of adolescence, 4) exploring the teenager's relationships with the community and 5) leading pupils toward adult reading.[5] These values present in work with adolescents and young adults are, of course, also realizable with individuals of other ages provided the essential conditions for effective bibliotherapy exist.

A questionnaire study of college freshmen and sophomores[20] attempted to explore some of the values achieved through voluntary reading. The students' responses to questions indicated that some found better self-understanding (28%), an ideal or model to emulate (33%), character traits they tried to imitate (30%), changed their behavior (34%), character traits life-problems in their reading analogous to their own (33%) and found some help in solving problems (20%). A small number (11%) claimed to have secured some help in selecting a vocation. Unfortunately, the author of this study made no attempt to test the validity of these student claims, as by personal interviews or other techniques. At best, the study permits us to conclude that about a third of his sample sincerely believed that voluntary reading had influenced their self-concepts, behavior, and vocational choices. In the discussion later of the inherent limitations in the bibliotherapeutic process, and other researches in its effectiveness, there are some clues as to the validity of this type of self-report study on the values of bibliotherapy.

THE PROCESS OF BIBLIOTHERAPY

If the expected values of bibliotherapy are to be achieved, we need more than simply a book and a competent reader. Russell and Shrodes[16] emphasize that the three personality mechanisms of identification, catharsis and insight, at least, must be present in the dynamic interaction. First of all, the reader must be able to identify with characters or elements of the story. He must recognize that he shares some such characteristics as age, sex, hopes, frustrations, and other problems of adjustment. Identification may result in augmenting the reader's self-esteem if he can conceivably admire the character with which he identifies. It may also increase his feelings of belonging and sharpen the outlines of his vague self-concept.

Sometimes, when an obvious personal identification is not possible, these effects occur through the mechanism of personification or hero-worship. Readers may identify vicariously, as it were, with the daring or bravado of a character and thus be moved to overt imitation. The wave of interest in coonskin caps and other articles of pioneer dress which swept through American children in recent years was a striking example of the impact of personification or vicarious identification with a beloved historical American character. Elements of personification of identification must be present in the interaction of the reader and the book before effective bibliotherapy can be initiated.

The process of bibliotherapy moves through identification to catharsis, a sharing of motivations, conflicts and emotions of a book character. Defined in psychological terms, catharsis is an active release of emotions, experienced either first-hand or vicariously. Catharsis goes beyond the simple intellectual recognition of commonalities as in identification or personification. It involves empathetic emotional reactions similar to those that the reader imagines were felt by the book character. Or, in another sense, the reader relives, insofar as his own emotional experiences permit, the feelings he attributes to a character in a story.

The third personality mechanism essential to bibliotherapy is insight. This effect is composed of such factors as seeing one's self in the behavior of the character and achieving awareness of one's own motivations, needs and problems. Here the reader must be able to recognize the similarities and differences between himself and the character. He must identify the character's problems with his own and react emotionally to this awareness. Then, reasoning by analogy, or perhaps by simple imitation, he may consider a course of action which will presumably enable him, like the character, to solve problems faced in common. It is wise to note that the simple achieving of insights does not always lead to the step of taking action intended to solve or end problems. Many troubled individuals may achieve insight and apparent understanding of the action necessary to secure relief. But they are prevented by personality defects or other factors beyond their control from implementing their insights with problem-solving behavior. As it might be phrased in the vernacular, the reader must progress from "He's like me" or "I'm like him" through "Gee, I feel the same as he does" to "I can do it just like he did" or "I can do it too." The final step of "See, I did it" may be the ultimate test of the effectiveness of the bibliotherapeutic process but in the opinion of some authorities is not an integral part of the success.

LIMITATION IN THE BIBLIOTHERAPEUTIC PROCESS

Both Russell[15] and Veatch[16] emphasize the need for freedom of choice for pupils if bibliotherapy is to operate successfully. There must be a permissive environment with no pressure to show results or to report on books. They feel that children must be able to read easily and well and that there must be a wide variety of reading materials of varying levels available. Russell also suggests that there should be no recommendations by the teacher but we would certainly not agree with this laissez-faire attitude. In our opinion, teachers and counselors can play a constructive role in suggesting or offering certain reading materials without necessarily creating antagonism or evoking outright rejection.

On the psychological side, there may be interruptions or barriers to the completion of the bibliotherapeutic process. Identification does not always lead through catharsis to insight. The reader may project his own motives onto the character and thus reinforce his destructive feelings without ever perceiving the possibility of solution of his problems. Or, the reader may vent his feelings on the character, using it as a scapegoat or whipping boy that is to blame for his frustrations. The reader may actively dislike the character because its problems remind him so strongly of his own unsolved conflicts. Tensions and anxieties of the reader may block or distort the expected constructive identification.

The therapeutic process may be halted for lack of social and emotional experiences on the part of the reader. Catharsis may be impossible because the individual has had no emotional experience which prepared him for empathy with the character's feelings. Or the vagueness of his self-concept may prevent him from recognizing the resemblance and from identifying with the story character. As Russell[15] has pointed out, the therapeutic efforts of reading must be reinforced by other experience. For example, attitudes and ideas gained from books must be supported by school and community influences, or must appeal to some felt need of the individual.

From the educational viewpoint, there are other problems to be met before the process of bibliotherapy can be successfully completed. Some authorities do not believe that the direct prescription of certain books for certain problems is feasible. Whether bibliotherapy will occur may be dependent upon such factors as the age of the reader, the present status of his problem, and his emotional state, not to mention his ability to profit from the prescribed reading. Postel[14] warns us that the use of inappropriate primary materials with a retarded upper-grade pupil may prolong dependency and immaturity or do other types of harm. There is often the need for guidance of the reader through discussion of the underlying causes of significant behavior of the literary characters. Role playing or dramatization may be necessary to evoke and ventilate the emotions essential to catharsis. Group discussion to facilitate the development of insights may also be desirable or essential. Thus the parent, teacher or librarian may need to play a significant role in supporting or furthering the development of bibliotherapy.

In her discussion of reading and the self-concept, Homze[6] re-emphasizes the fact that interaction between the pupil and the concepts offered in his reading occur constantly. The child is selecting adult models among the story characters, and building and clarifying his self-concept each time he reads, provided, of course, that his self-concept as a reader permits this interaction. If, on the other hand, he conceives of himself as a poor or non-reader, he will not be receptive to the ideas offered in books or be stimulated toward growth and change. Homze thus implies that the child with a negative self-concept regarding reading must first be helped to experience reading success before we can expect him to benefit personally from this activity.

In a brief historical review of ideas about bibliotherapy, Weingarten[21] cites a number of cautions. Certain authorities have pointed out that the process of reading is not the only means of effecting personal growth and thus it is extremely difficult to assess its contribution to personal-social adjustment, the self-concept, and other aspects of the individual's development. Weingarten also emphasizes that there is a danger that books may aid withdrawal into fantasy and thus promote poorer adjustment. This observation is, of course, an aspect of the mental hygiene of the classroom rather than a real criticism of the use of bibliotherapy, for no one assumes that a goal of this treatment process is to produce an individual who substitutes books for reality. Weingarten also points out that there may be a conflict between the goals of the teacher of literature and the bibliotherapist. Literature specialists are prone to insist that great literature should be read for its own values of appreciation and enjoyment. Therefore, it should not be selected mainly in terms of the students' needs for personal guidance. Although this conflict does exist in some quarters, it is completely artificial in our opinion. Both goals for reading good literature can exist simultaneously, for a student who is being helped to find personal guidance in some materials can also be expected to read others for other purposes. Those of us who believe in bibliotherapy are not suggesting that this is the only way to approach literature, or that the process should supplant all other legitimate types of reading. We are simply arguing that some effort to assist students in need of personal-social guidance through the use of books is most desirable. The extent to which this obligation is assumed by English teachers, teachers of literature, or any other teacher is dependent upon their judgment, their recognition of this importance of the students' problems, and their willingness and ability to make this approach.

Another article by Witty[22] cites several sources which suggest that bibliotherapy should be limited to situations involving obvious maladjustment only, and should be conducted under the guidance of a physician by a trained librarian. Such sources are obviously too impressed with the connotations of "therapy," ignoring the fact that almost any type of contact between a child and teacher has effects upon the child's personal and social development. We cannot afford to wait until the pupil's maladjustment reaches serious proportions before attempting to ameliorate it in the classroom. Nor can we expect physicians to have the time or training to direct the bibliotherapeutic efforts of teachers. As for librarians, we would welcome their participation in such efforts, but see no reason to believe that they are better trained in child development or mental hygiene than the average classroom teacher.

Some comment is certainly appropriate here concerning the competence of teachers and others to engage in bibliotherapy. The reactions of current psychologists and psychiatrists differ tremendously on this point. Russell and Shrodes[14] feel that teachers may proceed with caution. They will need as fundamentals—wide knowledge of books, broad and deep understanding of children and adolescents or of the troubled adult. They will probably have to reinforce the process by informal talks before and after bibliotherapy. In our opinion, the question is satisfactorily answered by the fact that teachers are and have been carrying on a successful form of bibliotherapy since the beginning of time. The average teacher transmits values and ideas, as well as facts, to most of her pupils. If this were not so, there would be no defense for our entire educational system except as a means of conveying purely factual information.

The crux of the problem of teacher participation in bibliotherapy is the degree of success she achieves in initiating the process and bringing it to fruition. As we have said earlier, the task is much more than simply bringing a book and a reader into contact. The teacher must be aware of her own limitations in effecting a working relationship with her pupils. Finally she must be conscious of the nature of the bibliotherapeutic process and the factors which hinder its development.

APPLICATIONS OF BIBLIOTHERAPY

The types of individuals and of human problems in which bibliotherapy may play a part are manifold. The process may be used for the improvement of attitudes, feelings, and personal and social values.

Such specifics as racial discrimination, stereotyped concepts of others, and disabling personality traits have been modified in readers of all ages. Bibliotherapy has been used effectively with delinquents, criminals, neurotic and even psychotic individuals. It has functioned as a preliminary to acting out solutions of common problems among groups of normal and disturbed individuals. One of its significant by-products may be the insight it gives the teacher or therapist concerning the student's personality and adjustment problems. In all these ways, bibliotherapy contributes to good general mental hygiene among those with whom it is used effectively.

Several large-scale attempts at bibliotherapy are recorded in the literature. One of these was conducted in Detroit for the purpose of improving citizenship through a better understanding of democracy.[13] As Cleary,[3] one of the authors of the summary report, points out, very little change appeared in the attitudes and values of pupils after one period of widespread, intensified effort. The project was then re-planned to include more specific interpretation and definition of democracy and democratic practices. Instead of generalizations, emphasis was placed upon specific situations in which these values could be practiced. Pupils were led to respond to specifics and to formulate generalizations gradually rather than the reverse procedure used earlier. With this revised approach, significant changes in democratic values and practices were found among the pupils.

The Intergroup Education in Cooperative Schools project[4] also showed a gradual development of more effective techniques in the use of bibliotherapy. The original list of books has been extensively revised and reworked. In the latest report of this project, stress is now placed upon the role of books in human relations teaching and upon effective methods of guidance rather than the simple prescription of books. The editors emphasize the importance of skilled discussion of books and offer a series of suggested steps for supporting the bibliotherapeutic process.

Other studies report the effects of group bibliotherapy in the first grade as well as other school grades. Katherine A. Pirie[10] read a number of selections to her first grade class and recorded the apparent impact by tape recorder. She found that the children identified with characters that helped them to find solutions to their problems. The selections also seemed to aid the children in identifying acceptable social behavior. In a study by Nila B. Smith,[17] of 500 pupils in grades four to twelve, sixty percent believed that their attitudes had been influenced by a specific piece of reading. These few examples from recent reports indicate the need for continued efforts to improve the effectiveness of the bibliotherapeutic process.

Evalene Jackson's effort to change racial attitudes[7] through selected stories illustrates another problem in the bibliotherapeutic process, that of the permanence of attitude changes. Her attitude tests showed a small but significant shift to a more favorable attitude toward Negroes after her students were introduced to certain readings. But the attitude changes were not necessarily lasting ones, as she found. This simple experiment may indicate bibliotherapy may need to be extended over some time, if permanent feelings or attitudes are to be created. It may also indicate that the process needs reinforcement by other than literary means, such as the impact of group attitudes, community attitudes, and active and obvious efforts by the teacher to provide verbal and behavioral reinforcement. This experiment also suggests that the teacher or bibliotherapist must consider providing opportunities for translating attitudes gained through reading into behavior. How real or permanent would an induced attitude of tolerance toward Negroes be for an individual who has little or no contact with Negroes? We already know that the simple acquisition of information does not insure a change in attitudes; and that a change in expressed attitudes is not necessarily reflected in behavior.

These gradual changes must be implemented, as shown in the simple classroom experiment described by Jane Webster.[19] After discovering that 35 of her first-graders feared the dark, Miss Webster read a carefully selected story to them each week for five weeks. The reading was followed each time by a free group discussion and sharing of experiences and reactions. Another small group was similarly exposed to a series of stories calculated to affect their fear of dogs. When interviewed three months after the bibliotherapeutic experience, twenty-nine of the thirty-five expressed reduction of fear of the dark, and all five in the second group had similarly changed in their fear of dogs. In fact, many of the children expressed positive feelings about the dark, night, being alone in bed, and dogs during the follow-up interview. The author modestly, and appropriately, makes no claims regarding the permanence of the apparent change in fears, nor does she claim to understand all aspects of the underlying dynamics. But she does demonstrate the possibility of effective bibliotherapy in the hands of an insightful teacher.

Helen Lodge[10] attempted to determine the effects upon students' concepts of the ideal person by an eight-week unit on biography. She found that pupil identifications of or with the ideal person were not materially influenced by this approach. In fact, interviews showed that books played a very small part in the concept of the ideal self. The influence of familiar adults was much greater in the pupil protocols. Again, we do not know whether the bibliotherapy failed in this experiment because of the length of time, the personality or techniques of the teacher, or the materials used.

Although she was concerned primarily with speech improvement through careful selection of literature, Marjorie Carey's article[2] had bibliotherapeutic overtones as well. She suggests that relaxation may be induced in tense children by acting out certain selected stories and poems. In our concern for the solution of personal and social problems through bibliotherapy, it is well to remember that literature may also serve to reduce or relieve some of the physical manifestations of these problems, such as tension, anxiety and physical rigidity.

Viola Kantrowitz, a teacher in a school for severely emotionally disturbed children, gives several brief descriptions of her bibliotherapeutic approach to these children.[8] By using materials centered around some vital interest of the child, she tried to involve them in helping themselves to read better. There were also some side effects of relaxing aggressiveness, tension and fears of the children when the work was concerned only with some topic of appeal to the individual child. It is questionable, of course, whether all the favorable changes in the personalities of these children that Miss Kantrowitz noted were due solely to her practices. However, using books and instructional materials which focused on an important interest of the child would certainly contribute to his feeling of acceptance and, perhaps, be reflected in more socially acceptable behavior.

The more didactic approach to bibliotherapy persists in some of the following items which simply match character traits or adjustment problems to specific books. Others offer suggestions for supporting the bibliotherapeutic process, as we have tried to do in this chapter.

BIBLIOGRAPHY

Jean DeSales Bertam, "Books To Promote Insights into Family and Life Problems," *English Journal,* 50 (November 1956), 477-482.

Muriel Crosby, Alexander Frazier and Carolyn Field, *Reading Ladders for Human Relations* 4th edition. (Washington: American Council on Education, 1963).

H. S. and G. L. Elliott, *Solving Personal Problems* (New York: Holt, 1936).

Geneva R. Hanna and Mariana K. McCallister, *Books, Young People and Reading Guidance* (New York: Harper, 1960).

Clara J. Kircher, *Behavior Pattern in Children's Books: A Bibliography* (Washington, D.C.: Catholic University Press, 1966).

Hannah M. Lindahl and Katherine Koch, "Bibliotherapy in the Middle Grades," *Elementary English,* 29 (November 1952), 390-396.

Metropolitan School Study Council, *Bibliography for Children's Reading* (New York: The Council, 525 West 120th Street).

Hilda Taba, *Literature for Human Understanding* (Washington, D.C.: American Council on Education, 1949).

Ethel R. Taylor, "Books for Character Education in the Primary Grades," *American Childhood,* 26 (November 1940), 43-44.

Ann G. Wolfe, *About 100 Books* (New York: American Jewish Committee). Other short lists keyed to particular age groups and their common adjustment problems are noted by Lindemen and Kling.[9]

A. R. Brooks, "Integrating Books and Reading with Adolescent Tasks," *School Review,* 58 (April 1950), 211-19.

E. Cohoe "Bibliotherapy for Handicapped Children," *National Education Association Journal,* 49 (April 1950), 211-19.

I. V. Eno, "Round Table, Books for Children from Broken Homes," *English Journal,* 38 (October 1949), 457-8.

A. Homze, "Children Face Themselves Through Books: A Bibliography," *Elementary English,* 41 (November 1964), 788-92.

A. Homze, "Interpersonal Relations in Children's Literature 1920-60," *Elementary English,* 43 (January 1966), 26-8, 52.

REFERENCES

1. Dorothy Bratton, "Reading for Therapy," *English Journal,* 41 (September 1957), 339-346, 361.

2. Marjorie Carey, "Children's Literature and Creative Speech," *Elementary English,* 36 (December 1959), 543-48.

3. Florence Damon Cleary, *Blueprints for Better Reading* (New York: H. W. Wilson, 1957).

4. Muriel Crosby, Alexander Frazier and Carolyn Field, *Reading Ladders for Human Relations* 4th edition. (Washington: American Council on Education, 1963).

5. Margaret A. Edwards, "Let the Lower Lights Be Burning," *English Journal,* 41 (November 1957), 461-469.

6. Alva Cross Homze, "Reading and the Self-Concept," *Elementary English,* 39 (March 1962), 210-15.

7. Evalene P. Jackson, "Effects of Reading Upon Attitudes Toward the Negro Race," *Library Quarterly,* 14 (January 1944), 53.

8. Viola Kantrowitz, "Bibliotherapy with Retarded Readers," *Journal of Reading,* 11 (December 1967), 205-12.

9. Barbara Lindeman and Martin Kling, "Bibliotherapy: Definitions, Uses and Studies," *Journal of School Psychology,* 7, No. 2 (1968-69), 36-41.

10. Helen C. Lodge, "The Influence of the Study of Biography on the Moral Ideology of the Adolescent at the Eighth Grade Level," *Journal Educational Research,* 50 (December 1956).

11. Sister Mary Agnes, "Bibliotherapy for Socially Maladjusted Children," *Catholic Educational Review,* 44 (January 16, 1946), 8-16.

12. Clyde Martin, "But How Do Books Help Children?" *Junior Libraries,* 1 (October 1955), 83-87.

13. Arnold R. Meier, Florence Damon Cleary and Alice M. Davis, *A Curriculum for Citizenship* (Detroit: Wayne University, 1952).

14. Harold H. Postel, "The Effect of Adapting Reading Materials to Seriously Retarded Pupils," *Elementary School Journal*, 37 (March 1937), 536-540.

15. David H. Russell, "Reading and the Healthy Personality," *Elementary English*, 29 (April 1952), 195-200.

16. David H. Russell and Caroline Shrodes, "Contributions of Research in Bibliotherapy to the Language-Arts Program," *School Review*, 58 (September and October 1950), 335-342, 411-420.

17. Nila B. Smith, "The Personal and Social Values of Reading," *Elementary English*, 25 (December 1948), 490-500.

18. Jeannette Veatch, "Children's Interests and Individual Reading," *Reading Teacher*, 10 (February 1957), 160-165.

19. Jane Webster, "Used Books To Reduce the Fears of First-Grade Children" *The Reading Teacher*, 14 (January 1961), 159-62.

20. Samuel Weingarten, "Developmental Values of Voluntary Reading," *The School Review*, 62, (April 1954), 222-30.

21. Samuel Weingarten, "Boundaries of Reading in Satisfying Needs," *Education*, 84 (April 1964), 481-9.

22. Paul A. Witty, "Meeting Developmental Needs Through Reading," *Education*, 84 (April 1964), 451-8.

Suggestions for
Further Reading

Walter T. Colville, "Bibliotherapy: Some Practical Considerations" *Hospital Progress* 41:138-142 (April/May 1960).

Armando R. Favazza, "Bibliotherapy: A Critique of the Literature" *Bulletin of the Medical Library Association* 54:138-141 (April 1966).

Julius Griffin, "Summary of Bibliotherapy Lectures Presented to the Professional Staff of Patton State Hospital" (Encino, Ca.: Griffin Clinic, 1959).

Norman Holland, *The Dynamics of Literary Response* (New York: Norton and Co., 1968).

Norman Holland, *Five Readers Reading* (New Haven: Yale University Press, 1975).

Jo Catherine Hynes, "Library Work with Brain Damaged Patients: A New Mode of Bibliotherapy" *Medical Library Association Bulletin* 60:333-339 (April 1972).

Artemesia Junier, "A Subject Index to Literature of Bibliotherapy 1900-1958." Master's thesis (Atlanta University, 1959).

Jack J. Leedy, *Poetry Therapy: The Use of Poetry in the Treatment of Emotional Disorders* (Philadelphia: Lippincott and Co., 1969).

Jack J. Leedy, *Poetry the Healer* (Philadelphia: Lippincott and Co., 1973).

Fred McKinney, "Explorations in Bibliotherapy: Personal Involvement in Short Stories and Cases." *Psychotherapy: Theory, Research and Practice* 12:110-117 (Spring 1975).

Karl Menninger, "Reading as Therapy" *American Library Association Bulletin* 55:316-319 (April 1961).

Eunice S. Newton, "Bibliotherapy in the Development of Minority Group Self-Concept." *Journal of Negro Education* 38:257-265 (1969).

Michael Shiryon, "Group Literatherapy: A Bibliotherapeutic Approach." Unpub. speech given at the Golden Gate Psychotherapy Society, San Francisco, (1970).

Michael Shiryon, "Twenty-five Years of Literatherapy" Unpub. speech given at the California State Psychological Assn., Los Angeles (1972).

Joseph Zaccaria and Harold Moses, *Facilitating Human Development Through Reading: The Use of Bibliotherapy in Teaching and Counseling* (Champaign, Illinois: Stipes Publishing Co., 1968).

PART

BIBLIOTHERAPY
AND
LIBRARY SCIENCE

Introductory Comments

Bibliotherapy is truly an interdisciplinary field in which librarianship has an active part. Although a surprisingly large number of articles on bibliotherapy are published in other professionals' journals, librarians' contributions to the literature cannot be underestimated.

Margaret Monroe's paper, "A Bibliotherapeutic Model for Library Service," is a fine introduction to the role of librarianship in bibliotherapy, and vice versa. She, and numerous other librarians, see bibliotherapy as a natural outgrowth of the other readers' services (reference and reading guidance) provided by librarians. "The bibliotherapeutic process is a potential in every reader's approach to the use of library resources." Out of this concept, she develops a model for service. Articles by Louis Rongione and Mildred Moody also present theoretic overviews of bibliotherapy from the librarian's point of view. All three articles exemplify differences in opinion, approach, and style so evident in the literature.

Margaret Hannigan and William Henderson's article represents the anecdotal or experiential type of writing still prevalent today. "Narcotic Addicts Take Up Reading" describes the bibliotherapy project conducted by the authors, two public librarians, in a unit for drug addicts in a correctional institution. "Bibliotherapy with Chronic Schizophrenics" by Rosa Horn Alexander and Stephen Buggie reports on a demonstration project, a mental hospital in San Jose, California. Alexander's experiment led to a subsequent long-term bibliotherapy project at Agnews State Hospital which was continued by the San Jose County Library when the hospital was closed in 1973. Clara Lack's article "Systems Analysis of A Bibliotherapy Session at Agnews State Hospital" is much more specific about the process of bibliotherapy and its results. Similarly, Arleen Hynes' paper, "Bibliotherapy in the Circulating Library at St. Elizabeths Hospital" is a detailed treatment of the use of bibliotherapy in a large mental hospital. The San Jose County Library project and the St. Elizabeths Hospital project are currently the two major bibliotherapy programs in the United States.

In a more theoretical vein, Evalene Jackson's article "Bibliotherapy and Reading Guidance: A Tentative Approach to Theory" is considered a landmark paper on the processes of bibliotherapy and their relationship to other forms of therapy and guidance. Ruth Tews, a frequent contributor on bibliotherapy since the 1940s and former librarian of the Mayo Clinic, is represented here by her paper "The Role of the Librarian on the Interdisciplinary Team." The concept of providing bibliotherapy by a team of professionals, rather than by one therapist, has been the subject of much debate over the years. This paper exemplifies the point of view that a team approach is necessary "if treatment is truly patient centered, geared to the patient's goal. . . ."

A Bibliotherapeutic Model for Library Service

by Margaret E. Monroe

While bibliotherapy is an art that aspires to the status of a science in "the application of literature as therapeutic adjuvants in medicine and psychiatry," librarians involved in bibliotherapy see their role more often as one of "guidance in the solution of personal problems through reading."[1] Further, librarians, on the whole, recognize their role in bibliotherapy to be related to the bibliotherapeutic process which is activated by the reader who is able to interact intensively with a book, film, recording or other created and authored analysis of human experience. In short the librarian recognizes that the bibliotherapeutic process is a potential in every reader's approach to the use of library resources. To the extent that the librarian understands the reader, knows the literature, is aware of the bibliotherapeutic potential of materials, she or he may make a decision to enhance the bibliotherapeutic potential of the library for the user by expanding the reader's awareness of the materials choices available. We will focus here on the bibliotherapeutic process as the basis for understanding the bibliotherapeutic potential of books, films and recordings.

THE BIBLIOTHERAPEUTIC MODEL

There are six steps in the Bibliotherapeutic Process:

Read or View or Listen

Those who cannot, or prefer not, to read, view or listen will not have bibliotherapy as a channel for life enhancement. And typically the work, whether short or long, may have to be experienced as a whole; skimming or sampling may prove useless except where excerpts have been carefully selected to represent the experience on which the bibliotherapeutic experience is to be based.

Identify with an Element in the Situation

Creative literature offers a choice of characters with whom the user may identify; didactic literature provides analysis of situations in which the user may find identity with his own. These identifications during the reading process must be strong and compelling, whether conscious or unconscious, and provide a motive force for experiencing the literature.

Experience Vicariously

From among those who can and will read, listen or view *and* who are able to identify strongly with a character or situation, some will enter so strongly into the experience offered that the use of the literature becomes a personal experience. They suffer, they struggle, they ponder alternatives, they solve and resolve as the character or author's analysis of the situation provides. Such users of book, film or recording allow themselves to live within the literature. Such vicarious experience is an essential aspect of the bibliotherapeutic model. Almost all children enjoy folktales in this fashion; all readers of poetry must be capable of vicarious experiencing to truly experience the art. Experiencing vicariously is a normal part of the use of literature. For those with emotional problems reflected in the literature experienced, such compelling identification is a normal effect arising from the importance of the problem to the user.

Catharsis

All Greek tragic drama relies on the viewers to watch, identify, and experience vicariously so that the moment of crisis and retribution, the denouncement of the play in which the chief characters find their fate, is in part a personal moment of truth for the viewer. He suffers the blow of fortune or triumphs with the character, and because he understands the meaning of this fate, he is "purged"; his burden falls from his shoulders, his problem is understood, and viscerally he feels psychological release, the cleansing power of the experience. The bibliotherapeutic process provides such catharsis for the reader, viewer, listener, whether he uses creative or didactic literature.

Insight

Once the psychological release is experienced, the reader, viewer, listener will suspend the vicarious experiencing and the intense identification with character or situation, and he reenters his own world. If the bibliotherapeutic process is to be said to occur, this reentry not only sustains the feeling of psychological release for at least a short time, but insight and understanding of the person or situation experienced become clarified; cause and effect emerge; evaluation of alternatives and solutions becomes conscious; and parallels to the reader, viewer, listener's own life situation are illuminated. This provides insight.

In the bibliotherapeutic model, insight is the climax of the process. Those forms of literature (westerns, light romance) which often offer only a superficial analysis of the human dilemma and therefore provide little basis for insight, nevertheless rely upon the first four steps of the bibliotherapeutic model, and some readers find them a source of catharsis. Lacking a basis for insight, such literature may become addictive in the reader's continued search for catharsis.

It is often said of a good children's book in relation to a particular child, "This is the time for her to read *Caddie Woodlawn*" or "I read *The Little Prince* at the wrong time and it meant nothing to me." The librarian's role in selecting materials is significant in providing suitability of the material at each step of the bibliotherapeutic process: readability, relevance of situation or character, closeness of the reading experience to that most needed by the reader, sound resolution of the life crisis, and meaningfulness of the insight likely to be induced.

Insight is so important to providing the bibliotherapeutic effect that librarians and others have used group discussion of literature as an impetus to development of insight. Insight cannot be imposed; it is based on revelation. In such discussion, the reading, viewing, listening experience is analyzed and relived at a more objective level as it is shared with others. One person's insight is compared with that of another, and a more rounded meaning often emerges. Insights then become available as tools to self-understanding. In a sense, this may be said to complete the bibliotherapeutic cycle. Two questions hover: How do we know that something has happened? And, to what good end have we taken the trouble to enable the experience?

Change in Attitude or Behavior

The bibliotherapeutic model includes a final step in the process; after catharsis and insight comes the measurable pay-off—a change in attitude or behavior. Research has demonstrated more wholesome or normal behavior or attitudes following a series of intensive reading and discussion sessions.[2, 3] If problems are resolved, guilt removed, hope restored, alternatives opened, then actions are privileged to change and attitudes toward self and others are revised.

Usually these changes and modifications are slight and observable only to the trained psychologist or family and friends. These changes have not been the goal for which the librarian strives, except in supporting such goals when set by a collaborating physician. Nevertheless, the librarian knows that these personally-generated effects flow from the user's interaction with book, film or recording and observes them following insight-producing discussion.

The fact that such positive behavior and attitude changes have been measurable and shown to be clearly associated with the reading and discussion process makes the bibliotherapeutic model a significant one for librarians.

THE ROLE OF LITERATURE IN HUMAN DILEMMA

Literature, whether print, film, or recording, may be categorized into two types: didactic literature and creative literature. These two types function somewhat differently in the bibliotherapeutic process; each type, however, has an important role.

Didactic Literature: Informs, Explains, Interprets

Didactic literature is designed to teach, to inform, to lead people to understanding. Many users of such literature do not seek and do not experience from the literature the "bibliotherapeutic effect"; they know, they understand and they can use the information, but they do not "experience vicariously" nor have the experience of "catharsis" upon which to base their insight. Others, however, project themselves into the descriptions of situation so strongly and compellingly that the selection of literature for them is a matter for a sensitive and aware librarian.

The literature on "the use of alcohol," for example, is a good illustration.[4] Knowledgeable authors, publishers, and film-makers have designed books and films in the area of alcoholism for highly specific groups of readers: the problem drinker, the spouse of an alcoholic, the young adult drinker, the young adult child of an alcoholic, etc. In this area of personal crisis, roles are sharply different, and the situations can be reflected on only if the material takes a sympathetic stance in relation to the particular reader's role. Anecdotal style is typical of such literature, allowing the reader to identify, although briefly, with such of the examples as he chooses. Without such "finding of oneself" in the book or film, the material has much less significance and may even turn the user away from the search for help. Librarians in evaluating and selecting such materials typically find it important to note the particular group of intended users. And in providing such literature to users, librarians deftly, swiftly and objectively yet sympathetically come to an understanding of the user's role in relation to the problem, so that the appropriate and useful material may be selected for use.

Creative Literature: Recounts, Relives, Creates

Creative literature reconstitutes the human experience, whether through the recounting of a life in a good biography, the reliving of the experience in fictionalized biography, the capturing of the essence of meaning in poetry, or the creation of a meaningful fictional situation, whether novel or short story. Drama is the essence of creative literature, although for many users the film version is an easier reenactment than is the reading of the printed play script. Similarly poetry, a difficult form for many, may be more accessible to understanding through the recorded oral interpretation by the poet or a sensitive reader.

The selection of materials for an individual reader imply the librarian's mandate to enter into understanding of the reader's problem to a point where the librarian can make reasonably good choices among potentially useful materials. For library users who are consciously seeking help—and many do!—the selection of the librarian from whom to seek assistance is his own, and he tacitly agrees to share the necessary information, up to a point. The librarian understands that there will be limits to what the reader is willing or able to share, and works tactfully, impersonally yet empathetically with whatever he is able to learn, to provide the appropriate materials from which the user makes his choice.

For the public librarian, limits are reached much sooner than for the librarian working in a mental institution or in collaboration with a therapy staff. As Dr. Karl Menninger often did, the psychiatrist may share his concepts of the kinds of materials the user might make best use of; or, to the knowledgeable librarian, he may share the nature of the problem and leave to the experienced bibliotherapist the selection of the kind of literature to be provided.

THE ROLE OF LITERATURE IN CRISIS FOR DIFFERENT GROUPS OF PEOPLE

Bibliotherapeutic materials have distinctive roles for three groups of people related to a human dilemma:

those experiencing the *personal crisis*

those who are *professional helpers* in the crisis

those who form *the human support system* to people with the personal crisis.

Most of the comments on the bibliotherapeutic process here have related to the person experiencing his own crisis. Bibliotherapy in its true sense applies to these people. But it is important for librarians to recognize that professional helpers must have such a capacity to "understand" emphathetically as reading creative or didactic literature "bibliotherapeutically" can provide. Further, the family and friends of those with the personal crisis often have the same kind of need for vicarious experiencing, catharsis and insight which the person at the center of the human dilemma also has.

Librarians are probably more frequently serving the "professional helpers" and those who form the "human support system" than those with the personal crisis. In the first place, there are a great many people involved for each individual human crisis; secondly, those related to the crisis rather than those directly suffering from it may be psychologically freer to seek assistance. The librarian's guidance, therefore, will often be to materials both for the seeker and, through him, to materials for the person experiencing the crisis.

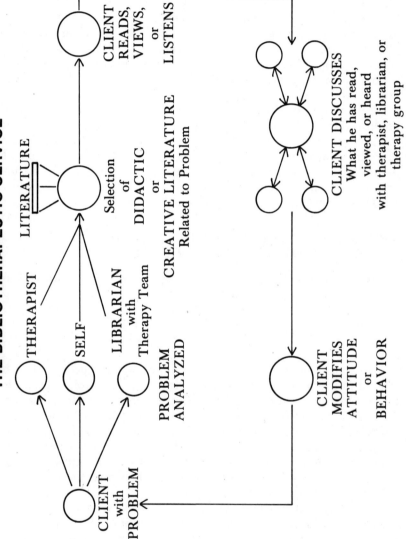

THE BIBLIOTHERAPEUTIC SERVICE

THERAPIST

SELF

LIBRARIAN
with
Therapy Team

PROBLEM
ANALYZED

LITERATURE

Selection
of
DIDACTIC
or
CREATIVE LITERATURE
Related to Problem

CLIENT
READS,
VIEWS,
or
LISTENS

CLIENT DISCUSSES
What he has read,
viewed, or heard
with therapist, librarian, or
therapy group

CLIENT
with
PROBLEM

CLIENT
MODIFIES
ATTITUDE
or
BEHAVIOR

THE BIBLIOTHERAPEUTIC MODEL FOR LIBRARY SERVICE

The process of bibliotherapy as a library service must be understood to be one that may be initiated by the client with the problem, by a therapist, or by a librarian in combination with client or therapist-with-client. The statement of the client's problem is never the librarian's; the librarian may assist in the analysis only in relation to what the librarian needs to know to make wise selection of the materials. These are important ethical considerations; no professional person ever has a mandate to move into personal knowledge except as that profession requires the knowledge necessary to the style of problem-solving which his profession openly offers.

The librarian must know which forms of literature (print, film, recording) the client handles with ease and satisfaction; must know enough of the client's situation in relation to the problem to select the materials reflecting best the aspects of the problem which need understanding and resolution; must assess (usually intuitively) the capacity of the client to sustain identification with the situation or characters for the duration of the selected materials, and reinforce that readiness to sustain the experiencing of the literature; and must provide the client any encouragement needed to undertake reflection and insight (whether through follow-up reading or through group discussion or conversation with others in the same dilemma or with a professional helper).

As the chart of the Bibliotherapeutic Process suggests, basically it is the client who must make most of the efforts—to read, to reflect, to discuss, to articulate insights, and to embody new understanding in changed behavior or orientation to the situation. All else is supplementary and supportive.

Finally, the model points to the fact that bibliotherapy is not a magic one-time thing, but a cyclic process, with small effects cumulating and the potential of major change coming in a series of small, nontraumatic transformations of attitude or behavior.

WHAT THE LIBRARIAN MUST KNOW TO SUPPORT THE BIBLIOTHERAPEUTIC PROCESS

The librarian who is to serve as bibliotherapist must:

Know the client (reader/viewer/listener) as a person
Know about the problem
Know the library resources and their potential for therapy
Know how to work in a team.

Know the Client

To the extent that the librarian is able to be acquainted with the library user (reader/viewer/listener), to know him not only in relation to his problem but to appreciate his talents and life experience in other areas, the librarian will be able to select materials that support his positive qualities as well as focus on his problem area. Further, this knowledge of the client by the librarian permits skillful, unobtrusive channeling of the discussion to allow him to express his ideas and experiences in group discussion sessions that follow the reading, viewing or listening. Finally, such knowledge enables the librarian to use an informed layman's level of perception of the problem without confusing the professor with the total person-as-person.

Know About the Problem

Basic knowledge of the major human problem areas is essential for the librarian working in bibliotherapy. Personal sensitivity must be enhanced by at least a knowledgeable layman's level of understanding of clinical interpretation of the patterns and problems associated with well-known mental illnesses. Equally important, the librarian must know the major traumas of life in their problem contexts; widowhood, alcoholism, deafness are only examples of the wide range of "things that happen to us" which have now well-plotted effects and associated problems. These must be understood by the librarian so that library materials and services can be brought to suitable assistance whenever appropriate. The intensity of the problems of widowhood for many require guidance to counseling and social programs; the complexity of alcoholism requires a many-faceted community support program with families, employers and the public at large; the social isolation of deafness must be understood for its effects on personality and remedied as completely as possible to sustain the person who undergoes this deprivation.

Know the Library Resources

Acquaintance with the problem, for the librarian, is most often through books and films. As the librarian undergoes this self-education, he/she accumulates a sophisticated judgment of the body of literature suitable for use by the client with the problem, useful to friends and family who seek to help, and of value to the professional helpers. Sharing of this knowledge through reading lists, bibliographies, oral interpretations in book talks or film showings makes an important contribution to alleviation of the problem in society.

The written record of these selective choices of materials for particular purposes is a highly important professional function. The experience can be shared widely. No librarian has time to develop the needed depth knowledge in every problem area, but must have available sound analyses of problems and of the related literature from which to work.

Each librarian serving as bibliotherapist, however, will find at least one area in which to make a unique contribution of materials analysis. The process of such analysis should be probing and definitive. *Alcohol Education for the Layman* represents one such librarian's journey into the problem and the literature, and this author can attest to the enormous rewards in personal understanding.[5]

Know How to Work in a Team

Because most librarians who serve as aids in the bibliotherapeutic process are not also trained psychologists or counselors, bibliotherapist librarians must have the skills of working in a team with trained therapists. The role of the therapist is to work with the client in diagnosis of the problem and determination of the treatment, while the librarian as member of the team consults on the selection of book, film or recording to be used, the environment for use, and may conduct the discussion of the literature with the clients. Further, the bibliotherapist librarian will report to the team and the therapist the effects of the use of literature which he/she has observed. The librarian reports overt behavior; the therapist interprets its significance. Further, the librarian turns to the therapist for assistance to the client when the bibliotherapeutic experience brings to crisis the client's understanding of the problem.

Such a team-oriented use of literature for therapy is logical and available within most institutional library contexts. The public librarian must seek to create a counterpart community team within the mental health professional group. Clinical counselors collaborative with such a program are probably the best answer to a very real need. A likely area for such experimental work would be in the homebound service to elderly.

Until such a team approach is possible for the librarian, the most effective involvement of the librarian in bibliotherapy is that of assisting and aiding the normal bibliotherapeutic effects to flow from the reader's interaction with suitably selected library resources, and enhancing the experience through the normal, benign effects of group discussion of such materials. Sensitive to the inevitability of the bibliotherapeutic process, the librarian—aware and knowledgeable—will observe and assist, and then may make a personal decision to move to further professional expertise.

REFERENCES

1. *Webster's Third New International Dictionary* (Springfield, Massachusetts: Merriam, 1961).
2. Harris C. McClaskey, "Bibliotherapy with Emotionally Disturbed Patients: An Experimental Study." Ph.D. dissertation, University of Washington (1970).

3. Lesta N. Burt, "Bibliotherapy: Effect of Group Reading and Discussion on Attitudes of Adult Inmates in Two Correctional Institutions." Ph.D. dissertation, University of Wisconsin (1972).

4. See Margaret E. Monroe and Jean Stewart, *Alcohol Education for the Layman* (New Brunswick, New Jersey: Rutgers University Press, 1959).

5. Ibid. While professional librarianship tended to ignore this publication, teachers responsible for developing programs of alcohol education were enthusiastic users, and families with alcoholic members expressed heart-felt gratitude for the volume.

Bibliotherapy:
Its Nature and Uses

by Louis A. Rongione

Over sixteen hundred years ago, a distraught and widowed mother approached her local bishop. She was overwhelmed with worry and apprehension because of the waywardness of her teen-age son. "I am no match for him," she told the bishop, "I do not know how to refute his horrible doctrines or correct his wicked conduct. Only you can disprove his errors; only you can lead him from darkness to light, from depravity to righteousness."

"No!" said the bishop. "He is not yet teachable. He is puffed up with pride at the novelty of his heresy and the conceit of his captious questions. Leave him alone. Only pray for him. He will find out for himself by reading, what his mistakes are and the depth of his depravity."[1]

Reading was the key suggested by the bishop to the cure of this boy's intellectual and moral blindness. Fifteen years later, this boy, now a professor of rhetoric, was perusing the *Epistles of St. Paul* when he came across the following passage: "Let us therefore throw off the deeds of darkness and put on the armour as soldiers of the light. Let us behave with decency as befits the day: no revelling or drunkenness, no debauchery or vice, no quarrels or jealousies! Let Christ Jesus himself be the armour you wear: give no more thought to satisfying the bodily appetites."[2]

The transformation which these words brought about are recorded in his autobiography: "I had no wish to read further; there was no need to. For immediately I reached the end of this sentence it was as though my heart was filled with a light of confidence and all the shadow of my doubt was swept away."[3]

The rest is history, the history of the triumph of truth over error, of virtue over vice, a complete cure effected by God's grace, through a wise choice of reading. A victory for bibliotherapy! The mother was St. Monica, the son was St. Augustine, a colossus at the crossroads of civilization, a genius whose books have influenced and enriched the culture of nations and brought solace and wisdom to millions of people for sixteen centuries.

Reprinted with permission from *Catholic Library World* 43:495-500 (May/June 1972). Copyright © 1972 by the Catholic Library Association.

The therapeutic value of books goes back beyond Christian antiquity to pre-Christian Egypt. Over the portal of the library at Alexandria, we find this inscription: "Medicine of the Mind." The Greek words can also be translated as: "A sanatorium for the mind," or "Nourishment for the soul."

Shakespeare, too, attests to the curative effects of books as is evident from these words:

> Come, and take choice of
> all my library,
> And so beguile thy sorrow.[4]

When matched to the patient at the appropriate psychological moment, books can influence the intellect, will, and emotions. For this reason, bibliotherapy may be called the pharmacy of the soul. To be effective, whether considered as an art or a science, bibliotherapy requires the cooperation of the patient, the physician, the psychiatrist, the therapist, the librarian, and others involved in the program.

Definition of Bibliotherapy

Helpful definitions of bibliotherapy can be found in the dictionaries of such fields as medicine, nursing, and psychiatry and in periodical literature of the last half century.

One definition which combines the essential elements found in most scientific statements is the following:

> Bibliotherapy is a program of selected activity involving reading materials, planned, conducted and controlled as treatment under the guidance of the physician for emotional and other problems. It must be administered by a skilled, professionally trained librarian within the prescribed purpose and goals. The important and dynamic factors are the relationships which are established, the patient's reactions and responses, and the reporting back to the physicians for interpretation, evaluation, and directions in follow-up.[5]

Objectives

The following are some of the objectives of bibliotherapy:

1. To teach a person to think positively and constructively and so to avoid negative and pessimistic patterns of thought.

2. To encourage a person to talk freely and honestly about problems which, in the past, fear, shame, or guilt made it difficult for him to discuss.

3. To help a person to analyze his attitudes and behavior with a view to understanding better his mental and emotional reactions to frustrations and conflicts.

4. To point out that more than one solution to a problem is possible and that some choice may be exercised in the way a problem is handled.

5. To increase a person's self-esteem in the realization of his intrinsic worth as a child of God and as a member of the various social institutions, such as, the family, the community, the church, the country, etc.

6. To stimulate his eagerness to seek adjustment that will lessen his conflicts, as he finds in books that others have successfully surmounted similar problems.

7. To assist a person to compare his problems with those of others so that his feeling of isolation may be dispelled and his fear of being different may be allayed.

8. To help the person to explore his own basic and mixed motivations and those of others when involved in particular situations.

9. To stimulate a person's imagination, enlarge his sphere of interests, and afford vicarious satisfaction without exposing him to the real dangers of certain actual experiences.

10. To provide guidelines of conduct and to reinforce, by precept and example, acceptable social and cultural patterns of morality which inhibit infantile, anti-social, even criminal behavior.

11. To assist a person to rise above merely material considerations and motivate him to see values in human and spiritual terms.

12. To provide therapeutically planned experiences which will encourage a person to face his situation honestly, reasonably, and realistically and to plan and carry to fruition a constructive course of action.

An Interesting and Challenging Career

Bibliotherapy is an interesting and challenging activity for librarians, provided they abide by basic relevant principles. To be effective, they must cultivate the proper personal qualities and acquire the necessary knowledge and skills. The bibliotherapist must realize the need for an interdisciplinary approach and be faithful to the ethical standards of bibliotherapy.

The relevant basic principles assert that there is sufficient evidence to support the contention that carefully selected reading has therapeutic value in cases of physical, psychological, emotional, and moral problems. Conversely, a poor selection of reading can be harmful in the same ways. It is naive to assert that reading can do no harm. We can state simply and unequivocally that if there are no bad books, then there are no good books. And, if there are no good books, then let us stop publishing such standard works as: *Children's Catalog; Junior High School Library Catalog; Senior High School Library Catalog; Books for Junior College Libraries; Books for College Libraries; Standard Catalog for Public Libraries.* Since all of these are "selected lists" the implication is that the books recommended are in some way, better or preferable to those omitted from these publications.

Personal Qualities of the Bibliotherapist

The personal qualities which the bibliotherapist must possess or cultivate include:

1. A balanced personality which implies emotional stability, physical well-being, mature judgment, and the ability to channel personal feelings and to direct them to the best interest of those whom he desires to help.

2. The ability to work with people, including the competence to instruct and the skill to supervise other personnel and associates.

3. The willingness to familiarize oneself with the community as well as the individual and to empathize with the misfortunes and shortcomings of others and to react with sufficient facility to be of help.

4. An understanding of the goal desired in each instance, together with a willingness to accept responsibility for the action taken, and the ability to assume, without reluctance and without arrogance, the authority necessary to meet each situation.

Knowledge of the Bibliotherapist

The necessary knowledge of the bibliotherapist should include more than a passing acquaintance with:

1. Literature for children, young adults, and adults.

2. The biological sciences of anatomy and physiology.

3. Elementary psychiatry.

4. Psychology in so far as it pertains to:
   a) Techniques of diagnosis, guidance, and counseling.
   b) The physically handicapped and the emotionally disturbed.
   c) Different kinds of ethnic groups.
   d) Principles of motivation and remotivation.
   e) Techniques of testing along with training in the interpretation of test results.

5. Sociology as it relates to:
   a) Medical and social problems of illness.
   b) Techniques of rehabilitation of the aging.
   c) Training in statistics and report writing.

Skills of the Bibliotherapist

Among the skills required of the bibliotherapist are the following:

1. The ability to discover a person's emotional, mental, and spiritual needs.

2. The aptitude to make valid interpretations of a person's reactions to readings.

3. The facility to understand and use the terminology of medicine, psychiatry, and psychology so that he can communicate effectively with the practitioners of these professions.

4. The competency to evaluate capacities, to assign specific books, to administer a suitable reading program, to review and evaluate the program constantly, and to make progress reports.

5. The discernment to discard the erroneous and irrelevant and to draw only warranted and valid conclusions.

Ethical Considerations

The ethical considerations require the bibliotherapist to adhere to a code of conduct which includes:

1. A willing assumption of the limitations of both the librarian and of bibliotherapy.

2. An acknowledgement of the potential contributions which the other professions can bring to bibliotherapy.

3. A strict observance of professional secrecy commensurate with the confidential nature of the responsibilities assumed.

It must seem at this point that it is the rare librarian, indeed, who possesses all these personal and professional qualities that we require of the bibliotherapist.

Perhaps no one person need have all of these qualities. What is necessary is that the bibliotherapist must be a librarian who goes beyond bibliocounseling or reader guidance and becomes a specialist. He should also avail himself of the services and competencies of other professionals outside the field of librarianship. Certainly, there is a need for a coordination of the efforts of the physician, the psychiatrist, the spiritual advisor, the nurse, the sociologist, the physiotherapist, the librarian, and others who must become involved if the reading program is to be beneficial and effective.

Particular Applications of Bibliotherapy

The particular applications of bibliotherapy are literally limitless. In the 1970 fall semester the author taught a course on Bibliotherapy to the Library Science students in the School of Graduate Studies, at Villanova University. Books were selected which applied to young people with the following problems:

1. Physical:
   - a) Blindness
   - b) Deformity
   - c) Deafness
   - d) Homeliness
   - e) Obesity
   - f) Speech Defects

2. Chronic Illness:
   a) Invalidism   b) Rheumatic Fever
                    c) Tuberculosis
3. Mental and Emotional Problems:
   a) Low Vocabulary   c) Mental Deficiency
   b) Mental Disturbance   d) Reading Difficulty
4. Poor Personality and Character Traits:
   a) Conceit   d) Loneliness
   b) Intolerance   e) Selfishness
   c) Irresponsibility   f) Timidity
5. Socio-Economic Problems:
   a) Alcoholism   f) Law & Order vs. Freedom
   b) Boy-Girl Relationships g) Poverty
   c) Drug Addiction   h) Racial & Ethnic Relationships
   d) Family Relationships   i) Violence
   e) Generation Gap   j) War & Peace

All of these categories were subdivided and, in each case, books, mostly fiction, were selected and recommended for application to and possible alleviation of the problems treated. By way of illustration let us mention just four out of the scores of books selected.

And Now Tomorrow, by Rachel Field, is applicable to the problem of deafness. *Hearts Courageous,* by William Herman, consists of inspirational stories of twelve people who overcame physical handicaps to achieve greatness. *The Bears on Hemlock Mountain,* by Alice Dalgliesh, might give some comfort to a person suffering from excessive shyness or timidity. The problems which might arise from being both Jewish and Black find a possible solution in *All American,* by John R. Tunis.

Most of the books, selected for use by school librarians, had special appeal for children and young people of grades K to 12. Other lists of books were compiled to meet the needs of librarians in the various types of hospitals, correctional and mental institutions, orphan asylums, etc.

Adverse Effects

Caution and caveats must be exercised for possible adverse effects in the applications of bibliotherapy. An implied parallel between the application of drugs in chemotherapy and the prescription of books in bibliotherapy will lead to the following cautions for their safe and effective use:

1. In cases of chronic illness, the indication in medicine is the proper use of drugs, and in bibliotherapy, the wise selection of books. We must remember, however, that prolonged illness produces emotional patterns quite different from those of people in good health or who suffer from an acute illness. Failure to recognize these differ-

ences would lead to failure in bibliotherapy and even worse in chemotherapy.

2. Contra-indication: usually, a reading program is of little or no value in acute forms of illness. Any reading done by patients who suffer from acute illness is simply for entertainment or diversion; rarely is its purpose for the proper understanding of the disease.

3. How much and for how long should a person read? Enough to help him cope with his problem. For instance, a diabetic person, suffering from marked insecurity, was harmed rather than helped when he read so much material on diabetes that he discovered discrepancies between caloric values found in various charts. So also did harmful effects follow in the case of a young mother of a child with rheumatic fever. She collected and read all the information she could find, and developed an over-protective reaction which became the cause of a cardiac neurosis in the child.

Limitations

This article, written by a librarian, is principally theoretic and makes no pretense of being scientific. Though clinical application is a logical and desirable outcome of our theorizing, such a step requires knowledge and training beyond the usual competencies of most librarians. In a relatively recent article, Armando Favazza is critical of most of the literature on bibliotherapy.

> The truth of the matter is that the vast majority of the literature on bibliotherapy is repetitiously shallow, anecdotal, unscientific, conjectural, confusing, propagandistic, and static.[6]

Perhaps this article suffers from the same general limitations. Inevitably, scientific methods and the clinical applications must be applied in the field of bibliotherapy. Such a course is necessary and desirable. With the incursion of the scientific and the clinical, however, I hope that we can avoid two possible pitfalls. One is the danger that science may inhibit and straight-jacket bibliotherapy as has happened when the scientific approach was applied to such areas of knowledge as classical, biblical, and historical studies. The second is the danger of succumbing to the subtle fallacy that a thing is not true unless proven to be so scientifically. Quite the reverse is the case. It is only because a thing *is* true that it becomes possible to prove it so scientifically.

Conclusions

The following are some safe and valid conclusions:

1. Despite some confusion and limitations, there is sufficient evidence to support the claim in favor of the therapeutic value of carefully selected reading.

2. Individual librarians ought to acquaint themselves with some of the super-abundant literature in the field of bibliotherapy.

3. Schools of library service must take a more active interest and institute courses, seminars, workshops, and clinical experiences in bibliotherapy. The course in bibliotherapy taught by the author at Villanova University in the fall of 1970 was very well received and occasioned sufficient response to warrant its being given again in the 1972 Spring Semester. Under consideration also is a follow-up course to include clinical experience.

4. Hospitals, mental and correctional institutions, as well as schools, should investigate the possible benefits of making use of people trained in bibliotherapy and bibliocounseling.

5. In addition to the therapeutic value, other benefits to patients and students can be reasonably expected from a wise choice of reading.

George Crabbe, in his poem *The Library,* gives an apt and artistic summary of some of the ideas advanced in this article.

> But what strange art, what magic
>   can dispose
> The troubled mind to change its
>   native woes? . . .
> This, books can do;—nor this alone,
>   they give
> New views to life, and teach us
>   how to live,
> They soothe the griev'd, the stubborn
>   they chastise.
> Fools they admonish, and
>   confirm the wise.[7]

REFERENCES

1. cf. St. Augustine. *Confessions* 3:12:21.

2. *Romans.* 13:12-13. (*New English Bible,* Oxford University Press, 1970).

3. *Confessions.* 8:12:29.

4. *Titus Andronicus.* Act IV, Sc. 1, 1. 34.

5. Armando R. Favazza. "Bibliotherapy: A Critique of the Literature." *Bulletin of the Medical Library Association,* LIV (April, 1966), p. 139.

6. *Ibid,* p. 138.

7. George Crabbe. *The Library A Poem,* (London: Reproduction by Anthoensen Press, November, 1966), p. 5, lines 6-13.

For Further Reading

Dr. Howard M. Bogard, "Bibliotherapy—For Whom and By Whom." *Association of Hospital and Institution Libraries Quarterly*, VI (Fall 1965) pp. 11-17.

Dr. John F. Briggs, "Adverse Effects from Bibliotherapy." *Hospital Progress*, XLV (July 5, 1964) pp. 123-125.

Christa H. Buswell, "Reading and the Aged." *Wilson Library Bulletin*, XLV (January 1971) pp. 467-476.

Patricia J. Cianciolo, "Children's Literature Can Affect Coping Behavior." *Personnel and Guidance Journal*, XLIII (May 1965) pp. 897-903.

Lonnie L. Emerick, "Bibliotherapy for Stutterers: Four Case Histories." *Quarterly Journal of Speech*, LII (February 1966) pp. 74-79.

Florence Grannis, "Philosophical Implications of Book Selection for the Blind." *Wilson Library Bulletin*, XLIII (December 1968) pp. 330-339.

E. J. Josey, "Reading and the Disadvantaged." *Negro History Bulletin*, XXVIII (April 1965) pp. 156-157, 159.

Archie L. Lejeune, "Bibliocounseling as a Guidance Technique." *Catholic Library World*, XLI (November 1969) pp. 156-164.

Clara E. Lucioli, "Out of Isolation." *Library Journal*, XCII (April 1, 1967) pp. 1421-1423.

Mildred T. Moody, "Bibliotherapy for Chronic Illnesses." *Hospital Progress*, XLV (January 1964) pp. 63-64.

Harold A. Moses and Joseph S. Zaccaria, "Bibliotherapy in an Educational Context: Rationale and Principles." *High School Journal*, LII (April 1969) pp. 401-411.

Austin L. Porterfield, *Mirror for Adjustment; Therapy in Home, School, and Society through Seeing Yourself and Others in Books.* (Ft. Worth, Texas, Manney Co., 1967).

Rev. Louis A. Rongione, "Science Fiction: The Psychological Aspects of Science Fiction Can Contribute Much to Bibliotherapy." *Catholic Library World*, XXXVIII (October 1964) pp. 96-99.

Caroline Shrodes, *Bibliotherapy: A Theoretical and Clinical-Experimental Study.* (Berkeley, University of California, 1950).

Ruth M. Tews, issue editor. "Bibliotherapy." *Library Trends*, XI (October 1962) pp. 97-228.

Ruth M. Tews, "Progress in Bibliotherapy," in *Advances in Librarianship*, I. Melvin J. Voight, ed. (New York: Academic Press, 1970) pp. 171-187.

Bibliotherapy for Chronic Illnesses

by Mildred T. Moody

The problem of chronic illness continues to grow as more patients are kept alive through advances in medical skill. According to the U.S. National Health Survey, an estimated 42 percent of the civilian non-institutional population has one or more chronic diseases; for 14.2 million persons the limitations are so severe as to result in inability or reduced ability to work, to keep house or go to school.[1] It is further estimated that there are two million people hospitalized for chronic illness, not counting those in mental or tuberculosis hospitals.[2]

For the acutely ill, the experience is merely an unpleasant episode, after which life moves on. Chronic illness, like an unwelcome guest, imposes a tyranny from which the patient cannot escape without the help of many people. It becomes a medical, psychological and social problem for which a team approach has been developed. This team includes library service as one of the rehabilitation therapies.

Reading as a pastime and means of gaining information is so taken for granted that its use as adjunctive therapy is often overlooked. What occupational therapy does for those who have a muscle-wasting disease, or recreational therapy does for those deprived of social interaction, bibliotherapy does for the intellectually deprived. In all three therapies the patient becomes the performer, the active participant, not merely the passive recipient. In each case, the handiwork, or the game, or the book is fitted to his particular level, his current need, and if possible acts as a bridge to a more advanced step in the rehabilitative process.

Intellectual deprivation can encompass a number of things the causes of which may be physical, mental or social. The victim of aphasia, for instance, will have to start recognizing words and reading from the simplest kind of books; the patient in a mental hospital may give a clue to solving the mystery of his disorder through the choice of a book or his reaction to a book he reads; the handicapped individual with restricted mobility will meet interesting people through their biographies, and see faraway places through the accounts of travelers.[3]

The dictionary defines *bibliotherapy* as "the use of selected reading materials as therapeutic adjuvants in medicine and in psychiatry; also, guidance in the solution of personal problems through directed reading."[4] To the hospital librarian this definition lends itself to a formula: good book selection + individual guidance + a definite goal = therapy. In a mental hospital bibliotherapy may be used as a specific part of diagnosis and treatment, and it is one of the techniques such as remotivation or psycho-drama. But bibliotherapy need not have so specific an application, although all reading cannot be considered therapeutic any more than casual handicraft is occupational therapy.

A recent study was made of the use of free time of ambulatory, chronically ill, elderly people.[5] Information was obtained from 167 patients through hour-long interviews by a social worker. Reading was the third most common activity, with TV or radio listening first, and "sitting and chatting" second. Of the group, 62 percent read often, 23 percent occasionally, for a total of 85 percent. The choice of reading was mostly newspapers, but often "uplift" books like the Bible were mentioned. It was not stated whether library service was available, but undoubtedly there would be more diversified reading by this group if the books were offered and some stimulus provided. Large public library systems have devised methods for reaching nursing homes and the home-bound, but there are countless institutionalized aged and chronically ill whose intellectual capacities have deteriorated because of the lack of suitable reading in a directed program.

Reading divides itself naturally into four categories: recreation, useful information, intellectual stimulation, and insight. There are elements of bibliotherapy in all four. An entertaining novel can be the means of discharging hostility as the reader identifies with a character, and vicariously works out the problem in the story. The novel which will help a vigorous, mature male patient is not the story which will produce a comparable psychological effect in the "little old lady from Dubuque," but in every book which the reader enjoys there is personal identification, and a measure of personal satisfaction, so that communication has been established. When the book is finished, the reader is reluctant to put it down and break the contact.

Reading for useful information is an important part of bibliotherapy with the chronically ill, because it helps the patient accept and overcome his handicap. He must learn about the nature of his disease; he must study ways in which the limitations imposed by his handicap can be mitigated, and there are excellent articles dealing with physical restoration which are suitable for patient use. These will give instructions on how to dress, or move about, or keep house with every conceivable type of handicap. There is excellent material for the home care of invalids for use by the patient and his family. Material on vocational rehabilitation, and reference material for both formal and informal educational pursuits should be available. Assistance to the chronically ill should be one of the primary objectives of library service since it is through training and reading that the patient will gain a measure of independence and re-enter the mainstream of life. He must make the effort himself, but he cannot do it without guidance.

Reading for intellectual stimulation is not easy reading, and requires a good deal of motivation. Stretching one's mental muscles can be as difficult and painful as physical exercise, and as necessary to one whose activities will be restricted for the rest of his life. The mind which thinks and explores can extend itself far beyond the limits of a confined body. The Adult Services Division of the American Library Association has developed a series of reading guides—*Reading for an Age of Change.*[6] Three subjects are included: "Space Science," "Contemporary Art," and "Intellectual Freedom." Reading from these guides is intended to broaden the scope of one's knowledge at a fairly high level, but there are reading lists for all levels, and reader's advisory services at any good library or state library agency, but the patient requires help in making the contact.

READING CAN TEACH ACCEPTANCE

Reading for insight comes when life has dealt a severe blow to a human being who follows it with the inevitable reaction: "Why?" Once the crisis of acute illness is past, the chronic phase allows time for introspection. Since the time of Job the question has been asked, "What have I done to deserve this?" There is not a pastor or hospital chaplain who has not been asked this question. This is a very sensitive concern of the hospital library and one that is often ignored. Books in this category can be of the greatest help, and the greatest offense. A recent phenomenon noted by hospital librarians is the present lack of interest in the "positive thinking" approach to philosophical and religious problems. Our present age of anxiety seems to engender a deeper and more personal sense of responsibility.

Reading is not only a good pastime for the lonely, it can teach acceptance of loneliness. In his essay, *God's Lonely Man,* Thomas Wolfe wrote, "The whole conviction of my life now rests upon the belief that loneliness, far from being a rare and curious phenomenon, peculiar to myself and to a few other solitary men, is the central and inevitable fact of human existence."[7] This is a condition which the chronically ill person must face and accept—not as a harsh and bitter fact, but as an opportunity to learn to know himself, accept and like himself, and be at peace with himself.

MEMORIES ARE IMPORTANT

One asset the chronically ill person has is his past. Dr. Joost A. M. Meerloo, writing on psychotherapy with the aged, presents a formula which every hospital librarian will understand: "Those who think that they have no future must be brought back to the past in order to accept the present."[8] In searching for a point of interest when helping a patient choose books, the most successful contact is established when some past moment of triumph, or pleasurable experience, is the basis for the selection. It can be the starting point for directed reading so that the past becomes the means of accepting the present. The subject can be almost anything—the place of one's birth, a childhood hero, a sport or activity in which one excelled, but it must be a subject which, when recalled, recreates a measure of self-esteem so that the individual says to himself, "I am still that person, there is hope for me yet."

Given the incentive, and the proper choice of books, the majority of chronically ill patients will do meaningful reading. The difficulty in many communities is the development of an adequate program. Books can be purchased, or donated, and space assigned, but what kinds of books, and who will be responsible for the collection and its distribution? It is unrealistic to expect every hospital to have a professional librarian on its staff; budgets do not permit it, and even now there is a shortage of trained librarians.

The Association of Hospital and Institution Libraries, which is a division of the American Library Association, is in the process of revising its standards for hospital libraries, and a very realistic approach to standards for small libraries is expected. Endorsement of the standards will be sought from national organizations which set standards for hospitals, including the Catholic Hospital Association. It is hoped that the over-all study of the problem will lead to publication of a series of manuals for the management of all types of small libraries in hospitals. The manuals would enable any hospital to organize and maintain a library that would be considered adequate for its size, with quality of content, and that could be manned by other than professional library personnel. The hospital, however, should establish contact with a professional librarian in the community who could act as consultant.

The need for recreational and rehabilitative services to the chronically ill is well-recognized, and the role of the library in this program is becoming more clearly defined. With hospital associations and library associations working together on the problem, there should soon emerge a pattern for service which will strengthen the rehabilitation team, and make bibliotherapy an adjunctive therapy which has real meaning.

FOOTNOTES

1. U.S. Department of Health, Education and Welfare, Public Health Service, *Areawide Planning of Facilities for Long-term Treatment and Care.* Report of the Joint Committee of the American Hospital Association and Public Health Service, 1963, p. 47.

2. James F. Conner, *Hospitalization for Long-term Illness,* in *Long-term Illness,* Michael G. Wohl, ed. (Philadelphia: Saunders, 1959), p. 3.

3. Orrilla T. Blackshear, "Public Libraries Serve the Aging," *Geriatrics,* 15:390-397 (May 1960).

4. Webster's *Third New International Dictionary* (Springfield, Massachusetts: G. & C. Merriam Co., 1961), p. 212.

5. Barbara Henley, L. Zeitz and G. Reader, "Uses of Free Time by Ambulatory Chronically Ill Elderly Patients," *J. Am. Geriat. Soc.,* 10:1,081-1,091 (December 1962).

6. American Library Association. *81st Annual Conference Proceedings,* Miami Beach, Florida: June 17-23, 1962, p. 66.

7. Thomas Wolfe, *The Hills Beyond* (New York: Harper, 1935), pp. 186-197.

8. Joost A. M. Meerloo, "Modes of Psychotherapy in the Aged," *J. Am. Geriat. Soc.,* 9:225-234 (March 1961).

Narcotic Addicts Take Up Reading

by Margaret C. Hannigan
and William T. Henderson

"Reading helps you get along better with people." — "On the outside, when you come from work, a good book will keep you out of trouble. I won't want to be on the streets so much. I'll stay home more. I feel I'll be able to get closer to my parents." — "I don't believe I ever read a whole book through before. Now I've started reading and I like it." — "Before, I used to think, 'Why should I read?' I wandered in the streets. I feel when I get out I'll be able to stay home more and read."

These are comments of young narcotic addicts who took part in a weekly group reading program at the New York State Vocational Institution at West Coxsackie recently.

Early in 1963, the Correction Department asked the Library Extension Division to conduct a bibliotherapy project as part of a special program for thirty young drug addicts who were nearing parole and who had been brought to the Institution from correctional institutions throughout the state. After several planning meetings, it was decided that the project would be a four-month demonstration and would take the form of reading groups similar to those conducted in many hospitals.[1] An attractive rotating collection of books would be supplied by the Mid-Hudson Library System to back up the program and materials for reading in the group session would be furnished by the Library Extension Division. Because of previous experience with reading groups, we were chosen to carry out the demonstration. It was by special dispensation that a woman was allowed on the team.

We should say a word about the men themselves since our readers may share some of the misconceptions about addicts which we ourselves had at the beginning. From our reading and from advice received from people we talked to, we were prepared to find a group of somewhat withdrawn, passive, unresponsive individuals — individuals, as someone said, who would be tough to work with. Instead we met a nice-looking, attentive group of normal-appearing young men comparable, perhaps, to a class of older students in a vocational high school. They were alert, responsive, interested and cooperative, due to

Reprinted with permission from *Bookmark* 22:281-286 (July 1963).

a large extent, no doubt, to the fact that they had not had access to drugs for some time. Their ages ranged from 17 to 26. While their educational classification was from low remedial through high school level, their differences in reading ability seemed to be an asset rather than a deterrent to the progress of the group. From the beginning the good readers helped the slow readers and the latter were able to accept assistance and correction from their fellows without resentment.

We were introduced to the men at a meeting at which officials of the Institution explained the special program being offered. Price Chenault, Education Director of the Department of Correction, in his talk pointed out that any benefits derived from the project would reach beyond the men in the group. He said that what happened in this program could well determine whether similar opportunities would be offered in other State institutions.

We, in turn, talked to the men about the benefits of good reading, referring to the indispensable *Wonderful World of Books* and citing actual cases where books and reading had helped individuals help themselves. Jointly we explained the reading group idea and showed some of the books which would be available for them to borrow. For our book talks we chose titles ranging from *The Family Book of Verse* (from which Mr. Henderson read "The Raven"), *Victory Over Myself* by Floyd Patterson, *Act I* (Miss Hannigan read the incident where Moss Hart, as a boy of 13, worked in the storage vault of a furrier), to Audel's *New Automobile Guide* and *The Occupational Outlook Handbook*. After a question and answer period, all but three of the men signed up for the program and checked out books they wished to borrow. It was heartwarming to see their pleasure and interest in examining the books and talking among themselves and to us about their selections. Several requested additional material they wished to read.

We would be less than honest to pretend that, at this stage, they joined the reading group for itself. The beautiful new books were a magnetic drawing card.

During the week following our meeting with the entire group, the 27 men who had signed up for the reading program were divided into four sections. Each section met with one of the librarians for a fifty-minute period, the major part of which was spent reading aloud short stories, plays, poetry, articles or excerpts from books. About ten or fifteen minutes were allowed for selecting and checking out material for their recreational reading. The men were encouraged to talk about their reading and to recommend books they enjoyed to others. Occasionally, we gave book talks aimed at broadening reading interests and experience.

We both regret the fact that we did not ask, early in the program, to have the men reassigned to two groups instead of four so that the length of the period could be doubled. It would have been so much more effective and satisfying if we could have finished a short story or one-act play at a sitting, with ample time left over for examining, sampling and talking about books. Although they politely made the best of the situation, the men, too, were disappointed about the inadequate amount of time. Almost all of them said they thought a session should last at least two hours and agreed that they would be willing to give some of their free time for this program.

Into our brief sessions we tried to cram many reading experiences and still make the activity pleasurable. We wanted the men to discover the enjoyment as well as the benefits of reading. We encouraged them to experience life vicariously through books and to become acquainted with many kinds of people and many places. We tried to make them realize the great variety of knowledge and ideas they would find in books. We wanted them to listen to what the authors were saying but to think for themselves.

Always conscious of the limited background of most of these men, and of the short time many had actually lived outside of prison, we tried to enrich their understanding through discussing words, ideas and unfamiliar points. For their part, the men impressed us by the way in which they entered into the spirit of whatever we were reading. They were often expressive and dramatic and their responses to material beyond their experience were appropriate and intelligent.

Everyone seemed to enjoy short stories and essays, with Harry Golden, O. Henry and Poe being among the favorite authors. One of our happiest selections was William E. Barrett's "Señor Payroll," a story of Mexicans working in the mills. It gave the Spanish-speaking men a chance to excel in reading the Spanish names and words, which they did with enthusiasm and ease. For once they were able to correct the pronunciation of the usually more glib members of the group.

Poetry had a special appeal to the men. Their taste ranged from old familiar favorites to modern "beat" verse and they liked to read it individually and in unison. One day we had a hilarious time with nonsense verse and tongue-twisters from *The Silver Treasury of Light Verse.* The Puerto Rican members, especially, were fascinated by this exercise and for a while everyone was chattering at his own pace and giggling at his own thick tongue. Then, to the librarian's discomfort, someone discovered a poem she had missed, "Cocaine Lil and Morphine Sue." Since everyone wanted to copy it, the only graceful thing to do was to provide paper and pencils and let them. Then they read it aloud with great gusto, one member explaining that "this is a little joke we have." While we never would have chosen this selection, we think the incident brought the men and the librarian closer together.

Even though the group had had little or no experience with drama, play reading proved to be the most popular activity of all. The men were entranced with the plays and vied with each other for good parts. Each play stimulated significant discussion centered around its particular theme and characters. With Goodman's "Dust of the Road" and Benet's "The Devil and Daniel Webster" it was the supernatural elements which added a new dimension to our reading. "The Lottery," based on Shirley Jackson's eerie and shocking short story of the same title, gave us an opportunity to talk about scapegoats and superstitions. The most effective of all was Arthur Miller's powerful "All My Sons," with situations and relationships which came close to the men's own experiences. It certainly deepened their understanding of people, their motives and actions, and gave them chance to judge the solutions to problems which some of the characters chose.

Since the over-all aim of the demonstration was to make reading so important in the lives of the men that they could depend on it to help them through periods of discouragement, stress or temptation, we took time to acquaint them with public library services. We encouraged them to use their public library. All are from New York City so it was a simple matter to distribute booklets with the location of branches and the description of library services and programs. At the suggestion of Katherine O'Brien, Coordinator of Adult Services, we also gave them the name of Robert Sheehan, Reader's Advisor at the central library, and urged them to go to him for guidance in their reading.

As the project came to an end, efforts were made to evaluate it. Dr. Glenn M. Kendall, Director of the Institution, authorized the newly appointed librarian and two counsellors to interview the men about what the reading program meant to them and how they thought it might help them after they leave the Institution. Due allowances must be made for their natural desire to make a good impression, especially since the interviews were taped. Even so, their responses, some of which have already been quoted, were impressive and meaningful. Many had discovered that they enjoy reading and learn from it. Some had made lists of books they want to read or buy. Books have become a topic of conversation among themselves and with other men "in the yard." Recognizing that a common aim is a necessary ingredient for success in a project like this, several commented that other inmates could benefit from taking part in a reading group if they really wanted to help themselves. In their own case, they identified their common problem with drugs as the bond which assured their trying to get all they could from the reading.

In evaluating our own part in the program, we recognize that other approaches and techniques might have been more effective than those we used. But we are convinced that our faith in our ability to reach these men by approaching them as fellow human beings was vindicated by their reactions which were always cooperative and appreciative. The comments of two of the men are typical of the attitude of all: "When we first started, I had the feeling that someone cared for me and was trying to help me . . ." and "I thought, 'They're helping me. I'll try to do my best'."

Dr. Kendall is convinced that the program should be continued at West Coxsackie and has arranged for Herman R. Rudolf, Librarian at the Institution, to conduct a similar program for voluntary participants from the inmate population. The Mid-Hudson Library System, through the director, Leon Karpel, and the Library Extension Division will continue to cooperate, on a limited basis, with the program.

Commissioner Paul D. McGinnis of the Department of Correction and his staff, particularly Deputy Commissioner Benjamin Weinberg and Director of Education, Price Chenault, have followed the project with interest and have initiated a plan for other state correctional institutions to offer this kind of directed group-reading activity for inmates. On the last day of the project at West Coxsackie, we conducted a workshop for representatives of six State institutions which included observing the reading groups in action. Plans are being pursued for obtaining funds for books to support the program and to improve the institution library collections.

The project demonstrating the benefits and pleasures of reading would not have been possible if groundwork for good library service in correctional institutions had not been laid over the years by people like Mr. Chenault of the Department of Correction and Marion H. Vedder of the Library Extension Division. It could well be considered a climax to their devoted efforts, especially if it will serve to justify the use of public money to develop library resources and services worthy of being an integral part of the rehabilitative program in every correctional institution in the State.

BIBLIOGRAPHY

H. T. Eaton, ed., *Short Stories.* (New York: American Book Company, 1951).
  "One Hour of Glory" by Mary R. Rinehart
  "One Minute Longer" by Albert P. Terhune
  "Some Can't Take It" by B. B. Fowler

Harry Golden, *Only in America.* (New York: Permabooks, 1958).
  "Buying a Suite on the East Side"
  "Carry-the-Books-Plan"
  "Causerie on Death"
  "The Show Must Go On"
  "The Vertical Negro Plan"
  "Why I Never Bawl Out a Waitress"

R. B. Goodman, ed., *75 Short Masterpieces: Stories From the World's Literature.* (New York: Bantam Books, 1961).
  "Absent Mindedness in a Parish Choir" by Thomas Hardy
  "The Bedchamber Mystery" by C. S. Forester
  "Charles" by Shirley Jackson
  "Fear" by Rhys Davies
  "Señor Payroll" by W. E. Barrett

O. Henry, *The Pocket Book of O. Henry Stories.* ed. by Harry Hansen. (New York: Washington Square Press, 1959).
  "The Cop and the Anthem"

Henry Hewes, ed., *Famous Plays of the 1940's*. (New York: Dell, 1960).
"All My Sons" by Arthur Miller

Paul Kazelka, ed., *15 American One-Act Plays*. (New York: Washington
Square Press, 1961).
"The Devil and Daniel Webster" by S. V. Benet
"Dust of the Road" by K. S. Goodman
"The Lottery," adapted from a story by Shirley Jackson

Stephen Leacock. *Laugh with Leacock*. (New York: Dodd, 1913).
"My Financial Career"

F. T. Palgrave, comp., *Golden Treasury of the Best Songs and Lyrical
Poems*. (Rev. ed., New York: New American Library, 1961).
"Elegy Written in a Country Church Yard" by Thomas Gray
"Invictus" by W. E. Henley
"O Captain! My Captain!" by Walt Whitman
"The Passionate Shepherd of His Love" by Christopher Marlowe
"The Seven Ages of Man" by William Shakespeare

E. A. Poe, *Great Tales and Poems*. (New York: Washington Square
Press, 1960).
"Hop-Frog"
"The Tell-tale Heart"

Samuel and Kathryn Rapport, eds., *Light for the Road*. (New York:
Harper, 1961).
"Whistle" by Benjamin Franklin

Alfred Stefferud, *The Wonderful World of Books*. (Boston: Houghton,
1952).
"The Book of Books" by Fulton Oursler
"The Joy of Reading" by Holbrook Jackson
"Our Reading Heritage" by T. V. Smith
"Reading Aloud Brings Ideas to Life" by E. C. Lindeman
"Reading Shows You What to Look For" by J. B. Haviland
"What Good are Poems?" by Thomas Riggs, Jr.

Oscar Williams, ed., *The Silver Treasury of Light Verse*. (New York:
New American Library, 1957).
"Cocaine Lil and Morphine Sue"
"The Dying Airman"
"Father William" by Lewis Carroll
"Father William Answers"
"For Loose Tongues"
"Jabberwocky" by Lewis Carroll

REFERENCE

1. See "Bibliotherapy: Its Part in Library Service" *Bookmark*
15:127-133, (March 1956).

Bibliotherapy with Chronic Schizophrenics: The Therapeutic Function of the Psychiatric Librarian in a State Mental Hospital

by Rosa Horn Alexander
and Stephen E. Buggie

Bibliotherapy has been recognized as a therapeutic tool for more than 30 years,[1] although the literature reveals no objective evaluation of controlled bibliotherapy in a state mental hospital. This paper reports an attempt to measure the effectiveness of the psychiatric librarian—in this case, a professional librarian with a firm background in psychology and psychotherapy—as a member of the treatment team.

At Agnews State Hospital an experimental design was adapted to fit an available group of 24 female chronic schizophrenics. The participating psychiatrist and ward charge selected one-fourth of the population from one ward according to the criteria of "accessibility" (emotional approachability) and "reading ability." He then divided them into three groups of eight—one to receive maximal librarian contact with the psychiatrist and ward personnel during the study; one to have minimal psychiatrist-librarian contact; and one as the control, receiving no bibliotherapy. All patients were undergoing drug and occupational therapy at the time.

The experimental bibliotherapeutic materials as approved by the psychiatrist consisted of six short stories and fiction passages, a standard collegiate dictionary, and a log kept by the patients.

Readings were selected with reference to the psychiatric category of the patients, chronic schizophrenia. As noted by Arieti,[2] the schizophrenic seeks escape from reality—from society, from emotion—with a progressive retreat of reason, and shows a syndrome of marked deterioration in conceptual thought. The librarian therefore selected works designed to:

Reprinted with permission from *The Journal of Rehabilitation* 55:26-27,42 (November-December 1967). Copyright © 1967 by The National Rehabilitation Association.

- develop attitudinal changes; for example, awareness that change must occur within the person
- foster acceptance of facts as a "reality anchor," with which feelings have little relevance; for example, acceptance of the fact of hospitalization, as rejection of this fact tends to block possible beneficial results
- encourage evaluation of another's attitude by considering that person's frame of reference
- gain some understanding of the various aspects of the term "love" as presented by contemporary writers through their stories
- initiate some concept of a person's unawareness of impaired judgment, and its effect upon the person's environment, in times of great stress and increasing emotional disturbance.

TO INTERPRET "LOVE"

The bibliotherapy for such attitudinal changes was based on interpretations of the term "love." The concept the therapist tried to convey to the participants was love as a spontaneous, outgoing act; as concern for another's welfare, distinguished by generosity of self, consideration, tenderness, and care for the other.[3] The six readings were introduced in ascending order of abstraction:

1. John Collier's "Thus I Refute Beelzy." This short story was selected to establish rapport between the groups and the therapist, since the work has an unexpected, humorous, and mystifying twist; it depicts a father's inability to communicate his love to his child.

2. O. Henry's "One Thousand Dollars," wherein love is depicted as both an expression of concern and a deprivation of self for another human being; it also illustrates the misunderstanding of a person's motives and acts by the rest of the world.

3. Carson McCuller's "A Domestic Dilemma" was chosen to show how an alcoholic wife's judgment becomes impaired without her realizing it; to show her growing self-pity and day-dreaming, and her unawareness of the effects upon her children and spouse; to demonstrate acceptance and tenderness in marital love by the husband's shouldering of burdens.

4. Marjorie Rawlings' "A Mother in Mannville" develops the theme of an orphan teenage lad's idealization of the mother-image; his spontaneous and generous little acts for the older woman as an expression of love; and his fear of direct expression, which affects the woman's perception of his feelings.

5. Selected passages from Samuel Butler's *The Way of All Flesh* (Chaps. 33-35) depict differences in perception of the same situations by a growing boy and by his parents; the value of money as a responsibility; and love as a social responsibility affecting other people's long-term welfare.

6. John Steinbeck's *The Pearl* relates how the desire for material gains may lead to deterioration of familial love; how the quality of an

object (the beauty of the pearl) is not affected by the manner in which persons perceive it; but how its value for the individual is affected by his desires.

Two reading sessions were devoted to each selection; each group met twice a week.

THE REALITY APPROACH

The ground rules of the reading sessions emphasized the reality-based orientation of the therapy.[4] The librarian insisted upon citation of a specific page and paragraph in discussions of the readings. The only "facts" accepted to substantiate opinions were the printed words. This method was used to: (1) form the habit of reference to sources of authority; (2) develop careful reading practices; (3) encourage formation of reality-based, factual opinions; (4) determine whether assigned reading had been done; and (5) limit the topics of discussion.

The therapist endeavored to transmit to the patients a positive expectation that they could and would do the reading, and that they were capable of engaging in meaningful discussion and answering queries with intelligence and common sense. She attempted to deal with them on a person-to-person level, to act increasingly as a moderator, and to become accepted gradually as a member of each group.

Since bibliotherapy was prescribed for the selected patients, the therapist made clear at the initial session that the participants had no choice as to attendance. To begin, each person was supplied with a copy of the book to be read, and reminded of her personal responsibility for its safekeeping and return. Each patient, in turn, was asked to read a paragraph or episode aloud, then requested to recount it in her own words.

Sometimes the therapist directed discussion with a question:

"Is this the kind of behavior one would expect from a child this age?"

"What do you think his father did for a living?"

"What do you think about the way the father talks?"

"Are they pleased to have him come home early?"

At the end of the first session, the patients were asked to continue reading the story, taking their copies with them, and to write out a brief summary of the story for the next session.

PARTICIPATION AND COOPERATION

At the beginning of the second session, the therapist explained the meaning and use of a log, i.e., a summary of the previous session. Patients took turns maintaining it. This served to: (1) develop a sense of responsibility to the group through task orientation; (2) develop attention and observation; and (3) provide a record for subsequent reference—by the participants themselves. To start each session, the last writer would read her recording of the preceding meeting. The group would then vote by a show of hands whether to accept or correct the log. Later, some patients would ask for a log reading for proof that they had actually made a statement attributed to them by another.

The dictionary was also used by the therapist to provoke discussion. Questioned as to a word's meaning, she would ask a member to read it from the dictionary, starting a group discussion; where several definitions were given, the group would decide which one was relevant to the story. When agreement appeared impossible, the therapist made the decision, at the group's request, giving her reasons and awaiting the group's confirmation.

In order to motivate further active participation, the therapist called for a secret vote as to which member of the group had contributed the most to discussion of each passage, the winner to retain permanent possession of that book.

Both experimental groups began to function as whole units. Members, for instance, joined to help search the ward for one of the group's misplaced book. Competition between the groups seem to help integrate the group members and foster the singular identity of each group.

MEASURING THE BENEFITS

Comments by both the psychiatrist and ward personnel, during the study, supported the librarian's subjective impressions that therapy group members were benefiting from the bibliotherapy techniques. A more definitive measurement, however, of changes in attitude and self-concepts was sought. A three-part evaluation method was developed: (1) pre- and post-therapy testing of each patient's self-concept, by card sorting of 18 statements adapted from Stephenson[5] (variance and covariance analyses were made of data in order to control for the differences in the additivity of treatment effects); (2) intelligence quotients obtained through use of the Institute of Living Scale;[6] and (3) post-therapy psychiatric evaluations.

It had been expected that the three groups would have mean scores on the pre- and post-therapy testing nearly equal at the beginning, and that the prescribed bibliotherapy would produce test results in the two experimental groups superior to that of the control. However, according to this test data, treatment effects were negligible, showing no significant differences before or after therapy. One could conclude that Stephenson's statements were not an adequate measure of improvement due to bibliotherapy.

Another difficulty was encountered when intelligence testing showed that the two therapy groups were not, after all, comparable to each other at the beginning of therapy. Tests also indicated that the control was not a comparable study group since its patients were much more severely impaired than the others.

Despite the inadequacies of these measuring devices, in the post-therapy psychiatric interviews most of the patients were rated positively on attitudes, changes in attitudes, task orientation, interaction capacity, and accessibility. Maximal patient interaction with therapist, psychiatrist, and ward personnel apparently had the greatest impact on the characteristic of task orientation. The psychiatrist's evaluations suggest that bibliotherapy did help to effect positive changes in these five categories.

The patients themselves remarked on attitudinal changes produced by the reality approach and other tactics employed in the bibliotherapy. Some who were not responsive to other types of group therapy soon were enthusiastically discussing the stories with other patients and with the ward personnel. Although the reading material at times was difficult for some, the challenging presentation appeared to inspire them to read and discuss the assignments. Participants remarked in astonishment that some patients had never been heard to talk on the ward before.

After the first week, ward personnel demonstrated greater confidence in the therapy program by intensified cooperation, climaxed by providing prizes and refreshments for the final session.

PROMISE FOR THE FUTURE

Bibliotherapy should continue to play an increasingly important function in the rehabilitation of chronic schizophrenics. Schizophrenic persons have shown ready response to the reality approach of bibliotherapy when it is presented in an interesting and challenging manner by a skilled therapist. With careful professional guidance, bibliotherapy can provide a significant "first step" in the rehabilitation of mental patients to become interacting members of society.

A significant finding of the study of which the above is a resume, and one which the study was not aimed at, is that with the application of bibliotherapy, a group of chronic schizophrenic patients, under ongoing drug therapy, *can learn to consistently perform tasks* heretofore considered beyond their ability.

REFERENCES

1. William C. Menninger, "Bibliotherapy," *Bulletin of the Menninger Clinic,* 1:263-274 (November 1937).

2. Silvano Arieti, *Interpretation of Schizophrenia* (New York: Robert Brunner, 1955).

3. Jose Ortega y Gasset, *Estudios sobre el amor,* transl. by Toby Talbot. *On Love: Aspects of a Single Theme* (New York: Meridan Books, 1957).

4. William Glasser, "Reality Therapy as Applied to Hospitalized Patients," *A. L. A. Bulletin,* 61:843 (July-August 1967).

5. William Stephenson, *The Study of Behavior* (Chicago: University of Chicago Press, 1953).

6. *Shipley Institute of Living Scale for Measuring Intellectual Impairment,* The Third Mental Measurements Yearbook (New Brunswick, N.J.: Rutgers University Press, 1949).

Systems Analysis of A Bibliotherapy Session at Agnews State Hospital

by Clara E. Lack

EXPLANATION OF THE PROBLEM

The large group bibliotherapy session on an open ward of fifty or sixty men was chosen for analysis because it was the most difficult and least rewarding for the therapist of the four bibliotherapy sessions held. The large group session had its rewarding aspects and values, but a large amount of energy was expended in trying to project the story, hold the interest of those in the circle and draw in those who were outside the circle. Attempts at discussion were sometimes discouraging because of distractions, irrelevant remarks and lack of response by so many of the men. Short stories that were considered "sure-fire" were well received by the men, but often little discussion followed.

The former bibliotherapist had read to the open ward, so a new employee did not want to initiate a change right away—that of sharing a story with a smaller group. One change had been initiated by the new bibliotherapist, that of introducing a play-reading group. Thus there was contact by the bibliotherapist twice a week, with the same ward. Previous experience had shown that two sessions per week were more productive than one session per week with the same group.

One of the ward doctors was a booster of the bibliotherapy program; thus this particular ward was the right place to experiment. The following is an example of systems analysis in decision making.

Motion Picture Model Bibliotherapy Session on an Open Ward

INPUT

From Environment:

Renewal of federal grant for program

U. S. Department of Education requested that a manual be written for training

Personnel from other institutions came to observe

Boundaries:

The large open room of a men's ward with about fifty or sixty men. The windows and doors are locked. There are varying degrees of mental illness: Some men are penal commitments; some are depressed and suicidal; some are catatonic; some are paranoid. Most of the men do not have ground privileges.

Operants:

Patients of the ward

Ward staff

Many distractions

Literature read

Patient's reaction to the story

Skill of leader in reading and leading discussion

Operations:

Reading of short story by leader

Some patients cannot hear because of distractions

Patient's identification with character in the story
    or
No identification with the story

Skill of leader in reading and drawing out patients for discussion

Rejection or acceptance by the group of patient's remarks

Rejection or acceptance by the group of each other

Insights from the story discussion

Hopefully application of insights to personal problems

SYSTEMIZATION AND INTEGRATION
OPERATIONS CONTROL

Resources	Constraints
Doctor is present	
Ward technicians are in and about	
Men are invited by doctor to form a semi-circle with their chairs	Some choose not to be in the circle

Resources	**Constraints**
	Some fold the laundry
	Some men mill around
	Some men are asleep on couches
	Some men are acting out an inner drama—sometimes silently, sometimes not
	Medication makes many patients drowsy
	Staff from other wards come through to get patients for various reasons
	Jets fly overhead at regular intervals
	Noises from bathroom immediately adjacent
A staff bibliotherapist who reads well and who likes people	Great emotional energy is expended in projection to such a varied group with so many distractions
Can have a coffee break after the sessions	
Can talk over session with librarian	
Bibliotherapist has office in patient's library to make selections of literature	Much time is taken in literature search
	Must have emotional involvement
	Budget is limited for materials
	Patient's attention span is short
	Reading must not be longer than fifteen minutes
Leader leads discussion after reading	
Some men very open and responsive to literature and leader's warmth	Some men very resentful at hospitalization. Therapy is resisted.
Leader attempts to draw out patients	
	Some men make disconnected, irrelevant remarks, but seek recognition.

Resources	Constraints
Leader retells or summarizes the part missed	In large room with many distractions, some men cannot hear
Leader able to come to ward twice weekly	Patients forget leader if not seen at regular intervals
	Rapid turnover of patients
Leader takes requests for books after group breaks up	Time limitations. Men get very restless after 40 or 50 minutes.

ANALYSIS

I. Pay-Off

A. Other ward personnel are relieved for other duties—paperwork or concentrated attention to few patients not participating

B. Relieves tension and boredom

While the men are listening and discussing, they are not fighting each other

C. Doctor can observe patients in group interaction

II. Attainments

A. Refreshment

Attention is good by those in the circle

Usually several outside the circle become interested

There is always some favorable comment about reading

B. Socialization

1. *Group participation*
discussion does take place but only by five or six men

2. *Group interaction*
sometimes takes place between those that discuss

most men just sit

no way of knowing how they perceive

after several sessions some withdrawn men do participate

C. Self-insight—Identification

1. Discussion participants see themselves in the story
2. Indeterminate whether men who just listen gain any self-insights from the reading or discussion

   3. Smaller group would enable leader to ask each man to participate
   4. Participation might be greater if were fewer distractions

D. Preparation for other therapy

   1. Patient's responsiveness
       those who take part in discussion usually want to take part in play reading on another day
   2. Type of response
       helps doctor form judgment regarding other therapy relative to patient's needs

E. Ego-building

   1. Each comment is considered attentively
   2. All men are encouraged to express themselves

III. Alternatives

A. Smaller group

   1. Do not read to large ward group
   2. Explore with doctor possibility of bibliotherapist taking a small group of doctor's patients to barber shop
   3. Do not go to the ward except to escort patients to the library for a bibliotherapy session
       —would need doctor's permission
       —penal commitments can only be escorted by ones or twos
       —patients cannot ride in staff cars without clearance
       —walking is fine in good weather

TRANSFORMATION CONTROL

Monitoring

   Written evaluation of each session by leader of literature and discussion
   Verbal report to librarian of each session
   Doctor present at sessions
   Patient's feedback is asked for and received

TRANSFORMATION FACILITATION

Emergizing

   warm feelings between patients and leader
   patient's relief at self-expression

ego building for patient when ideas are accepted

new focus for patient—relief from own suffering

librarian and doctor satisfied with program

leader feels successful and useful

Maintenance

continue search for appropriate literature

build up bibliograpy of tried materials

leader learns men's names

OUTPUT

Analysis - Relevancy and Adequacy

1. Important for patients to have new social situation—respond to expectations
2. Several patients say they like smaller groups (play reading group meets in visitor's room)
3. Fewer distractions would permit greater involvement

Adjustment

I. Testing of alternative number 2—Bibliotherapist taking several of doctor's patients to a side room

A. Doctor willing that smaller group go to barber shop (only small room available)

B. Only twelve could fit into barber shop

C. Eight men joined the group

D. Doctor led group of men who did not move to barber shop

Objective of small group: More group interaction and broader participation

Resources	Constraints
Men can hear story in small room without interruptions and noises of ward	Men in various stages of reality contact
The story read had elicited very favorable response with another group of men	Only one man in the group responded to the story's actual meaning
All but one man responded in some way	Little group interaction.
Leader did not have to expend as much emotional energy to project the story	Doctor could not be present except briefly

II. Pay-Off

More men had opportunity for expression

Doctor had smaller group and found it useful

Leader did not have to work as hard at projecting story

III. Evaluation

A. Story did not meet objective

B. Small group did not produce more group interaction

C. Although all but one man responded in some way

D. Easier to hear and conduct discussion without interruptions

E. Responses were as varied and rambling as in large group

F. Opportunity for men to respond more than once because of small group

G. Objective perhaps not realistic in view of varied emotional condition of men

IV. Probable Course of Action

A. Doctor agreeable to any arrangement most comfortable for bibliotherapist

B. The two smaller groups will be maintained on Wednesdays

The play reading group will continue on Mondays

Bibliotherapy in the Circulating Library at Saint Elizabeths Hospital

by Arleen Hynes

The librarian in the mental health hospital has a unique opportunity to serve patients. The very milieu of the hospital library is one of warmth, acceptance and little distinction between patients and staff. The non-clinical setting is a significant factor in serving to establish the library as a bridge between the hospital and the world from which the patient came and to which he hopes to return. Opportunities to develop a bibliotherapy program add a special dimension to other available services.

Bibliotherapy, the healing that lies in the written word, is and has long been a field that librarians have nurtured out of the very essence of their work. It is the librarians' profession to know books and their contents, to be familiar with old and new literature, to cherish the universality of beauty of experience that the writer has captured, to be motivated by a deep desire to share these splendors with others and to see the library as a melding point for others. Bibliotherapy enables the librarian to bring the beauty and universality of literature to patients, beauty being its own therapy. In addition the librarian-bibliotherapist, especially when working as a team member with the psychotherapist, brings her professionalism and expertise about literary materials to focus on the emotional needs of the patient.

The librarian interested in bibliotherapy will already have had courses in psychology and literature in her college background and will have continued her education in both of these fields. In addition, courses in group dynamics and experiences in facilitating bibliotherapy activities are necessary. The Association for Poetry Therapy has set standards for certified poetry therapists; those qualified are permitted to use the initials C.P.T. as a title. Psychotherapists, nurses, librarians and social workers are among those listed as having the basic qualifications for further study and experience before certification. The American Library Association has long had a committee on bibliotherapy, and published articles on the subject have appeared for the last forty years in library publications.

Librarians have been grateful users of the books *Poetry Therapy* and *Poetry the Healer* edited by Jack Leedy, M.D. These publications have given standing to the librarians' efforts while they have narrowed the field to poetry. However, Dr. Leedy refers to the entire gamut of reading materials when he states in *Poetry Therapy* "Today, bibliotherapy (which has been defined as the process of assimilating the psychological, sociological and esthetic values from books into human character, personality and behavior) holds a firmly established position with such other modes of healing as occupational therapy, art therapy, music therapy and dance therapy. In many mental hospitals, the library plays a significant role in the total recovery program." [1] Obviously, we agree.

Bibliotherapy in practice varies with the vision of the bibliotherapist and with the specific goal and character of each group. Approaches, selections of material, methods of conducting the group and goals always vary with the individual therapist. Furthermore, the therapist finds that even when the same literary materials are used, it is exciting to experience the unique reactions of each group. There are many modes of conducting sessions that result in a continuum of activities on the bibliotherapeutic scale. A listing of the different modes will be made and the methods used at the Circulating Library noted.

Individual therapists meet with individual patients to discuss materials. While this particular mode might be very effective, it is not a feasible form of bibliotherapy for the Circulating Library.

Reading materials aloud to a group is the next step on the continuum. The librarian, technician or trained volunteer reads aloud to patients on their ward. At this most basic level, the humor, the beauty, the poignancy, the rhythm or the message provides an enriching experience for those interested in listening. Some beauty or concept has been introduced into the patients' consciousness that would not have been added without this personal effort. To achieve any degree of success the cooperation of the ward staff is helpful. They may turn off the television and help to quiet some patients so others can listen or even share the experience. In this mode, no discussion is elicited and the moment of enrichment is the goal.

Reading and/or writing together is a mode in which the sophistication of the materials and presentation will vary widely depending on the capacity of the group members and psychological depth that the therapist is reaching for. The members of the group choose the materials and read aloud, or they may write creatively and discuss their efforts.

Facilitator directed reading and/or writing groups seems to be the most common mode used for bibliotherapy groups and is the one used most often in the Circulating Library. The facilitator chooses and reads the materials aloud or asks specific members to do so. The art of reading materials effectively is regarded as important since bibliotherapy is a form of communication. The goals of the group in relationship to the significance of communication may vary and this should be kept in mind when deciding upon the importance of the interpretive reading. The facilitator also decides upon how the group will participate in choosing the theme or the form the writing will take. For instance, if a poem on hope was read, members would be asked to write about that theme if they so desired. The group climate as a whole is sympathetic, cohesive, intuitional and non-coercive. When literature is read, typed copies are usually provided for each member. We have also found it helpful to keep two files, one of authors and one of titles, of all materials used with a brief notation of when, where and how the piece was received.

For almost four years bibliotherapy groups have been held in the drug addiction unit that is a derivative of the Synanon program which stresses self-responsibility.[2] We were invited by the members, not the staff, to lead an hour-long weekly poetry seminar. We have used a great deal of poetry, some plays and creative writing. Each selection was discussed with great insight although the educational level of most members was low and they were generally unfamiliar with poetry. For instance, we read some examples of Japanese haiku, an art form with which they were unacquainted, and then each group member wrote his own haiku, a description of an emotion that he wanted to communicate. My personal belief is that addictive youth are extremely sensitive people and that is one reason why they respond so enthusiastically to poetry.

Occasionally in the drug unit and in others we read the words to a popular song, play the music on the cassette tapes that the library provides and then discuss the ideas. The songs are effective because the youths are familiar with them and the message is written in the vernacular. The music adds to the emotional impact. Many popular songs raise very provocative questions. Simon and Garfunkel's "I Am a Rock" quickly brought to the surface a discussion of whether people should insulate themselves from feelings, should never cry or love others.

With very old and disturbed patients or young and unlettered children, we may read a poem or story aloud and ask each person for a one-word response or a one-line response. A blackboard may be used to record these reactions and the total group response is considered a "poem." This and other adaptations have been described in Kenneth Koch's *Wishes, Lies and Dreams.*[3] Other media such as tapes, prints of paintings and photographs have also been used to stimulate the senses.

Directed reading and discussion is an early form of bibliotherapy. A number of popular mental health books, as well as fiction and drama, are considered by some to be helpful in improving self-understanding and in recognizing and learning to solve difficult problems. Menninger's *The Human Mind*[4] and Beers' *The Mind That Found*

Itself[5] are classic examples used to aid self-understanding. Hilda K. Limper, a librarian who has served as Chairwoman of the Troubled Child Subcommittee of the American Library Association, has compiled lists of books useful to those who work with troubled children.

Without the benefit of a psychological study we cannot truly assess the value of a project we carried out with both the young drug addicts and the middle-aged men in an Alcoholics Anonymous Unit. We excerpted Erich Fromm's *The Art of Loving*[6] into twenty-three sections and gave typed copies to the group members. As we read, we paused to define the terms or clarify a concept. Poems and stories were often presented to clarify and reinforce an idea. It is interesting to note that both groups applied the readings to their rehabilitation programs and to themselves. Comments indicated that they had gained a new understanding about the significance of respecting and loving themselves before they could expect to respect and love others. Fromm's writings reinforced the idea of the individual's responsibility to himself and the commitment to change, both of which were stressed in the two respective programs. The group members seemed to regard their bibliotherapy experience as successful but could that be due in part to the fact that we were invited to join the drug addiction program and that the A.A. members forfeited their lunch hour to come to the library for the reading group? It appears that where members join freely in a bibliotherapy activity, it is more likely to be successful. Even more significant is the fact that these are addictive patients in self-discovery programs.

Team leadership consisting of a bibliotherapist and a mental health worker has proved to be a mutually supportive mode of cooperative bibliotherapy. In the last year the librarian has had the privilege of working with two psychologists and a clinical nurse specialist in three on-going weekly groups. The group members were chosen by the staff who knew the patients. The librarian chooses the literary materials and reads aloud to the group which is often furnished with copies of the selections. The co-leaders work together to ask appropriate questions or to make statements which enable the members to delve as deeply as possible into their reactions. The goals, the mode of procedure, the balance between personal esthetic enrichment and the depth of psychological insight are the product of the mutual cooperation of the co-leaders as well as the over-all mental states of the patients in the groups. For instance, in one group, which consists of over twenty chronic patients, our goal is simply to introduce some new ideas and awaken some perception of beauty. It is difficult to gauge the success of the larger groups, but in the smaller ones it is possible to sense some progression of relationships, insights and some improvements in the ability to communicate.

A final step in the continuum of bibliotherapy demands more of the participants than any mentioned previously. The group members all read the selected materials before they arrive at the discussion meetings. In this mode of bibliotherapy the group and its leader decide on the goals, what will be read and how the discussion will be structured. The group might choose to read a novel, biography, poem, drama, short story, mental health book or an informational article. The group meets regularly and discusses what they have read.

An excellent doctoral thesis on bibliotherapy was written in 1972 by Lesta Burt, a librarian, in which this method was used to test whether the reading and discussion of literature in a prison might bring about improved attitudes toward self and others. The study concluded that socially acceptable attitudes may be fostered by group book discussions.[7]

The artist has created, or reported, a form of bibliotherapy we have not mentioned. In Solzhenitsyn's "Cancer Ward"[8] Yefrem Podduyev is facing death, as are all the others in his ward. He is very restless until he finds a little blue book. Then he goes around the ward asking everyone the question the story brought to mind. "What is it men live by?" Tolstoi said it was that men live by not worrying about their own problems but by the love of others. Solzhenitsyn demonstrates the result of effective bibliotherapy, he changes his behavior. Instead of stomping up and down between the beds railing at everyone to recognize his fate, he becomes quiet and spends hours silently contemplating this great mystery, able, at last, to prepare for his own death.

REFERENCES

1. Jack Leedy, ed., *Poetry Therapy* (Toronto: J. B. Lippincott Co., 1969), p.11.

   Jack Leedy, ed., *Poetry the Healer* (Toronto: J. B. Lippincott Co., 1972).

2. Lewis Yablonsky, *Synanon: The Tunnel Back* (New York: Penguin Books, 1965).

3. Kenneth Koch, *Wishes, Lies and Dreams: Teaching Children to Write Poetry* (New York: Chelsea House Publishers, 1970).

4. Karl Menninger, *The Human Mind* (New York: Alfred Knopf, 1930).

5. Clifford Beers, *The Mind that Found Itself: An Autobiography* (New York: Doubleday, 1937).

6. Erich Fromm, *The Art of Loving* (New York: Harper and Row, 1956).

7. Lesta Norris Burt, *Bibliotherapy: Effect of Group Reading and Discussion on Attitudes of Adult Inmates in Two Correctional Institutions.* Doctoral Thesis, University of Wisconsin, (1972).

8. Alexander Solzhenitsyn, *Cancer Ward* (New York: Farrar, Straus & Giroux, 1969), Chapter 18.

Bibliotherapy and Reading Guidance: A Tentative Approach to Theory

by Evalene P. Jackson

The literature of therapy is vast. The literature of bibliotherapy is with few exceptions couched in terms of "perhaps" and "maybe." This paper is no less tentative although it takes into account some promising, if slight, evidence.

The writer is not a bibliotherapist, but by experience and affinity one who is interested in the provision of reading guidance to persons who have not sought and who may not need clinical help. This guidance consists of bringing about effective encounters between people and books and is an accepted part of the library's educational program. That education is not clearly separable from therapy has been recognized by some educators of adults. Benne notes this fact in his statement of reasons for seeking the presidency of the Adult Education Association: "At one end education does seem akin to therapy, and at the other end it seems it must include much more. Many factors contributing to alienation are not rooted in the personality at all but in the disorganization of our communities and societies."[1] Educators, he holds, must become students of personality. He is recognizing that one of the major tasks of education is the reduction of this alienation in individuals and in society. The librarian is apparently attempting to educate by means of books. It is unlikely that he can ignore the therapeutic aspects of reading.

If he functions as part of a therapeutic team or works within a hospital, the librarian is likely to be concerned primarily with bibliotherapy. The milieu in which he works or, rather, the complex of doctors, nurses, occupational therapists, and others will to some extent govern what he does, even if his only assignment is to provide recreation.

"Bibliotherapy and Reading Guidance: A Tentative Approach to Theory," by Evalene P. Jackson reproduced with special permission from the publisher, *Library Trends* 11:118-125 (October 1962).

If the results of reading are therapeutic, the elements by means of which the results are achieved will be the same regardless of whether the reader be a patient or simply a library patron. In either case, if the librarian's knowledge of personality is more than superficial, he will recognize that he has some guiding theories in regard to the developmental process by means of which organism becomes individual.

The interpersonal theory of Harry Stack Sullivan seems a promising context in which to consider the role of reading. The organism which becomes reader brings into the world little more than a bundle of potentialities. To what extent these potentialities are limited by native endowment is uncertain. The organism will seek satisfaction in ways that are determined by the culture. The self which emerges is the result of approval and disapproval by significant others: mothers, fathers, siblings, etc.: "Tendencies of the personality not approved by these others, tendencies strongly disapproved, are disassociated from the awareness of the child."[2] A tension in the body of an anxious parent is a rejection as well as a verbal rebuke or an act of punishment. And the result in the child is organic: "Throughout life the pursuit of satisfactions is physically determined by an increased tone in some unstriped muscles."[3] If an individual, and particularly a gifted individual, disassociates a large number of motivational systems, tensions are created by wants of which he is unaware, and he is likely to experience difficulties. One becomes what he is by interaction with the interpersonal situations of which he is a part. Life is a patterned sequence of these.

If significant others were not limited by being human, the possibility of the healing acceptance of books might not be such an important means of transcending these limits. In Sullivan's conception the book itself may be a significant other: "In general, any frame of reference whether constituted by real people, imaginary people existing only in books . . . along with one other real person, can make up an interpersonal situation."[4] On this basis one may propose that the variety and richness of books are means of counteracting the meagerness of the environment and the limits of those who are parts of interpersonal situations. This provides a rationale for considering the role of the book in the prevention of alienation both from oneself and from others. Rollo May has stated that, *"The common, objective aspect of these neurotic problems* [of our times] *is that the individual . . . cannot experience himself as a self in his own right."*[5] Unless one has a real valid attitude toward the self, he will be unable to experience others as valid and real. "It is not that as you judge so shall you judge others, but as you judge yourself so shall you judge others. Strange but true so far as I know and with exception."[6]

What elements are involved when bibliotherapy, be it implicit or explicit, preventive or curative, takes place? Alice I. Bryan noted the relevance of the mind-body relationship in 1939.[7] This stresses the unity in the biological world which insures that changes at one level will produce changes at another level. As Whitaker and Malone put it:

> Physical changes have very clear psychological effects, and presumably the reverse is also true: the interpersonal changes the psychological; the psychological changes the physiological; and the physiological changes the anatomical. . . . In the human organism, one finds much the same continuity of functional levels. In keeping with recent developments in biological theory, thought and ideation are viewed as highly integrated feeling, feeling as highly integrated emotion, emotion as highly integrated physiological change, and physiological change as simply a highly integrated electro-chemical change.[8]

A book which arouses emotion will in turn bring about physical changes.

One analysis of the literature of bibliotherapy is interesting for its critical scrutiny of medical literature. Dewey Carroll,[9] to whom this paper is greatly indebted, has found the mechanisms involved to be insufficiently described to be useful for testing. The majority of those described fall into three categories:

> Those through which the reader identifies himself with characters and experiences in the reading materials and abreacts repressed unconscious affects in regard to the material absorbed; those through which the reader integrates the intellectual understandings and emotional experiences contained in the reading material into combined intellectual and emotional insights into his own personality and life situation; and those through which the reader vicariously expresses or sublimates his instinctual impulses in a socially acceptable manner and effects their redirection toward socially acceptable goals.[10]

Carroll also concludes that no serious effort toward a conceptual analysis has been made outside of the framework of psychoanalysis. Two studies which he suggested for further consideration are interesting.

On the basis of a study by Ericson,[11] Kaufman and Taylor[12] propose that a writer creates and resolves a conflict in the reader. By means of this the reader resolves his own conflict. Ericson reports the cure of one neurosis by the resolution of another which he induced hypnotically. The fiction for Kaufman and Taylor constitutes an artificial neurosis. Lee,[13] in the second of the two studies, attempted to understand the therapeutic effects of reading in both psychological and aesthetic terms. The creativity of the author is the result of his need to make restitution for the destruction of some object toward which he is ambivalent. The reader who experiences the form which the author creates as beautiful identifies himself with the subject matter. The appeal of the subject matter is unconscious and due to his resolution of the Oedipal conflict in some pregenital stage of his development. Since the creation of the artist is beautiful, the reader is able to recognize his unconscious tendency projected upon the work of art. This process involves both recognition of the attitudes of the artist and his ability to impose form upon materials.

Two studies to which Carroll did not have access provide some evidence in regard to dynamics. Caroline Shrodes[14] has found a unifying rationale for the effects of reading imaginative literature in psychoanalysis, field theory, and aesthetics. In this context it should be remembered that Sullivan may be considered a field theorist. These effects, she holds, are the dynamics. In one case study, and in several less fully reported instances, she found that three processes were present which correspond to phases of psychotherapy: identification, including projection and introjection, catharsis, and insight. Identification is an adaptive mechanism by means of which the reader, largely unconsciously, increases his esteem for himself by affiliating with another person or persons. In projection the reader attributes his own motives and emotions to theirs. Miss Shrodes uses the words *catharsis* and *abreaction* synonymously to denote the "uncensored and spontaneous release of emotion."[15] Insight is the emotional awareness of motivation. The aesthetic experience facilitates psychodiagnosis while at the same time it provides experiences by means of which the reader grows. While didactic literature may have therapeutic effects, imaginative literature makes possible an emotional experience without which therapy cannot take place. Esther Hartman[16] offers additional evidence of identification and some evidence of abreaction.

The reactions of Miss Hartman's subjects with characters and situations in stories tend to correspond with their own experiences in interpersonal situations. The reactions among younger persons tend to be intensified when characters whom they have read about are of their own age level. Parents respond in two ways to the characters in one story, both as parents and as children.

The human tendency toward symbolization which Sullivan recognizes utilizes the Freudian mechanisms of identification, projection, and introjection. The distortion of symbols, which may facilitate psychodiagnosis, is the mechanism which Freud calls transference, "whereby emotion is directed at a given stimulus in terms of a previous affective experience."[17] Apparently in reading one is able to incorporate materials by means of responses in which identification, projection, and insight are involved. The way in which the reader organizes his field, of which the literature under consideration is a part, depends upon that field, but is also structured by what the reader brings to the situation. His use of literature is facilitated by elements that attract him although he may be largely unaware of these elements. What, in this process, has become of the vital presence of the therapist?

Is the book, itself, therapist? Is it possible that a particular book may offer to a particular reader the kind of acceptance that Rogers believes to be necessary in the therapeutic situation?[18] Miss Shrodes,[14] as has been seen, found evidence of effects analogous to early stages of therapy. However, it seems dangerous to substitute books for persons. Sullivan suggests that one other person must be present in the situation when the book becomes the significant other. Perhaps it is in this context that we should consider the role of the librarian.

Only as he functions in his role of bibliotherapist, a particular and limited kind of therapist, may the librarian be considered in that capacity. Yet the relationship between reader and librarian may be a relationship in which the growth of one or both participants is fostered or inhibited. Two kinds of therapy have been recognized—explicit and implicit.[19] For explicit therapy one goes to a psychotherapist. Implicit therapy, however, is a resource of the culture, present under some circumstances for those who can find and make use of it. The hospital librarian is frequently involved in the provision of the first kind. Philosophy, purposes, and techniques are to some extent set by the clinical situation of which he is a part. The reader's adviser may provide guidance in the implicit sense. Neither adviser nor reader will always be aware of when such guidance takes place. Under some limited circumstances the adviser may function as a bibliotherapist in the explicit sense. In either case the dynamics are the same, and insofar as personal characteristics are concerned, desirable attitudes on the part of the librarian are similar.

The librarian must, of course, know books and readers as well as the effects of bringing the two together.[20] Possible dynamics have been specified. As yet we know little of effects. The librarian puts his knowledge of books at the disposal of the reader who has sought help for purposes of his own.

Rogers' discussion of the characteristics of the helping situation might well be digested by all who provide reading guidance. This is a relationship in which one of the participants intends "that there should come about in one or both parties, more appreciation of, more functional use of, the latent inner resources of the individual."[21] Basic to all such relationships are (1) the ability of the helper to be fully what he is at any moment; (2) his ability to form a helping relationship with himself; that is, to be positively aware of and acceptant of one's real feelings; and (3) the capacity to experience warmth, interest in and liking for another. An attitude of evaluation will hinder the relationship.

While knowledge of bibliographic sources is indispensable to this librarian, he must have a tremendous first-hand knowledge of books. There is a good reason for this knowledge in a situation with therapeutic potentialities. The practice of individual book selection is likely to remain an art although there is no reason that it should not eventually rest upon scientific foundations. This practice, by the way, is also true of the ministration of a doctor to a particular patient. As an art, book selection requires imagination. Titles that occur spontaneously in response to an expressed need may sometimes be the best selections. There are occasions when selections will be based upon careful and serious study.

It will be necessary to know as much as possible of the person because his response to material is determined by his predispositions. In a clinical setting this information may be supplied. When it is not supplied, as in the situation of the reader's adviser, considerable skill in interviewing may be requisite, along with the ability to respond honestly and warmly to another person. Selections of books should provide a variety of choices among which the reader may make his own decisions. This kind of guidance may take place on many levels from the most casual to one of considerable depth. The importance of the casual contact as a beginning should not, however, be overlooked. While imaginative literature is promising, there are times when carefully planned courses designed to provide a more formal learning experience will be required. Situations in which the individual reader may interact with others are desirable.

Discussions of books in which the librarian as well as the patron may grow and change are important. In private conversations or in groups, provided that the nonevaluative atmosphere is maintained, the effects may be as therapeutic for the librarian as for the reader.

It is possible that the librarian's perception of his own need and his desire for these effects may be requisite. An examination of a number of therapies, in particular those of Fromm, Rogers, Whitaker and Malone, and Rollo May reveal the presence of this wish and need on the part of the therapist involved. Librarians who do not wish to participate in these processes may not function as effectively as those who do.

The ends for which bibliotherapy or guidance is exercised will vary. The adviser or bibliotherapist may attempt to show the reader that others have met problems very similar to his own, that more than one solution is possible. The adviser may also attempt to provide insight into motivation, necessary facts of choices among values tending toward those that are human rather than material.[22] These are specific objectives and should be viewed within the context of ordering and guiding conceptions which take into account the purposes of therapy or of guidance. These vary among schools of thought. The therapeutic effects of reading must be viewed as part of a larger question: What are the effects of reading? As yet we know little of these.[23] The fusion of field theory, psychoanalysis, and aesthetics attempted by Miss Shrodes seems promising as an approach. The conception of the book as the field, or as part of the field, points to more studies of content in terms of symbols, situations, characters,[24] and conflicts presented.[25] As yet we lack descriptions of the voluntary reading of different personality types. Does it vary with type? The descriptive survey might be a beginning, but case histories and perhaps depth analyses in which reading can be seen in relation to the organization of personality and within the context of life itself would be most revealing. Experience suggests that a book with the same theme as another will appeal to one reader but not to another. For instance, both Flannery O'Conner and Charles Williams have been deeply concerned with salvation, but the symbol systems of the two writers are so different that those who respond with pleasure to one are often repelled by the other. Although reactions of distaste may tell a physician something, it is doubtful that abreaction and identification occur if the individual refuses to read the book. Fantasy may be more effective with one type of reader or realism with another, but with what kinds? Do neurotic persons tend to prefer fantasy? These questions are among those that need to be answered. Librarians are, it would seem, sufficiently equipped to explore some of them. Depth analyses are, of course, beyond librarians. Students of literature, librarians, and therapists all will be involved if we obtain the kinds of answers that are necessary.

One final question: Are librarians equipped to provide bibliotherapy, either implicit or explicit? Some of them may be good implicit therapists. Some have learned to contribute as bibliotherapists. This is an area now somewhat neglected by library schools. In the future the continuing education of librarians should provide opportunities for students to consider and discuss books in interpersonal situations in which helping relationships are possible. Where are substantial courses available which are devoted to adult reading guidance, let alone a substantial course in bibliotherapy? The education of some librarians should also include advanced courses in psychology and literature.

When one considers the shortage of persons who can provide some kind of help for those who need it, librarians trained to provide help both implicitly and in explicit situations seem to be a resource too valuable to ignore.

REFERENCES

1. K. B. Benne, "Why I ran for President of the A.E.A." *Adult Leadership*, 4:7 (January 1959)
2. Harry Stack Sullivan, *Conceptions of Modern Psychiatry* (Washington, D.C.: William Alanson White Psychiatric Foundation, 1947), p. 43.
3. *Ibid.*, p. 22.
4. Patrick Mullahy, "The Theories of Harry Stack Sullivan." In Patrick Mullahy, ed. *Oedipus: Myth and Complex* (New York: Hermitage House, Inc., 1952), p. 301.
5. Rollo May, "Historical and Philosophical Suppositions for Understanding Therapy." In O. Hobart Mowrer. *Psychotherapy: Theory and Research* (New York: The Ronald Press Company, 1953), p. 24.
6. Sullivan, *Conceptions of Modern Psychiatry*, p. 7.
7. Alice I. Bryan, "Can There Be a Science of Bibliotherapy?" *Library Journal*, 64:774 (October 15, 1939)
8. C. A. Whitaker and T. P. Malone, *The Roots of Psychotherapy* (New York, The Blakiston Company, 1953), p. 18.

9. Dewey E. Carroll, "The Psychological Mechanism Involved in Bibliotherapeutic Reading." Unpublished paper prepared in the Emory University Division of Librarianship (1955).

10. *Ibid.,* pp. 30-31.

11. M. H. Ericson, "A Study of an Experimental Neurosis Hypnotically Induced in a Case of Ejaculatio Praecox," *British Journal of Psychology,* 15:37-50 (1955).

12. F. W. Kaufman and W. S. Taylor, "Literature As Adjustment," *Journal of Abnormal and Social Psychology,* 21:233-234 (September 1936).

13. H. B. Lee, "Projective Features of Contemplative Aesthetic Experience," *American Journal of Orthopsychiatry,* 19:101-111 (January 1949).

14. Caroline Shrodes, "Bibliotherapy: A Theoretical and Clinical-Experimental Study." Unpublished Ph.D. dissertation, University of California (1949).

15. *Ibid.,* p. 14.

16. Esther A. Hartman, "Imaginative Literature As a Projective Technique: A Study in Bibliotherapy." Unpublished Ph.D. dissertation, Stanford University (1951).

17. Shrodes, "Bibliotherapy: A Theoretical and Clinical-Experimental Study," p. 111.

18. C. R. Rogers, *On Becoming a Person* (Boston: Houghton-Mifflin, 1961), pp. 39-57.

19. Whitaker and Malone, *The Roots of Psychotherapy,* pp. 49-50.

20. Alice I. Bryan, "The Psychology of the Reader," *Library Journal,* 64:10 (January 1, 1939).

21. Rogers, *On Becoming a Person,* pp. 39-40.

22. Alice I. Bryan, "Personality Adjustment through Reading," *Library Journal,* 64-576 (August 1939).

23. Lester Asheim, "Research in Mass Communication and Adult Reading," *Library Trends,* 6:120-121 (October 1957).

24. Hartman, "Imaginative Literature as a Projective Technique."

25. Kaufman and Taylor, "Literature as Adjustment."

The Role of the Librarian on the Interdisciplinary Team

by Ruth M. Tews

Bold, new approaches! What an exciting challenge for us librarians in hospitals and institutions! The climate is right; the need is great for all of us to set up realistic and meaningful guidelines to achieve better library service. We play an important function in the "therapeutic society" of today. It is wise and of utmost significance, that we librarians spend some time examining our role, as we start formulating "bold, new" guidelines.

Let us use the classic questions of the journalist: Who, What, When, Where, How and Why. Who are we? What do we have to do to qualify as members of the Team: When, where and how do we justify our position?

Today's discussion should give us a base, a framework on which we build our profile. Tomorrow's papers should lead us nearer to analyzing the Why of our work. Understanding who we are, what is expected of us, and why we are doing it, should lead us to setting up realistic guidelines, reaching toward goals we seek.

Determining one's role is a most important and also difficult task. One must first answer honestly these questions: where do I belong? what are my functions and how are they to be coordinated with those of other specialties?

There is a sobering challenge in establishing one's role as a librarian—the challenge of honestly facing oneself by oneself. Are we librarians or are we Capital T Therapists or are we both? These questions trouble us. For this reason, let us take a few moments, reviewing some of the concepts that have been discussed during the past week.

You have heard them before but think of them as being repeated for emphasis. When we have assessed what is expected of us, and fit what we have to offer in this structure, we should be able to define our role.

In Margaret E. Monroe, *Reading Guidance and Bibliotherapy in Public, Hospital and Institution Libraries*, pp. 57-62. Reprinted with permission from the University of Wisconsin Library School and the author.

An "approach" is a manner of advance toward full knowledge or experience. Your keynote speaker used Shakespeare's simile of a "tide leading to fortune" which we must take or "lose our ventures."

In modern usage, an approach is the ramp leading to the freeway. To the experienced and competent driver, who knows and follows the rules, it is a means to an expeditious "tide" and "current" leading to his destination. To the uninitiated, it is an area of frenetic activity, with strong overtones of rivalry, tension, frustration and aggressiveness. When one considers the latter meaning of the word, it is obvious that "Approach" may not be enough. It seems to follow that we must have something more; we must have "what it takes" to be able to follow through. Socrates' advice: "Know thyself" is still valid today.

There are many definitions. By now we know that "team" is a concept which has about as many meanings as there are users. The team is a structured group, with a leader, usually the consultant physician. When there is none assigned, the group will elect its own leader. We know, too, that there are hazards in team work which mar its effectiveness; such as diffusion, and conversely, overextension of roles by individual members.

There is a growing concern in getting people to interact more, in making a team function effectively as well as efficiently. We *need* to work as a team, to understand each other better. If we don't, chaos and confusion will take over, so much so that we may even lose sight of our objectives.

Big business is presently experimenting with a very dramatic and radical change in the structuring of its work-flow chart. You all know the traditional organizational chart which is composed of rectangular boxes connected with rigid lines. The new concept allows for more freedom of interaction of people. The rigid structure is discarded for one where work-flow is planned in "islands," with channels for communication connecting between and among related areas.

What makes a team of specialists effective as well as efficient? Its members! Each of the members must have three necessary features— (1) the ability to contribute some knowledge the others do *not* have, (2) a willingness to receive and absorb what the other members offer, (3) the ability to make decisions and carry out the plans in his area, as it relates to the goals set up, without conflicting with those of the other members.

What should the librarian be; what arts must the librarian possess to establish his role and to work effectively? There are three areas in which the librarian requires skill and knowledge: (1) Professional skills of librarianship; (2) Ability to implement this knowledge into action, to elicit team work, to work effectively with people; (3) Self-knowledge.

Before discussing the first area of concern in establishing one's role, permit me to give you a small vignette of myself and how I function in my work. I am a librarian. Whether I am functioning in my role as part of the rehabilitation team or in my role as administrator of a large and active library volunteer program, I am a Librarian.

Because of my training, experience and continued activity in personal advancement, I can consider myself a specialist in working with patients. What I do as a librarian contains therapy and is considered part of the total patient care. When I work, I use all my skills and arts to achieve an interpersonal relationship—a relationship which can be a dynamic factor in predisposing the reader to new experiences. When I first see a patient, therapy starts. He is displaced, in a threatening environment; he may be angry or irritated. Some vital quality tells him there is mutual respect; there is interest and concern for him as a person. Out of this relationship, rapport is established. During this time, I may be acting on several levels; there may be the elements of the role of the social worker, the counselor, the activities therapist, the physical therapist, perhaps even of the psychologist. As part of this active involvement, the patient becomes aware of, recognizes and trusts me as a therapist—not a capital T therapist but as a capital BIBLIO-therapist, capital LIBRARIAN.

Let me give you just one illustration from my experience. Bruce was referred to the library early in his hospitalization. An impasse had been reached, in the planning for his treatment. The librarian was asked to try to establish a level of communication, to arouse interest, to raise his morale, through the use of the library. This was difficult; Bruce was completely paralyzed following a bad accident; in addition, a tracheotomy had been performed to facilitate breathing; this prevented prolonged talking. He had also regressed into a depression of hopelessness. It was obvious that I would need to operate on many levels. First I had to give of myself, so that he could trust me, that he could learn to know me as one of many who wanted to help him, not as a paralyzed patient, but as a person whom we like, that I had something to offer. Once this barrier was broken, I could proceed to try the resources I had available as a librarian, the means which could help him. In his case, my contribution was the breakthrough for further treatment and rehabilitation.

I am not an active member of a structured interdisciplinary team. My contacts with the individual members are informal and occur when my services are indicated or when I have information which is pertinent and may be helpful.

It would have been satisfying to tell you that I am an active member of the team. Such is, however, not the set-up at the Clinic. We are a diagnostic center. The average stay in the two hospitals in which our patients are hospitalized is very short. Only a small percentage of our patients are what may be called long-term. Realistically these conditions do not make for productive and prolonged work involving bibliotherapy. However, I am an "island" and as John Donne said, "not entire of myself but a piece of the continent, a part of the main." There is interaction between and among the various specialties and the channels of communication are kept flowing. How? We interpret our role through our work with patients, our follow-through on referrals, our involvement of ourselves and our program with all services of the hospital.

We have a message to transmit, namely: the inter-relatedness of writing to life.

Our department at the Mayo Clinic has developed a public relations program—call it "advertising our mission" in which we attempt to reach all those who have direct contact with the patient. This is done through formal lectures as part of continuing education for the graduate nurse, the supervisors, special nurses; as part of the curriculum in nursing art for the student nurse, the practical nurse, nurses aides, physical therapists, etc. The library program is presented as a part of the total patient care, an important factor in the psychological adjustment of the patient. Through the normal, non-threatening atmosphere and activity, the patient is helped to feel himself a human being and not only a patient with a number. Each incoming group of residents in psychiatry is given a seminar on bibliotherapy and its effectiveness in group therapy.

One of our widest-reaching influences is through our volunteer program. Prospective library workers must go through a formal training and orientation program, consisting of ten hours of lecture covering the philosophy of hospital librarianship, the technics, and the elements of book selection. In addition, before acceptance on a regular schedule, the worker spends six hours of field work in the department. These women are trained to work in a professional area, doing independent work, but always under supervision and within clearly defined limits.

Our public relations program is effective and patients are benefited by this personal concern which comes from the whole staff. This is evident from the calls and referrals we receive from all levels. One shining example is the LPN who regularly comes to the library between the librarian's visits, to select books for her patients on the orthopedic surgical service. She will select armsfull, for the newly admitted patients, for those who have finished the books the librarian left, for those she feels are now ready to read. She will refer to the librarian those problems in sensitive areas, such as the patient who has special needs, perhaps because he is depressed, handicapped, or being a problem on the clinical area.

THE PROFILE OF THE LIBRARIAN

A most restricting factor in the growth and recognition of hospital librarianship is the lack of a profile of the librarian. What is a hospital librarian? an institutional librarian? What distinguishing characteristics and backgrounds do they have?

Technical knowledge in librarianship must be there, certainly. But this does not make a hospital librarian. In order to work with the other specialties in the health science fields, we must have acquired additional knowledge and experience and have developed a sensitivity to people and their needs.

The hospital librarian must have developed a body of professional knowledge about reading and its therapeutic application in order to function effectively and efficiently in fulfilling his role. Most important, this knowledge is necessary if there is to be any communication leading to action. Throughout and part of this communication is this hidden quality, an undefinable skill, a sensitivity, which sets therapy in motion and establishes interpersonal relationships, respect, mutual trust and understanding. When this is established with patient, and shared with the other disciplines, a bond has been formed, connecting librarian, patient, and the staff. Collaboration with specialists demands professional competence on all levels. We librarians today face a great challenge. The time is here when we must take our mission more seriously than we do ourselves.

We, in the health sciences, must be able to show *why* we are concerned about the individual and his needs and what we, as librarians have that he needs but perhaps doesn't know he needs nor how to acquire it.

Professional knowledge, experience, plus conviction and faith in one's mission should result in security in one's purpose, in satisfaction and reward. There is an "if" in this process, if there has been effective communication.

What am I trying to tell you? Just this. In our development of our hospital library profession and its unique aspect, bibliotherapy, we seem not to be communicating or relating on an effective level. Our message seems to lack the proper stimuli. Jesse Shera wrote that a quarter of a century ago, Pierce Butler had charged, though librarians "know very well *how* to do things, they have only vague notions *why* they do them." Now in 1968, a similar criticism is still being voiced. Shera continued "the truth is that we have not succeeded in establishing our professional purpose." Perhaps it is as one of the speakers in Kansas City put it, "We are operating with *third* generation computers but *first* generation librarians."

Who's to blame? We are suffering from a malady Dean Asheim called, "a reluctant profession and a resistant education." There are hopeful signs, however. This Institute is one; here we are attempting to define our role, so that guidelines may be set up, to lead to more effective ways of using our knowledge and achieving our goals.

This Spring, also, a curriculum guide for library careers in hospitals and institutions was prepared by a committee in the ALA's Library Education Division. The leaflet is to serve as a means of information and recruitment for the student in high school, college, and at the graduate level.

Realistically approached, the guide lists courses for specialized training which "will qualify the librarian to participate in the remedial, therapeutic and rehabilitative care of the individual."

As part of the basic structure of the curriculum, there must be a balance of the behavioral and biological sciences. In addition to library technics and an extensive knowledge of literature and a personal awareness of the benefits of reading the librarian must also know human nature and understand personality growth. As part of the therapeutic milieu, the librarian must have a knowledge of the techniques of group leadership and individual guidance. The most important of the electives are those dealing with communications and interpersonal relationships; social studies, speech, psychology, group dynamics, including information of the psychopathology of the individual. Such a curriculum will supply the professional expertise the librarian needs, not only for personal assurance but also in establishing one's role as an expert with the client and with one's peers.

With comparable training, scientifically oriented, such as that of the occupational therapist, what distinguishes the two? It is, of course, the role that each plays in the treatment of the patient.

Have you ever wondered why occupational therapists have progressed as far as they have? It is because they have defined and have been able to communicate their own distinctive functions and roles within the framework of the concept, "curing by doing," or the involvement of the patient in doing something for himself, and for a purpose.

We librarians can operate within the team as the specialists. We are professionals and can bring to the team professional competence as well as the traditions, values, and standards of the profession. What we do is to articulate and relate our distinctive contribution, not only within the team but in our day by day, person-to-person contact. Unless we do this, we do ourselves, our profession, and the team a disservice.

Professors Bundy and Wasserman, in their splendid article, "Professionalism Reconsidered," "suspect that the hallmark of the librarian who functions as a true professional is reflected in the nature of his relationships. He constantly expands upon his circle of contacts, reinforces and strengthens existing relations." The warnings they voice are direct and clear, when they write: "As long as professionalism remains so weak and so ill-understood, libraries will remain unable to solve not only their immediate problems but they will be unprepared and so unable to make the radical adaptations necessary to meet rapidly shifting and growing requirements put upon them." Under these conditions, they warn, outside intervention will move in, either by direct action or by using alternatives to meet the needs.

We hospital librarians should not fear that we will disappear unless we continue to cling to standards which have outgrown their usefulness. At San Francisco ALA, a speaker used the phrase: "Yesterday's standards are today's millstone and tomorrow's tolling of the bell."

We must continue to expand our horizons, to grow, to adapt our concepts to changes which are occurring. This is part of putting our training and knowledge to use. It is a vital part in the implementation of our knowledge into action. This past week you undoubtedly discussed the changes, the rapid development of the behavioral sciences. You heard how concepts of treatment are changing as part of the psycho-sociological approach to problems in our culture. We, too, must be flexible and be able to adapt our methods so that the contribution we make on an individual basis or as consultants is a dynamic one.

We come now to the implementation of what we know, the where, when and how of the hospital librarian. First, let me review briefly what is expected of us.

The team will expect from us professional competence. It will demand that we can formulate and articulate what we are doing as librarians, as it relates and pertains to the whole concept of treatment. These are some of the things that will be expected:

> That we organize a library service that is meaningful and structured on the principles of therapy.

> That we not only have the qualities and qualifications of a specialist, but that we can relate them as a contribution.

> That we show the inter-relatedness of the book to life; of book content to overt behaviour as it can be related to therapy.

> That we can evaluate the role of the librarian in the planning of the goals for the patient.

> That we can evaluate the nuances and changes of behavior; to keep records and make reports with intelligent observations and evaluations.

> That we are able to analyze literature for its emotional content to fit the patient's need, and to act as support and reinforcement in individual and group therapy.

> That we can be flexible, to be able to re-evaluate our program to fit the emotional situation; as when a patient suddenly regresses and all plans must be changed; this offers a challenge to all.

Emerson wrote it well: "Don't say things. What you *are* stands over you the while and thunders so that I cannot hear what you say to the contrary."

What are we? Can we interpret what we do, simply and directly? What is the distinguishing feature of our work; what do we do that the others can't do?

Certainly we cannot point to the books we use. We don't hold the key to literature. The library service? It is valid to say that the library and the reading of books are remedial activities. However, no matter how well it has been planned, or how carefully the books have been selected, the library remains a static thing by itself. Someone must make us into the vital, living force—a means of therapy, which it can be.

The librarian's mystique lies in the ability to act as an intermediary, as a catalyst in establishing the fusion between book content and reader.

How is this done? Communication is the key—the key to treatment in the librarian-patient relationship, in the guidance to emotional involvement of the patient with the content of the book. Communication is the key to staff relationship, also.

Miss Moody, in a recent paper, stated "We must become communication analysts, because communication involves people, people exchanging ideas, people changing attitudes, people reacting by behaving in ways that benefit themselves and their fellowmen."

The librarian cannot be an isolationist, whether working on a team or alone.

Planning the library activities involves inter-team collaboration. Better understanding of the philosophy of other disciplines results; the treatment of the patient will improve, and of great importance this collaboration will also help dispel some of the misconceptions to which library service is still vulnerable. Comments such as "a nice service, helps occupy the patient's mind," are still heard. When we interpret our role effectively, it will be evident that we have the training, the capacity to present reading as a normal activity which is related to a patient's everyday life and which, used as a specific treatment, aids his psychological adjustment.

Example: Plans were being formulated for a diabetic patient whose condition would necessitate a radical change in her life. She was a successful business woman, a hair stylist and owner of several beauty salons. Progressive blindness would prevent her return to active duty. This she refused to accept by denying her failing eyesight. Under the direction of the physician, the social worker and librarian worked together. It was our function to interpret to her that she was still a successful business woman, still capable of further work, that there were other "eyes" which would help keep her mind alert, knowledgeable, and capable of expanding. Both the social worker and librarian kept each other informed of the slightest progress. The first sign of growing acceptance of her failing eyesight occurred when she a tried a magnifying glass. Her final acceptance of the talking book service helped make a bridge so that the social worker could take over. Plans could then be started for vocational rehabilitation.

We must remember this, however, communication is a two-way street, a system which has to be built so that there is *in*-coming as well as out-going communication. Both channels must be kept open.

The librarian should be aware that if treatment is truly patient centered, geared to patient's goal, then coordination should occur almost automatically, as each service considers the patient's needs rather than his own prestige. Assumed here is that there is participation and understanding of the functions and duties of each member by each member. No one service can say it was responsible for the rehabilitation of the patient. Each one has contributed of his services, in the treatment and guidance which lead to rehabilitation.

In the process of establishing interpersonal relationships are many factors. I shall cite only a few which must be present, whether we are operating on the verbal or non-verbal level of communication. They are:

Appreciation of the role, functions, and professional status of each other. This involves understanding not only one's own abilities but also one's limitations, the feelings that arise. We must not only recognize our own status, but derive satisfaction in maintaining it, within its potential and also its limitations.

Interpretation of one's role, what one hopes to accomplish for the patient, stated clearly, succinctly and simply.

Security in personal and professional competency and ability.

Communication in letting others know what is going on as well as learning what others are doing. This is an on-going process, reaching throughout the hospital and beyond.

Attitudes—a non-competitive and non-possessive attitude toward the patient. There should be understanding and acceptance of realistic goals of each patient.

Integration of treatment recommendations, a pooling of thinking and abilities.

Let us go back briefly to my original questions. What we must be and what is expected of us, I have tried to outline for you. The When, Where, and How, we have seen occurs through communication, on all levels, reaching throughout the institution and beyond, on an ongoing basis. The Why, a combination of all these factors, I shall try to tell you tomorrow.

One question is left: Who are we? This is something one frequently forgets to ask. Self-evaluation is not easy. If we want to be successful in establishing ourselves and our profession, we must know ourselves. How do we affect others? Are we over-aggressive, defensive about our role? Do others respect us for our contribution? Do we expect them to like us and the rest then takes care of itself? What is holding back the development and recognition of our program? Could it be you and I?

Each one of you write your interpretation of your role. Ask your family sometime what it is you do; what does your volunteer think? How do you interpret it to the physician, to your dinner partner at a banquet, to a teenager who may be interested in the profession? And lastly, to our own profession of librarianship.

A good working hypothesis is that where the heat is, there also will be found the light for the next step forward. For us, it is the guidelines to further development.

We are living in a culture of many changes and we as librarians are unrealistic if we think we will remain untouched. Jesse Shera in an article stated: "To Thomas Huxley's classic question propounded over a century ago, 'What are you going to do with these new things?' Librarians have given only the Luddites' answer, 'Destroy them before they destroy us.' But it was the Luddites who were destroyed, they were hanged, and librarians could suffer even a worse fate—they could be ignored."

Suggestions for
Further Reading

Alice R. Brooks, "Developmental Values in Books" in F. Henne, et al. *Youth, Communication, and Libraries* (Chicago: A.L.A., 1949).

Margaret C. Hannigan, "The Librarian in Bibliotherapy: Pharmacist or Bibliotherapist?" *Library Trends* 11:184-198 (October 1962).

Arleen Hynes, "Bibliotherapy Training Program at St. Elizabeths Hospital" in Rhea Rubin, *Using Bibliotherapy: A Guide to Theory and Practice* (Phoenix: Oryx Press, 1978).

K. G. Keneally, "Therapeutic Value of Books" from F. Henne, et al. *Youth, Communication, and Libraries* (Chicago: A.L.A., 1949).

Clara Lack and Bruce Bettencourt, "Bibliotherapy in the Community" *News Notes of California Libraries* 67:372 (1973).

David J. McDowell, "Bibliotherapy in a Patients Library" *Bulletin of the Medical Library Assn.* 59:450-457 (July 1971).

Margaret Monroe and Rhea Rubin, "Bibliotherapy: Trends in the United States" *Libri* 25:156-162 (1975).

Mildred Moody and Hilda Limper, *Bibliotherapy: Methods and Materials* (Chicago: A.L.A., 1971).

Melvin C. Oathout, "Books and Mental Patients" *Library Journal* 79:405-410 (March 1954).

Rhea J. Rubin, ed., "Bibliotherapy." *HRLSD Quarterly* 1:1-27 (entire issue) (October 1975).

Ruth Tews, "Bibliotherapy," in Allen Kent and Harold Lamour, eds., *Encyclopedia of Library and Information Science* (New York: Marcel Dekker, 1969), pp. 448-457

PART

IV

FOREIGN
PERSPECTIVES

Introductory Comments

The International Federation of Library Associations (IFLA) Hospitals Subsection devoted a program to the topic of bibliotherapy in 1974. At that meeting, a representative from Germany reported that a bibliography of bibliotherapeutic materials, organized by topic, was being prepared in her country; the project is still underway. Representatives from other countries asked questions and expressed interest in the status of bibliotherapy here. The papers presented were all by Americans because the conference was held in Washington, D.C. (The best of them appear in sections II and III of this volume.)

Numerous articles on bibliotherapy have appeared in foreign journals during the last two decades. These are interesting, although less sophisticated in style than the American ones, containing primarily exhortatory and anecdotal material. German and Scandinavian library and medical journals in particular have carried relevant articles. Unfortunately, most have never been translated into English.

British library publications have long discussed the use of literature for therapeutic purposes. Two typical English articles are reprinted here. Duncan Leys' was published as part of a text on hospital libraries in 1965. He expresses his concern that "in our preoccupation with the application of the physical sciences to medicine, we have tended to forget that bodies belong to people." He feels that the use of literature can undo the depersonalization of the hospital setting and can relieve the loneliness of the patient. "Therapeutic Aspects of a Library Service to Hospital Patients" was published a decade later by S. D. Coomaraswamy, a clinical psychologist. She too stresses the psychological implications of illness and hospitalization and states that library service can "energize and motivate" patients. In Sweden and the other Scandinavian countries, bibliotherapy is used mainly with physically ill hospital patients and is seen as an "occupational therapy" rather than as a psychological one. "Reading Therapy in the Service of the Sick" discusses the philosophy of library service in Swedish hospitals. Medlicott's article on bibliotherapy in a psychiatric hospital in New Zealand emphasizes the potential problems in using literature with patients. He correctly observes that "both librarians and therapists need to know the books they recommend and the patients they recommend them to."

"Books and Empathy Help Troubled Children," is included here because it represents a simple research project dealing with children, the second most widely used population in bibliotherapy experiments. Altmann's Canadian study is especially noteworthy because it emphasizes the attitude of the bibliotherapist in addition to the method of bibliotherapy.

"Suggestions for Rehabilitation and Bibliotherapy in South African Prisons" is interesting as the author is admittedly influenced by the growing awareness of inmates' library needs in the United States. But, the prisoner typology and material classification suggested is far from acceptance in America today. The attempt to classify types of fiction by "criminal types" is the sort of study that was popular in the U.S. in the 1920s through the early 1950s. Moerdijk's article is, however, one of few on bibliotherapy in South Africa which has appeared in English.

Russia has long demonstrated its interest in the therapeutic aspects of literature. In 1916, Nicholas Rubakin formulated a unique theory of reading, "bibliopsychology." Lenin was only one of Rubakin's eminent followers. Rubakin devised tests and formulae to categorize books by their effects on readers. "The special method of bibliopsychology consists of statistical evaluation of the excitations experienced by the reader during the process of reading." He theorized that readers, too, could be classified by their reactions to books. "Having worked out a numerical coefficient for a given reader at a given time, we can arrive at his coefficient applicable in general." Materials could then be scientifically selected for each individual to insure certain results. Included here is Sylva Simsova's essay on Rubakin and his work. Nearly a half century later, in 1962, one Russian republic established a central office for bibliotherapy research and training. A. M. Miller discussed this and other recent developments in Russia in his article "The Reading Matter of Patients."

This section of foreign articles demonstrates widespread interest in bibliotherapy, although admittedly the most sophisticated use of bibliotherapy and research is currently concentrated in the United States.

The Place of Literature in Healing

by Duncan Leys

Librarianship is an honoured and ancient profession: not quite so ancient, but a good deal more honoured than that of doctoring. I understand very well that I am as little entitled to offer my thoughts on the arts of poetry and prose writing as the least experienced member of the community of librarians, whether professional or amateur, salaried or voluntary. My sole qualification for writing this chapter is that we are now, I am glad to say, colleagues in the art of healing and that I have spent forty years watching and talking to people in bed in hospital or institution, people of all ages from the newborn to the very old; people who expected to be in bed for only a few days; people who knew they would never be active again; people whose lives were ending and who knew this was so; attractive, intelligent people; lively and receptive children; experienced and wise old men and women. But also the dull, repulsive, even offensive; the silent, dour, withdrawn, the sad, the uncouth, the ignorant, opinionated, the aggressive, the anxious and resentful.

Not every person who occupies a hospital bed is seriously ill and not every child in a home, or old person living alone, feels himself to be abandoned. But nobody suffers illness without some diminution of his powers. Even a relatively trivial illness can cause a lot of anxiety. Part of the duty of physician or nurse, or of the guardian of a child robbed of his family, is to make an effort to find out what sort of people they are for whom he or she has accepted responsibility, what their experiences have been, and how much they understand about their situation and are affected by it. The effect of all illness or deprivation is to cause a certain withdrawal of interest in affairs, a concentration upon oneself and a limitation of curiosity about events and still more of curiosity about ideas.

We have passed through, or rather are slowly emerging from a bad period in nursing and doctoring. The last fifty years have seen explosive enlightenment in the science of medicine, but have also witnessed in our practice of medicine a most lamentable display of

Reprinted with permission from The Library Association, London, 1963, Chap. V, pp. 44-50, in *Hospital Libraries and Work with the Disabled*, M. E. Going, ed.

ignorance and complacency. In our preoccupation with the application of the physical sciences to medicine we have tended to forget that bodies belong to people, and that people are the most complex wholes known to us, unique and individual and indivisible. There is an infinite variety of human beings, and during illness, and especially in the condition of hospital life, personality is displayed to us in a unique way. We break down, as it were, because of the need for intimacy, the ordinary defences which the individual erects round his personality and which makes him look like everybody else. Some individuals live at a high pitch of excitement, making the very most of their opportunities of living, full of resources in themselves. But there are many who have only a slender support, an equilibrium precariously adjusted and easily overturned by adversity or injury or sudden change of circumstance. These are the sort of people whose interests are so narrow that if one has to be abandoned, as in retirement from active work, they become easy victims of depression, and even die from lack of genuine desire to live. But everyone who is cut off from his everyday habit of life, and is not a voluntary recluse, is to some extent put off his balance. A serious illness (or, which is as much to the point, an illness which he believes to be serious) is likely to have made him apprehensive about his work and his family, but mostly anxious about himself, of possible permanent injury or even risk of losing his life. This is likely to be followed, as soon as it is relieved, by boredom and often enough the patient is not really conscious that it is boredom which affects him. I have often seen a man lie in bed all day, merely watching what goes on around him, not really conscious of the need for some activity, exchanging gossip about the staff or his own symptoms: he would not describe it as boredom, but for the most part passivity of this kind does in fact retard recovery. One sees the same thing any day in a long railway journey: if there is not quickly established a chatty atmosphere in the compartment, then for hours some of the passengers will gaze out of the window, their minds either occupied with daydreams or, as often I believe, with nothing at all.

But of all the sensations which the hospital patient experiences, I think the most difficult to bear is loneliness: a loneliness which so often nobody makes any effort to relieve. Sympathy is not a natural phenomenon, but a cultivated sentiment, something which belongs to civilization. Sick people, and old, helpless people, even deprived children with their griefs and resentments, make demands upon the healthy and free which are by no means always welcome. The instinctive response to the news of someone else's illness is one of aversion or boredom, of "How does this affect me?" It may mean more work, more obligations. The need to display sympathy and to offer help is something we are taught or learn by experience, and about which we need to remind ourselves constantly. If we have ever been seriously ill ourselves we are possibly helped in the effort to understand another person's need in sickness, but our own painful experiences tend to be forgotten, by a merciful dispensation, and the ability to put oneself in another man's shoes is a strictly limited one.

I imagine that most people will have read Cecil Woodham-Smith's life of Florence Nightingale. Miss Nightingale suffered the lot of most reformers, and, after years of recrimination and neglect during her lifetime, later achieved canonisation. Although her popular reputation is rather that of a disciplinarian who regarded a clean and tidy bed, personal hygiene and a properly scientific attitude to illness as all-important, her own *Notes on Nursing* are informed by an intelligent regard for the sensibilities and intellectual needs of patients as people. For example, she remarks how an individual can be thrust back into dependence and prevented from regaining the self-confidence and self-respect which indicate recovery from illness, by a too protective attitude. True, in hospital work, the fault has usually been on the other side, and in the present anxiety to keep patients actively employed, to prevent them from hibernating as it were, current medical fashions have gone too far. A degree of inactivity and irresponsibility can be regarded as one of the legitimate compensations of illness for many people who are ordinarily overpressed. I think especially of mothers of families, who are often breadwinners also, and of unmarried women earning their living and spending their leisure caring for old fathers and mothers. Social service is too much subject to fashion. It would no doubt have shocked many of my own teachers if they could have heard me speak of medical practice as a branch of social service, yet this is in fact as reasonable a description of my work as it is of yours. The present fashion is to insist on activity as a healing process. As so often happens, a truth, even an elementary truth, has been forgotten, restated, hailed as a new discovery and then formalised to a regime. It is not good for people, even for sick people, to allow themselves to abandon all the activities of health which involve mental or physical effort; yet an enforced period of rest and relative idleness can certainly bring an indirect benefit in relief from the usual effort of living and working. Some people have in fact a pathetic desire to find in illness a relief from the perplexities, irksome responsibilities and actual physical labour of life. And there are many of us who find some consolation, when a not too threatening or painful illness overtakes us, in the mere fact of being solitary. Unfortunately, in hospital we are rarely solitary and our surroundings are not often conducive to tranquil thoughts. It is an obvious mistake to employ, in an undiscriminating way, the doctrine that activity of some kind is an essential part of treatment. Here is one example of this wrong-headed, unthinking, rule-of-thumb application of the present medical fashion. Day-rooms and play-rooms, i.e., places where convalescent patients can accustom themselves to getting about after an acute illness, are the exception rather than the rule in hospital, and we have all desired them. In the fracture ward of one hospital, the management of which had been sensible enough to provide such rooms, all the ambulant patients, willy-nilly, were made to sit all day in chairs ranged round the walls, elbow to elbow.

Some of the bad practices of hospital wards and of homes for children and old people are relics of an outworn charity tradition. Not perhaps as much relics as one would wish. Hospitals, as we know them, are of recent date. You would, I am sure, be profoundly shocked by some of the things which were seen when critical observers appointed by the Ministry of Health made a survey of hospital accommodation and service shortly before the National Health Act came into operation. Society has, even now, not fully accepted its obligations to the sick and the aged. When I was a house-physician in one of our London teaching hospitals, the sister of the ward would call out, when I appeared, "Papers away!" and nobody, however remote from us, was allowed, while I was in the ward, to look at a book or to speak. This attitude still survives, quite actively. The patient was someone to whom things were given, a humble seeker for charity, and an attitude of grateful conformity was required of him. Doctors, nurses, committee members, official visitors, almoners and even masseuses were people apart, to be regarded with some awe. Their service to the patient was, if you like, a high duty. Consciousness of duty can be a useful personal discipline: but it is a bad guide to the sort of sympathetic personal relationship with the people upon whom the patient depends for his care.

It is very easy for people to become anonymous in hospital or institution. One finds it, even now, not uncommon for people working in hospital to forget to use common courtesy titles, or to take the trouble to learn people's names. Mr. Brown gets called plain Brown, as if he were on charge in a police court, and Mrs. Brown becomes "Grannie" or "Dear." One hears people referred to as "No. 7" or even "The appendix in No. 7." People treated like this cease to become people and are merely numbers, bodies, diseases. And when you are anonymous, personality begins to disintegrate. My reference to the police court is not altogether inapt. There are plenty of likenesses between hospital patients and prisoners. We don't speak about "admitting" and "discharging" people from hotels and holidays camp, nor, if the head waiter is annoyed when we refuse the roast beef, does he express himself to us in strong disapproval. The compulsory religious ward service of many of our hospitals is an affront to the sensitive dissenter or agnostic.

Working against all these inimical features of a hospital illness or of life in an institution there are sensitive individuals who have cultivated the capacity to be something more than an expert technician, to be able to sympathise, and to act as counsellor and friend, and as substitute for mother, wife or daughter, husband or son. Among these you, with your books, your informal offer of friendly interest, and your confidence of having something valuable to offer, take your place. You have the advantage of appearing to the patient as offering something to be rejected or accepted as he wishes. All the rest of us have, in some manner, authority over him. We may do things to him or for him which he finds not unpleasant, and even desirable, but our visits and ministrations are things which he cannot escape, and often he very much desires to escape them: everything we do is advertised as for his good. You are all only too familiar with the sort of gambit we employ, the still all too common stereotyped manner of pretence identification of interest which lends itself so readily to caricature: "We mustn't let ourselves get lazy, must we, No. 9?" You have no temptations in that direction, no need to force yourselves or your wares upon a helpless victim, no obligation to be an improver of his mind or conduct. You offer him what? Distraction, entertainment? Perhaps, if he is in the mood, a good deal more—enlightenment or the genuine relief which comes from the understanding of good art in any form, the purging of the emotions, a glimpse of heaven.

There is, of course, to be cultivated, the judgment of what to offer. This is something which cannot be taught or learned except by experience of life itself: poetry or prose, fiction, biography, travel; the who-dun-it or Tolstoy, to satisfy the needs of a child, an adolescent, a student at university, all the seven Shakespearean stages of life, all the gradation of capacity. We cannot any of us genuinely share another's thoughts, but we can be receptive, undogmatic, and learn to be shrewd judges of character. In general the sick person will want to follow his everyday habit in reading. But there are likely to be certain qualities of writing which are of more value than others to people who are going to be cut off for a very long time from normal activity or who have to face a daily experience of pain and discomfort. I have a notion that in literature, as in other things, you can destroy your capacity to enjoy good things by indulging always in the second-rate, and therefore lose a lot of the refreshment which books should give. I also have a prejudice about who-dun-its, regarding them as very unsatisfactory kinds of reading, and offering very little opportunity for "losing oneself," which should be the object of reading at all.

At times of crisis, doubt or depression, we all have our own special resources in the arts, and if I mention one or two of mine in literature it is only as illustration, and not because I suppose them to have any special value for everyone, although I know that I share them with many. A. E. Housman, whose work someone has called "the last trickle of classical poetry in England," in the simplicity of his language and style, and his mood of self-reliance, is a constant resource. Mark Rutherford, now very much outmoded, retains for me a charm which is sustaining. But for serenity and powerful interest the characters of Trollope's novels, almost inexhaustible in number, offer in themselves a library for the sick-bed.

I found myself, when sick, with no desire whatever for humour. This may be a peculiarity of my own, and I think there should usually be plenty of room for it, especially the unexacting kind of farcical writing of a Thurber. Again, to speak from my own experiences as a patient, and this opinion is reinforced by that of my friends, the sick and convalescent man is usually quite incapable of sustained mental effort, especially in an unfamiliar field. I tried, and failed, to satisfy a long-felt desire to make acquaintance with modern philosophy; on the other hand, when I was able to read in company and discuss, I could enjoy the effort greatly as a convalescent, and it seems to me that there is an idea here for development in wards for the chronic sick—i.e., of play and poetry readings, or even the reading aloud to a group. There is nothing new in this; I can remember my mother doing just this for old ladies in the poor-law institution near our home. Literacy is precarious; for most people there is no continuing incentive in company or atmosphere to encourage development of a taste for reading: many houses, even quite prosperous ones, remind one of the man wishing to give his friendly neighbour a Christmas present and asking whether a book would be acceptable, receiving in reply "Oh I don't think so, thank you, we have one." There are many people, not by any means always people who work with their hands, who never open a book, although they can read. I knew one doctor who never read anything but comics. Thrown on their own resources, away from their hobbies and gardens, their enforced idleness may become a real burden. Practical occupations may satisfy, but many will also welcome a reintroduction to literature through some book, perhaps more inspiring than anything they ever were offered before. Others, even less fortunate, may be unable to read, and like the cook in one of Ivy Compton-Burnett's novels, be ashamed to confess it. I hope you are not high-brow; the comic or picture book is not literature but can be all the same a resource.

Healing and health are only other forms of "Whole." I am whole when I am myself—an individual, not a mere bed number—master of my fate. Books can help greatly to restore that wholeness, to convince me, the sick person, that I am far removed from the young man who said "Damn, at last I've found out what I am; I am something which moves in predestinate grooves, not even a bus but a tram."

Therapeutic Aspects of a Library Service to Hospital Patients

by S. D. Coomaraswamy

Hospital library services began as diversionary measures for patients and have developed to meet many divergent needs. The resources of most libraries are seen to be diversional, educational and therapeutic. This library is an integral part of this hospital offering a range of passive and active services to meet definable aims which I will detail later on.

Hospital libraries are called upon to cater for the needs of infinitely varied clients. Patients often have many empty hours to pass with apprehensive thoughts about their pain, illness, personal problems, work and finances. Books are usually evocative and can rescue patients from their isolation. Books make valuable sources of knowledge about human beings and their activities which become available to patients. Opportunities can arise for disciplined use of the imagination we call "empathy," which is an inner and often an obscure experience. Books become highways of communication, making readers sensitive and insightful. Literature can be used to sensitise patients to human situations, to deepen their understanding and enrich their contacts with other people. Legends, fables, plays, anecdotes, all become avenues of communication.

In looking at the therapeutic aspects of such a library service to patients, one needs to study the significant challenge we face in treating patients in general and psychiatric patients in particular.

Let us consider:

THERAPEUTIC VALUE OF LIBRARIES FOR PATIENTS IN GENERAL

When persons become patients they are usually overwhelmed with feelings of apprehension, inadequacy and often experience a loss of dignity and self-esteem, even though educationally and professionally

Reprinted with permission from *Health and Welfare Libraries Quarterly* 2(2-4):29-32 (June-December 1975).

competent. Fears relate to loss of bodily organs and functions; these constitute threats of personal survival. Patients are often required to play a submissive role in that decision-making has to be given over to specialists.

These aspects have psychological implications for patients. How do we energise and motivate them to remain mentally active, interested, without too much preoccupation with their illness? e.g.

    (a) children who are injured, suffering disease or disability due to brain damage.

    (b) a young man who has sustained double amputation of both legs and is withdrawn and uncommunicative.

    (c) patients awaiting surgery.

    (d) patients in continual pain.

The challenge here would be to initiate and sustain short-term concentration. Communication may develop from passive reception of information from books to active participation in discussions. Libraries are required to devise, acquire and provide a range of items to stimulate and support "patient-readers." There would be a widening of horizons and perspective. Patients' personal needs may become clearer with new opportunities to waken and foster latent and residual abilities. Patients recovering from head injury may look at pictures and illustrations as an alternative to staring into space. Reading short stories to them may enable them to remember more and more of the plot. A game technique may be adopted to offer progressive help to the brain-damaged with inverted speech and receptive aphasia. This may develop into educational rehabilitation with the help of teachers and speech therapists. Play-sets become made available for play-reading groups in the Occupational Therapy department as a development from quiz games.

Patients exercise selection of reading material — being guided to books to help in their rehabilitation into new or previous occupations — technical or otherwise . . . e.g. nurses, engineers.

THERAPEUTIC VALUE OF LIBRARIES FOR PSYCHIATRIC PATIENTS IN PARTICULAR

Here I speak mainly from my experiential perspective.

Therapists and patients are constantly in a process of self-discovery . . . with each other, within themselves, in poetry and literature. The chief aim in psychological treatment of patients is to initiate, establish and maintain communication. Communication, as I understand it, is two-ways, then many-ways. To quote an extreme instance, even the mute psychotic is communicating the 'impasse' he has arrived at for those who have eyes to see or ears to hear. The angry, the desperate, the cynic, the withdrawn, all have their language systems, their unique styles of emitting verbal or non-verbal signals. Time does not allow me to expand on this.

Therapist's knowledge and understanding of patient's daily living experiences and their cultural, emotional and intellectual background enable the gaining of communication with the patient.

Reading material needs to be considered, evaluated and matched for the characteristic needs of patients. The levels of sophistication of the patients, their goals, the degree of relatedness and closeness between patient and therapist would guide the suggestions of reading matter the therapist makes to individual patients, as compared to material for group reading or discussion.

Poetry is acknowledged to be a powerful therapeutic tool in helping patients in general and psychiatric patients in particular to get in touch with their feelings and powerful emotions, so as to identify and work through them. Poetry provides catharsis . . . as significantly as though an analyst were interpreting for them.

There are noted similarities between the language of schizophrenics and poets—paleologic, neologisms, metaphors and so forth (Dr. Forrest).

It is necessary to select poems patients can readily understand— poems with a fairly clear message and a good sense of rhyme and rhythm—poems that tell a story, cultural poems and poems of childhood reminiscences, perhaps extracts from the Bible.

Chronic schizophrenic patients with long-term periods of 40 years in hospital would have very limited attention spans. They need short-term goals to make them accessible for communication and socialisation and self-expression. These patients require more directive leadership. We need first of all to create opportunities for them to relate to each other and to the therapists, so that gradually they may share feelings and experiences through the media of poetry, drama and general literature.

Poetry becomes a therapeutic medium with groups where characteristics of group members periodically change. It is a flexible therapy which may help patients with overwhelming feelings of inadequacy and depression. This may become a self-generating research activity. Patients identify with poets like William Cowper (1731-1800) who studied law for 12 years, but attempted suicide when it came to examinations and was committed to an asylum at St. Albans. Patients become able to project feelings and reveal more of themselves than otherwise. William Blake (1747-1827) experienced hallucinatory visions without necessarily destroying his life. Group reading of poetry elicits discussions before any identifying about author is provided.

Group members attempt writing poetry for groups to respond to before author's own interpretation. In this way the alienation of chronic alcoholics comes forth in the bitter, arrogant, sarcastic and often insolent remarks during repetitious bouts of being drunk.

The problems of conflicts become externalised in Robert Frost's "The Road Not Taken" because of divergent goals—this stimulus opens floodgates of information hitherto suppressed.

Should reading material be censored? This is a matter for serious consideration by the Therapist in relation to particular patients. Themes of relevance for self-exploration range from motives for suicide and rejection to anger, turbulence and violence. The Therapist should establish a framework within which he and his patient are comfortable and with which they can cope.

Books portraying strife and hope, the value and inevitability of personal experiences, family and personal relationships and friendships can introduce humour, compassion and tolerance. Communications within families are of profound significance.

There are many gifted, sensitive persons whose relationships into adult life are still marred by over-possessive relationships and lingering guilts. Patients often select themes of particular significance to them.

It is a fascinating challenge, however, to consider that an intellectual understanding about the reason for our difficulties in itself removes them.

For example, Simone de Beauvoir "Memories of a Dutiful Daughter, " "The Prime of Life," Saul Bellow "The Victim," M. Drabble "Jerusalem the Golden," "The Millstone."

Can we not thus transfer patients' energies spent on purposeless rituals and obsessions and compulsive addiction into the purposeful activities of trying to obtain information and insight from books and discussion on the nature of their anxieties? This is the track I am trying to follow into the unexplored regions of the human mind. It would be very useful if practitioners could share their experiences through group discussions such as this.

Advice by librarians would be welcome on studies of themes such as:—

1. Deprivation in childhood.
2. Problems of puberty and adolescence.
3. Family interaction.
4. Courtship, marriage—the ordinariness of crises and family's unspectacular failure to cope.
5. Emotional interaction in intense personal relationship, individuals bound together by emotional needs, often neurotic needs, such as Iris Murdoch described where there is discussion of ambivalence, unacknowledged rivalries in significant relationships when other relationships challenge the patterns with which they have coped. For example, "An Accidental Man." The pervasive effects of early conditioning, the restraints imposed on oneself and others close to one, the poverty of communication between individuals can be brought into conscious awareness of the usually self-absorbed psychiatric patient.
6. Ageing—the sensitive views expressed by writers on the losses and confusion in old age can enlighten both therapist and patient.

7. Grief and loss—the problem of adapting to new conditions such as the removal of a breast or the death of a spouse, for example, are dealt with by P. Mortimer in "My Friend Says It is Bullet-proof." Physical or psychological loss can leave a person with a feeling of being maimed.
8. Themes of disabling guilt, the interjection of guilt by the victim who is scapegoated by society, e.g. B. Malamud's "The Fixer."
9. Deviance in behaviour which may often be outside one's personal experience can be insightful, e.g. incest, indecent assault, homosexuality.
10. The psychopathology of crime would lead us into an understanding of criminal behaviour where labelling often obscures the values of good and bad.

The individual's attempts to find self-respect, self-worth through the insidious upsurge of mental illness may become a search for identity and healthy self-acceptance. The saddest casualties in society are often those who destroy their own potential resources because of sexual guilt.

Solzhenitsyn's "Cancer Ward" is a monumental discussion about an individual's right to self-determination.

BIBLIOGRAPHY

1. Peggy Card, "Poetry as a Bridge to the Lost," R.N.: 3236249 (March 1969).
2. D. V. Forrest, "Poiesis and the Language of Schizophrenia," *Psychiatry* 28: 1At (February 18, 1965).
3. Edward Connery Lathem, ed., "The poetry of Robert Frost" (New York: Holt, Rinehart & Winston, 1969).

Reading Therapy in the Service of the Sick

by Barbro Schmidt

Modern medical science seeks to consider the sick person as a unity, and stresses the need for awareness of the interplay between soul and body in order to achieve a correct judgment on a case. There is interaction between the mental and physical functions. Obvious changes in digestion, temperature or blood pressure can result from intense emotional states, as of anger, remorse or fear, or from crises of feeling such as disappointment, worry and anxiety. It is, furthermore, a well-known fact that a number of illnesses—for example, digestive disorders, heart illnesses, asthma and diabetes—are usually accompanied by certain types of emotional disorder.

We can seek to prevent and alleviate a proportion of these emotional disorders by mental guidance, influence, therapy. It is as a form of mental therapy that we regard bibliotherapy or reading therapy, whose task is to endeavour, with the aid of specially selected literature, to create that balance which is requisite to the regaining or maintaining of mental health. All kinds of informed library work among hospital patients can be regarded as reading therapy in the broad sense. In America, reading therapy is also used as an integral part of the psychiatric care of mental patients. In psychiatric clinics and mental hospitals there, scientific experiments are carried out to ascertain what literature lends itself to therapeutic use in the case of different forms of illness, and to find ways of stimulating the patients into reading.

Reading is not only a means of driving away boredom during a stay in hospital. Reading of well-chosen literature can stimulate the depressed and calm the over-excited. Reading arouses new interests, and prevents the patient's thoughts from circling around his own ego and his own illness. The book not only gives diversion, comfort and encouragement for a while, but can also make a positive contribution to the recovery of health, through giving mental equilibrium and heightened joy in living.

Reading therapy can also be regarded as a form of occupational therapy. There is now complete recognition of the need to complement

Reprinted with permission from "The Hospital Library in Sweden," Pamphlet #23 (London: The Library Association, 1962).

the purely medical hospital care with some kind of occupational therapy. Even the patient who feels himself to be in a state of mental balance must be provided with opportunities for various forms of occupation during his enforced free time. "Freedom from occupation is no rest, and a mind without thoughts is a mind with troubles." For the majority of hospital patients, reading of good literature is one of the best forms of occupation. Reading is, for most patients, the occupation which involves the least strain; and they can begin to read when their strength is still greatly diminished. Reading is also a form of occupational therapy which easily lends itself to adaptation to the needs of everyone.

In those hospitals which have a well-organized patients' library, the doctors and associated members of staff have come to set high store by the hospital librarian's work among the patients. The library gives the patients encouragement, entertainment and help with studying. In all clinics, books are welcomed as friends and comforters. The patients of each clinic, however, have their own special characteristics, which influence their need of reading as a form of therapy. Reading is of especial value in certain kinds of illness. I should like to give a few illustrations which bear out that this is the case.

In medical clinics there are patients with duodenal ulcers who are undergoing prolonged courses of dietetic treatment; there are also heart patients, diabetics and rheumatics, all with their own particular mental difficulties, which stand in direct relation to the various types of illness, and the treatment to be undergone. To be able to relax through reading affords the patients direct recreation. For patients in ear clinics, who, on account of deafness or diminished hearing, feel themselves isolated, and become melancholy and wrapped up in themselves, reading gives the best contact with the outside world, and at the same time affords good entertainment. For patients in skin clinics, reading can be of direct therapeutic importance through distracting attention from an irritating itch.

Patients in lung clinics have an especially great need of reading. Lung tuberculosis reduces physical strength in general, and tuberculosis patients are often subject to depression, for which good light reading can be an effective therapeutic solution. On account of the risk of infection, many of the patients must be kept in strict isolation, which can give them a feeling of being outcasts from the community. Through the protracted course of their illness, they are debarred, too, from their profession, for a matter of months or years. Doctors, for their part, strongly emphasize the value for tuberculosis patients of seeking to maintain contact with the world of work through utilizing their time in hospital for private study—study within their own sphere of work, language study, or study by way of training for a new occupation in which to earn a living on their emergence from illness.

Patients in rheumatic clinics often have crippled limbs, which confine them to bed, and prevent all forms of manual occupation. Reading constitutes one of their few recreational outlets. The proneness to relapses in this illness creates a special strain upon the spirits of rheumatic patients. Their zest for living is not so great on the second or third time they come to the clinic, as the first time. Patients in a surgical clinic need to have their thoughts distracted, by reading, from the imminent or recently undergone operation, which must stand out for each patient as a highly incalculable and dangerous element. The same applies in the case of patients in gynaecological and maternity clinics, who have come in for uterine operations, or who have undergone miscarriages or confinements with severe complications. The biological functions peculiar to women are closely related to women's emotional life, and disorders in them are particularly liable to create a depressed emotional state.

Long-term patients in orthopedic clinics can, with the help of the library, use their enforced free time in regular study towards improvement in their work, or in preliminary study for a new occupation, if they are going to be numbered for the future among the partially disabled. To be only partly fit for work, through loss of mobility in some form or other, is a mental as well as physical strain, and those thus afflicted need an extra dose of spiritual courage, which well-chosen reading can give. Many patients in plaster jackets or bandages are forced into immobility such as gives little chance of any recreation other than reading. It is a great advantage for people who have to leave hospital with a disability to have learned to find good friends among books.

Many clinics have large children's departments where the "book auntie" is a highly esteemed and longed-for guest. Toddlers look at picture books. School children read fairy tales and adventure stories, and it often happens that they read them aloud for their younger companions.

The library should be of great significance for the patients in psychiatric clinics. The librarian responsible for the choice of their reading matter ought to know these psychiatric patients personally. "It is as unsuitable to bring uncontrolled literature into a psychiatric hospital as it is to allow visitors to bring food to patients with abdominal illnesses," says an American doctor.

If they are to be able to meet the patients' many-sided reading requirements, all hospitals ought to have modern libraries. The larger hospitals should have specially trained hospital librarians; the smaller ones should at least be able to get competent library service from the nearest municipal library. It has taken us some time to grasp the significance of this.

It is in the interests of society to seek to prevent a prolonged stay in hospital from leading to a weakening of the patients' mental and moral forces. It happens not infrequently that patients return to everyday life with regained physical health, but without any positive desire to get down to work with hand or brain. They have grown into the habit of letting the day pass in idle chatter, card games, or the reading of inferior weeklies. They want to go on being taken care of and being objects of commiseration, and have no desire to try out their power of personal achievement. A good library service can actively contribute to the prevention of such a development. Reading can give spiritual help and stimulation, and can contribute to the restoration of the patient's mental and moral health. "A healthy mind in a healthy body" is an old motto which we ought to set ourselves as a precept, not least in the treatment of our hospital patients.

Bibliotherapy

by R. W. Medlicott

Reading is the major source of intellectual growth and an important source of emotional growth in any modern community. In a specialised community such as a psychiatric hospital the provision of background reading material is essential. Sitting rooms should have the local papers and one or two current periodicals such as *Time* or *Newsweek* and the *Listener*. Dictionaries and something of an encyclopaedic nature of which *Pears* is the simplest should be on hand. A set of an easily handled encyclopaedias such as *Everyman's* would be ideal. It is essential that any temptation for a hospital to accept out-of-date magazines and "old" books be resisted and that "dated" periodicals be removed and burnt. The average waiting-room collection of tattered magazines is depressing and must be avoided at all costs. As well as sitting-room material a hospital should have a small library and access to larger libraries. At Ashburn Hall, for example, a library is supplied and changed three monthly by the Country Library Service Division of the National Library. The selection of books from the van is made by a small group of patients and any interested staff member and the borrowing and changing of books organized by the patients. The monthly list of accessions supplied by the National Library makes available an extensive source of technical books for those who wish to order. In addition, the Dunedin City Public Library generously allows borrowing facilities to Ashburn Hall patients who care to use its resources. One might add to this reading background the provision of visual stimulation through carefully selected pictures for the walls. Reproductions should be avoided and a selection of the works of New Zealand artists gradually built up.

What has been discussed so far is the necessary background to a psychiatric facility—bibliotherapy only in the broadest sense. Bibliotherapy involves the planned use of reading material as part of a treatment programme. The term "therapy" should not be used if there is no planning and no attempt to assess the benefit or otherwise of what is offered. There is an extensive literature on bibliotherapy which involves the use of reading in all aspects of medical treatment, but curiously enough a dearth of accounts of specific plans and assessments so that in fact the field has not been explored to any depth.

Reading no doubt can provide much the same dynamic elements

Reprinted with permission from *New Zealand Libraries* 38(4):205-208 (August 1975).

as are inherent in psychotherapy, namely universalisation, identification, catharsis, and hopefully, insight. Communication, in the novel in particular, is of man to man. While information is important, these mechanisms cited are more powerful in their effect on the personality. Any stirring of the imagination has, however, potential for both constructive or destructive development. In the rest of this paper, rather than attempt to delineate reading programmes specific for different types of patients, the author will discuss some of the pros and cons of reading which he thinks should be considered when bibliotherapy is discussed. He takes this approach because he believes that it is an axiom that anything potentially constructive is also potentially destructive.

The possible ramifications of the influence of reading are so complex that one can only abstract certain aspects. Although there is obvious overlap the object of the use and abuse of reading will be divided into use of literature either as a source of information or as a stimulus to the imagination.

Three types of books used as sources of information will be discussed briefly, general mental health books and books on child-rearing and sexuality. There is a wide variety of general mental health or mental hygiene books which discuss the personality and the mental processes which lead to health or illness. Western man is increasingly preoccupied with health and one must expect a constant stream of popular books on psychiatry. Books like those written by Karl Menninger have stood the test of time and there are many others which are highly informative. It is unfortunate that there are not more studies on the assessment of the effects of such reading on segments of both patient populations and the public. As a psychiatrist one undoubtedly finds both patients and their relatives better informed now than in previous decades. As a psychiatrist, however, one finds definite limits to their helpfulness. The pseudo-sophisticated psychological intelligentsia show remarkable readiness in interpreting the unconscious sources of behaviour both in themselves and in their friends. This seldom, however, is reflected in mature behaviour. Commonly one finds amongst such psychologically preoccupied individuals highly destructive life patterns and it is often clear that they use their intellectual knowledge to avoid rather than strive for real change. With patients in psychotherapy the author advises against psychological reading as such reading is almost invariably used as a defence against deep involvement in treatment and serves to avoid real emotional change.

In the more specific areas such as child-rearing and sexual information in spite of their value books have many defects. Popular writers have used Freud throughout the whole of the twentieth century as the corner-stone of a permissive, often intensely selfish ethic. Freud was certainly not permissive, and although he explored primarily individual psychology he was well aware that the individual could only achieve maturity in a co-operative or sharing relationship with his fellows. Benjamin Spock, who is deservedly universally read, has had recently to recast much of what he wrote about child-rearing. Books on sexual information are helpful, but educators and psychiatrists do have to beware that a text is no alternative to discussion. Most sexual difficulties arise not from the absence of factual knowledge but through repression and emotional distortion of knowledge which is freely available. Many texts do not emphasise sufficiently the interpersonal aspects of sexuality. In other specific areas such as intellectual handicap books are often of tremendous value, especially to parents. Again, of course, personal discussion with experienced workers is essential.

In the imaginative sphere books are the real treasures of a literate society. Life without "poetry" using the word in its broader sense, is sterile. Novels, biographies, mythological, and religious writings are endless sources of inspiration. At the same time so powerful a stimulus to imagination can be destructive. The tendency to morbid day-dreaming accentuated by reading is more of a problem than many realise. Life demands the acceptance of reality and its avoidance in daydreams of glory and excitement in the identification with fictional characters can only lead to inadequate relationships with others and psychological malfunction. It is however, through indoctrination and in the stimulation of morbid interests that reading can be most destructive. In the national sphere, Nazi indoctrination led to a mass perversion and untold destruction. Frederic Wertham in the *Seduction of the Innocent* and *A Mark for Cain* warns that a diet of violence cannot help but be destructive. It is possible for patients to surround themselves with books which make any constructive approach to life extremely difficult. One patient's personal library was entirely devoted to philosophies propounding the meaningless of life and to stories of murder and suicide. The Manchester Moors murderers, Brady and Hindley, dieted on Neo-Nazi literature, sadistic books, and horror films. Their short sadistic career was one of the most sordidly tragic episodes in recent crime history.

In the sexual sphere books supplying sexual information have been discussed. In the wider field of literature novels with the sensitive portrayal of sexual relationships, normal and abnormal, have a positive value. However, much erotic literature is little more than hard-core pornography. Such works have little respect for reality; they ignore consideration of the mutual development of the sexual partners and ignore the responsibility for the children of selfish liaisons. Tenderness is absent and ultimately hard-core pornography resorts to sado-masochism to stimulate jaded appetites.

Returning to the more specific requirement of bibliotherapy both librarians and therapists need to know the books they recommend and the persons they recommend them to. They need to avoid the Scylla of paternal authoritarianism and the Charybdis of uncritical permissiveness. As a psychiatrist, while one can use the recommendation of reading constructively, one has to avoid indoctrinating others with one's personal prejudices.

Books and Empathy Help Troubled Children

by H. Altmann and B. Nielsen

Influence of Bibliotherapy on Self-Esteem

Rob was a slight boy, the youngest of nine children. During his first year at school, he showed promise of becoming a good student, but was now slow, anxious and over-sensitive. He liked playing games with his brothers and sisters, but otherwise preferred to do most things alone. Rob was one of 18 pupils from grades four and five in the Calgary Public School System chosen to participate in a special four-month study. A project was designed to investigate the influence of bibliotherapy of children's self-esteem and to examine the relationship between the librarian's attitude and the success of the program. The librarian was evaluated on her level of empathy, respect for the child and the genuineness of her concern.

Bibliotherapy is a relatively new term, coined to describe the use of directed reading in the solution of personal problems. It is regarded as a potentially useful tool, which school librarians and counsellors can use to help a troubled child. Several writers report the success of this technique in dealing with handicapped children, those who are unusually fearful or experiencing problems with their personal relationships. Researchers claim that reading and discussing books, specifically chosen for an individual, can help him to overcome or alleviate emotional and behavioural problems. The reader identifies with a character suffering personal difficulties resembling his own and gains insight into his problem after seeing how someone else copes with a comparable situation. A child may discover an alternative line of action which gives him greater command in difficult circumstances. Like adults, children with low self-esteem lack the capacity to deal with their environment. An environment which may itself have spawned their sense of inferiority. Several researchers have indicated that bibliotherapy, like any other form of therapy, will only work in an empathic atmosphere. They set out certain basic qualifications for a good bibliotherapist, which include physical well-being, emotional

Reprinted with permission from *The Canadian Library Journal* 31:284-287 (1974).

stability, a pleasing personality and an understanding of, and a feeling for, what goes on when one person talks and another listens. In addition, the bibliotherapist (librarian or counsellor) should be humane, intelligent and informed about human behaviour and books. It has been suggested that the method of treatment is less important than the attitude of the bibliotherapist. The study, therefore, set out to examine this concept.

A Calgary elementary school, with a trained and qualified librarian, was chosen for this study. The librarian had received no training in the core conditions. Thirty fourth and fifth grade students, with observable low levels of self-esteem, were selected by the teachers. Pupils involved in formal counseling or guidance sessions were not included. The pupils were asked to fill out a self-esteem inventory, and the 18 pupils with the lowest scores were chosen as the subjects. Homeroom teachers were asked to complete a behaviour rating form for each child involved in the investigation. At the end of the investigation the two forms were readministered.

Core Conditions

The librarian was rated on the core conditions of empathy, respect and genuineness.

Empathy refers to the helper's ability to accurately understand another person's feelings, experiences and meanings, and to accurately communicate this understanding to that person.

Respect is the communication to the person helped of a very deep concern for his value as an individual and of a commitment to the realization of his human potential.

Genuineness refers to the spontaneous communication between counsellor or librarian and the student of personally relevant and immediate feelings and experiences indicating genuine concern and involvement.

Procedures

The 18 children having the lowest self-esteem scores were randomly assigned to three groups of six pupils, designated as groups A, B and C.

Group A

The six children in Group A were each seen in a preliminary interview to determine their reading interest. The questions were designed to release the general details about their family, favourite activities and one current "worry." As a group, they were then introduced to the resource collection.

Selection of Resource Collection

A resource collection of 75 books was chosen from the library of the school participating in the study. All books used in the program were read by the librarian, and the books were selected on the basis of reading interest of the participating children, as indicated in the preliminary interview. As the children's interest in problems became more apparent through subsequent interviews, books were added to the collection. In addition to the reading interest of the children, and general book selection principles widely used by children's librarians, other factors considered in choosing specific books included a well-constructed plot, vigorous and strong characterization, an authentic setting, and an interesting theme, together with an appealing style and an understandable vocabulary level. Reading scores of the pupils in the study were considered helpful in assessing the suitability of the books. Special consideration was given to books with an attractive format and good illustrations. The characters in each book exhibited high self-esteem or improved their self-esteem by overcoming personal problems.

The children were asked to assist the librarian in finding out what books appealed to them, and each freely selected their first book. Other books, which the librarian felt might particularly interest each child in the group, were put on display. These children were interviewed individually on a weekly schedule for 12 weeks. The sessions, which averaged 25 minutes in length, were recorded. The discussions included retelling what occurred in the story, reviewing the apparent feelings and behaviour of a specific character, identifying (or making an effort to identify) a similar incident drawn from the experience of the pupil or from other reading he had done, exploring the potential consequence of the behavior of the book characters, and drawing conclusions or making generalizations based on these factors. Besides providing an opportunity for the student to talk about his books and compare personalized experiences, the interviews also allowed the investigator to help the child select new books which were thought to relate to his needs. Each child was allowed ample time to discuss his reaction to the books and any other matters of interest to him. It was the child's prerogative to end the interview.

Groups B and C

The six children in Group B had contact with the librarian only while the inventory forms were filled in and at one combined group meeting. At this meeting, the children were shown the same reading resource collection as Group A, and were encouraged to read as many books as they liked. The children in Group C had no contact with the investigator, except for making out the self-esteem inventory.

Results

Although no statistically significant results were achieved, the data indicated that the change that did occur in Group A (or the group receiving bibliotherapy) was in a positive direction. But, when rating the librarian for empathy, warmth and genuineness, it was found that the ratings were all below the suggested levels for being helpful.

Discussion

It was assumed that a re-evaluation of self-esteem involving bibliotherapeutic techniques, would result in the adoption of a new and enhanced self-image. However, if other factors in a child's life were contributing to the maintenance of his original self-image, the effects of the treatment may have been cancelled out, resulting in no change.

Since the level of empathy, respect and genuineness of the librarian were well below those necessary for the personal growth of the students, no changes in self-esteem should have been expected. These findings lend support to previous studies showing that therapy involving low levels of empathy, respect and genuineness produce little, if any, improvement (Carkhuff, 1968; 1969b; 1969c; 1971; Dickenson and Truax, 1966; Holder, Carkhuff and Berenson, 1967; Mickelson, 1971; Truax and Carkhuff, 1967; Truax and Mitchell, 1971).

An individual examination of the data of the experimental group indicated that two children had made substantial improvement on both instruments in comparing the prepost tests. The interesting aspect of this finding was that, in both cases, the librarian was functioning at levels of empathy, warmth and genuineness required to be helpful. A significant implication of the present investigation is that perhaps more attention should be given to the type of training we are providing students who are entering the field of library science, teaching and counseling. If these people are to influence self-esteem, or any other personal difficulty, a high level of facilitative functioning is essential to understanding the specific need of a child requesting a library book or a student seeking counseling.

While many research efforts have emphasized *the method* as the contributor of change, the attitude of the counsellor has been greatly underplayed. How important, and of what significance are these variables in bibliotherapy? Will the concern displayed by the bibliotherapist relate to the level of understanding and effect the actual selection of a book? Is this not the crucial element which could greatly influence the initial motivation and pursuit of the reading material by the student?

While this study did not find statistical significance, the trend toward increased self-esteem exhibited by those students in Group A would seem to indicate that bibliotherapy warrants further investigation. Higher process ratings of the librarian in the later sessions would suggest that more time may perhaps be required to establish better rapport with children. Further, it would seem advisable for a librarian to have education in counseling techniques and bibliotherapy before using this technique as part of a library program.

Suggestions for Rehabilitation and Bibliotherapy in South African Prisons

by Eugéne Moerdijk

The South African Department of Prisons is concerned with the process of rehabilitation. This is the process from which the prisoner should emerge as a free citizen with a higher educational level, an acceptance of the social norms and a more stable emotional outlook than he had when he first entered the prison.

A programme is therefore formulated that will embrace all the basic needs and interest of the prisoner. This is an enormous undertaking in South Africa, as there are over 88,000 White and non-White prisoners p.a. in 217 institutions. Added to this is the fact that the average White prisoner reads far more than the normal user of the public library, probably five times as many books. The problem of providing reference material is aggravated in South Africa by the fact that over 2,000 illiterates are in dire need of study and writing materials. The Department of Prisons offers a 9-month educational course for these illiterates.

The prison library service is inadequate in South Africa although the library is an obvious answer to the problem of providing the literature that may stir ambition, provide knowledge and prepare the inmate for his post-institutional life. Through this store of knowledge the inmate is encouraged to take a spontaneous part in his own rehabilitation.

In short, the library is an agency within the correctional institution that provides a wholesome neutral middleground where the need for education, recreation and personal development of the inmates can be served.

Theory:

Speculation about the characters of our fellow men and women is an important activity, since how else can one try to understand their

Reprinted with permission from *Libri Natales* 11-15 (July 1974).

behaviour and the reasons for this behaviour? This activity is of primary importance to those whose task it is to rehabilitate offenders against the law.

Dr. Adolphe Ferriere, a modern psychologist, distinguishes 12 main psychological types; it seems that for the most part this typology has bearing upon the criminal's character, and shows how his personality itself can be the reason for crime. Using 7 of Dr. Ferriere's headings, I have attempted an outline of a prisoner-typology:

Impulsive type. Adults who are incapable or only slightly capable of adaptation will remain at this level; consequently frustration may lead to crime.

Primitive type. It should be realized that not all criminals are aggressors—"hard-boiled eggs": a certain percentage of the criminal population belongs to the primitive type, the people who are naturally docile and easily led, at times, to do anything suggested to them.

Heroic, imaginative type. The desire to become a leader and to be respected may be so exaggerated as to encourage such a person to become an unlawful political leader, for instance, if no other medium of leadership is available to him.

Traditional type. Here there is the danger of rousing to rebellion people who, having been too long repressed, suddenly break free and do so in an aggressive manner.

Individualistic type. This type may overemphasize the importance of success in his life, and to achieve it with more speed he may resort to crime, the short cut to success that so seldom triumphs.

Emotional type. A disturbed emotional balance will inevitably lead to social disharmony and crime.

Uneasy type. An introvert who always prefers his own ideas to the standard ones of his society, may *actively* reject social norms; this may mean negation of the law.

It is impossible to regard the causes of crime in any single-tracked manner but one might say that serious and habitual criminality may be due to undeveloped intelligence, a lack or moral sense or an absence of emotional stability. These factors lead to individuals being caught by the law for infractions against the community codes which they either do not understand or do not accept.

Except in the case of mentally abnormal criminals, (only a small percentage of the total criminal population), it is safe to say that bibliotherapy is an efficient means by which the criminal may be cured of his social maladjustment. A great deal will, of course, depend on his own effort. It becomes necessary, therefore, to study not only the psychological types, but also the types of books which may be used as tools in the rehabilitation program.

A SUGGESTED POLICY FOR THE SELECTION OF BOOKS:

Of course prison inmates should be encouraged to either begin or continue the development of their interest in the field of non-fiction; the most aimless-seeming person has *some* faint light of interest, which, given some attention, could be kindled into something meaningful. There is a very wide variety of non-fictional subjects, some of which are here listed as possible constituents of a book selection policy:

Arts, Biography, Business, Drama, Economics, Education, Geography, Government, Health Education, History, Hobbies and Games, Home Economics, Languages, Literature, Mathematics, Medical Sciences, Mechanics, Music, Nature Study, Oceanography, Philosophy, Psychology, Religion, Science, Technology, General Reference Material, e.g. dictionaries, directories, maps, encyclopedias, etc. and at least one current daily newspaper (perhaps several copies) to be kept in the reading room.

Fiction can play an even more important part in bibliotherapy. It is particularly with this type of reading material that careful choice must be made for the prison library and careful guidance given to each prisoner so that he will read suitable books; this, of course, must be done very tactfully.

A selection of fictional material and a grouping of various types of books with the 7 main "criminal types" may be done as follows:

Plot stories: detective, adventure, romance; novels characterized by action and suspense—primitive, traditional, emotional and uneasy types.

Love stories: novels with emphasis on emotional interest, but not psychological or analytical in treatment—individualistic and uneasy types.

Humorous and satirical stories: all 7 types.

Supernatural stories: all 7 types if they so desire.

Problem novels: philosophical, political, economic and social issues—emotional, uneasy and primitive types.

Character and Psychological studies: primitive, traditional and emotional types.

Stories involving Special Groups or Backgrounds: occupational groups, special races, animals personified, rural life, historical novels—all 7 types.

Whatever the book selection policy may be, every endeavour must be made through it to reach and develop the needs and interest of prison inmates. It should therefore be part of the librarian's task to find a little time to scan the prisoners' personal histories kept on file.

Example of the effect of books:

Extract from personal file: ". . . unable to think clearly, confused unsure of himself and disinclined to make descisions; relies on guidelines provided by others . . . "

Librarian's conclusion (based on extract and personal contact with inmate): "inmate is a primitive type. Librarian's decision regarding suitable books, i.e. a collection from which the inmate is to make his *own* choice:

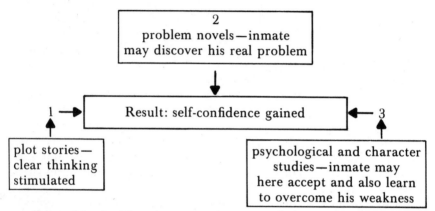

From this the librarian may pinpoint a *basic* need in the reader, but no librarian can hope to discover the deepest need; the reader himself must discover this, and through what better medium than books?

There is still much to be thought about regarding prison library services; the aim of this discussion is, therefore, not to offer any final solutions to the problems, but to open up some new ideas and to suggest ways of supplementing the existing rehabilitation programme.

BIBLIOGRAPHY

1. Adolphe Ferriere, *Psychological Types and the Stages of Man's Development,* tr. by Wyatt (Ransom, 1958).
2. Jeanette Haward Foster, "An Approach to Fiction through the Characteristics of Its Readers." *Library Quarterly,* v.6. (April 1970).
3. *Handbook of South African Libraries* (1970).
4. K.C. Harrison, *Libraries in Scandinavia* (2nd rev. ed., 1969).
5. International City Managers' Association. *Local Public Library Administration.* Municipal Management Series (Chicago, 1964).
6. Jean Spealman Kujoth, ed., *Libraries, Readers and Book Selection* (1969).
7. Thomas Landau, *Encyclopedia of Librarianship* (3rd ed. London, 1968).

8. "Connecticut Prison Inmates Producing Union Catalog" *Library Journal* (March 1969).

9. "Two Library Projects Launched in New York Prisons" *Library Journal* (April 15, 1972).

10. Kathleen R. Molz, "Burning Yourself Out: The Prisoner's Right to Read" *Newsletter on Intellectual Freedom* (September 1972).

11. Sue Opipare, (a.o.), "Breaking into Jail" *Library Journal* (September 1971).

12. *Paperbound Books in Print* (November 1971).

13. P.A.G. Reitz, *Die plek wat die openbare biblioteek inneem in die behandelingsprogram van gevangenig.* South African Libraries Conference issue (December 1970), Vol. 38.3.

14. (The) Rhodesian Librarian. *Library Services in Rhodesia*, Vol. 2., no. 3. Supplement (July 1970).

15. Nicholas Rubakin, *Bibliopsychology*, tr. by M. Machee and J. Peacoch (1968).

16. Jeffrey Schrink, *A State Correction Department in Search of a Library Policy* (Indiana Dept. of Correction). *Library Occurrent*, vol. 23. (1970).

17. S. David Thurman, comp., "Access to Legal Reference Materials" *Law Library Journal*, vol. 62. (1969).

18. Kimball Young, *Personality and Problems of Adjustment* (1947).

19. Ernestus Von Busse, *Libraries in the Federal Republic of Germany — Prison Libraries.*

Nicholas Rubakin and Bibliopsychology

by Sylva Simsova

Otlet in his *Book about the Book*[1] includes bibliopsychology as an important section of bibliology.

Yet the science of bibliopsychology is and always has been unknown in the English speaking world. With the exception of one article[2] in a psychological journal nothing has been written about it in English; the works of its founder, Nicholas Rubakin, have not been translated and the existence of the Institute of Bibliopsychology in Switzerland has never been noted by the library press. When Rubakin died in 1946 only two brief obituaries appeared, one in the Library Journal[3] and the other in the Bulletin of the International Bureau of Education.[4]

Rubakin was better known during his lifetime on the Continent of Europe, though only in a few countries, particularly the Netherlands and Czechoslovakia. His native Russia was in two minds about him and after his death found it convenient to let him fall into oblivion. Switzerland, the country of his adoption, had a similar attitude to him, though for different reasons.

At the present time only Poland shows an interest in him because there the study of reading is given great prominence among librarians. I owe my discovery of Rubakin to two articles in the Polish Bibliotekarz.[5]

This article is intended as a bibliographical guide to the literature about bibliopsychology and its founder. I shall attempt a brief evaluation, partly historical, showing why Rubakin's ideas developed the way they did, and partly practical, assessing the relevance of bibliopsychology to librarians today. In the limited space I cannot attempt a detailed description of the contents of bibliopsychology and readers are advised to consult the sources listed in the footnotes if they wish to study the subject further.

NICHOLAS RUBAKIN

Rubakin's personality is closely interwoven with the science of bibliopsychology which he formulated more or less singlehanded. Romain

Reprinted with permission from *Libri* 16(2):118-129 (1966). Copyright © 1966 by Danmarks Biblioteksskole.

Rolland in his Journal for the year 1916 describes Rubakin as follows:

> A man of sixty, with a grey beard and thick hair, healthy, smiling and vibrating with thought . . . An original scientist, a great worker, always absorbed in his studies of bibliopsychology. He is dreadfully literate; to my question if his works can get into Russia he answered: "Forty seven of my books are forbidden, but one hundred and three are in circulation and that is enough . . ." He has seven million readers, more than Gorki and the popular novelists . . .[6]

Rubakin's industry was one of his outstanding features. Combined with his idealism, it produced a total commitment to work, bordering on fanaticism. In this respect he is a typical Russian "intelligent":

> . . . Russian "intelligents" were not only individuals sensitive to some ultimate values and ideas, they were also totally committed to and completely identified with them. These ideas absorbed the "intelligents" to such an extent that, like a lover with his beloved, they did not hesitate to play out their whole lives around them. And having made some single set of ideas their only point of reference, they turned into men of conviction and principles, bent upon ideologizing every sphere of their relations to people, including even the ties of friendship.[7]

Although the above passage refers to the "intelligents" of an earlier generation it could well be applied to Rubakin, for it was in the atmosphere of the revolutionary intelligentsia that he was brought up and his temperament always carried signs of that influence.

His personal life was guided by his work. He did not hesitate to sacrifice his own and his family's comfort in the interests of his cause. He was permanently short of money and whatever money he had he put into his books.

He was basically a lonely man in spite of the fact that he corresponded with several thousands of readers. Friendly to all he had but a few real friends, the main ones being Paul Otlet and Adolphe Ferriere who were both idealists, men of original thought and reformatory zeal like him and who, like him, are on the way to being forgotten.

This is only one of the main contradictions in Rubakin's Pnin-like character. Romain Rolland in an attitude of tender amusement describes his weaknesses:

> . . . He explained to me his plan, with a great deal of confusion, as always and in a terribly abstract fashion. (I cannot understand how such a man, so completely lacking a gift of translating his ideas into a realistic narrative, could have attracted such a large reading public.) I believe that the Russians have a more abstract mind than us.[8]

Rubakin mastered the art of living with contradictions as can be well illustrated by a brief summary of his political adventures.[9]

His mother, his wife, his son were all revolutionaries. He himself was expelled from Russia after persecution by Czarist regime. Yet the Revolution disappointed him. Rolland reports that in 1918 Rubakin was on the verge of suicide. To ease his conscience he planned to write moralizing tracts for a Christian Science campaign, although all his previous life, starting with his first publication at the age of 15, he campaigned against religion. The Swiss authorities did not trust him, having mistaken him for a Bolshevik, and his son was dismissed from his post in France for the same reason. After a visit to a library conference in Czechoslovakia in 1919 he had difficulties in getting a reentry permit to Switzerland. He did not return to Russia after the Revolution and he was condemned for his idealism and eclecticism. In spite of that he was offered a Soviet pension in 1934 which alienated him from some of his emigre friends and strengthened the suspicions of the Swiss authorities. He bequeathed his library of 230,000 volumes and his manuscripts to the Lenin Library. For ten years the material remained unused and nothing was written about him. The tenth anniversary of his death was commemorated by his son in an article in which he pleads that his father's work be not forgotten because, in spite of the idealism and eclecticism for which he has justly been condemned, much valuable material was to be found in it.

RUBAKIN'S WORK

Rubakin's life was dedicated to books which he saw as a powerful instrument of enlightenment. In this he was influenced by his mother who took part in the revolutionary movement of the 1860's concerned mainly with the spread of education and who employed him in her library since he was 13.

During his long life (he died in 1946, aged 84) he worked with books in many different capacities: as an author, publisher, librarian, book collector and reader.

He wrote 280 books of popular science and it is for these that he is best known in Russia—as well as 49 books for advanced readers. His archive contains two unpublished novels.

He compiled two large recommending bibliographies on the lines of Sonnenschein's "Best Books." The first one, "Among Books"[10] brought him both the friendship of Lenin, who contributed the section on Bolshevism, and Lenin's condemnation because of Rubakin's open mind on other subjects—yet another example of the contradictions mentioned earlier. Rubakin's second bibliography "The Practice of Self-Education"[11] contained a practical application of bibliopsychological principles: every book was classified not only by its subject, but also by its psychological type and intellectual level.

Rubakin had a strong desire to help the advancement of education among those who needed it most. On completing his university degree he was denied the right to teach in any educational institution because of his revolutionary activities. As a result of this he turned his energies to education through books. Apart from the two large bibliographies, he compiled 15,000 individual programmes of reading and kept up a vast correspondence with readers who let themselves be guided by him through his "University of the Home." He worked out a system of studies by which any reader, using books suited to his temperament, could attain encyclopedic knowledge in five years.

His correspondence with readers helped him to an insight into the process of reading which he made use of not only in his theoretical studies, but also in the process of improving his own style of writing.

In his later years, having assembled a large amount of material, he concentrated on formulating the principles of bibliopsychology.

THE INSTITUTE OF BIBLIOPSYCHOLOGY

His first outline in the form of a lecture to a joint meeting of Institut J. - J. Rousseau and Institut International de Bibliographie in 1916, was received enthusiastically and both institutes sponsored the founding of the Institute of Bibliopsychology.[12]

This institute was probably very small, based on Rubakin's library in his own house in Lausanne. Even during the war he carried out a great deal of work and experimentation and published the results in his two-volume *Introduction à la psychologie bibliologique* Paris 1922.[13] This is a standard work on bibliopsychology and should be studied by those who want to delve deeper into the subject. The important chapters are Chapter 1 as a general introduction and Chapter 7 which describes the "special method" of bibliopsychology and outlines the whole range of bibliopsychological studies. Unfortunately the work has not been translated into English. A short summary can be found in Turin's article quoted above.[2]

The Institute continued to function until Rubakin's death in 1946. It is not quite certain what happened to it afterwards. It is known that Rubakin's papers were transferred to Russia in 1948. Yet in 1949 Marie Bethmann claimed that the work of the Institute was being carried on by Prof. Ferriere and herself. I would be grateful for any information about the Institute's activity after 1946.[14]

LAWS OF BIBLIOPSYCHOLOGY

A book is not a transmitter of contents, rather it is a book on which readers can hang their projections. The reader objectifies his psychic phenomena by attributing them to the book. Every reader knows only his own projection and not the book itself.

The author does not communicate through his book. The content which he expressed in it is perceived in a distorted way by the reader. Reality is replaced by language and readers have to guess the reality that is being referred to.

There are two forces at work during reading: the author's mind which created the book and the reader's mind which recreates the book in pursuit of its own ends.

It is a well-known fact that two readers will retain two different impressions of the same book, or that the same reader turning to his

favourite book after a number of years finds it different and even dis-
appointing. It is possible to find thoughts in a book which the author
never put there, just as it is common not to see those thoughts which
he did. For apparently irrational reasons a book will appeal to a reader
one day although a month previously he could not bear it.

All these experiences support the first law of bibliopsychology
(*Law of Humboldt-Potebnia*): "The book and its elements, including
every one of its words, are instruments of stimulation which produce
within the reader's psyche experiences which are particular to that
psyche; and it is not an instrument for relaying experiences. All
linguistic signs only stimulate mental states, they do not transmit
ideas. The meaning of a word, the contents of a book are subjective
psychological phenomena."

Rubakin adds to this that the reader is not static and therefore his
reading of the same text undergoes a change as he himself changes.

The theoretical background of bibliopsychology has been adversely criticised in Russia because of its idealistic basis. Rubakin's conception is founded on Semon's theory of the mnema.[14] This brings us to
the second law of bibliopsychology (*Law of Semon*): "All verbal
phenomena have a biological basis in engrams, memories of past
impressions which are stored in the mnema."

There are two kinds of engrams: primary and secondary. The
former are marks left by the individual's meeting with reality, the latter are fictitious constructions that often have nothing in common with
it. Through reading, secondary engrams are called up, grouped in new
combinations and created anew. The difference between primary and
secondary engrams corresponds to the difference between reality and
projection of reality.

Bibliopsychology does not see the reader's mnema in isolation divorced from its social setting (*Law of Taine*): "The total of a man's
engrams, i.e., his mnema, is conditioned by the environment, race and
historical moment."

One branch of bibliopsychology is given the name of bib-
liosociology. Among the problems which interested Rubakin was how
society produces its authors and how books spread in it (diaspora bib-
liologica).

The fourth law of bibliopsychology is also connected with the
social setting (*Law of Tarde*): "The greater the inter-mental exchange
among the ancestors of two given individuals,—an exchange which
created a common ground of thoughts, feelings, patterns of
behaviour,—the easier it will be for them, when they meet, to communicate to each other the state of their soul."

The fifth law is an extension of the fourth (*Law of Hennequin*): "A
book has the strongest influence on the reader whose psyche is organized similarly to that of the author, i.e., whose psychological type is
similar to the author's." This law is very important for library work.

METHOD OF BIBLIOPSYCHOLOGICAL STUDY

The book and the author are seen as natural phenomena which can be subjected to exact study. As the reality described in the book is, by its nature, elusive even to the investigator, because he also perceives it in the light of his own projections, bibliopsychology invented a system of measurement aiming at objectivity.

The process of reading a certain book by a certain reader is observed and recorded under controlled conditions. From this conclusions may be drawn about the reader on the one hand (book acting as reagent on the reader) and the book on the other (reader acting as reagent on the book). The system of measurement is called "special method" of bibliopsychology. (Described below).

Side by side with his "special method" Rubakin used questionnaires. He compiled a number of them, and some of them can be found as supplements in his *Introduction à la psychologie bibliogique.*[13] His early surveys in Russia were based on questionnaires and he used the same method in his last international enquiry started together with M. Bethmann in 1931.

Both methods rely a great deal on introspection either in the form of self-observation or experiments carried out by the subject on himself. The results of introspective processes are carefully collected with the greatest objectivity on the part of the investigator. Rubakin claims this synthesis of a subjective and objective method to be one of the outstanding features of bibliopsychology, although to us it may appear as one of the weakest.

In his passion for bridging the gap between opposites he also ascribes to it a synthesis of qualitative and quantitative measurement, the former being the classification of psychological phenomena recorded during reading, the latter the statistical summary of classifications recorded.

Bibliopsychological study is done at several levels:

a. *Verbal* bibliopsychology is the study of phenomena produced through the influence of individual words.

b. *Interverbal* bibliopsychology is the study of relationships between words in a text. To understand the difference between verbal and interverbal bibliopsychology the reader is asked to classify the words of the text back to front, and some time afterwards in the usual way, i.e. from beginning to end.

It is to this part of bibliopsychology that the 'special method' belongs. During reading, the meaning of each word of a sentence shifts constantly in connection with interverbal changes.

Some words create a strong stimulus producing a very high potential in the mnema. The smaller the capacity of the mnema the higher the potential, just as a large quantity of water poured into a narrow container lifts the level of the water very high. This explains, e.g., why

individuals with a poor mnema can be more easily influenced by propaganda than individuals whose mnema is rich.

Elsewhere Rubakin says about propaganda, which has been one of
his favourite topics of enquiry: "It would seem that it is sufficient to set
in front of the reader some books to act on his mnema in a desired way.
Many people think that propaganda has a strong influence, but they
are wrong as the book itself has no power. The strength of the book is
to be sought in the mnema. The mnema is not created by one or more
books but by life itself (i.e. primary engrams)."

c. *Supraverbal* bibliopsychology is the bibliopsychological synthesis of
words in a given context. It studies the results of stimulation by a
whole phrase considered as a meaningful unit.

This part of bibliopsychology is the easiest one to accept as it is
nearest to the conventional study of books and reading, involving
phenomena such as comprehension, appreciation, aesthetics .

Yet there is a difference in the bibliopsychological approach. Literary theory and history see the book as a cultural phenomenon. But to
bibliopsychology books are primarily natural phenomena although at
the same time their cultural and social value is not denied. "Bibliopsychology is to literature what acoustics is to music," says Rubakin.

The "special method" is frequently criticised for not studying
phenomena on the supraverbal level. It is, however, not possible to go
on to the study of supraverbal phenomena without first studying the
verbal and interverbal phenomena.

"SPECIAL METHOD" OF BIBLIOPSYCHOLOGY

The "special method" studies the process of reading which has
been artificially slowed down so that it is possible to observe very small
sections of the process, i.e. reactions to single words, with some interverbal influences.

To see how the method works I have, on a small scale, repeated
one of Rubakin's experiments. I cannot claim my conclusions to be
totally valid as my sample of readers (eight) was too small, the passages
selected too short (two passages of 73 words each), and the classification of psychological phenomena too simplified (ideas, images, sensations, emotion, volition, instincts, action). However, this is how it was
done:

The selected passages were written down in individual words, with
one word to a line, and this slowed down the reading process so that
the readers could immediately record their reactions to the individual
words of the text rather than to the text as a whole. They were free to
classify each reaction under one or several categories or to leave a
blank.

In comparing the reaction of each reader to the two passages, a
pattern emerges which can best be expressed by the amount of devia-

tion shown by the average for each passage against the overall average reaction for the two passages combined:

	Ideas	Images	Sensations	Emotion	Volition	Instincts	Action
Average reaction to Jevons & Powys com.	42	14	12	6	11	2	2	12
Average reaction to Logic by Jevons	41	21	9	3	8	3	3	13
Deviation	−1	+7	−3	−3	−3	+1	+1	+1
Average reaction to a novel by J. C. Powys	43	7	16	9	13	1	1	11
Deviation	+1	−7	+4	+3	+2	−1	−1	−1

The main deviation in Jevons (+7) appears under the heading "abstract ideas," while in Powys the three main deviations (+4, +3, +2) appear under "images," "sensations," "emotions." It could be said that the same conclusions could be reached by common sense, as the first is a textbook of logic, the second a work of fiction. Common sense certainly confirms the finding on this point, but some finer points, not immediately apparent, are revealed in the statistical summary—among them, for instance, the fact that two readers (one of them male) recorded an emotional reaction to Jevons which is above average not only for Jevons, but also for both works combined. Another interesting feature is that the reactions to Powys tend to be of a more complex nature and therefore each had to be recorded under several categories. Instances of an "echo" can be observed, where words without an emotional content (e.g. conjunctions) call forward an emotional reaction because of the context in which they appear.

In my simplified version of the experiment I have concentrated mainly on the average reaction. Rubakin's interest was always in the individual reader for whom the average reaction provided only a background. This can best be illustrated by the following analysis taken from his *Introduction à la psychologie bibliologique.*

A simultaneous study of the book and the reader

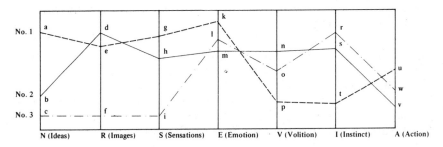

1. The curve of given reader reading a given book.
2. The curve of an average book read by the average reader.
3. Curve of a given book (same as No. 1) read by the average reader.

From this graphic representation the following conclusions can be drawn:

Characteristics of the Reader

He is of an abstract type (aN > bN > cN). Therefore his ability to think is below average (dR > eR). On the other hand the book has evoked in him more concrete images than in the average reader (eR > fR). This can be explained by the fact that this reader easily remembers sensations (gS > hS). This cannot be attributed to the qualities expressed in the book (iS < hS). The reader is emotional (kE > mE) because the book has impressed him more than the average reader (kE > lE). The book failed to move his sense of volition (pV < oV < nV). The instincts of this reader are not well developed (tI < sI < rI). This is a characteristic of an abstract type (aN > bN > cN) although the book is not in itself abstract (cN < bN). The book calls out more action in this reader than in the average reader (uA > wA > vA), but this depends on his emotions not on his volition. (kE > uA).

Characteristics of the Book

The book is less abstract than the average book (cN < bN), but it cannot be called a concrete book, i.e. a book rich in images (fR < dR). It calls out very weak memories of sensations (iS < hS). Compared with the average book it calls out more emotions (eE > mE) and instincts (rI > sI), therefore it acts strongly (wA > vA) through emotions not volition (lE < oV). The volitional phenomena called up by it are fewer than those called up by the average book (oV < nV). A strong effect on instinct is typical for this book (rI > sI).

It would be interesting to attempt this type of investigation on a larger scale and to go into all the possible ramifications of the "special method" described by Rubakin in Chapters 7 and 8 of his *Introduction à la psychologie bibliogique*. This would enable us to collect material for the study of various phenomena connected with the process of reading. A collection of this kind could hardly hope to equal Rubakin's own which occupied him throughout his long life, but it would have the advantage of being related to the readers and books which we know (Rubakin tested and described mainly Russian literature and Russian readers) and of being accessible (Rubakin's material is in the Lenin Library).

Having acquired a taste for this type of experiment I am at present working on an analysis of the reactions of 80 readers to 20 texts by nine authors. I hope to publish the results in due course.

PRACTICAL APPLICATION OF BIBLIOPSYCHOLOGY

On the basis of bibliopsychological study, books and readers can be classified into types. These are not psychological types, but reading types. Types of readers should not be identified with types of people. Readers are people, but people are not necessarily readers. The type to which a reader belongs can best be defined by his reaction to a text in the process of reading.

This has practical application in library work where the right type of book should ideally reach the corresponding type of reader. Rubakin advocated the creation of a catalogue which would, against each entry, show a psychological classification in addition to classification by subject. While the idea of the "right book to the right reader" is more than acceptable to us today, a catalogue on the lines of Rubakin's suggestion is not a very practical proposition in these days of constantly changing stocks. He demonstrated this type of catalogue in his "Practice of Self-instruction"; this was an annotated static collection of the best books of all ages and for this his method was suitable.

Another field where the knowledge gained through bibliopsychological study can well be applied is book production. Rubakin explains how he studied the "compositions" (letters) of his readers to make his own style more comprehensible. An author who wants to have a strong effect on his readers should choose his words according to the type of reader for whom he is writing. That way he will arouse in their minds the psychic states exactly as he wishes.

In his own writing Rubakin achieved this aim with great success. While reading his "Introduction" I was impressed by the clarity of his exposition, in spite of the fact that I was handicapped by an imperfect knowledge of the language.

BIBLIOPSYCHOLOGY TODAY

For us, the main value of bibliopsychology lies in the insight it gives into the minds of readers during the process of reading and into the structure and style of writing in books. If these two points were applied in practice they would lead to improved personal service in libraries and to the production of books which are aimed better at each particular group of readers.

In conclusion I would like to emphasize that two things are needed before we can make full use of the wealth of material contained in Rubakin's work: One is the translation of his works on bibliopsychology into English and the other their discussion and evaluation by librarians and psychologists.

Possibly we may find that bibliopsychology has little to offer to us today. Yet in the absence of other works in this much neglected field we cannot afford to ignore what has been done so far.

ADDENDUM

In recent years a revival of interest in Nicholas Rubakin has taken place in the USSR since Nikita Khrushchev's speech at the Third Congress of Soviet Writers when he mentioned his admiration for Rubakin. Several articles have appeared in various journals and the most important of these are two which describe the contents of Rubakin's archive: IVANOVA, L. M.: Archiv N. A. Rubakina . . . in Sovyetskaya Bibliografia, 1962, No. 3, pp. 98-109. IVANOVA, L. M. and others: Archiv N. A. Rubakina . . . in Zapiski otdela rukoposey Gosudarstvennoi Biblioteki SSSR imena V. I. Lenina, vol. 26, 1963, pp. 63-206.

Some previously unpublished correspondence has been published in "Zapiski . . ." for 1962 and 1963, including letters to Rubakin from Maxim Gorki and Romain Rolland. Archive material has also been reprinted in an article by Mashkova, M. V.: G. V. Plecharov i "Sredi knig" N. A. Rubakina . . . in Sovyetskaya Bibliografia, 1963, No. 6, pp. 83-101.

REFERENCES

1. Paul Otlet, *Traite de documentation: le livre sur le livre* (Bruxelles, 1935), pp. 32-35.

2. Mrs. Lydia Turin, "Dr. N. Roubakin on Biblio-psychology," in *Psyche* (formerly Psychic Research Quarterly) (April 1929), pp. 74-93.

3. *Library Journal* (Jan. 1st, 1947), p. 94.

4. *Bulletin of the International Bureau of Education,* Vol. 20, No. 81, p. 168.

5. K. Kosteniczovna, "Nikolaj Rubakin," in *Bibliotekarz*, 1947, No. 9-10, pp. 130-131; J. Ankudowicz, "N. A. Rubakin." in *Bibliotekarz* 1960, No. 11-12, pp. 345-351.

6. Romain Rolland, *Journal des annes de la guerre* (Paris 1952), p. 699.

7. V. C. Nahirny, "The Russian Intelligentsia," in *Comparative Studies in Society and History,* Vol. 4., No. 4. (July 1962), pp. 403-435.

8. Rolland, *Journal,* p. 1413.

9. A. N. Rubakin, "Nicolai Alexandrovich Rubakin," in *Sovetskaia Bibliografia* (1957), pp. 42-50.

10. *Sredi knig* (Moskva 1911), 2 vols.

11. Praktika samoobrazovania (1914).

12. Summary of the lecture together with a short biography of Rubakin in Adolphe Ferriere, "Le psychologie bibliologique d'apres les documents et les travaux de Nicolas Roubakine," in *Archives de Psychologie* (1917), pp. 7-132.

13. Nicolas Roubakine, *Introduction à la psychologie bibliologique*, 2 vols. (Paris, 1922). A shorter summary which excludes the "special method" of bibliopsychology is Nicolas Roubakine and Marie Bethmann, "La psychologie de la bibliotheque populaire" in *Institut International de coopération Intellectuelle:* Mission sociale et intellectuelle des bibliothèques populaires (Paris, 1937), pp. 127-175.

14. R. Semon, *Die Mneme* (Leipzig, 1904).

15. Marie Bethmann, "L'Institut Robakine de Psychologie Bibliologique à Lausanne," in *Rev. Doc.* No. 1. (1949), pp. 17-18.

U.S.S.R., 1970:
The Reading Matter
of Patients

by A. M. Miller

For a long time the important role which the printed word plays in the healing of human suffering has been known. Since the book accompanies modern man from his birth until his last day on earth, it is naturally also of supreme importance in sickness. We are concerned here with the use of those powerful psychological influences which books and, in the first instance, works of creative literature, can work on the minds of sick people.

The reading of patients must be influenced to help the patient and his mental condition. Soviet library science considers the reading of various groups of readers as one of its main concerns. An important aspect of this problem lies in the selection of the patients' reading matter in such a way that the quickest possible rehabilitation is achieved.

Since the foundation of bibliotherapy 70 years ago, librarians and doctors have collected extensive and interesting data. One bibliography of bibliotherapy contains 400 titles.

Many Russian doctors and persons in pursuit of culture have, in the course of several centuries, maintained in their writings that books are as indispensable as drugs.

A great surging forward in the use of books in the battle for quicker recovery and for the maintenance of the best qualities of the human personality, followed the publishing of the excellent book *Idealism as a Psychological Factor* by the well-known Russian intern A. Jarotsky, Professor of the University of Jurjew (Tartu). "By the term 'idealism' we mean in this book" (writes Jarotsky) "not the philosophical technical term (i.e. the idealistic as opposed to the materialistic view of life) but the specific mental condition — the striving after an ideal (i.e. psychological idealism)."[1]

Reprinted with permission from *International Library Review* 4:373-377 (1972) and V.A.A.P., Moscow. Copyright © 1972 by Academic Press, London.

In his book Jarotsky was not only writing for his colleagues but also for patients so that they should find in themselves the high moral qualities for their battle with sickness. The work of Jarotsky contains many examples which indicate the importance of books in the creation and maintenance of the state of mind of the patient.

In the early months of the Great Patriotic War (1940-45) a group of members of the Kharkov Scientific W. C. Korolenko Library compiled a recommended bibliography *What to Read*[2] which was published in an edition of 1,000 copies for field hospital libraries. It contains a select list of reading matter for the wounded, quite independent of their general education, and systematized according to their interests. Librarians of military hospitals obtained assistance which helped them to work with the wounded.

After the war some articles of the older Soviet psychiatrist, Professor M. P. Kutanin, were published to direct the attention of the medical and librarianship world to the problems of the reading of the sick.

There are now 4,000 libraries functioning in hospitals and sanatoria of the U.S.S.R. These libraries collect medical technical literature for hospital staff as well as literature for patients. In the large hospitals (those with more than 300 beds) there is a professionally qualified librarian who must possess special training. In several Republics, e.g. in the Moldavian S.S.R., there is a librarian in every clinic quite independent of the number of beds.

Books intended for the reading of the sick are housed in special rooms, where possible they are stored separately from the stock of medical literature.

Libraries with qualified librarians in charge of good accommodation and large bookstocks include: the Moscow City Eye Hospital, the Moscow Botkin Hospital, Republic Clinic Hospital of the Moldavian SSR in Kishinev, the Central Psychoneurological Hospital for the Ministry of Railways in Kharkov, the sanatoria of the Ministry of Defence in Kislovodsk, "Fros" in Yalta, and the "Kisegatsch" for the Chelyabinsk Region.

What is the role of the library in the course of treatment for patients? Here doctors must have the deciding word and above all the psychotherapists. A firm bond between librarians and doctors is essential. In the Ukrainian Institute for Medical Education in 1962 there was established the Chair of Psychotherapy, Psychohygiene and Psychoprophylaxis which is held by Professor I. S. Velvovsky. The terms of reference of the Chair consists also of the working out of scientific methodology and the naturalization of bibliotherapy into the practice of sanatoria. Many plans were made to use the libraries in the sanatoria of the Ukraine for therapeutic purposes. The experience so gained was then to be published and distributed to other sanatoria.

The clinical basis of the Chair is the Sanatorium "Berjosovsky mineralnye vody." Here there has been created a consultative advice center for bibliotherapy. It consists of eight persons—four doctors and four librarians. To this advisory center there also belong scientists as well as practising members of both professions.

The center intends from 1970 onwards to publish methodological and instructive materials for hospital librarians. In order to instruct the librarians of the sanatoria of the Ukrainian S.S.R. on the basis of medical psychology and on the reading of the sick in sanatoria, a permanent seminar will be held in the autumn of each year. Each group of librarians, consisting of 10-12 persons, will receive instruction for a whole week.

Since 1968 lectures on bibliotherapy have been held by the author of this paper at the Chair for Psychotherapy of the Ukrainian Institute for Medical Education. Besides libraries with bookstocks of 6,000 volumes for patients in the sanatoria, there is a special library for bibliotherapy with its own book stock and two senior professional librarians who specialize in medical psychology and psychotherapy (the author and a research assistant).

The task of the librarian-bibliotherapist consists of studying the effect of literature on the emotional condition of the patient. He must predict, where possible, the reaction of the patient to what he has read.

Professor I. S. Velvovsky has prepared the following classification of mental conflicts for the purposes of treatment quite independent of the character of the situation influencing the person's mind:

1. Conflicts of honour.
2. Conflicts, which from inherited and acquired disturbance of the organism, result in defects and distortion.
3. Conflicts caused by the bitter loss of near relatives, the death of loved ones, and similar works.
4. Conflicts on the basis of tragedy in love.
5. Conflicts on the basis of hindrance in activity and the lack of success in creative plans.
6. Conflicts which arise from everyday situations.

This scheme is only partially valid, for the neurotic condition of patients is due to many causes. The largest group are patients whose neurosis is the result of chronic somatic infection.

To use bibliotherapy correctly to its fullest extent one must use fully psychological and technical methods. The schematic and methodic principles for bibliotherapists who work in contact with the psychotherapists may be summarized as follows. We consider it necessary to recommend books whose hero is to be found in similar circumstances to those of the patient. It is not only a case of choosing books whose hero conquers the condition of depression and despair but also of its deactualization (according to J. S. Velvovsky, V. N. Ivanov, and W. N. Mjasistchev).

Sick persons should not be given pessimistic books, or books with plots based on a series of happy accidents, since, after the reading of this sort of literature, the sick person will find his condition more tragic.

Books chosen for bibliotherapy should have an attractive layout, a comfortable format and a range of contents suitable for the patient.

Foreign bibliotherapists, particularly French and American, pay great attention to the decoration of the library, to the book trolley for transportation of books into the sickroom, as well as to the appearance of the librarian and his deportment.

The library staff should not force books onto patients. The patient must have the impression that he has chosen the book himself. After contact between the library assistant and the patient has taken place, which is based on trust and confidence in the librarian, a recommendation is possible. The main task is to lead the patient without any feeling of compulsion to those books which are necessary for him.

Many patients maintain that a good book will help them to forget pain. Apart from this the patient has, while reading, a mental diversion, fewer contacts or friction with other patients and the hospital staff, and fewer ungrounded complaints.

We set ourselves the goal to work out for the patient a proper relationship to his illness and to his future so that, despite his illness, he remains a human being in the true sense of the word.

Soviet authors have written many heroic books which evoke enthusiasm and lead on into the great life. Above all there are *How Steel was Tempered* by N. Ostrovsky, *Fortune* by P. Pavlenko and *In Spite of All the Dead* by V. Titov. Foreign novelists have had a healing influence also in the books *Prickles* by Ethel M. Voynich, *Stand Up and Walk* by Henri Bazin and *I Can Jump Puddles!* by Alan Marshall.

A twenty-year-old female patient confined to bed suffering from severe sclerosis wrote, after she had read the book of the coal-miner W. Titov who had an accident, lost both his hands and became an author: "This book has taught me belief in mankind and in life. And therefore I will no longer have evil thoughts about myself and about others; no loss of will power; no wish to commit suicide. I am now ashamed to think back to the time when I had such thoughts."

A list of suitable books has been compiled. We do not confine ourselves to this list but make use of the whole stock of the library and borrow also from mobile libraries from the municipal library.

In our sanatorium for liver, stomach and intestinal complaints, as for the neuroses which result from these complaints, there is a department of psychotherapy. The psychotherapists recommend all patients to use the hospital library. Some are advised to visit the special bibliotherapy collection.

Each patient stays in the sanatorium for 26 days. He is sent to us in the special bibliotherapy library with a short history of his complaint and the character of his infection and the degree of his neurosis. We study the patient as a reader, clarify possible causes of his neurosis, and compile a plan of reading for him.

To establish a basic guide to the treatment of bibliotherapy and for an objective view of the results of treatment in the sanatorium, including the therapeutic effects of the book, a psychological examination of the patient is carried out.

After processing the results we compile an individual plan of reading for the patient. The plan is handed to the patient on a special form. Each plan contains 6-12 books. We will also compile a plan for home reading.

One of our patients has written about the book of the Soviet prose-writer L. Borissov's *Parents, Education, Poets:* "This book gives the impetus for a completely new evaluation of books. It comes down to the fact that we have got ourselves so used to books and to reading that we, or so it seems to me, have begun to regard it as something quite usual and everyday like eating and work. After I had read Borissov's book, and had analysed my impression, I understood quite clearly that books, favourite books, are a source of joy, happiness, good feeling and courage in life. They are helpers in our moments of sadness, they are the joy of the heart in life."

We discuss with the patient every book read and ask to write briefly about the book if it has particularly influenced him. In doing this we explain to the patient that he does not need to analyse the book or give his critical evaluation of it. "We are interested in knowing what feelings you had when reading this book, what concerned you most, made you happy or sad, and what conclusions you draw for yourself from this book." The pages of readers' diaries have for us extraordinary value.

The experiences of our colleagues in the Soviet Union and abroad, as well as our own, permit us to say that the study of the influence of reading on patients is an important and noble task which should be carried out everywhere.

REFERENCES

1. Alexandr Jarotsky, *Der Idealismus als lebenerhaltendes Prinzip* (Wiesbaden, F. Begmann, 1908) (Jurjew, 1909).

2. *What to Read. Bibliographical material for hospital libraries* (Kharkov, 1941), 48 pp.

Suggestions for
Further Reading

Rauni Aalto, "The Book Selection Problem in a Mental Hospital" *Scandinavian Public Library Quarterly* (March 1970), pp. 168-175.

Marcus S. Crouch, "Work with Disabled Children and Slow Learners" in Mona Going, ed., *Hospital Libraries* (London: The Library Assn., 1963), pp. 155-161.

Franz Grempel, "The Naturing Process in the Fairy Tale" *Zeitschrift fur Klinische Psychologie and Psychotherapie* 19:301-322 (1971).

M. Kiss, "Literature in the Hospital: Considerations of a Hospital Library" *Deutsch Krankenpflegez* 27:14 (1974).

H. Sojogren, "Some Personal Reflections on the Theme: Patients, Doctors and Books" in *The Hospital Library in Sweden* (London: The Library Assn., 1962), pp. 21-28.

APPENDICES

APPENDICES

A. Selective, Annotated Bibliography of Monographs on Bibliotherapy and Related Topics

Ronald A. F. Alvarez and Susan Calhoun Kline, *Self Discovery Through the Humanities II: Images of Aging* (Washington, D.C.: The National Council on the Aging, Inc., 1977).

This book represents an eight week program of self-enrichment through literature designed for the Senior Center Humanities Program of the National Council on Aging. Included are stories, poems, and excerpts selected to elicit discussion of aging; discussion questions; and suggested further readings.

William K. Beatty, ed., "Proceedings of A.L.A. Bibliotherapy Workshop in St. Louis, June 25-27, 1964" special issue of *A.H.I.L. Quarterly* 4:1-60 (entire issue) (Summer 1964).

Short position papers from librarians, psychiatrists, an activity therapist nurse, social worker, occupational therapist, and psychologist are included with introductory materials and a transcript of the inter-disciplinary discussions. These papers were originally presented at the important bibliotherapy workshop financed by the National Institute of Mental Health and sponsored by the American Library Association.

Bruno Bettelheim, *The Uses of Enchantment: The Meaning and Importance of Fairy Tales* (New York: Knopf, 1976).

Bettelheim explains how children find meaning to their lives through fairy tales. The first half of the book examines the internal processes of enjoying fairy tales and the psychoanalytic principles involved. A detailed discussion of ten stories comprises the rest of the book.

Eleanor Frances Brown, *Bibliotherapy and Its Widening Applications* (Metuchen, N.J.: Scarecrow Press, 1975).

This recent book on bibliotherapy is actually a full length review of the literature. The author states in her preface that she is a "reporter" only and the book's lack of cohesion and point of view obviously result from that approach. It is valuable, however, as a review and guide to the literature.

Eli Greifer, *Principles of Poetry Therapy* (New York: Poetry Therapy Center, 1963).

Greifer was the founder of poetry therapy; he instigated its use at the Creedmoor State Hospital and at the Mental Hygiene Clinic of Cumberland Hospital (Brooklyn, N.Y.) in the 1960's. His book has two parts: the first is a speech given at the American Society of Group Psychotherapy and Psychodrama on April 12, 1963; the second is a reprint of "Psychic Ills and Poem Therapy" which he originally published as a book chapter in 1968.

Molly Harrower, *The Therapy of Poetry* (Springfield, Ill.: Charles C. Thomas, 1972).

Harrower theorizes that poetry *is* therapy and that creating verse is part of normal development. She uses her own poetry to trace the "poet-self" through the various stages of development and to demonstrate the many uses of self-created poems.

Norman Holland, *The Dynamics of Literary Response* (New York: Norton, 1968).

Based on a study of five readers, Holland's work examines the processes of reading and reacting to literature. This book, and his two others, provide much of the background necessary to understand the "how" of bibliotherapy.

Jack J. Leedy, ed., *Poetry Therapy* (Philadelphia: Lippincott and Co., 1969); and *Poetry the Healer* (Philadelphia: Lippincott and Co., 1973).

These two compilations of original essays are the basis for the Association of Poetry Therapy and for poetry therapy as it exists today. Note especially Edgar and Hazley, Meerloo, Leedy, and Forrest in the first volume; Pietropinto, Rothenberg, Buck and Kramer in the second. Leedy is the founder of the Assn. for Poetry Therapy.

Arthur Lerner, ed., *Poetry in the Therapeutic Experience* (New York: Pergamon Press, to be published in 1978).

A forthcoming anthology of new articles on poetry therapy edited by the founder of the Poetry Therapy Institute, which broke off from the Assn. for Poetry Therapy in 1973.

Libri 25 (2) (1975).

This issue of *Libri* includes the transcripts of speeches on bibliotherapy presented at the Internation Federation of Library Associations (IFLA) General Conference, 1974, in Washington, D.C. These articles are also available through ERIC and a few of them appear in this book.

Sister Mary Corde Lorang, *The Effect of Reading On Moral Conduct and Emotional Experience* (Washington, D.C.: Catholic University, 1945); and *Burning Ice: The Moral and Emotional Effects of Reading,* (New Y rk. Scribner's, 1968).

Sister Mary's attempt to study the relationship of reading material and its effects on adolescents led to her conclusion that "if a book has an effect on the reader, the effect of a good book will almost certainly be good and the effect of an objectionable book will almost certainly be bad." Because case studies are the basis of her work, she has no quantitative or substantive results. Her books are recommended here because they exemplify the "educated opinions" that bibliotherapists and anti-censorship groups must deal with.

Margaret E. Monroe, ed., *Reading Guidance and Bibliotherapy in Public, Hospital, and Institution Libraries* (Madison, Wi.: University of Wisconsin Library School, 1971).

A compilation of ten short speeches given at the University of Wisconsin Library School. Articles by Monroe, Lyman, Moody, Hannigan, and Tews are included.

Mildred T. Moody and Hilda K. Limper, eds., *Bibliotherapy: Methods and Materials* (Chicago: A.L.A., 1971).

The first fifty-four pages of this slim volume are a simple explanation of bibliotherapy and description of example programs. The rest are booklists for "troubled children"; unfortunately most are reprints of previously published bibliographies. Note that the "methods and materials" chapter of the text uses a very broad definition of bibliotherapy and therefore includes programs which are not currently considered bibliotherapy.

Rhea Joyce Rubin, ed., "Bibliotherapy" issue of the *HRLS Quarterly* 1:1-27 (entire issue) (October 1975).

A short issue of the journal is devoted to bibliotherapy and includes a historical overview, three articles by current bibliotherapists, a bibliography of bibliotherapy reference materials 1970-1975, and a survey to be completed by people using bibliotherapy.

Rhea Joyce Rubin, *Using Bibliotherapy: A Guide to Theory and Practice* (Phoenix: Oryx Press, 1978).

This is the textbook designed to be the companion to *A Bibliotherapy Sourcebook*. It stresses the interdisciplinary roots of bibliotherapy and the three types of bibliotherapy. It also deals in depth with methodology and with education and certification for bibliotherapy. Included are extensive bibliographies for use with children and with adults.

Gilbert Schloss, *Psychopoetry: A New Approach to Self-Awareness Through Poetry Therapy* (New York: Grossett and Dunlop, 1976).

Schloss' theory of poetry therapy is drawn from Jacob Moreno's concept of "psychopoetry" or the use of poetry in psychodrama and group psychotherapy. This volume is composed primarily of five case histories and poems written in psychopoetry sessions.

Sister Miriam Schultheis, *A Guidebook for Bibliotherapy* (Glenview, Ill.: Psychotechnics, Inc., 1976); and *Classroom Teachers' Manual for Bibliotherapy* (Ft. Wayne, Indiana: Benet Learning Center, 1977).

In her first book, Sister Miriam discusses her use of bibliotherapy in tutoring sessions with children in her learning center. The second volume, which is an unbound workbook, is the stronger work and contains suggestions on techniques, procedures, and materials in addition to introductory material.

Sylva Simsova, *Nicholas Rubakin and Bibliopsychology* (Hamden, Conn.: Archon Books, 1968).

Three essays by Rubakin, a librarian, editor, and prolific author; and three pieces about him are included. Although his theories are ignored now, they make fascinating reading.

Ruth M. Tews, ed., "Bibliotherapy" issue of *Library Trends* 11:97-228 (entire issue) (October 1962).

This is the one collection of papers of bibliotherapy to read if you plan to read only one. The issue is out-of-print but available at most libraries. It includes articles by a psychotherapist, a psychologist, a nurse, and an occupational therapist in addition to articles by seven librarians.

Paul A. Witty, ed., "Satisfying Needs Through Reading" issue of *Education* 84:451-493 (April 1964).

Witty, himself a regular author of articles on bibliotherapy in education, edited this issue containing eight specially written pieces. Perhaps the best two are his own, "Meeting Developmental Needs Through Reading" and "Bibliography on Developmental Needs."

Joseph S. Zaccaria and Harold A. Moses, *Facilitating Human Development Through Reading: The Use of Bibliotherapy in Teaching and Counseling* (Champaign, Ill.: Stipes Publishing Co., 1968).

Written totally from the educator's point of view, this book barely mentions libraries. But it is more complete than either the Moody-Limper book or Brown's book in both theory and examples. Beware the bibliography which contains many errors.

B. List of Theses and Dissertations on Bibliotherapy

Eleanor Young Alsbrook, *Changes in the Ethnocentric of a Select Group of College Students as a Function of Bibliotherapy.* Ed.D. dissertation, Univ. of Illinois at Urbana-Champaign (1970).

Anthony Joseph Amato, *Some Effects of Bibliotherapy on Young Adults.* Ph.D. dissertation, Pennsylvania State Univ. (1957).

M. H. Appleberry, *A Study of the Effect of Bibliotherapy on Third Grade Children Using a Master List of Titles from Children's Literature.* Ph.D. dissertation, Univ. of Houston (1969).

Roslyn Beitler, *The Therapeutic Application of Children's Books.* M.A. thesis, Univ. of Chicago, (1976).

Erna Below, *Behavior of Ten to Twelve Year Olds as Influenced by Bibliotherapy.* M.A. thesis, Wisconsin State College—Milwaukee (1956).

M. L. Brinkman, *The Value of Directed Reading for Personal-Social Adjustment on the Ninth Grade Level.* Ph.D. dissertation, Northern Illinois Univ. (1954).

Alyce Burmeister, *An Experimental Application of Group Bibliotherapy to Improve IntraGroup Relations in a Sixth Grade Class.* M.A. thesis, Wisconsin State College—Milwaukee (1952).

Lesta Norris Burt, *Bibliotherapy: Effects of Group Reading and Discussion on Attitudes of Adult Inmates in Two Correctional Institutions.* Ph.D. dissertation, Univ. of Wisconsin—Madison (1972).

G. R. Carlsen, *A Study of the Effects of Reading Literature About the Negro on the Racial Attitudes of Eleventh Grade Students in Northern Schools.* Ph.D. dissertation, Univ. of Minnesota (1948).

A. L. Carter, *An Analysis of the Use of Contemporary Black Literature and Music and its Effects Upon Self-Concept in Group Counseling Procedures.* Ph.D. dissertation, Purdue University (1974).

Linda Crowley, *Bibliotherapy: An Annotated Booklist for Use in a Program of Bibliotherapy in an Elementary School.* M.A. thesis, Oregon School of Education (1965).

J. R. Dixon, *The Effects of Four Methods of Group Reading Therapy on the Level of Reading, Manifest Anxiety, Self-Concept, and School Personal-Social Adjustment among Fifth and Sixth Grade Children in a Central City School Setting.* Ph.D. dissertation, Univ. of New York at Buffalo (1974).

Frank L. Fisher, *The Influence of Reading and Discussion on the Attitudes of Fifth Graders toward American Indians.* Ph.D. dissertation, Univ. of California—Berkeley (1965).

R. L. Hagen, *Group Therapy or Bibliotherapy in Weight Reduction.* Ph.D. dissertation, Univ. of Illinois—Urbana (1970).

H. E. Hand, *Modern Novels in Senior High School English: A Study Concerning Practices and Opinions of Teachers of High School English in the State of Michigan.* Ph.D. dissertation, Univ. of Michigan (1959).

Esther A. Hartman, *Imaginative Literature as a Projective Technique: A Study in Bibliotherapy.* Ph.D. dissertation, Stanford Univ. (1951).

E. G. Herminghaus, *The Effect of Bibliotherapy on the Attitudes and Personal and Social Adjustment of a Group of Elementary School Children.* Ph.D. dissertation, Washington University (1954).

E. E. Hoyser, *Therapeutic Non-Directive Play with Low Achievers in Reading.* Ph.D. dissertation, Oregon State University (1971).

David Gerald Jarmon, *Differential Effectiveness of Rational-Emotive Therapy, Bibliotherapy, and Attention-Placebo in the Treatment of Speech Anxiety.* Ph.D. dissertation, Southern Illinois University (1972).

J. A. Johrden, *Bibliotherapy for Children: A Selective, Annotated Bibliography 1950-1962.* M.A. thesis, Catholic University (1964).

A. J. Junier, *A Subject Index to the Literature of Bibliotherapy.* Ph.D. dissertation, Atlanta Univ. (1959).

C. K. Kimoto, *The Effects of a Juvenile Literature-Based Program on Majority Group Attitudes toward Black Americans.* Ph.D. dissertation, Washington State University (1974).

Norman Anthony King, *The Effects of Group Bibliocounseling on Selected Fourth Grade Students Who Are Underachieving in Reading.* Ed.D. dissertation, Univ. of the Pacific (1972).

Johanna Wiener Lessner, *Melpomene and Psyche: The Synergy of Literature and Psychology.* Ph.D. dissertation, U.S. International Univ. (1973).

Mildred Letton, *Individual Differences in Interpretive Responses in Reading Poetry at the Ninth Grade Level.* Ph.D. dissertation, Univ. of California (1958).

I. R. Lewis, *Some Effects of Reading and Discussion of Stories on Certain Values of Sixth Grade Pupils.* Ph.D. dissertation, Univ. of California-Berkeley (1967).

D. K. Livengood, *The Effect of Bibliotherapy on Peer Relations and Democratic Practices in a Sixth Grade Classroom.* Ph.D. dissertation, Univ. of Florida (1961).

W. D. Loban, *Adolescents of Varying Sensitivity and Their Responses to Literature Intended to Evoke Sympathy.* Ph.D. dissertation, Univ. of Minnesota (1949).

H. C. Lodge, *The Influence of the Study of Biography of the Moral Idealogy of the Adolescent at the Eighth Grade Level,* Ph.D. dissertation, Univ. of California (1953).

Sister Mary Cordes Lorang, *The Effect of Reading on Moral Conduct and Emotional Experiences.* Ph.D. dissertation, Catholic Univ. (1945).

R. R. Lowdermilk, *Attitude Shifts from Reading and from Radio Programs Listening.* Ph.D. dissertation, Ohio State University (1939).

Louise Lyon, *Bibliotherapy in the Elementary School.* Ph.D. dissertation, U.C.L.A. (1959).

Harris Clark McClaskey, *Bibliotherapy with Emotionally Disturbed Patients: An Experimental Study.* Ph.D. dissertation, Univ. of Washington (1970).

Gloria Mattera, *Bibliotherapy in a Sixth Grade.* Ph.D. dissertation, Pennsylvania State University (1961).

H. C. Meckel, *An Exploratory Study of Responses of Adolescent Pupils to Situations in a Novel.* Ph.D. dissertation, University of Chicago (1946).

R. Miller, *Attitude Change through Bibliotherapy.* M.A. thesis, Univ. of Missouri (1965).

Barry Morris, *An Investigation of Personality Change through Bibliotherapy.* M.A. thesis, Univ. of Regina, Canada.

D. Muilenberg, *Personal Involvement in Short Stories.* M.A. thesis, Univ. of Missouri (1965).

Pauline Opler, *The Origins and Trends of Bibliotherapy as a Device in American Mental Hospital Libraries.* M.S. thesis, San Jose State College (1969).

V. B. Ponder, *An Investigation of the Effects of Bibliotherapy and Teachers Self-Others Acceptance on Pupils' Self-Acceptance and Reading Achievement Scores.* Ph.D. dissertation, Univ. of Southern Mississippi (1968).

Judith Putzel, *Toward Alternative Theories of Poetry Therapy.* Ph.D. dissertation, Univ. of Massachussetts (1975).

J. B. Read, *A Psychological Investigation of Poetic and Non-Poetic Uses of Paralogia.* Ph.D. dissertation, Georgia State Univ. (1975).

J. D. Reynolds, *Attitude Change by the Stimulus of the Oral Interpretation of Poetic Literature.* Ph.D. dissertation, Ohio State Univ. (1966).

J. W. Ring, *A Study of the Interpretation Processes Employed by Selected Adolescent Readers of Three Short Stories.* Ph.D. dissertation, Ohio State Univ. (1968).

C. E. Rogers, *Individual Differences in Interpretation Responses to Reading the Short Story at the Eleventh Grade Level.* Ph.D. dissertation, Univ. of Arizona (1965).

Joel Royalty, *A Rationale for the Use of Bibliotherapy as an Independent Form of Psychotherapy.* M.A. thesis, Univ. of Missouri (1975).

M. B. Saper, *Bibliotherapy as an Adjunct to Group Psychotherapy.* Ph.D. dissertation, Univ. of Missouri—Columbia (1967).

F. L. Shirley, *The Influence of Reading on the Concepts, Attitudes and Behavior of Tenth, Eleventh, and Twelfth Grade Students.* Ph.D. dissertation, Univ. of Arizona (1966).

Caroline Shrodes, *Bibliotherapy: A Theoretical and Clinical-Experimental Study.* Ph.D. dissertation, Univ. of California (1949).

I. R. Squire, *The Responses of Adolescents to Literature Involving Selected Experiences of Personality Development.* Ph.D. dissertation, Univ. of California (1956).

J. W. Stephens, *An Investigation into the Effectiveness of Bibliotherapy on the Reader's Self-Reliance.* Ph.D. dissertation, Univ. of Oklahoma (1968).

V. A. Stone, *Personality Factors in Immunizing against Source of Content of Persuasive Messages.* Ph.D. dissertation, Univ. of Wisconsin (1966).

R. H. Tauran, *The Influence of Reading on Attitudes of Third Graders Toward Eskimos.* Ph.D. dissertation, Univ. of Maryland (1967).

Lester Lee Tobias, *The Relative Effectiveness of Behavioristic Bibliotherapy, Contingency Contracting, and Suggestions of Self-Control in Weight Reduction.* Ph.D. dissertation, Univ. of Ill. at Urbana-Champaign, (1972).

C. J. Tsimpoukis, *Bibliocounseling: Theory and Research Implications For and Applications in Counseling and Guidance.* Ph.D. dissertation, Univ. of Wisconsin (1968).

M. L. Turner, *Bibliotherapy and Its Place among the Sciences.* M.A. thesis, Univ. of Missouri (1967).

C. R. Veley, *Literature and the Emotions: A Psychology of Literary Response.* Ph.D. dissertation, Pennsylvania State Univ. (1970).

Charles M. Whipple, *The Effect of Short Term Bibliotherapy on the Personality and Achievement of Reformatory Inmate Students.* Ph.D. dissertation, Univ. of Oklahoma (1968).

James Oliver White, *The Assessment of a Program in Bibliotherapy for Black Helpers.* Ph.D. dissertation, Univ. of Illionis at Urbana-Champaign, (1972).

T. R. Zentner, *The Effects of Bibliotherapy and Level of Reading Ability on Self-Concept.* Ph.D. dissertation, Univ. of Montana (1974).

T. R. Zentner, *The Effects of Bibliotherapy on Depressed Behavior in Prison Inmates.* M.A. thesis, Univ. of Montana (1972).

B. J. Zucaro, *The Use of Bibliotherapy Among Sixth Graders to Affect Attitude Change toward American Negroes.* Ph.D. dissertation, Temple Univ. (1972).

C. People Resources and Organizations on Bibliotherapy

1. Association for Poetry Therapy. 799 Broadway, Suite 629, New York, N.Y. 10001.

   This is a membership organization of people interested in poetry therapy. You can join for $10.00 per year and receive their newsletter (published irregularly) and announcements of the annual poetry therapy conference. The A.P.T. also certifies poetry therapists.

2. Bibliotherapy Committee of the Health and Rehabilitative Library Services Division of the American Library Association. c/o A.L.A. 50 E. Huron Street, Chicago, Ill. 60611.

   A.L.A. founded its first committee on bibliotherapy in 1939 and has had one off and on since then. The committee has been responsible for a workshop, numerous surveys, publications, and programs. Membership is by appointment only but all interested observers are welcome at its meetings twice a year.

3. Bibliotherapy Discussion Group of the Health and Rehabilitative Library Services Division of the American Library Association. c/o A.L.A. 50 E. Huron Street, Chicago, Ill. 60611.

   The Discussion Group is an offshoot of the Bibliotherapy Committee. It was founded by Rhea Rubin in 1975 for people interested in bibliotherapy but not necessarily on the more formal committee. The membership fee is $2.00 for members of HRLSD and $4.00 for others; included in the fee is a subscription to the quarterly newsletter and a directory of members.

4. Bibliotherapy Research Institute. c/o Psychology Dept., Columbus College, Columbus, Georgia 31907.

   Begun in 1977 by Dr. Franklin Berry, the Institute hopes to develop and guide research funded through grants and private funds.

5. Bibliotherapy Round Table. c/o Circulating Library, St. Elizabeths Hospital, Washington, D.C. 20032.

   Arleen Hynes, the librarian at the Circulating Library, has coordinated the Round Table for five years. It holds annual programs, usually in conjunction with the Mental Health Librarians (below) for which there is a fee.

6. Institute for Study of Bibliotherapy, Inc. c/o Benet Learning Center, 724 W. Fourth Street, Fort Wayne, Indiana 46808.

   Sister Miriam Schultheis' institute concentrates on bibliotherapy with elementary schoolchildren.

7. Mental Health Librarians of the American Psychiatric Assn., 1700 18th Street NW, Washington, D.C. 20009.

The librarian for the A.P.A., Jean Jones, heads this very informal group which activates periodically to sponsor a program in conjunction with the A.P.A. Hospital and Community Psychiatry conferences.

8. Poetry Therapy Institute. 16917 Ventura Blvd., Encino, Ca. 91316.

Arthur Lerner, a psychologist, founded this organization in 1973 after breaking off from the Association for Poetry Therapy. It is a training institute rather than a membership group and offers courses and workshops in poetry therapy.

INDEX

Index

Compiled by Susan Ruth Stein